W9-DFK-368

The World of Marcus Garvey

*with best wishes
your obedient servant
Marcus Garvey*

Frontispiece reproduced courtesy of Schomburg Center for Research in Black
Culture, The New York Public Library, Astor, Lenox and Tilden Foundations

The World of MARCUS GARVEY

Race and Class in
Modern Society

JUDITH STEIN

Louisiana State University Press
Baton Rouge and London

Copyright © 1986 by Louisiana State University Press
All rights reserved
Manufactured in the United States of America

Designer: Albert Crochet
Typeface: Linotron Palatino
Typesetter: G & S Typesetters, Inc.

Louisiana Paperback Edition, 1991
00   99   98   97   5   4

LIBRARY OF CONGRESS CATALOGING IN PUBLICATION DATA

Stein, Judith, 1940–
   The world of Marcus Garvey.

   Bibliography: p.
   Includes index.
   1. Garvey, Marcus, 1887–1940.   2. Afro-Americans—
Biography.   3. Universal Negro Improvement Association—
History.   4. Black nationalism—United States—History.
5. Afro-Americans—Race identity.   I. Title.
E185.97.G3S8   1985   305.8'96024 [B]   85-7084
ISBN 0-8071-1236-4 (cloth)
ISBN 0-8071-1670-X (paper)

Published with the assistance of a grant from
the National Endowment for the Humanities

The paper in this book meets the guidelines for permanence
and durability of the Committee on Production Guidelines
for Book Longevity of the Council on Library Resources. ∞

To the memory of my father
George Stein

Contents

Illustrations

Acknowledgments

This book could not have been written without the help of many persons who cheerfully gave of their time and good will. Especially in the beginning, when the search for evidence seemed an insurmountable barrier, numerous persons—archivists, friends, and even an unknown man whom I happened to chat with outside the Schomburg Library—gave me leads and encouragement. I cannot list each person who aided a project that took over ten years to complete, but I wish to acknowledge that my debts are enormous.

The courtesy and intelligence of librarians and archivists were unfailing. The following persons were especially helpful: Joseph B. Howerton and John E. Taylor of the National Archives; the entire, peerless staff of the Schomburg Center; Ann Shockley and Jessie Carney Smith of Fisk; Daniel T. Williams of Tuskegee; Oscar L. Sims of the University of California at Los Angeles; and Ester Daniello of the Federal Bureau of Investigation.

Tom W. Shick generously took time from his own work in the Liberian State Archives to retrieve several important letters. Kenneth Clark facilitated my use of a portion of the UNIA papers when I was cornered by bureaucracy. Lionel Yard not only shared his UNIA material with me but tolerated my presence in his study each Saturday for months. Marion Alexander made available her father's correspondence. The late Thomas W. Harvey gave me his time and also let me use the UNIA records in Philadelphia's old UNIA headquarters on Columbia Avenue. F. Levi Lord talked with me for hours about his UNIA experiences; his sense of humor tempered my seriousness and liberated my thinking.

Numerous friends and colleagues were unfailingly helpful and encouraging. In particular, Eric Foner and Martin R. Waldman gave me important criticism and advice at crucial points in the formation of the ideas behind this book. Robert Twombly reproduced many of the photographs. My students at the City College of New York gave me continual criticism, sometimes when they were not aware that I was testing ideas on them.

The style of the book was improved by my friend Barbara Probst Solomon and my mother, Anne S. Stein. Beverly Jarrett and Catherine F. Barton of Louisiana State University Press were always encouraging, friendly, and professional. I also appreciate the fine work of my editor, John Easterly, who is a skillful editor, stylist, and historian. I am grateful for financial support from the Research Foundation of the City University of New York, the National Endowment for the Humanities, and the American Philosophical Society.

Abbreviations

Age	New York *Age*
C.O.	Colonial Office, Great Britain
F.O.	Foreign Office, Great Britain
MG	Marcus Garvey
MID	Military Intelligence Division
NW	*Negro World*
RG	Record Group

The World of Marcus Garvey

Introduction
The Problem of Garvey and Garveyism

"Supreme Jamaican Jackass," "Black Imperial Wizard," "Moses," "Savior," "fascist," and "communist" were some of the epithets used to describe Marcus Garvey in his lifetime. His early years gave no hint of the later controversies. He was born in 1887 in a small town in northern Jamaica. Garvey's search for a career forced him off the island to Central America, England, and finally, in 1916, the United States. Along the way he discovered that his own thwarted ambitions were part of the larger problem confronting the entire black race. Both, he believed, could be resolved simultaneously with Pan-African politics. Garvey founded the Universal Negro Improvement Association (UNIA) in Jamaica and extended it to other West Indian islands and Africa, but it was strongest in the United States. From 1919 through 1923, Garvey and the UNIA built a steamship line, sponsored colonial expeditions to Liberia, staged annual international conventions, inspired businesses, endorsed political candidates, fostered black history and culture, and organized thousands. But Garvey's power proved to be brief. He was tried and found guilty of mail fraud in 1923 and imprisoned in 1925. His sentence was commuted by President Coolidge in 1927, when he was deported to Jamaica, where he tried and failed to revive the UNIA's power. He left Jamaica for England in 1935, where he continued to speak and write until his death in London in 1940.

A small UNIA survives today. Diverse racial leaders—Malcolm X and Michael Manley, Muslims and Communists, businessmen and politicians—testify to Garvey's continuing influence. Kwame Nkrumah named Ghana's merchant marine the Black Star Line, after the UNIA's fleet. Garvey is a national hero in Jamaica, and schools, taxi fleets, parks, and restaurants in the United States are named for him.

Although Garvey rests securely in the pantheon of black leaders, there is no consensus on the nature and measure of his contribution. Harlem newspaperman Roi Ottley maintained soon after Garvey's death that the UNIA leader had "set in motion what was to become the most compelling force in Negro life—race and color consciousness, which is today that ephemeral thing that inspires 'race loyalty' the banner to which Negroes

1

rally, the chain that binds them together." A Jamaican scholar, Trevor Munroe, honored his countryman as the "organizer of the first international mass movement of black people." An American historian, E. David Cronon, agreed that Garvey "attracted the attention of the colored world to a degree never before achieved by a Negro organization" but concluded that he "sought to raise high walls of racial nationalism at a time when most thoughtful men were seeking to tear down these barriers." The different appraisals reflect the political judgments that shape and guide all historical writing, from the openly partisan to the professionally objective.[1]

The absence of a full set of raw materials for biography and history makes sound scholarship on Garvey and the UNIA a difficult task. The Justice Department seized, and subsequently destroyed, UNIA records in 1922 when it indicted UNIA leaders. The UNIA's factional wars led to the destruction and scattering of other organizational papers. The bulk of Garvey's personal papers was destroyed in the London bombings of 1941 and 1942. Even the useful set of Garvey papers now being published is incomplete.[2] Other scattered papers of individual UNIA locals and members have survived by chance. The incomplete record, the accidental survival of papers that might not be representative, and the heavy weight of sources from government investigatory bodies make writing about Garvey a hazardous undertaking.

Yet the past is not tranquilized so easily. The rise of black militancy in the 1960s rekindled the debates of the Garvey era despite the absence of adequate historical sources. Historians John Hope Franklin and Theodore Draper dismissed Garveyism as "Negro Zionism," a back-to-Africa movement that became, in practice, a utopian retreat to a psychological Africa within the United States. Draper concluded that the nationalism of the Garveyites had "little or nothing to do with their immediate lives, with their own time and place." Sympathizers of the black nationalism of the 1960s reversed these judgments. Theodore Vincent and Tony Martin cataloged the movement's businesses, newspapers, political organization, and protest activities in the United States. Their work demonstrated that sympathy for a subject can impel the diligent research that yields better history. Both asserted that Garvey and the UNIA were at the forefront of Afro-American and Pan-African politics in the 1920s. To Cronon, Franklin, and

1. Roi Ottley, "New World A-Coming": Inside Black America (Boston, 1943), 81; Trevor Munroe, The Politics of Constitutional Decolonization: Jamaica, 1944–62 (Kingston, 1972), 18; E. David Cronon, Black Moses: The Story of Marcus Garvey and the Universal Negro Improvement Association (Madison, 1955), 221–22.
2. Robert A. Hill (ed.), The Marcus Garvey and Universal Negro Improvement Association Papers (10 vols. projected; Berkeley, 1983–).

Draper, Garvey was interesting and unique but irrelevant. To Martin and Vincent, however, Garvey was interesting mainly because of his unique relevance. Neither camp relinquished contemporary politics long enough to comprehend the historical Garvey.[3]

The debates about Garveyism also raise issues in black social history. The Draper-Cronon view is rooted in a view of black migration and racism best articulated by E. Franklin Frazier. Frazier concluded that the new urban experience for blacks was disruptive, even "pathological." If this was true, mass politics would be rooted in desperation, not promise. Indeed, Frazier judged Garveyism to be the bankrupt product of deep alienation.[4]

The Vincent and Martin studies, though often innocent of social history, implied that blacks were untouched by the transition to the city and that they responded simply to the racism of Western societies and the poverty of established racial organizations. Although both scholars were married to the view of Garvey's political uniqueness, their work meshes with a trend in black urban history that detects continuity, not disjunction, in the northern black communities. Both assume the distinctiveness of the black urban experience and implicitly depart from recent trends in social history that attempt to integrate the black experience with the broader social transformations of modern societies. Politically, this approach typically locates the dynamic of black politics in leadership and minimizes internal changes and social classes within the black community and often the larger society as well. Although the black middle class frequently plays the role of whipping boy, the social bases of political differences are rarely analyzed seriously.

Speaking to the polemical issue, I support Martin's and Vincent's conclusions that Garvey addressed and attempted to solve the economic, political, and cultural problems of black life. Garveyism was not an escape to a psychological or real Africa. However, unlike them, I do not find that the UNIA's militance and black nationalism were earlier and more comprehensive versions of the racial politics of the 1960s. Garvey did not successfully combine the later movement's goal of civil rights in the early 1960s with that of racial self-determination after 1965. Despite Garvey's rhetoric and ambition, which Martin and Vincent uncritically accepted as achievement, the UNIA was unable either to extract black rights from ruling powers or to

3. John Hope Franklin, *From Slavery to Freedom: A History of Negro Americans* (3rd ed.; New York, 1967), 489–92; Theodore Draper, *The Rediscovery of Black Nationalism* (New York, 1970), 48–56; Theodore Vincent, *Black Power and the Garvey Movement* (Berkeley, 1972); Tony Martin, *Race First: The Ideological and Organizational Struggles of Marcus Garvey and the Universal Negro Improvement Association* (Westport, Conn., 1976).

4. E. Franklin Frazier, "The Garvey Movement," *Opportunity*, IV (1926), 346–48.

create institutions capable of uniting the race. Garveyism cannot be either a model or a hobgoblin for contemporary politics. The UNIA was a historical movement anchored in specific class and race relationships and ideologies.

This book stresses the particular roles that blacks enact in the societies they inhabit. Insofar as it speaks to issues of continuity and discontinuity in black history, it opts for discontinuity, especially in the important arena of politics. Garvey self-consciously departed from the past. But this formulation is too blunt to analyze the movement in the United States, not to mention in the Caribbean and Africa. I have also found the line of analysis that characterizes behavior as either pathological and disorganized, on the one hand, or communal and adaptive, on the other, to be too morally and politically loaded to be useful.

Instead, an analysis of the different classes within black communities seems to explain the appeal of Garveyism better than other frameworks. Certainly, the dynamics of the movement—its development over time, its Pan-African components, its strengths and weaknesses, and its inner conflicts—seem chaotic without understanding the various expectations that different classes and regions had. This internal explanation is harnessed to an analysis of the structural forces of the outside world that profoundly affected the black experience both within and outside the UNIA—wars, depressions, and world politics on the largest scale but also the smaller events in the economies, politics, and class relations of particular communities. Finally, the movement was shaped by the character of race relations, which varied from place to place, set limits on race contacts, and defined the space Garveyism could occupy. Underlying the UNIA's politics was a profound social upheaval that affected all parts of the black world. This phenomenon cannot be reduced to racism.

For black people the period of Garvey's life, from 1887 to 1940, was dominated by the massive pressures that an expanding capitalism and alien governments placed on rural blacks whether they were American sharecroppers, West Indian peasants, or African farmers. The "new imperialism" at the end of the nineteenth century was accompanied by a trumpet volley of racism, but racial discrimination and racism were dependent variables. The racial experience, though pervasive, was not monolithic; it was not identical for black farmers and businessmen, lawyers and laborers, Africans and Afro-Americans. But the uprooting of old and the creation of new social roles, relations of production, and ideologies were everywhere at the center of the black condition.

During the years before World War I, one part of the black community, an international elite of blacks in the United States, the West Indies, and Africa, dominated racial politics. Unlike most blacks, the elite applauded the triumphant institutions, values, and power of capitalism. But capitalism had eroded old ways of life without creating enough "careers open to talent"—places in the new society for the ambitious sons of displaced peasants and artisans—and racial bars were often used to allocate the scarce places. The black elite excoriated the new order's racial discrimination, which denied men like themselves the places of prestige and social advancement that their talents and achievements merited. In classic fashion they tried to construct "black," "colored," "African," and "Afro-American" institutions to create the opportunities they were denied. These different adjectives reflected the unique boundaries and history of the black world. Although all the nationalists and most blacks were race-conscious, not all race-conscious blacks were nationalists. Nationalist solutions to the problems of race and racism were the products of class experiences and were best suited to the redress of elite ills.

The specific goals of the nationalists varied. Few advocated independent states, but all worked to create institutions that historically have been the infrastructures of modern nations—schools, pressure groups, businesses, intellectual societies. The black elite debated only which ones could be created at a particular time and which blacks should control them. The controversies were heated, but they rarely engaged most blacks, because the institutions at stake were the modern ones dominated by the elite.

Garvey accepted this racial agenda. His UNIA and its leading creation, a steamship company named the Black Star Line (BSL), were unique because Garvey attempted to enlist the masses behind the elite model of progress. Although initially the recipe appeared to unite the race, in time the BSL replicated the divisions of the bourgeois world within the UNIA. And instead of creating the economic power that could demand equal rights, the BSL suffered the fate of other small enterprises competing against economic giants. The UNIA survived the decade, but Garvey's racial appeals did not overcome the workings of modern institutions.

The Great Depression, which destroyed many of the racial businesses of the 1920s, dealt the final blow to the UNIA's route to racial progress. National and racial movements after World War II were equipped with more effective ideologies to unite blacks and confront Western governments. In Africa and the Caribbean, national independence, not business, became the means to provide opportunity and confront racism and Western power. In the United States, the ending of Jim Crow and disfranchisement were equivalent means to similar ends.

After World War II, nationalists addressed the social issues directly, not merely the color line, discrimination, and the uneven growth of progress. They incorporated working-class modes of politics: the boycott, sit-in, strike, and demonstration replaced the petition, lawsuit, parade, and business. The masses came late to nationalist goals and played a subordinate role in nationalist politics, but they were essential for success. Garvey had eyed the power of mass organization during World War I. While his appeal attracted thousands, he could not effectively or permanently mobilize them behind the elite goals he had made his own.

Garvey's international movement was peopled by ambitious artisans, small businessmen, and uprooted workers. Its methods and visions were simultaneously shaped by the fatalism of the powerless, the utopias of hustlers and charlatans, the promises of mass movements, and the ideologies generated by the new social transformations of World War I and the 1920s. Garvey imposed his views and personality on the UNIA but was forced to accommodate to the movement he created and to larger world history. The movement was untidy but not without form. Using old and new sources, I have tried to tell Garvey's story in a way that illuminates our understanding of a critical era in American and world history. This book has been enriched by new material from the Federal Bureau of Investigation, interviews with Garveyites, and a more diligent search for evidence in standard government and private collections. It has also been informed by new reflections on the world that Garvey confronted. Although Garvey's ideas were always animated by his current purposes and usually lacked the objectivity of distance, the necessary effort to see things his way yielded insights that modified my understanding and challenged and revised some of the conclusions in the historical literature.

1 / Pan-Africanism Before Garvey

Pan-Africanism, the ideology that freed Garvey from the provincial politics of Jamaica, was a complex and imprecise, if passionately held, set of racial beliefs joined to defend and advance black equality and progress. Triggered by a new Western assault, a "new imperialism" that had colonized most Africans and disfranchised most Afro-Americans by 1900, it was a modern blueprint for achieving racial equality through the economic, technological, social, and political development of all areas where black people lived. Because Pan-Africanism lacked organizational continuity, common practices, and even common goals, it is best understood historically through its diverse expressions and leading advocates.[1]

Pan-Africanism was created by an international black elite that included persons from West Africa, the Caribbean, the United States, and occasionally England, the boundaries of the old Atlantic slave trade. They were lawyers, teachers, social workers, journalists, students, civil servants, and churchmen—modern men who made up only a small minority of the black world. (White men like them were also only a small minority in the larger world.) They were an elite because their occupations did more than mark the individual attainment of high status. Serving black people, they simultaneously purveyed new power, new ideas, and new possibilities. Unlike the black majority, they easily established and severed ties as they moved from place to place in search of careers and advancement, goals unknown to the masses. Most blacks were sharecroppers, peasants, and farmers. Whatever their legal status, blacks in the New World were already subject to the growing and intrusive world economy, which involved them in the problems of international competition, overproduction, and the collapse

---

1. The literature on nationalism and Pan-Africanism is vast, but E. J. Hobsbawm's *Age of Capital* (New York, 1975) and "Some Reflections on 'The Break-Up of Britain,'" *New Left Review*, no. 105 (1977), 3–23, make useful distinctions between nineteenth- and twentieth-century nationalism. Anthony D. Smith's *Nationalism in the Twentieth Century* (Oxford, 1979) and Benedict Anderson's *Imagined Communities: Reflections on the Origin and Spread of Nationalism* (London, 1983) are fresh syntheses. On Pan-Africanism, see J. Ayodele Langley, *Pan-Africanism and Nationalism in West Africa, 1900–1945* (Oxford, 1973), and Imanuel Geiss, *The Pan-African Movement* (London, 1974).

of prices. The blacks of Africa labored in a world plagued by the traditional hazards of agriculture, such as famines.

During the midnineteenth-century Era of Emancipation, the elites had believed that progress was readily attainable through the capitalism, enterprise, technology, science, reason, and individualism of the West. The abolition of black slavery convinced them of the validity and universality of Enlightenment ideals of liberty. They believed that each new school, business, and church, and the growing number of men like themselves on both sides of the Atlantic, promoted the new civilization. Cultural assimilation, or Westernization—the attainment of the Western ideals of wealth, education, and character—was the antidote to race prejudice.

Dramatic personal experience often produced the most loyal converts. James Horton, the son of an Ibo, was rescued from slavery by a British squadron and later became a physician and businessman in Sierra Leone, the West African colony Britain founded for free blacks and freed slaves in 1787. Horton was certain that "if Europe . . . has been raised to her present pitch of civilization by progressive advancement, Africa too, with a guarantee of the civilization of the north [Europe], will rise into equal importance."[2] During the same period, Frederick Douglass, an escaped slave and abolitionist in the United States, set out to "inspire our young men with manly ambition, and lead our whole people onward in the party of civilization." The assumed connections between the growth of capitalism and the death of archaic labor systems and between economic abundance and social progress were powerful arguments for Western superiority.[3]

The new imperialism, offspring of the economic crisis at the end of the nineteenth century, threatened the elite's vision of progress by erecting new barriers to professional and business careers. The earlier age of exploration and trade had given way to an era of colonialism and investment. Black leaders began to discover that Western progress was not universal but was wielded by nation-states. Indeed, implicit in Western cultural dominance was the idea of the racial inferiority of black people.

In 1900, thirty-seven men of color participated in the first Pan-African Conference to protest the new racial balance of power. They met in London because their purpose was to inform and influence public opinion in the leading colonial power of the world. Although they spoke out against brutality, forced labor, and land expropriations, the delegates were more worried about the by-products of the new imperialism—an uneven social progress and a widening gap between the races. Several of the delegates

2. Robert W. July, *Origins of Modern African Thought* (New York, 1967), 116.
3. *New National Era*, September 8, 1870, October 12, 1871.

contrasted the growth of representative institutions in white Canada and Australia with the persistence of traditional colonial rule in Britain's colonies composed of Negroes; the Americans cited Jim Crow and disfranchisement in the United States. All enumerated other, less dramatic but real obstacles to racial advancement. One American, W. E. B. Du Bois, expressed a common fear that "the problem of the Twentieth Century" would be the problem of the color line, "a white effort to limit black progress and development."[4]

The delegates invoked the old egalitarian ideals in their appeal to Western public opinion. Du Bois hoped that "the spirit of Garrison, Phillips and Douglass" would not "die out in America." But he and his racial brothers were no longer convinced that the progress they backed was a historic given. Blending idealism and careerism, they prescribed as a solution a heavy dose of collective self-help and racial businesses, schools, and culture.

The Pan-African voices were barely audible to the optimistic, imperial celebrants of the new century. The blacks had come together more out of weakness than strength. No delegate represented a popular organization. The cultural gap between the modern elite and most black people was wide. Western civilization was neither benign nor attractive to the masses in the postslavery era. In the Caribbean and in the southern United States, Afro-Americans experienced Western culture as the plantation, from which they fled if possible to farm their own land, away from the economy and culture of the white and colored elites. In Africa, Western civilization fractured traditional economies, hierarchies, and religions but also withheld compensatory spiritual or material progress. Depending upon the intrusion and balance of forces, the masses battled, protested, passively accepted, or migrated from Western power. The black elite's neutrality or opposition to the popular resistances often earned them the suspicion of the masses. In turn, the elite, not commanding popular allegiance, did not call for political democracy or independence.

The delegates at London did begin to speak up for the majority. But their cataloging of popular injuries was more an obligatory ritual mandated by their new ideology of racial solidarity than a genuine agenda for political action. Lacking a political theory, black leaders substituted clichés— British fair play, Christian ethics, American democracy—for precise analysis of the forces at work in the new imperialism and for effective solutions to the problems it had brought.[5]

4. Owen Charles Mathurin, *Henry Sylvester Williams and the Origins of the Pan-African Movement, 1869–1911* (Westport, Conn., 1976), 49, 63, 68, 165–69.

5. Wilson J. Moses, *The Golden Age of Black Nationalism, 1850–1925* (Hamden, Conn., 1978), 141.

Failing to attract countrymen of other classes, the elites of different regions joined together now as Pan-Africanists. The American churchman Alexander Walters declared that in matters of race there were "no geographic lines" and "no national limitations" to racial consciousness and identification. Pan-Africanism, which took into account place, race, and history, encompassed the critical experiences—slavery, emancipation, racism, and imperialism—necessary for a modern resistance. Nevertheless, the virtues of Pan-African ideology were insufficient to sustain organization. The Pan-African Association, child of the 1900 London meeting, quickly disintegrated.[6] During the years before World War I, no other Pan-African gathering took place. However, Pan-African thought and feeling drove individuals throughout the urban centers of the black world and inspired elites in West Africa, the United States, and the Caribbean to confront the arrogance of the West and the tyranny of tradition. Marcus Garvey learned from each regional variety.

Although Garvey never visited Africa, he absorbed a great deal of its politics and problems from Africans and Englishmen when he was in London from 1912 to 1914. The idea of Africa was always a powerful force in the black imagination, but dramatic changes in the real Africa nourished the new racial nationalism. European nations ruled scattered enclaves on the coast in 1879. During the next eleven years, five million square miles, inhabited by over sixty million Africans, were seized more or less according to a blueprint that Europeans had created at the Berlin Conference in 1885 to adjust their conflicting claims. By 1903, Europeans were sovereigns of all but six of Africa's forty political units.[7]

The modern African elite occasionally protested the excesses of colonial rule, but they did not question colonial legitimacy. Edward Blyden, a West Indian–born African scholar and Liberian statesman, the leading theorist of Pan-Africanism, welcomed the extension of British rule to the hinterlands behind Sierra Leone and praised the French conquest of Dahomey for freeing "a great country from the cruel savagery of the ages and throwing it open to the regenerating influences of an enlightened nation." He praised the British protectorate over the Niger Delta, which "abolished barbarous customs and suppressed marauding practices" of inland traders. An advisor to colonial governors, Blyden even advocated the ending of Liberian independence.[8] At the same time, Gold Coast lawyer J. E. Casely

6. Mathurin, *Henry Sylvester Williams*, 76, 165–71.
7. Roland Oliver and J. D. Fage, *A Short History of Africa* (Harmondsworth, England, 1962), 185; J. D. Hargreaves, "West African States and the European Conquest," in L. H. Gann and Peter Duigan (eds.), *The History and Politics of Colonialism, 1870–1914* (Cambridge, England, 1969), 199–201.
8. Hollis Lynch, *Edward Blyden: Pan-Negro Patriot* (London, 1967), 187–89, 141–45,

Hayford portrayed a grand imperial future, with the African "hinterland opened to commerce and civilization," free of "inter-tribal jealousies," united by "railways, telephones, and the electric telegraph—with a central national assembly—with a common literature . . . with common religion." For these black professionals, detached from power and popular allegiance, colonial rule would destroy the local loyalties and culture that prevented the imagined national or racial community.[9]

The new African intellectuals married two intellectual traditions. They continued to uphold, especially in their rhetoric, the optimistic, liberal mode of the emancipation generation. Rooted in the commercial relationships between Europe and Africa, it assumed that free trade would bring steady progress and civilization to Africa. A laissez-faire attitude toward cultural development complemented the laissez-faire economics. The second arose out of the new imperialism, which brought European governance and foreshadowed economic monopoly and modern forms of production like the plantation, which required capital and expertise. The new African intellectual, as much as the European, came to believe that economic development and progress required more planning and efficiency, which inevitably must be imported from Europe. Racial development would also require more direction.

Today, calling for European capital and practices might appear to be a strange prescription for enhancing African culture and progress. The black elite saw no conflict between their means and ends. Racial theory provided the escape hatch for the elite's support of imperialism. Foreign power was necessary to destroy the local divisions and inefficient practices of traditional culture, but alien races could not create an African nation. So long as cultural assimilation had been the goal, the case for elite leadership was flawed because, theoretically, whites as well as blacks could teach Africans the secrets of Western civilization. But like the Europeans, the new African intellectuals made race and nation the principal motors of history. Blyden asserted that the races were distinct, "each . . . endowed with peculiar talents." The duty to create a "nationality" out of the racial material was an "ordinance of nature." Moreover, "no people can rise to an influential position among the nations without a distinct and efficient nationality." The task of politics and leadership was to develop nature's program. Colonial rule would permit the African elite to create the nation, the nationality that would eventually lead to the nation-state.[10]

198–201, 209. Garvey read Blyden's writings when he was in England. MG to Sir Frederick George Kenyon, October 8, 1913, in Robert A. Hill (ed.), *The Marcus Garvey and Universal Negro Improvement Association Papers* (10 vols. projected; Berkeley, 1983–), I, 27.

9. Cited in July, *Modern African Thought*, 444.

10. Cited in Lynch, *Edward Blyden*, 209; July, *Modern African Thought*, 211, 221.

Although loyal to the new imperialism, the modern men observed uneasily the faster growth of foreign companies, the discriminations in the British Civil Service, the appointment of Europeans to head churches, and the segregated housing and social life that appeared in Africa in the 1890s. The improvement of tropical medicine made it possible for more Europeans to enter the interior and occupy the administrative and clerical posts that the elite claimed. All of a sudden, leadership in the church, education, government, and business—the social institutions of the nation-state— was closed to men who saw them as routes to power and prosperity for themselves and their people.[11]

The new barriers caused the elites to turn to the traditional leaders, whom they had earlier ignored or opposed. They could not win allegiance on the basis of their own grievances or their future national vision. So they now began trying to defend traditional Africa rather than enlighten it. The modern elite of Lagos attempted to protect the land titles of Yoruba countrymen in the hinterland. Creoles in Sierra Leone transmitted protests against the hut tax and other popular grievances that accompanied the consolidation of British rule on the West Coast. Some modern men adopted native dress and exchanged Christian names for traditional ones. The modern elites championed the past, however, to promote the new order, and they created new political forms that displaced traditional authority. The traditional elites accepted the modern elites' aid because they lacked knowledge of the new government's ways and faced competition in territories they had formerly controlled. Because of the internal conflicts within traditional societies, many chiefs were no more able to mobilize people than the Westernized elite.[12]

The Aborigines Rights Protection Society (ARPS), established on the Gold Coast in 1898 by African lawyers and merchants, was a typical elite instrument. It was created to oppose a proposed law to transfer authority over unused land to Britain for the purpose of preventing tribal chiefs from leasing lands to European speculators anxious to exploit minerals and timber. But the act of British regulation carried with it the assumption of Brit-

11. In 1883, Africans held 9 of 43 high posts on the Gold Coast. In 1908, of 274 civil service appointments, only 5 were held by Africans, and 4 of these were in the junior rank. African doctors were excluded from the British Medical Service in 1902. G. I. C. Eluwa, "National Congress of British West Africa· A Study in African Nationalism," *Présence Africaine*, no. 77 (1971), 131–49; July, *Modern African Thought*, 274–91; E. A. Ayandele, *The Educated Elite in Nigerian Society* (Ibadan, Nigeria, 1974), 84; Patrick Cole, *Modern and Traditional Elites in the Politics of Lagos* (Cambridge, England, 1975), 111.

12. July, *Modern African Thought*, 125–28; Cole, *Modern and Traditional Elites*, 75; Philip Ehrensaft, "The Political Economy of Informal Empire in Pre-Colonial Nigeria, 1807– 1884," *Canadian Journal of African Studies*, VI (1972), 479.

ish dominion. Both the traditional and modern elites feared the favored position that Europeans would win if the Crown succeeded in regulating the land alienation they all practiced.[13]

Although the ARPS defended the African view of imperial rule, which denied British sovereignty over land, the elite's instrument of protest challenged traditional dominion. The ARPS was financed by the chiefs but controlled by the modern men. Transcending the structure of tribal institutions, its form was the preeminent bourgeois political channel, the pressure group. ARPS methods were legal and reasonable, unlike indigenous protest, which threatened and menaced.

A colonial official concluded that "if one wished to stir up trouble . . . all one would have to do would be to suggest that the land of the native is about to be taken away from them." The British expropriated land in Kenya and other parts of Africa even though it caused trouble. But in West Africa the peasant farm was judged to be a cheaper, more efficient mode of production than the plantation. Hence, there the African view of sovereignty also won the allegiance of British merchants. The combination of traditional and elite African and British forces carried the day.[14]

The elite's ambition for leadership and power in the empire made its defense of traditional Africa contingent, *i.e.*, subject to reforms carried out by its members, who felt they could "draw out the best qualities innate in the . . . Native" and "develop and improve" his culture according to "scientific principles."[15] The modern elite's first loyalty was to their places in the new society. When challenged by white foreigners, they constructed a racial front; when contested by traditional or democratic forces in Africa, it claimed expertise and eventually the bourgeois right to rule. In 1921, Casely Hayford declared that the African educated class "buys the motorcars, the patent boots, the high collars, the fine shirts, builds the fine houses." Those who paid taxes should govern. Racial and national appeals to the masses were weak because Pan-African practice rationalized social snobbery and elite privilege.[16]

The global economic growth and shift in the balance of trade in favor of agricultural exports in the years between 1900 and World War I moderated the conflicts between tribal and modern leaders. Pacification of the hin-

13. July, *Modern African Thought*, 318, 338–41; Cole, *Modern and Traditional Elites*, 75.
14. Cole, *Modern and Traditional Elites*, 89–90.
15. Casely Hayford, "Gold Coast Native Institutions with Thoughts upon a Healthy Imperial Policy for the Gold Coast and Ashanti," in Henry S. Wilson (ed.), *Origins of West African Nationalism* (London, 1969), 322–31.
16. July, *Modern African Thought*, 457; Langley, *Pan-Africanism and Nationalism*, 115–24; Ehrensaft, "Pre-Colonial Nigeria," 480.

terlands had facilitated economic development. The building of roads and railways expanded the market for minerals and agricultural products. Merchants and landowners grew wealthy, educated Africans taught and Christianized an enlarged population, and lawyers mediated the conflicts between old and new in their societies. The modern elite extended its economic power, and the sons of chiefs acquired Western education. Although the top positions went to the Europeans, twentieth-century imperialism required numerous subordinate cadres for state and corporate bureaucracies. The Westernized elite grew in numbers.[17]

Most Africans were untouched by the new progress. But their traditional leaders, who had wielded power in the past, were dependent upon the new wealth. There were few poor chiefs. Power and wealth had always been joined. Yet, the levers of prosperity were no longer in the hands of chiefs. The traditional elite invoked ancient sanctions to maintain their control over the land and labor, but their success was dependent upon the fortunes of an uncertain world economy whose only constant was change. Novelties appeared in the countryside: railroads, schools, and, occasionally, white men—intrusions, not transformations. Most Africans still used the agricultural methods of their ancestors. The expanding market produced new wealth but did not increase the productivity of the farmer and laborer. Modernization was thin. It offered new opportunities and power to individuals who possessed the tools of the West. Their knowhow and contacts naturally increased their influence inside the colonial state. The urban Africans saw British rule as a model and as the source of opportunity for advancement on all fronts. Although their acceptance of the new sovereignty did not blind them to the rise of new discriminations, it narrowed the potential social base that could be marshaled to oppose them.

Garvey embraced the African nationalists' sense of racial discrimination, inequality, and hierarchy and their fervent belief that the riches and future of Africa could be secured by black men with modern techniques of organization and production. The idea of unlimited African wealth fueled Garvey's hopes for the Black Star Line; his plans to develop the independent, black republic of Liberia paraded the latest Western economic methods. But because modernity was only a thin veneer in Africa, Garvey was first forced to organize and accumulate capital in the New World, where there were many more men who shared his goals.

The Afro-American elite, like its African counterpart, was the heir to

17. Henry S. Wilson, *The Imperial Experience in Sub-Saharan Africa Since 1870* (Minneapolis, 1977), 207, 240–41; Anthony Hopkins, *Economic History of West Africa* (New York, 1973), 216.

the politics of the emancipation generation. New World slavery had destroyed the traditional allegiances and loyalties of the past by severing the power and ways of life that underlay a man's conception of himself as an Ibo, Ashanti, or Igba. Slavery created a people who considered themselves black, African, or Negro—all synonyms for the same person. Unlike the African lawyer Casely Hayford, who hoped that economic development would remove the traditional allegiances of the past, Afro-American leaders did not have to compete with traditional leaders for their loyalty. More positively, the ideals of Western civilization as expressed by the Republican party in the United States proved attractive to many of the former slaves. Even though they would have preferred to work their own land, they were now citizens, with the right to contract their own labor and the right to vote. In some ways, Republicanism succeeded. The party prevented the most blatant attempts to shackle black labor and legislate racial restrictions in occupations. It began a public education system. Black farmers ate more and enjoyed greater autonomy than black slaves had. But they did not achieve the independence that was the crux of their idea of freedom or that was expressed in the classic formulations of the Republican party. Blacks' independence had been challenged by antagonistic southern planters during Reconstruction. After 1877, prospects were permanently destroyed by the new investors in the forest and mineral regions of the South and West, the nation's interior empire. Although the new expansion was called development, not imperialism, and although most of the new capitalists were Americans, not foreigners, the black and white natives of the South viewed them as aliens. Despite a spirited political resistance during the 1890s, American farmers and sharecroppers, black and white, individually and collectively, in both racial and interracial groups, were unable to resist the new power.[18]

The losers were deprived of political power. Restriction of suffrage resolved the labor problems of southern planters, strengthened the power of the region's new capitalists over their workers, and disarmed the remnants of agrarian radicalism and potential political opponents. Because formal color bars would have violated the Fifteenth Amendment, new laws and amendments to state constitutions applied a variety of nonracial hurdles—literacy tests, poll taxes, and bureaucratic technicalities—to prospective voters. The destruction of the black electorate was a prerequisite to the crescendo of court-sanctioned Jim Crow legislation designed to separate and

18. Kenneth Stampp, *The Era of Reconstruction, 1865–1877* (New York, 1965), 126–31; C. Vann Woodward, *Origins of the New South, 1877–1913* (Baton Rouge, 1951), chaps. 2, 3, 5, 9.

thereby control and subordinate the black population. Some blacks voted under the new conditions, but without the possibility of mass voting, black ballots secured only small improvements, generally for the urban elite—a school, a park, a paved street.[19]

The reformed southern political system was an American equivalent of colonial government in Africa. Even though the Afro-American elite were loyal during the political upheavals of the 1890s, they were also victimized. Like the new African leaders, the Afro-Americans now urged racial self-help and uplift through the institutions of the victorious system. Booker T. Washington, the principal of Tuskegee Institute in Alabama, was one of the first to choose the winning side. Like Blyden, Washington believed that the schools, businesses, and values of the modern nation-state were appropriate models for black progress. He established new organizations like the Tuskegee Institute and the National Negro Business League to promote black entrepreneurship. He convinced some of the leading capitalists who invested in the South to contribute money and time to Tuskegee.[20] They believed they were training a race of laborers. Washington hoped to create black captains of industry. Like the African elite, Washington discovered that he needed the help of more traditional bodies. He cultivated the leaders of black churches and lodges, organizations with mass influence, and agencies of capital accumulation, functional equivalents of the tribal associations in Africa.[21]

Although Washington opposed the new proscriptions and was frequently disappointed by the racial views of his white allies, he was rarely disheartened, because he genuinely believed that access to public facilities and even the ballot would be easily won when blacks accumulated wealth. Race recognition and equality were dependent upon "a large number of individual members of the race demonstrating beyond question success in controlling their own individual business affairs." Like Blyden's acceptance of imperialism, the Afro-American elite's accommodation to disfranchisement was rooted in a view of progress that made capital accumulation the race's first order of business. The implicit abandonment of participation in politics magnified racial divisions. To demonstrate the injustice of racial discrimination in Nashville, Tennessee, a black minister maintained that "between the best and worst elements in Negro society . . . there is as wide

19. J. Morton Kousser, *The Shaping of Southern Politics: Suffrage Restriction and the Establishment of the One-Party South, 1880–1910* (New Haven, 1974), chap. 9.

20. Louis Harlan, *Booker T. Washington: The Making of a Black Leader, 1865–1901* (New York, 1972), 274; Robert Factor, *Black Response to America: Men, Ideals, and Organization from Frederick Douglass to the NAACP* (Reading, Mass., 1970), esp. 197–200.

21. Factor, *Black Response to America*, 227–36.

a social gulf as exists between the best and worse Anglo-Saxon people. But the white man almost never considers this fact in estimating the social merits of the Negro race." Such an argument, which emphasized class division, was not a political formula likely to produce racial unity.[22]

The white and black elites' solution for the mainly landless masses was hard work and education. Lacking the franchise, however, blacks could not protect the value of their labor or demand a fair share of the public educational budget or even the new philanthropic allocations. Southern schools had usually been segregated, but they now began to become grossly unequal. And secondary schools like Tuskegee became tolerable to the planters when they saw that Washington's rhetoric of social uplift left undisturbed their cheap labor by affecting only a few, by deferring change to the future, and by removing potentially unruly elements of the laboring population to the cities.[23] Although Washington's ambition to create black Carnegies was not realized, the numbers of black businessmen and professionals grew in the economic expansion of the first two decades of the twentieth century. Each success story confirmed Washington's wisdom. His fame spread internationally and encouraged numerous young men like Marcus Garvey to seek aid and advice from the master.[24]

But the erosion of black rights was not stemmed by the bromides of white philanthropy, black achievement, or racial institutions. A new organization, the National Association for the Advancement of Colored People (NAACP) was created in New York in 1909 to protect the lives and rights of voteless southern blacks. Like the ARPS in West Africa, the NAACP was a pressure group. Initially mainly white, over time the NAACP attracted modern blacks, recent critics of the new political order. W. E. B. Du Bois, a founder and editor of the NAACP's *Crisis* magazine, had advised blacks in the 1890s that "they must not expect to have things done for them—they MUST DO FOR THEMSELVES; that they have on their hands a vast work of self-reformation to do, and that a little less complaint and whining, and a little more dogged work and manly striving would do us more credit and benefit than a thousand Force or Civil Rights bills." He assented to "legitimate efforts to purge the ballot of ignorance, pauperism and crime" and granted that it was "sometimes best that a partially developed people should be ruled by the best of their stronger and better neighbors for their own good" until they could rule themselves. Du Bois became an opponent of Washing-

---

22. Booker T. Washington, "Storm Before the Calm," *Colored American Magazine*, I (1900), 200–201; "Southern City Negro," *ibid.*, XVII (1909), 193.
23. Henry Bullock, *A History of Negro Education in the South* (New York, 1967), 123.
24. Harlan, *Booker T. Washington*, 252–53; Woodward, *Origins of the New South*, 336.

ton's recipes only when the steady acceleration of Jim Crow and mob violence demonstrated that black achievement and excellence were no guarantees of the ballot or of equal treatment.[25]

Although Washington's critics expressed their racial grievances more openly, they did not create a new politics, because they carried too much of the baggage of the past with them. Archibald Grimké, scholar and NAACP leader, believed that the first years of the twentieth century were an age of "industrialism and democracy."[26] The assumed coincidence had been the foundation of the liberal faith in the Emancipation Era. But evidence of the correlation was becoming harder and harder to find. The liberal state was not inevitably democratic. Disfranchisement was the spouse of industrialism in the South, and in 1896 the Supreme Court validated Jim Crow in the landmark case *Plessy* v. *Ferguson* and subsequently sanctioned most of the various voting barriers. On the other hand, federal courts concluded that many of the worst violations of black rights, such as lynching, could not be remedied because they were local and state matters. In the end, legal rulings depended upon the power the NAACP marshaled in the North. But most northern whites interested in the race question followed Washington's counsel in the South and preferred the advice of the new National Urban League in the North. Created in 1910 for the purpose of adjusting individual migrants to urban work and life, the Urban League merged the black elite's goal of racial uplift and the northern businessman's interest in integrating a growing but still auxiliary black labor force within its bastions. The NAACP's use of agitation and protest, its demands for equality, had no place within the hierarchical structures of the modern corporation.

Failing to attract elite whites, the Young Turks also failed to enlist the black masses in the North or the South. W. E. B. Du Bois attributed the stagnation of the NAACP to the gulf "between the aspirations of the leaders and the understanding of the masses." His view that the problem was one of communication acknowledged the problem but ignored the primary causes: the "Talented Tenth's" elitism and its ossified understanding of northern society and politics.[27]

Although connected to black southerners through family and sentiment, the northern elite viewed southern questions through the lens of its own interests. The North offered blacks broader economic opportunity and relief from the southern system's omnipresent racial subordination.

25. W. E. B. Du Bois, "The Conservation of the Races," in Howard Brotz (ed.), *Negro Social and Political Thought, 1850–1920* (New York, 1966), 490; Du Bois, *The Autobiography of W. E. B. Du Bois* (New York, 1968), 208.

26. Archibald Grimké, "Modern Industrialism and the Negro," in Brotz (ed.), *Negro Social and Political Thought*, 464–80.

27. Cited in Factor, *Black Response to America*, 354.

Even so, the new northern corporations blocked the growth of independent black enterprises at the same time they excluded non-Anglo-Saxons from managerial positions. And new professional associations impeded the careers of black scholars, doctors, nurses, lawyers, and teachers through licensing powers, education, and social connection. Even when the barriers were not racial, black achievement did not lead to power and influence. Ironically, these same forces that limited the careers of the elite encouraged a migration of rural blacks to cities. The new workers created a market for the services of black businessmen and professionals, and also had the numerical clout to demand new racial representation from indifferent urban political bosses. Thus, migration worked in several ways to erode the ideological and social basis for dissent.

American black nationalism, like its African cousin, did not offer a precise blueprint for racial progress. The nationalists of the North disagreed about which institutions ought to be racial. All agreed that black businesses and politics were desirable; many believed that black hospitals should be constructed; only a few supported racial public schools. Although the new enterprises were often launched in the name of the masses, they were, at best, remedies for elite grievances and often built at the expense of mass interests. They were not associated with political surrender, because, unlike the new racial institutions in the South, they were not accompanied with the imposition of overt racial setbacks like Jim Crow and disfranchisement. The political economy of the North did not need the elaborate rituals of black subservience and exclusion practiced in the South. Northern black leaders did not have to tarnish their ideology of racial pride with submission to racial subordination. They often protested discrimination vigorously, and sometimes effectively. But they also recognized the tacit necessity to accommodate to the larger business and political elite, and they distanced themselves from popular forces, both black and white.

The northern elite, like the southern, had bridged the gap between its rhetoric and its practice by affirming the primacy of racial bonds: the strengthening of the black middle class and the creation of black captains of industry and a Talented Tenth were seen as equivalent to racial progress. The solution was hegemonic because alternatives were nonexistent. America's "domestic" imperialism had destroyed the institutions of nineteenth-century popular power—Republicanism, Populism, and industrial unionism. Most blacks were rural southerners. Before the migration of World War I, only one million were northerners, and they were scattered, making up 5 percent of Philadelphia and Pittsburgh, 2 percent of New York and Chicago, and barely visible in the censuses of Detroit, Cleveland, and

Newark. Southern, disfranchised, Jim Crowed, and unorganized, most blacks could not actively dissent from the middle-class agenda.

When Garvey came to the United States in 1916, he had already accepted the methods and goals of elite politics. Therefore, he eyed Afro-American achievements—Tuskegee in the South, the racial businesses and voluntary organizations in the North—and ignored the problems. His enthusiasm was especially warm because of the contrast between black progress in the United States and the stagnation he observed in Jamaica and other Caribbean colonies. Garvey's evaluation of the West Indies was not unique. Most of the ten islanders who had attended the Pan-African Conference in 1900 remained in England or settled in Africa. The few who returned to the West Indies cultivated Pan-African sentiments and ideology but found few ways to create the kinds of racial enterprises and associations that were in the United States.[28] Jamaican history revealed that the new Pan-African solutions rested upon economic development, not racial sentiment.

The new imperialism had bypassed the British Caribbean for the glitter of Africa and the Far East. Garvey's Jamaica, once Britain's richest colony, was typical. In 1906 an English traveler found the island "more than half derelict and wholly without the attraction of wealth and promise." Jamaica's economic problems were not recent. Its economy had stagnated in the postslavery period. The sugar industry in 1865 employed only twenty thousand freedmen, one-fifth of the labor force worked under slavery. The inefficiency of production became visible when Jamaican exports faced the competition of beet sugar and sugar grown on virgin soil, and the dismantlement of the protective system that had guaranteed a market in England. The surviving, reorganized estates required large amounts of capital, not workers.[29]

The inadequacies of capitalist agriculture spawned a rival, subsistence economy. Through purchase, renting, and squatting, freedmen acquired land. By 1860, Jamaica had 200,000 peasants, increasingly independent of the ruling authorities and their civilization. The peasant pioneered in the development and production of bananas and began to produce for the market. In 1890 farmers owning less than twenty acres produced 39 percent of the island's exports. But the new economy had limits. Responding to world trade, it succumbed to it. Peasants could not compete with United Fruit's

28. Mathurin, *Henry Sylvester Williams*, 165–71.
29. John Henderson, *Jamaica* (London, 1906), 2; Gisela Eisner, *Jamaica, 1830–1930: A Study in Economic Growth* (Manchester, England, 1961), 169–70. The decline in sugar production both preceded emancipation and was accelerated by it. Franklin W. Knight, *The Caribbean: The Genesis of a Fragmented Nationalism* (New York, 1978), 240.

far-flung banana empire or sell enough provisions to the sugar estates to prosper. Without a marketable crop and without additional land, the black peasantry became impoverished. As in other parts of the world, distress reached a zenith in the depression of the 1890s. Capitalist agriculture proved more durable, but the plantation still did not generate sufficient work for Jamaicans. If the peasants or their sons had been able to find industrial jobs on the island, their condition might have been difficult but not hopeless. However, colonies had not been founded to compete with home production. Imperial commercial restrictions and the absence of cheap sources of power aborted new industries.[30]

So Jamaicans went abroad to places where wages often doubled and trebled the rate on the island. One hundred thousand left to build new railroads in Central America and work on the banana plantations that had made them necessary. They dug the Panama Canal, and they cultivated sugar on other islands, like Cuba, where it was profitable. Jamaicans participated in the economic development of the new imperialism, but their labor did not alter their own society. Many Jamaicans at this time emigrated permanently. Those who returned used their earnings to prop up the peasant communities they had left.[31]

Jamaica's modern elite had been loyal to the plantation economy and to British rule. When one dissenter, George Gordon, championed the peasant cause, the leading colored newspaper accused him of disregarding "political decency and propriety" by seeking "popularity with the greasy unwashed mobocracy of the island." After peasants rebelled against the local legal system in 1865, the white and colored elite together surrendered Jamaican self-government to the Colonial Office. The planters acknowledged that they could not rule without the full complement of powers they possessed as slaveholders. As historian Ken Post observed, the colonial state stepped in to govern, because no other class was strong enough to replace the planters. A Legislative Council of appointed men took the place of the elected assembly in 1866. Colonial rule in Jamaica became one model for the new imperial regimes imposed on Africans at the end of the century.[32]

30. Woodville K. Marshall, "Notes on Peasant Development in the West Indies Since 1838," *Social and Economic Studies*, XVII (1968), 253–56, 261–62; Eisner, *Jamaica*, 179–80, 225, 228–30.
31. G. W. Roberts, "Demographic Aspects of Rural Development: The Jamaican Experience," *Social and Economic Studies*, XVII (1968), 277.
32. Mavis C. Campbell, *The Dynamics of Change in a Slave Society: A Socio-Political History of Free Coloreds in Jamaica, 1800–1865* (Rutherford, N.J., 1976), 299, 331–36; Ken Post, *Arise Ye Starvelings: The Jamaican Labour Rebellion of 1938 and Its Aftermath* (The Hague, 1978), 35.

Although the colored elite supported the new British power, it had not yielded its goal of leading Jamaica. Before the cataclysm of 1865, a British officer commented that the "colored party . . . now looks to have at no distant date the command of the Assembly." Many white landowners had migrated to England during the immediate postemancipation labor conflicts and ensuing depression. Some whites urged replenishing the racial stock with white settlers from Great Britain, but Jamaica's economy did not attract the ambitious and adventurous. Therefore, the colored elite looked forward to political power won by default. Unlike equivalents in Afro-America and Africa, it rarely attempted to construct racial alliances with the black rural population. Its 1906 slogan JAMAICA FOR THE JAMAICANS was not a call for the union of Jamaicans against imperial rule but only a demand by the colored elite that they, rather than white men, be allowed to administer a British colony. The colored elite's continuing prejudices against men of dark skin disqualified the growing number of accomplished blacks from the competition.[33]

Most of the modern men of Jamaica were light-skinned and had been free at the time of emancipation. The children of black slaves and whites, the free caste of 35,000 members had equaled the numbers of whites but was overwhelmed by the 310,000 black slaves. The ending of legal discrimination based upon color, part of the progress of emancipation, allowed more men of black skin to achieve and succeed in the modern professions, once the preserve of the light-skinned elite. By 1911, four of the seven non-whites in the Legislative Council were Negroes.[34]

Although the modern men of Jamaica were divided by color, they all prescribed British capital as a cure for the island's problems. Many more, however, migrated to places where capital investment was more abundant. Jamaican nationalism was weak because its prerequisite—economic growth—was too frail to retain its ambitious men, like Marcus Garvey.[35]

Nationalist politics in the United States, West Africa, and the Caribbean were created by a modern elite schooled in Western culture during the period preceding World War I. Their goal was progress, whereas the majority of blacks, who were farmers, valued independence and self-sufficiency. Therefore, the elite relied upon the Western governments to destroy traditional and popular forms of organization and politics so that capital accu-

33. Henderson, *Jamaica*, 116–17.
34. Campbell, *Dynamics of Change*, 331–32; H. A. Will, *Constitutional Changes in the British West Indies, 1880–1903* (Oxford, 1970), 252, 271, 288, 290. By 1900, the council included elected men, but only a fraction of the population had the right to vote until 1944, when universal suffrage was instituted in response to the riots and strikes of 1938. Post, *Arise Ye Starvelings*, 39.
35. Mathurin, *Henry Sylvester Williams*, 88–92, 105–205.

mulation, the life blood of the new society, could proceed. This new class effectively relinquished black suffrage in the southern United States and self-government or independence in the Caribbean and West Africa. Despite their compliance, they were discriminated against and excluded from the highest posts of the new order. In the three main regions of the black world, the elite assumed that racial institutions modeled on the dominant ones of Western society were the solutions to their new problems. They argued, too, that these modern institutions would benefit all blacks, that racial bonds could dissolve the color, class, cultural, and regional divisions within the black world. Despite the rhetoric, however, their solutions were not popular, because they were peripheral to the lives of most blacks. Elite ideas received a hearing, however, wherever men and women were uprooted and thirsted after careers and social progress. As the effects of capitalism overwhelmed traditional communities, more black men and women became potential converts. Marcus Garvey's early life was one variation of a common experience.

2 / In Search of a Career Open to Talent
The Early Life of Marcus Garvey

The footfalls of the modern world were subdued in St. Ann's Bay, a small town and port on the northern coast of Jamaica. Marcus Garvey was born there in 1887, not far from the waterfalls of Roaring River, an international mecca for lovers of romantic scenes. But the local people's admiration of nature was necessarily tempered by their experiences with tropical hurricanes and economic distress. The hard life of the area had its impact on the Garvey family: Garvey's mother, Sarah, bore eleven children, but only Marcus, the youngest, and one sister reached adulthood. In addition, in the 1890s the decaying peasant economy undermined residual family bonds and affection.[1]

Garvey's grandfather and father were master masons. His father was well read, though without formal education. Marcus Garvey, Sr.'s quest for self-improvement was typical of artisans wherever they lived. His world was not the peasant's. He was Mr. Garvey to everyone in the family and village. A resident in the town recalled that "he always acted as if he did not belong among the villagers." In industrial nations men like him had been the core of working-class organizations and also of industrial stability. "The intelligent artisan," as the British middle class would call him, played both roles. But in Jamaica the artisan played neither. Garvey's father was a modern man with no modern role to play. His work as a stonemason was dependent upon the prosperity of the villagers. Mr. Garvey had once built houses; now he made tombstones. The women of the family were also affected. Searching for additional income, Sarah Garvey became a petty trader, cook, and housekeeper while Marcus's sister, Indiana, entered domestic service in England. Some of the family's land was lost during the 1890s, though the particulars are undocumented. Garvey, Sr., used the courts frequently to defend his claims. Whatever the specific merits of his pleadings, numerous other landowners of the area lost their titles at this time to the market and to the Crown's seizure of squatters' land. Sarah Gar-

1. Amy Jacques Garvey, *Garvey and Garveyism* (Kingston, Jamaica, 1963), 3–7.

vey retained a small plot, owned jointly with a brother, from which she grew the allspice and citrus she traded. The experiences of the Garvey family—shrinking landholdings, migration, domestic employment, and petty trading—are common in peasant societies in decline.[2]

While he was still in primary school, Garvey was apprenticed to his godfather, Alfred E. Burrowes, a printer. Poor relations with his father and the stagnant local economy probably ruled out his father's trade, stonemasonry. Stimulated by the books and newspapers he read in Burrowes' printshop, Garvey went to the big city, Kingston, in 1906, after working briefly at a branch of his godfather's printery. Garvey brought his mother to the city after a hurricane had destroyed her crops. His parents had parted sometime before. Sarah Garvey found work as a domestic but disliked city life. She died in 1908. Garvey thrived, though he sometimes experienced the discomforts of the country boy in the slick city.[3] Minor setbacks in informal debates, a popular pastime, only drove him to improve his oratorical skills.

Garvey worked as a pressman with P. A. Benjamin and Company, a pharmaceutical business that printed its own labels and advertising leaflets. Many years later, the retired head of the firm told the Jamaican writer Richard Hart that Garvey was one of four men employed in the printery. According to Hart, assertions by Amy Jacques Garvey, Garvey himself, and historian David Cronon that the young Garvey was a foreman at Benjamin's are questionable. It seems unlikely that a young man barely out of his teens would be made foreman or even that there would be such a position in a small shop. Working as a printer extended Garvey's world but also brought larger problems. In 1908, he joined other printers in an unsuccessful strike. One of the founders of the union, A. J. McGlashan, recalled Garvey's participation but denied Cronon's assertion that Garvey was a strike leader.[4]

Garvey does not seem to have been hurt by his union activity, because he found a new job easily in the government's printing office. He somehow scraped up enough money to begin a short-lived newspaper, *Garvey's Watchman*, in 1909. He also joined the National Club, founded by S. A. G.

2. *Ibid.*, 7; Ken Post, *Arise Ye Starvelings: The Jamaican Labour Rebellion of 1938 and Its Aftermath* (The Hague, 1978), 40–42.

3. A. J. Garvey, *Garvey and Garveyism*, 3–7; MG, "A Journey of Self-Discovery," in John Henrik Clarke (ed.), *Marcus Garvey and the Vision of Africa* (New York, 1974), 71–73.

4. Richard Hart, "The Life and Resurrection of Marcus Garvey," *Race*, IX (1967), 219–20. There are many gaps in our knowledge of Garvey's work experience. At his trial in 1923, he mentioned that he had worked for the United Fruit Company in Kingston. *Marcus Garvey v. United States of America*, 267 U.S. 607 (1924), 2210.

"Sandy" Cox, a lawyer and longtime legal clerk in Jamaica's government service. Although the club elected two of its members to the Legislative Council, the victory did not produce new opportunities for Garvey.[5]

He left Jamaica in 1910. Perhaps he could not find what he would have called suitable work. He subsequently claimed that he set forth to discover whether the black condition in other places was the same as in Jamaica. Because many of his future explanations of his behavior professed similar detachment and disinterest in personal goals, it is useful to evaluate Garvey's account of his decision. Garvey rendered his ambitions and dilemmas in the language and formulas of the heroic biographies of the Victorian age. Inevitably, the great trials encountered by the hero began with family dramas. One day when he was still a boy, Garvey was helping his father build a vault for a coffin. At lunchtime, the father climbed the ladder, immediately pulled it up, and left his son alone and hungry in the dark, unfinished vault. The boy's cries received no answer. The menacing specters of dead men were dispelled only in the sleep brought on by Marcus' hunger and fatigue. His father awakened him roughly: "Boy, this is a lesson to teach you never to be afraid." Another time, his father attempted to send him to a reformatory for delinquents after he was caught in some boyish prank. Luckily, the magistrate did not agree. Young Garvey's fright was calmed by his mother, who was warm, affectionate, and religious. These incidents, and presumably others like them, scarred the relations between father and son. Typically, Garvey at first refused to aid his father when the latter was hospitalized as a pauper at the time of Garvey's greatest success in the United States. Although Garvey relented, the episode revealed a vindictiveness caused by the hurts he had endured as a boy. In maturity, Garvey was merciless with opponents; he often cried when frustrated or rejected.[6]

But his personal vulnerability was concealed behind a public facade. Garvey's two wives, not he himself, recounted his childhood experiences with his father, and associates and reporters documented his refusal to aid his father. Garvey's public portrait of his father was more favorable but also more abstract. In an essay he wrote for a popular American magazine, the *Century*, in 1923, he described his father as a man of "brilliant intellect

5. A. J. Garvey, *Garvey and Garveyism*, 7.
6. Amy Jacques Garvey, "The Early Years of Marcus Garvey," in Clarke (ed.), *Garvey and the Vision of Africa*, 31; Amy Ashwood Garvey, "Marcus Garvey: Portrait of a Liberator" (Typescript in possession of Lionel Yard, Brooklyn, N.Y.), 10, 181–91. Amy Ashwood's biography is the best source for Garvey's early organizing experiences in Jamaica because she accompanied him. The work is free of the spleen one might have expected after an unpleasant divorce. Its capsule biographies of many Garveyites and rendering of numerous incidents in the history of the UNIA are invaluable.

and dashing courage. He was unafraid of consequences. He took human chances in the course of his life, as most bold men do, and he failed at the close of his career. He once had a fortune; he died poor." The description omitted his own relationship with his father and was a counterpoint to a vignette concerning his mother, whom he portrayed as warm, charitable, and forgiving—"the direct opposite of my father." The qualities he attributed to his father and mother have been confirmed by other accounts. But Garvey provided only heightened, often idealized distillations of his early experiences. As a boy, he refused to be whipped by a teacher, he recalled. "It annoys me to be defeated; hence to me, to be defeated is to find cause for an ever lasting struggle to reach the top." As a printer's apprentice, he was "strong and manly, and I made them respect me. I developed a strong and forceful character, and have maintained it still."[7]

In Garvey's world, men act alone against hostile forces. The scene of the contest is a "world of sin, the flesh, and the devil." Whether this conclusion was the child's or the man's, whether it was expressed in religious or secular language, it was the fountain of all his actions. The social context disappeared in the battle. We are not told about the causes of his father's poverty or about the early difficulties that forced Garvey to assert his strength. We are not informed of his purposes.[8]

The world of contending forces was animated by personal, not social, motivation. Garvey encountered the world of privilege and rank at the threshold of adult life. As a child at play and in school, he was not conscious of the significance of racial differences, he recalled. When he was fourteen, a white girl who was his friend was sent off to school in Scotland while he went to work. To Garvey, the girl's parents had sent her abroad "to separate them and draw the color line because he was a 'nigger,'" not because children of white Methodist ministers in Jamaica were routinely sent abroad to complete their education. Even if his understanding of the reason for the separation was accurate, his response to it seems to contradict his interpretation: "I simply had no regrets." Such indifference seems a more appropriate state of mind for the racial leader than for the boy of fourteen. In fact, as a young man, Garvey had boasted to Alfred Burrowes that he planned to marry a "Spanish-Irish heiress."[9]

Similarly, Garvey's descriptions of his early working years show him journeying from the hostile world of his childhood to the personal self-

7. MG, "A Journey of Self-Discovery," 71–73.
8. *Ibid.*, 70.
9. *Ibid.*, 72; MG to Alfred E. Burrowes, March 2, 1914, in Robert A. Hill (ed.), *The Marcus Garvey and Universal Negro Improvement Association Papers* (10 vols. projected; Berkeley, 1983–), I, 35.

assertion of his maturity, without confronting either an intervening social structure or occasional states of self-doubt. He "had to make a fight for a place in the world. It was not so easy to pass on to office and position." It was probably difficult. Yet he tells us, "I had not much difficulty in finding and holding a place for myself, for I was aggressive." Garvey's accounts of his emotions and desires fit neatly into the Victorian cosmology. But in the real world, an adult's aggression, ambition, and strength—qualities Garvey claimed proudly—usually come alloyed with earlier fears and frustrations, which are not so readily shed.[10]

Garvey's self-conception and view of the world were class formulas for success. The attainment of "self-mastery" and "character" was necessary for poor men and women to transcend the lot of the many to achieve a firm and respectable place in society. Marcus Garvey, Sr.'s pedagogy, harsh according to present methods of child rearing, was necessary for the task. If he could not transmit sufficient land or a prosperous trade, he could instill character, a valuable asset to do battle, to struggle for existence in a hostile world. For many persons, the achievement of the qualities became the surrogate for the achievement of the goal. But Garvey was neither satisfied with acquiring the qualities of character nor successful in translating them into a secure social status in Jamaica.

His decision to leave the island was undoubtedly colored with ambitions, personal doubts, political perceptions, restlessness, and desire for adventure. His destination was not exceptional. In 1911, nearly thirteen thousand Jamaican emigrants left the island. Most of them went to Central America, where at least sixty thousand Jamaicans labored. Rapid expansion of banana cultivation made Costa Rica a magnet. Garvey's uncle obtained employment for him as a timekeeper on one of the United Fruit Company's plantations. Garvey began a newspaper, observed the exploitation of workers, and experienced the frustrations of improving the conditions of migrant and alien agricultural labor. Although his petitions to local British consuls were ignored, Garvey won a small reputation as an agitator who demanded the rights of British subjects for his people. From 1910 through 1912, he traveled to Ecuador, Venezuela, and Colombia, and throughout Central America. Opportunity continued to elude him. Returning to Jamaica in 1912, he discovered the island offered no more than before. Garvey resumed his travels, this time in England and on the Continent.[11]

Garvey's important experiences in London were intellectual and politi-

10. MG, "A Journey of Self-Discovery," 73.
11. *Ibid.*; A. J. Garvey, *Garvey and Garveyism*, 7–8; H. A. Will, *Constitutional Changes in the British West Indies, 1880–1903* (Oxford, 1970), 300–302.

cal. He took courses at Birkbeck College, which eventually became a branch of the University of London meant for working-class youths without the standard preparation for the university. But his major instruction took place outside the academy. Garvey spent hours in the visitor's gallery of the House of Commons, where he heard Lloyd George and others debate the issues of the day. While he was dismayed at their discussions about the colonies, he acquired, like other young colonials, a "peculiar fondness for England." A Guianese, T. Ras Makonnen, explained the city's attraction for young men from the provinces of the empire: "Despite the suffering of our people, there was never a gloomy moment, particularly when we realized how much we could do in England: write any tract we wanted to; make terrible speeches; all this when you knew very well that back in the colonies even to say 'God is love' might get the authorities after you!" Garvey listened to others and spoke himself in Hyde Park. The wealth, knowledge, freedom, and range of culture in England must have awed him, as it did others, and must have made Jamaica seem very provincial.[12]

Britain's elite culture did not offer likely avenues for him to attain the power it flaunted. The blacks living in London supplied more accessible models. Small and cosmopolitan, the racial community in Britain lacked the social stratification of the colonies and United States. Garvey entered the thick of this world when he went to work for the fascinating Dusé Mohamed Ali, who knitted together many of the prewar relationships among British humanitarians, black students, and African and European businessmen.

Ali was a Sudanese-Egyptian actor, journalist, and businessman living in England. In July, 1912, he launched the *African Times and Orient Review* (*ATOR*), "a Pan-Oriental, Pan-African journal at the seat of the British Empire . . . [to] lay the aims, desires, and intentions of the Black, Brown, and Yellow Races—within and without the Empire—at the throne of Caesar." Africans, Afro-Americans, whites, Indians, Chinese, and Arabs contributed. Ali's editorial offices served as a center for Africans seeking commercial relations with British businessmen. Eclectic in opinions, the *African Times* expressed abuses in British colonies, promoted African businesses, and reported the major achievements of the black and colored world. In short, it embodied the loose theory and untidy practice of prewar Pan-Africanism.[13]

Garvey worked briefly as a messenger at the journal's office and published an essay on the West Indies in the October, 1913, issue. The personal

12. A. A. Garvey, "Marcus Garvey," 25, 36; T. Ras Makonnen, *Pan-Africanism from Within*, ed. Kenneth King (Nairobi, Kenya, 1973), 123.
13. Imanuel Geiss, *The Pan-African Movement* (London, 1974), 223; Ian Duffield, "The

and intellectual contacts with the men connected with the magazine revealed the usefulness of Pan-African contacts and perhaps motivated him to expand his ambitions beyond Jamaica and the West Indies to encompass the black world.[14]

When Garvey returned to Kingston in July, 1914, a newspaper report that he had been "to England for a course of study" did not do justice to his education there. A better indication of his thinking was the announcement of his new organization, the Universal Negro Improvement Association and African Communities League (UNIA) on August 1, 1914, the anniversary of the emancipation of Jamaican slaves. The UNIA's goals were

> To establish a universal confraternity among the race.
> To promote the spirit of race pride and love.
> To reclaim the fallen of the race.
> To administer to and assist the needy.
> To assist in civilizing the backward tribes of Africa.
> To strengthen the imperialism of independent African states.
> To establish commissaries or agencies in the principal countries of the world for the protection of all Negroes, irrespective of nationality.
> To promote a conscientious Christian worship among the native tribes of Africa.
> To establish universities, colleges and secondary schools for the further education and culture of the boys and girls of the race.
> To conduct a worldwide commercial and industrial intercourse.

If the language seems archaic to modern ears and lacks the direct style of Garvey's earlier and later writings, the broad scope revealed modern ambitions. Garvey's goals were clothed in the expressions of the religious mission, whose schools and economic enterprises were often vehicles of development in the colonies. But the international racial institutions, Garvey's agency of change, emerged out of the Pan-African ideas and activities he had come in contact with in London.[15]

Garvey's program for Jamaica was remarkably similar to the blueprint for modernization common among the Pan-Africanists.

Local (Jamaica) Objects
To establish educational and industrial colleges for the further education and culture of our boys and girls.

Business Activities of Dusé Mohamed Ali: An Example of the Economic Dimension of Pan-Africanism, 1912–1945," *Journal of the Historical Society of Nigeria*, IV (1969), 571–600.

14. MG, "The British West Indies in the Mirror of Civilization," in Clarke (ed.), *Garvey and the Vision of Africa*, 77–82; John Bruce to Major Loving, January 13, 1919, file 10218-261/39, and I. Newby to Lieutenant Colonel H. A. Pakenham, November 22, 1918, file 10218-261/36, Military Intelligence Division (hereinafter cited as MID), in Record Group 165, Records of the Department of War, National Archives.

15. Daniel T. Williams has reprinted the first statement of UNIA goals in his *The Perilous Road of Marcus Garvey* (Tuskegee, Ala., 1969).

To reclaim the fallen and degraded (especially the criminal class) and help them to a state of good citizenship.
To administer to, and assist the needy.
To promote the better taste for commerce and industry.
To promote a universal confraternity and strengthen the body of brotherhood and unity among the races.

Garvey's idea to end discrimination and exploitation through the creation of instruments of improvement did not emerge spontaneously. His program of uplift came to him as a result of contact with something that he judged superior—the civilization he had observed in London.[16]

Garvey's essay of 1913 on the West Indies contrasted sharply with his thinking at the time of the launching of the UNIA. In the essay he had stressed the production of wealth by Negro labor, the inhuman treatment of slaves, and their heroic revolts. "With the characteristic fortitude of the African," he wrote, "the Negroes shouldered their burdens [after slavery] and set themselves to work, receiving scanty remuneration for their services. By their industry and thrift they have been able to provide themselves with small holdings which they are improving, greatly to their credit." He had excoriated the society that permitted "intellectually inferior" white youths to receive the civil service positions that blacks merited.[17]

A year after his return to Jamaica, Garvey denied "the intention of the society [UNIA] to belabour any race question in this country as some may be inclined to believe. . . . What concerns us here is the development of our people and country. As a society we realize that the negro people of Jamaica need a great deal of improvement. The bulk of our people are in darkness and are really unfit for good society. To the cultured mind the bulk of our people are contemptible—that is to say, they are entirely outside the pale of cultured appreciation." The small farmers were no longer heroic, thrifty, or self-improving: "Go into the country parts of Jamaica and you see there villainy and vice of the worst kind, immorality, obeah, and all kinds of dirty things are part of the avocation of a large percentage of our people and we, the few of cultured tastes, can in no way save the race from injury in a balanced comparison with other people, for the standard of races or of anything else is not arrived at by the few who are always the exceptions, but by the majority."

The achievements of the few would always be limited by the condition of the majority. Therefore, the UNIA "set itself the task to go among the people and help them up to a better state of appreciation among the cultured

16. Ibid.
17. MG, "The British West Indies," 81.

classes, and raise them to the standard of civilized approval. To do this we must get the co-operation and sympathy of our white brothers."[18] Garvey's analysis of Jamaican history and society led him ineluctably to the conclusion that what was required was not racial conflict but the uplift and direction that Edward Blyden and the new nationalists had prescribed. Soliciting white elites was as important as organizing rural blacks for the huge task.

A year of personal difficulties only confirmed Garvey's rather pessimistic intellectual conclusions. He had founded the UNIA with his future wife, Amy Ashwood. Ashwood, born in 1897 in Port Antonio, Jamaica, spent her early years in Panama, where her father ran a bakery and restaurant, and then in Colombia. At eleven, she had returned to Jamaica to attend high school. She met Garvey at a debate at the Baptist church hall in Kingston. The proposition to be argued was "Morality does not improve with civilization." As Amy Ashwood described her romance with the young man, they became instantly devoted to each other, and their dreams for their own personal and racial liberation mingled. She claimed that the motto of the UNIA, ONE GOD, ONE AIM, ONE DESTINY, referred initially to their personal bonds and vows. The young man once wrote to her:

> Your Napoleon is longing to see you, longing to gaze into your beautiful eyes in fond devotion, let no mother, no father, no sister, no brother stand in the way of the redemption of Africa. I will always worship at your shrine.
>
> > Your devoted Napoleon,
> > Marcus[19]

Romantic barriers were almost as great as the pair's political difficulties. Amy Ashwood's parents forbade her to see Garvey, because they suspected that a young man struggling to sell greeting and condolence cards and tombstones would not be able to support a wife. The young lovers, with the help of the Ashwoods' maid, found ways to overcome the prohibition, in the manner of French bedroom comedies. Taking advantage of her father's absence and his business credit, Amy rented a house in Kingston to serve as UNIA headquarters. Eventually, the two must have won some parental tolerance, because they worked together on the UNIA for two years.[20] By 1916, however, the UNIA had attracted only one hundred mem-

18. MG, "Universal Negro Improvement Association: Address Delivered by the President at the Annual Meeting," Kingston *Daily Gleaner*, August 26, 1915.

19. Lionel Yard, "The First Amy Tells All" (Typescript in possession of Lionel Yard), 41.

20. Amy Ashwood's mother was reported to be an officer of the UNIA at this time. Kingston *Daily Chronicle*, August 3, 1915.

bers. The Ashwoods dispatched their daughter to Panama while the two young lovers vowed eternal devotion.[21]

Garvey attributed his organizational failures to the hostility of the "colored gentry." The "retrograde state of the Negro . . . is attributable to the callous indifference and insincerity of those Negroes who have failed to do their duty by the race in promoting a civilized imperialism that would meet the approval of established ideals." The colored opposition presented him with a dilemma. He "had to decide whether to please my friends and be one of the 'black-whites' of Jamaica, and be reasonably prosperous, or come out openly and defend and help improve and protect the integrity of the black millions and suffer." Choosing to try to improve the masses, Garvey won the hatred of the colored elite, who convinced Jamaican whites, "afraid of offending the 'colored gentry' of Jamaica," to oppose his plans.[22]

It is likely that Garvey's denunciation was triggered by the government's rejection of his petition for Crown lands to begin a school for delinquent boys. The particular plot he sought was set aside for houses for civil servants, most of whom were probably colored. Given Garvey's intentions, however, the conflict seemed to be more a matter of competition for a limited amount of land than a question of ideology. Although Garvey was dark-skinned, like the majority of Jamaicans, he was not a leader in the mold of George Gordon, championing the interests of the peasants and opposing the ruling classes of Jamaica. Quite the contrary. His principal supporters appear to have been whites—clergymen, businessmen, and colonial officials. UNIA meetings highlighted the attendance of prominent Jamaicans, preached class conciliation, and affirmed loyalty to Britain.[23]

Garvey's critics included the black elite, as well as the colored elite, and also other black dissenters. When an article by him that had come out in the British magazine *Tourist* in June, 1914, was reprinted in the leading Jamaican newspaper, he was roasted by numerous opponents. The article claimed that Jamaicans lived "in an atmosphere of equality and comradeship." A Jamaican labor leader, W. G. Hinchcliff, and a former comrade in the National Club, Alexander Dixon, attacked him for his portrayal of Ja-

21. A. A. Garvey, "Marcus Garvey," 80. Richard Hart claimed that colonial officials, alarmed at Garvey's agitational activities, were about to imprison him on a charge of vagrancy when associates rented premises for him to conduct a school. Hart's account implies, without supporting evidence, that the UNIA was at that time more effective than the accounts by Garvey and Amy Ashwood suggest. Hart, "Life and Resurrection of Garvey," 22.

22. MG, "A Journey of Self-Discovery," 75; MG, "A Talk with Afro-West Indians," in Clarke (ed.), *Garvey and the Vision of Africa*, 83–84.

23. A. A. Garvey, "Marcus Garvey," 42; MG, "A Journey of Self-Discovery," 75; Kingston *Daily Chronicle*, November 28, 1914.

maica as an "island paradise" and particularly for his negative remarks on the character and culture of the common people. Garvey was forced to call a meeting to defend himself. He refused to retract his indictments, reiterated the need for improvement, and warned all Jamaicans to avoid politics. Garvey's arrows were occasionally aimed at the colored gentry of Jamaica. They also targeted "black professionals" who married colored or white women, black ministers and teachers, "moral cowards," and black men with "money and education who think they are white and colored." Garvey was indicting Jamaica's middle class. By the time of World War I, it included increasing numbers of blacks, but its older color separation was always a reference point in political discourse. Garvey also praised the British Constitution as "free and liberal," dispensing "justice to everyman within the state." [24]

The majority of black Jamaicans were also indifferent to Garvey's efforts to "raise them to the standards of civilized approval." During the first year, he had spent most of his time lecturing in Kingston. He held his first meeting outside of the capital city in October, 1915, at St. Ann's Bay. At one meeting in his hometown, the audience laughed at his speech. Garvey burst into tears. The people's reaction was probably prompted as much by the procedures of the meeting as by its object. The treasurer forgot the speech that Garvey had written for him and then neglected to call for the collection. Despite one's sympathy for Garvey's predicament, it would be inaccurate to credit the broad rejection of these amateurish meetings to racial or ideological opposition. Nevertheless, Amy Ashwood bitterly recalled that "not one soul in St. Ann's Bay helped us with a penny." [25]

After Garvey failed to obtain the government land, he began to solicit funds to build a school modeled on Tuskegee. Garvey attributed his decision to become a race leader to his reading of Booker T. Washington's classic autobiography, *Up From Slavery*, on the ship voyage from London to Kingston. Once back in Jamaica, Garvey had written to Washington, explaining his work and asking for assistance. Washington invited him to visit if he came to the United States but withheld a contribution—the standard reply to admiring unknowns. [26] If Garvey's account is accurate, his inspiration was not unique. After attending the Tuskegee Conference on Africa in 1912, some Jamaican teachers and students petitioned the government to

24. MG, "The Evolution of Latter-Day Slaves: Jamaica, a Country of Black and White," *Tourist*, XIX (June, 1914), 61–63, reprinted in Kingston *Daily Gleaner*, July 13, 1914; responses to it are in the issues of July 14, 15, 18, August 14, and September 25, 1914; Kingston *Daily Chronicle*, August 26, 1915.

25. A. A. Garvey, "Marcus Garvey," 48–50.

26. MG to Booker T. Washington, September 8, 1914, Washington to MG, September 17, 1914, both in Booker T. Washington Papers, Library of Congress.

establish a school like Tuskegee on the island. A former colonial governor of Jamaica perceived the reasons for their failure to convince: "The theory of special training in productive manual labor . . . has always flourished less where the power and economic incentive to adopt that method of improving him has been absent." In Jamaica, there was no political or economic motive to create a better-educated labor force. The perennial shortage of teachers, even with the opening of the Government College in 1870, and small budgets revealed official indifference. In theory, children through the age of fourteen attended primary schools administered by the Anglican church. Garvey had attended primary school, but he was not part of the 1 percent to receive secondary education. Numerous Jamaicans who wished secondary education and teacher training went abroad to Tuskegee or other American universities where ambitious young men could work to pay for their education.[27]

On April 12, 1915, Garvey wrote again to Washington, sending him newspaper reports about UNIA meetings and emphasizing the similarity of his own approach to Washington's. He also stressed his white support and black opposition. Washington renewed the invitation to visit Tuskegee. He died later that year, but his successor, R. R. Moton, visited Jamaica in February, 1916. Garvey tried and failed to meet Moton, but he was able to send him a memorandum. In it Garvey wrote that the "'race problem' is a paradox. I personally would like to solve the situation on the broadest humanitarian lines. I would like to solve it on the platform of Dr. Booker T. Washington, and I am working on those lines hence you will find that up to now my one true friend as far as you can rely on his friendship, is the whiteman." He attached a long list of whites from the Jamaican establishment who "have come to my assistance to help me along."

Although Garvey appeared to hew the Washington line, his specific plans must have been vague, because a newspaper announcement of his departure to the United States on March 1, 1916, declared simply, "Mr. Garvey will be leaving Jamaica shortly on a lecturing tour through the West Indies, North, South and Central America, in connection with the movement." Once again, Garvey followed a route traveled by other Jamaicans, who were beginning to migrate in greater numbers to the United States.[28]

27. MG, "A Journey of Self Discovery," 73; Sydney Haldane Olivier, *White Capital and Coloured Labour* (London, 1929), 188; Mavis C. Campbell, *The Dynamics of Change in a Slave Society: A Socio-Political History of Free Coloreds in Jamaica, 1800–1865* (Rutherford, N.J., 1976), 335–36.

28. MG to Booker T. Washington, April 12, 1915, Washington to MG, April 27, 1915, in Washington Papers; MG to R. R. Moton, February 29, 1916, in Robert Russa Moton Papers, Hollis Burke Frissell Library, Tuskegee Institute, Tuskegee, Ala.; MG, "A Talk with Afro-West Indians," 83–87.

Garvey lodged with a Jamaican family in Harlem and found part-time work as a printer. His initial associations were made through John Bruce, a retired civil servant and popular journalist, the American distributor of Ali's *African Times*. Bruce contributed five dollars to the school Garvey proposed to build in Jamaica and gave Garvey introductions to leading black New Yorkers, including W. E. B. Du Bois. Initially, Garvey made little impression. Slowed down by the pneumonia he contracted shortly after he arrived, he was well enough by June to lecture in Boston. By the end of the year, he had visited Philadelphia, Pittsburgh, Baltimore, Washington, and Chicago. In early 1917, he toured the South and visited Tuskegee. Although he received neither the attention more prominent people did nor official endorsement for philanthropic support, Garvey was pleased with his visit.[29]

In his first year in the United States, Garvey met numerous racial leaders, but he did not raise much money for the school. He usually spoke in churches. Handbills portrayed him as a professor or orator who had addressed "packed audiences" in England, on the Continent, and in the major cities in the United States. He often assessed the position of "the Negroes in the West Indies after 78 years of emancipation" or evaluated the "world position of the race." After the talk, he asked for financial contributions. Itinerant lecturers like Garvey were fair targets for local delinquents. In Detroit, Garvey suffered head cuts at one church meeting where some boys pelted him with stones. Luckily, Ashwood, who had joined him in the United States in September, 1918, and was with him at the meeting, obtained the money for two tickets to Virginia from a sympathetic Jamaican dentist. But other problems confronted the pair in Virginia. A minister permitted them to speak before his congregation but, aware of the potential loss for his church, he stipulated that they not try to collect money. While feverishly preparing flyers to announce their meeting, they discovered that the cleric had a mistress who might be used to overcome his financial restrictions. The two sent a telegram, under the woman's signature, requesting an urgent meeting with him. While he was away, Garvey and Ashwood took up the collection. When the minister discovered the trick, the pair appeased his rage with $100 of the $500 they had received.[30]

Despite an occasional windfall, Garvey barely covered his expenses. But the accountant's ledger was not the only measure of his progress, especially in terms of his education. Once in the United States he realized that

29. John Bruce to Major Loving, January 13, 1919, file 10218-261/39, MID, in RG 165; A. A. Garvey, "Marcus Garvey," 77–78.
30. Flyer, March 23, 1917, reproduced in Amy Jacques Garvey, *Black Power in America* (Kingston, Jamaica, 1968), 13; A. A. Garvey, "Marcus Garvey," 53–60, 107, 111.

Washington had been only the most prominent of a group of racially conscious leaders. Eight months after his arrival in Harlem, Garvey judged "the American Negro . . . the most progressive . . . in the expansive chain of scattered Ethiopia. Industrially, financially, educationally and socially, the Negroes of both hemispheres have to defer to the American brother, the fellow who has revolutionized history in race development."[31]

For Garvey, black business enterprise now replaced black education as the critical civilizing agent for the race. He was impressed with "the active part played by Negro men and women in the commercial and industrial life of the nation." He predicted greater achievements in the future: "The acme of American Negro enterprise is not yet reached. You have still a far way to go. You want more stores, more banks, and bigger enterprises." And under American tutelage West Indians could "dress as well as the Negroes in the North of the United States, [and] . . . live in good homes . . . with furniture on the installment plan."[32]

Garvey's celebration of the blacks of the United States and racial business was not the result of new ideology. Pan-Africanism did not prescribe a precise route to progress. The choice of which institutions were critical always involved a certain amount of expediency. But inevitably the idea of the Jamaican school paled before the new economic opportunities, especially those created in the United States by the European war.

31. MG, "West Indies in the Mirror of Truth," in Clarke (ed.), *Garvey and the Vision of Africa*, 89; Eliezar Cadet to H. Dorsinville, January 13, 1919; and MG, speech at meeting of Baltimore UNIA, December 18, 1918, enclosed with W. H. Loving to Director, MID, December 20, 1918, file 10218-261/33 and 34, MID, in RG 165.
32. MG, "West Indies in the Mirror of Truth," 89, 91.

3 / Garvey and the Politics of Agitation

When Garvey arrived in New York in 1916, the heady changes unleashed by World War I had already begun to limit the power that had been exercised by the dominant classes in America since the 1890s. America's mobilization and then, in 1917, American entrance into the war enhanced the power of the masses because nations fighting wars need additional labor and loyalty from civilians as well as from soldiers. Popular demands summarily rejected in prewar years became negotiable. "The people" became part of the citizenry, and their representatives entered councils of state. But the leading classes in America discovered that the resulting popular awakening could not always be contained. The success of the Bolsheviks in Russia convinced many that traditional patterns of life and exploitation could be ended most effectively through revolution, not reform, and right away, not in the future. Using proverbial sticks as well as carrots, the government tried to isolate, neutralize, and destroy organizations like the Industrial Workers of the World (IWW) and the Socialist party, which worked to escalate popular demands.[1]

Race relations were not immune from the domestic dynamics of war. Overriding southern preferences and army blueprints, Secretary of War Newton Baker authorized a new fighting division and an officer training school for blacks to enhance Afro-American morale. New black appointments in the War and Labor departments acknowledged "the ability of the Negro leaders to influence and control their race." In towns and cities, the "best Negroes, most trusted by the white citizens of the community," manned the Negro Workers Advisory Committees of the Council of Defense. They often won better school facilities, paved roads, and fairer treat-

1. William Leuchtenburg, *The Perils of Prosperity, 1914–1932* (Chicago, 1958), 142; N. Gordon Levin, Jr., *Woodrow Wilson and World Politics: America's Response to War and Revolution* (New York, 1968), 164, 168; John Bodnar, *Immigration and Industrialization: Ethnicity in an American Mill Town, 1870–1940* (Pittsburgh, 1977), 125; Melvin Dubofsky, *We Shall Be All: A History of the Industrial Workers of the World* (Chicago: 1969), 349–452; James Weinstein, *The Decline of Socialism in America, 1912–1925* (New York, 1967), 119–78.

ment from the local white elites. At the least, many leading blacks made gains in status withheld before the war.[2]

New employers of black labor were not far behind the government. Prewar patterns of race relations were dissolving principally because of the new demand for and value of black labor. One-half million blacks migrated to work in northern factories during the war, replacing alien workers who had returned to their homelands and filling the large demand for new labor on the part of industries bloated by military orders. Corporations turned to the National Urban League, the NAACP, and academic institutions such as Tuskegee, Hampton, and Fisk for supervisors, foremen, and social workers to recruit and manage the new laborers and organize their leisure time.[3]

The signs of racial progress were everywhere. John Clark, executive secretary of the Urban League of Pittsburgh, noted that the "large wages" paid to migrants had caused churches to embark upon "ambitious plans." "Salaries of Pastors in some instances have been boosted three and four times." The head of the Chicago Urban League counted three new black banks and numerous new black businesses.[4] Racial gains crossed the Mason-Dixon Line. Even sharecroppers benefited from twenty-seven-cent-per-pound cotton. National goals to increase production and sell Liberty Bonds carried the war propaganda into the most isolated and backward areas of the South. A former governor of South Carolina acknowledged, without pleasure, that the state's Negro population could no longer be contained, because of "the liberating world forces set loose by the war . . . this moving spirit of world democracy."[5]

W. E. B. Du Bois' optimism overcame his usual skepticism on racial matters. In his famous *Crisis* editorial of July, 1918, "Close Ranks," he said: "We of the colored race have no ordinary interest in the outcome [of the

2. Arthur E. Barbeau and Florette Henry, *The Unknown Soldiers: Black American Troops in World War I* (Philadelphia, 1974), 56–59, 70, 89; Captain J. E. Cutler to R. R. Moton, September 7, 1918, Moton to Emmett Scott, December 17, 1917, in Moton Papers; Farm Bureau Service to Secretary of Labor, May 7, 1918, Chief Clerk's File, in Record Group 174, Records of the Department of Labor, National Archives; report on Jackson, Miss., n.d. [November, 1917], in Box 86, National Urban League Papers, Library of Congress.

3. The records of Tuskegee, the National Urban League, and even the NAACP are full of requests for trained blacks. See also *Age*, September 23, 1918.

4. John T. Clark to Walter White, November 19, 1919; T. Arnold Hill to White, November 14, 1919, Box C-319, in NAACP Papers, Library of Congress. Between one-half and two-thirds of small black businesses in 1920 had come into being since 1917. John Harmon, Arnett G. Lindsay, and Carter G. Woodson, *The Negro as a Businessman* (Washington, D.C., 1929), 25.

5. Thomas Hemmingway, "Prelude to Change: Black Carolinians in the War Years, 1914–1920," *Journal of Negro History*, LXV (1980), 222.

war]. That which the German army represents today spells death to the aspirations of Negroes and all darker races for equality, freedom, and democracy. Let us not hesitate. Let us, while the war lasts, forget our special grievances and close our ranks, shoulder to shoulder with our own white fellow citizens and the allied nations that are fighting for democracy." It appeared that the strategy fashioned by the black middle class during the past decade had succeeded, that the Negro would progress, guided by racial leaders and organizations through the expanding social opportunities of industrial America.[6]

Other developments, especially in the South, revealed the unevenness of racial gains. Shielded by the Supreme Court's protection of local government, states passed "work or fight" laws to keep low-paid southern labor at traditional rural jobs. Moreover, because the government acted to foster mobilization, not deliberate racial change, bureaucrats sometimes reinforced the planters' objectives. Secretary of Labor Wilson appointed white southerners to oversee federal agencies in the South. The new manager of the federal employment office in New Orleans declared that "the first thing he was going to do was to see that 'Niggers' were stopped from going North."[7] The Wilson administration often yielded to southern opposition to federal labor standards. George Haynes withdrew the Division of Negro Economics, the racial bureau of the Labor Department, from Florida after lumber barons confused "the effort of the Department of Labor and [that of] radical agitators." The Georgia-Florida Sawmill Association in Jacksonville had demanded that the bureau advise blacks not to join a union attempting to organize the workers. When the official informed the lumbermen that the department was neutral, he became part of the enemy. John H. Kirby, president of the National Lumber Manufacturers Association, even refused to meet with black agents of the Labor Department: "In the South we tell negroes what to do; we do not take counsel with them," he said.[8]

The weakness of the racial gains was not that they were incomplete, but that they were not certified in law or guaranteed by alterations in critical southern institutions. Southern employers raised wages when necessary, just as Democratic registrars enrolled some black voters. In both cases, the southern elites mediated and shaped the process of change. They opposed

6. *Crisis*, XVI (1918), 111; Du Bois' support of the war was similar to the broader movement among prewar progressives and some socialists who identified Wilson's acceptance of some of their reforms with permanent alterations in society and government.

7. Walter White to John Shillady, October 26, 1918; H. McConcio to Shillady, October 9, 1918, Box C-1, in NAACP Papers; R. R. Moton to L. M. Hooper, October 7, 1918, Albion Holsey to Moton, June 19, 1918, in Moton Papers.

8. George Haynes, "Memoranda," March 22, 25, May 17, 1919, Division of Negro Economics, in RG 174; Washington *Post*, April 3, 1919; *Age*, May 31, 1919.

granting blacks the right to form labor unions and the right to vote, and they fought organizations pursuing such goals. Although federal officials often pressured the South, the administration did not mandate national standards.

Garvey's plan to found a school in Jamaica was tame fare in this world of rapid change. But Garvey's quick intelligence and opportunism kept him flexible and at the forefront of black agitation. Much of his learning took place on Harlem street corners, classrooms for every change blacks experienced during the war. Soapbox orators flayed old targets like Moton and new ones like Du Bois. Garvey listened to others and spoke himself on Jamaica and the British Empire. His first formal lecture in the United States in May, 1916, was not propitious. Plagued with nervousness and the barbs of hecklers, Garvey fainted and fell off the platform. But he soon learned to master himself and others.[9] He was cheered in June, 1917, at a meeting to launch the Liberty League, a new pressure group in Harlem. Although we lack the text of his speech to the audience of two thousand, he reportedly echoed the common call for new racial leadership.[10] Immediately afterward, Garvey scheduled "A High-Class Benefit Concert . . . to Establish an Industrial and Trades Institution" in Jamaica, to be held at St. Mark's A.M.E. church in Harlem on June 26. He sent free tickets to prominent American leaders, including R. R. Moton of Tuskegee. The relatively high price of the ticket—a dollar—revealed that Garvey was directing his appeal primarily to the black elite. But the failure to attract large audiences to help finance the Jamaican school combined with his new opportunities in the United States to convince him to set up his base of operations in New York. He created a branch of the UNIA in New York at some point between the summer of 1917 and early 1918. Changing his geographical base, Garvey simultaneously changed his political methods.[11]

A letter he wrote to the editor of the New York *Tribune* at this time was an indication of his growing militancy. The race riot that erupted in East St. Louis, Illinois, on July 2, 1917, was a legacy of the city's bitter class conflict. Capitalists had openly played off blacks against whites to defeat a recent drive to organize workers. The competition in the factories deepened the contest for scarce housing and recreational facilities in one of the most brutal and corrupt cities in the United States. A rumor about a new black "in-

9. A. A. Garvey, "Marcus Garvey," 84; "Account by W. A. Domingo of Marcus Garvey's St. Mark's Church Hall Lecture," n.d., in Robert A. Hill (ed.), *The Marcus Garvey and Universal Negro Improvement Association Papers* (10 vols. projected; Berkeley, 1983–), I, 190–92.

10. Hubert Harrison, *When Africa Awakes* (New York, 1920), 9–13.

11. Garvey, in an article in *Current History*, XVIII (September, 1923), 95, gave 1918 as the founding date. The *NW* of August 2, 1919, placed the date in May, 1917. Possibly a group was established in 1917, but the formal date of incorporation was 1918.

vasion" from the South triggered a riot that ended only after thirty-nine blacks and nine whites were killed. Garvey's letter in the *Tribune* questioned Theodore Roosevelt's analysis of the riot, especially his accusation that organized labor was responsible for the violence. To Garvey the issue was not economic but racial. He believed that "labor troubles can always be settled by arbitration or something other than war." Racial conflict was eternal. Citing Secretary of Navy Josephus Daniels, a southerner, Garvey predicted that the next war, the real war, would pit the white race against the darker races. The East St. Louis riot was not a local or American incident but the first shot of the worldwide racial struggle.[12]

Garvey engaged Roosevelt directly and by name; he vied indirectly with Fred Moore, editor of the city's leading black newspaper, the New York *Age*.[13] Moore had become editor in 1907 when Booker T. Washington took control of the newspaper. The recipient of Republican patronage positions, Moore was active in the New York Urban League and Negro Business League. He had declared in the *Tribune* that the "representative Negro does not approve of radical socialistic outbursts, such as calling upon the Negroes to defend themselves against the whites." Moore's use of the Tuskegee approach of parlaying the image of the docile Negro into racial gains marked him as Old Guard. In 1917, the advocacy of self-defense was a litmus test of militance, dividing old from aspiring leadership. Garvey's assertion in his letter that race relations would be conducted through struggle, not conciliation or petition, placed him squarely in the militant camp and also separated him from his own past.

To embrace racial conflict was to downplay appeals to leading whites and even racial self-help. But organizational weakness forced Garvey to place the decisive racial conflict in the future. He signed his letter simply "Negro Traveller and Lecturer." He did not mention the UNIA, which at this point was small, still based in Jamaica, and incapable of taking advantage of the new ideas and emotions brought by the war. He continued to solicit the aid of leading whites. He asked Theodore Roosevelt, Nicholas Murray Butler, the conservative Republican president of Columbia University, and George Battle, a leading Democratic lawyer, to speak to the UNIA and to contribute to its campaign to erect a building.[14]

Garvey's dilemma was shared by a group of young agitators in Harlem

12. A. A. Garvey, "Marcus Garvey," 39; New York *Tribune*, July 11, 1917. See also Elliott Rudwick's *Race Riot at East St. Louis, July 2, 1917* (Carbondale, Ill., 1964), the definitive study of the riot.

13. New York *World*, February 24, 1927.

14. MG to editor, New York *Tribune*, July 11, 1917.

who were struggling to create a politics suitable to their new racial consciousness, which had been forged by the intellectual climate of America, the escalating race and class conflicts surrounding them, and their new sense of racial power. Although the political camps were not fixed or unbridgeable, there were two basic sets of ideas around which leaders conceived of new organization: the first was the nationalist, "race first" ideology, and the second was the working-class ideology in the forms of both trade unionism and socialism. Hubert Harrison, the founder of the Liberty League, was the leader of the "race first" militants. His open agitation against "lynching, segregation, Jim Crow, peonage, and disfranchisement" was an assault against the Republican politics of Tuskegee and its northern satellites.[15]

Although Harlem blacks, like blacks throughout the country, voted Republican, the party of Lincoln had long ceased to represent them accurately. Vestigial Republicanism masqueraded as urban politics in New York. The black GOP boss of New York was Charles Anderson, a protégé of Booker T. Washington. Appointed collector of customs for the Port of New York by Theodore Roosevelt, Anderson preferred the discreet infighting of elites to the open warfare of ward politicians.[16] Even if his personal qualities had been different, Democratic control of city politics depreciated the promises of Republicanism. GOP allegiance was a luxury only New York's wealthy could consistently afford. Black Democrats were regularly created out of the ambitions of local businessmen and professionals and out of the disappointments of Republican office seekers. But the small social base and narrow bill of complaint made it possible for Tammany boss Richard Croker to create a racial fiefdom run by Harvard-educated Ferdinand Q. Morton, who, like Charles Anderson, carried the priorities of the elite that dominated racial politics. Both eyed visible, high-status appointments, not the working-class jobs that built urban machines.[17]

This situation drove numerous blacks to attempt to break out of the coffin of conventional politics. Splinter groups were born, and died, over particular issues or candidates. Hubert Harrison's new Liberty League seemed more promising than most because he represented broader intellectual and political experience than the typical Harlem hopeful. Known as the Black Socrates, Harrison excelled at the indoor and outdoor popular lec-

15. Harrison, *When Africa Awakes*, 9–13.

16. Charles Anderson to Emmett Scott, October 23, 1916, in Emmett P. Scott Papers, Soper Library, Morgan State College, Baltimore, Md.

17. Ira Katznelson, *Black Men, White Cities: Race, Politics, and Migration in the United States, 1900–30 and Britain, 1948–68* (London, 1973), 67–71.

ture that was a leisure activity for thousands in the cities. He was born on St. Croix in the Virgin Islands in 1883. He taught school on the island but left to travel in Europe and study at the University of Copenhagen. He came to New York in 1900 and passed a civil service examination for a position of postal clerk. Harrison paid for his political independence, for in 1911, after he had publicly criticized Booker T. Washington, Anderson had him fired from the post office. Shortly after, Harrison joined the Socialist party.[18]

Harrison was attracted to the Socialists' modern intellectual views. "As a man of the 20th century," he was "thoroughly disgusted" with the "seventeenth century mode of translating ideas" displayed by leading black intellectuals.[19] He was also drawn to the militant activism of the Industrial Workers of the World, the syndicalist movement for industrial unions. But his own life as a teacher in P.S. 89 on 135th Street did not go well with his new enthusiasms. The interracial school lacked the ambience his racial ambitions required. He complained to a friend that he taught "two white pupils to every colored one." Therefore, in 1916, he resigned his position "to give myself exclusively to work among my own people."[20]

Harrison did not approach his people as a socialist. Ironically, when young blacks like A. Philip Randolph and Chandler Owen began to adopt socialism during the war, he became their principal intellectual opponent in Harlem. Randolph recalled that Harrison thought the "Negro's knowledge" was "too limited to develop a vanguard in the field of revolutionary change." Harrison believed that education—the attainment of enlightenment and knowledge—was a prerequisite for, not a by-product of, socialism. His new politics was based instead on the experiences of national-

18. "Reminiscences of A. Philip Randolph," 153, Oral History Project, Butler Library, Columbia University, New York; Charles Anderson to Booker T. Washington, October 30, 1912, in Washington Papers; Chicago *Defender*, December 29, 1927.
19. Hubert Harrison to James Weldon Johnson, May 12, 1915, in James Weldon Johnson Papers, Beinecke Rare Book and Manuscript Library, Yale University, New Haven, Conn. Harrison's remarks were a response to William Ferris' *African Abroad; or, His Evolution in Western Civilization, Tracing His Development Under Caucasian Milieu* (2 vols.; New Haven, 1913). This work, a curious catalog of race history and political analysis, displayed conventional thought on race traits and civilization bound together with a Whiggish view of progress. He wanted Negroes to be "history-makers, wealthy, and distinguished, the prerequisites to being treated as a man." But Ferris also claimed that "Anglo-Saxons always win in science, business, and politics." The thrust of his message was that if the race would come "to a consciousness of itself," progress would be inevitable. See Vol. I, 407, 268.
20. Hubert Harrison to John Bruce, October 25, 1915, in John Bruce Papers, Schomburg Center for Research in Black Culture, New York Public Library; Harrison, *When Africa Awakes*, 7–8.

ist movements during the war. He wrote in September, 1917, that blacks "must follow the path of the Swadesha movement of India and the Sinn Fein movement of Ireland. The meaning of both these terms is 'ourselves first.' Any man today who aspires to lead the Negro race must set squarely before his face the idea of 'Race First.'"[21]

The consequences of the new inspiration were not self-evident, because blacks were a minority in America and Harrison was not demanding independence but equal rights for all Americans, black and white. Speaking in Boston, Harrison urged "the colored people [to] rise against the government, just as the Irish against England, unless they get their rights." The translation of the rising militant temper into politics was not obvious. Harrison had vainly hoped that the July riot in East St. Louis would "enlarge rapidly the membership of the Liberty League of Negro-Americans which was organized to take practical steps to help our people over the land in the protection of their lives and liberties." A local call-to-arms met other barriers. New York lacked the racial climate, violent tradition, and targets of the South—Jim Crow, disfranchisement, lynching. State laws outlawing school segregation and banning discrimination in public facilities deprived the militants of rallying issues available in other northern cities. Although passionately held, the doctrine of "race first" boiled down to a political manifesto demanding "what the Irish and Jewish voters get—nominations on the party's ticket in our own districts." Harrison's new politics registered the fact that semirural, white, middle-class Harlem was being transformed into "the Negro Metropolis." In 1914, the Urban League estimated Harlem's black population to be nearly 50,000. By 1920, the number had increased to 73,000, equal to about half the black population living in the five boroughs composing New York City. The simultaneous exodus of whites from Harlem created a large racial district, the prerequisite of ethnic politics.[22]

Harrison was pleased, therefore, when Harlem sent the black lawyer and realtor Edward Austin Johnson to the state assembly in 1917. Harrison had supported Johnson's campaign. But it soon became obvious that the new black politicians had won out over the new black politics. The rising racial consciousness found a conventional outlet in the Republican party, with minimal racial dividends in New York or the nation. The Liberty League floundered. After only a few issues Harrison's new newspaper, the

21. "Reminiscences of Randolph," 153; Harrison, *When Africa Awakes*, 40.

22. Baltimore *Afro-American*, June 30, 1917; Harrison, *When Africa Awakes*, 15–16; Gilbert Osofsky, *Harlem: The Making of a Ghetto: Negro New York, 1890–1930* (New York, 1963), 122–23.

Voice, was in financial trouble. In October, he asked the central committee of the Socialist party in New York for financial support for the newspaper. He was turned down.[23]

Although at the time Harrison interpreted the Socialist rejection as confirmation of his "race first" philosophy, he rejoined the party in March, 1918, only to resign again in September. Harrison vacillated between the Socialists and the militant businessmen and professionals in Harlem's pressure groups who aspired to control local Republican politics. He found comfort with neither. The militant bourgeoisie preferred the racial power of conventional Republican politics to Harrison's Liberty League, and the Socialists rejected Harrison's financial requests because they were already contributing to a new black socialist magazine, the *Messenger*, edited by Randolph and Owen, two young men who also headed a new Socialist political club in Harlem and who were the leading exemplars of the working-class ideology as a means to racial progress.[24]

Asa Philip Randolph was the son of a minister in Jacksonville, Florida. The family was poor, but Asa and his brother James knew the Bible and Shakespeare, as well as the heroes of black history. After completing high school, the brothers briefly tasted the irregular work that southern cities offered blacks. Asa went to New York in 1911. Laboring at odd jobs, he immersed himself in the study of politics, history, and economics in the evening classes at the City College of New York. There he read Marx and met young American Marxists and other radicals who championed the struggles of the IWW in the textile mills of Lawrence, Massachusetts, in 1912 and a year later in Patterson, New Jersey.[25]

Randolph's wife introduced him to Chandler Owen, a graduate of Virginia Union College and a student at Columbia University. Owen, from a more affluent family, was more interested in Negro society than the sober Randolph. While Randolph introduced Owen to Marx and socialism, Owen encouraged Randolph to read Lester Ward and other American sociologists of the academy. They became instant friends and began to meet at Randolph's apartment with other young intellectuals—Cyril Briggs, W. A. Domingo, Theophilus Lewis, Joel Rogers, Lovett Fort-Whiteman—future activists in Harlem politics. Their discussions found a practical outlet in January, 1917, when the president of the black Headwaiters and Side-

23. Osofsky, *Harlem*, 170; "Minutes of the Central Committee," October 21, 1917, in New York Socialist Party Papers, Tamiment Library, New York City.

24. Harrison, *When Africa Awakes*, 21, 40, 55–60, 74–75; "Minutes of Central Committee," March 27, September 18, 1918, in N.Y. Socialist Party Papers.

25. "Minutes of Central Committee," October 10, 1917, in N.Y. Socialist Party Papers; Jervis Anderson, *A. Philip Randolph: A Biographical Portrait* (New York, 1972), 1–67.

waiters Society of Greater New York asked them to edit its monthly magazine. Randolph and Owen, who had been looking for office space for the Independent Political Council, their Sunday talk group, accepted happily. Promised editorial freedom, the two were dismissed in August when they began writing about the exploitation of the ordinary waiters by the "aristocratic" headwaiters, who conducted a subcontracting system, selling uniforms to the sidewaiters at exorbitant prices and winning kickbacks from the uniform manufacturers. But the friends continued to publish the magazine, now renamed the *Messenger* and financed by Randolph's wife, whose hairdressing business produced steady income for the family. The first issue of the *Messenger*, which came out in November, 1917, billed it as the "Only Radical Negro Magazine in America."[26]

The pair's independence took political form as they reached for influence and power. On October 10, eleven days before Harrison asked the Socialist party to aid the *Voice*, Randolph and Owen offered to rally Harlem behind Morris Hillquit, the Socialist candidate for mayor. They established a lively Socialist club in the Twenty-first Assembly District. The party did well that fall. Hillquit received 145,332 votes, four times more than the party had polled in 1912, and finished third behind fusion candidate John Mitchell and Tammany victor John Hylan. With pride, the *Messenger* announced that the Socialists received one-quarter of the black vote and elected ten Socialist state assemblymen, seven aldermen, and one municipal judge. Although the black Socialists on the ballot did not win office in Harlem or in statewide campaigns, their performance was promising.[27]

But what did it mean to be a black Socialist or a "race first" leader in 1917 or 1918? The various leaders argued in friendly rivalry, yet often cooperated in joint ventures. Despite his slogan "race first," Harrison was a member of the Socialist party from March to September, 1918. Like the "race first" men, Randolph, the Socialist and exemplar of the working-class ideology, warned blacks not to "depend on white men and white women to work out the problem. We have too long relied on white people. . . . You have got to get it yourself." He asserted that it was time "for a great mass movement among Negroes." One difference between the two groups was that black Socialists judged unions to be the most effective social vehicle for racial power, whereas the "race first" men were more likely to root the new militancy in the new black business community. Harrison announced that "the new day that has dawned for the Negroes of Harlem is a day of

26. "Reminiscences of Randolph," 142–48, 162–68.
27. *Ibid.*, 168–74, 219–21; "Minutes of Central Committee," October 10, 21, 1917, in N.Y. Socialist Party Papers; Anderson, *A. Philip Randolph,* 92–94; *Messenger,* I (January, 1918), 11.

business accomplishment." But such differences were not of great significance. The Socialists Randolph and Owen, despite their working-class
ideology, were not working-class organizers. They lectured before a wide
variety of black groups. And Harrison spoke to workers as well as to businessmen, and supported the IWW. Each of these leaders lacked the weight
of an organization to implement his analysis and demonstrate its superiority over those of rivals.[28]

Within this arena of spirited but friendly competition, Garvey was
closer to the "race first" men than to the Socialists. But he joined the Socialist Randolph on January 2, 1919, to create a new Pan-African organization to promote African interests at the Paris Peace Conference. In doing
so, Garvey parted with his "race first" mentor, Hubert Harrison, who believed the foray into the international arena was premature and wasteful of
scarce resources needed on the home front.

The black agitation had been marked with a new African consciousness, which was generated as much out of Washington as Africa. Woodrow Wilson's Fourteen Points of January 8, 1918, had called for "a free,
open-minded and absolutely impartial adjustment of all colonial claims,
based upon a strict observance of the principle that in determining all such
questions of sovereignty the interests of the populations concerned must
have equal weight with the equitable claims of the government whose title
is to be determined."

But the politics of nationalism practiced by the great states was narrower than its rhetoric. Only the disposition of German, not British or
French, colonies was debated at Versailles. Wilsonianism ruled out out-
right annexation, but it also ruled out instant independence. The British
Labour party and some European Socialist parties advocated interna-
tionalization of the German and Ottoman empires. A mandate system for
the peoples judged incapable of immediate self-government was a useful
compromise. Europeans would rule, though not possess, the former colonies. Afro-Americans from Moton and Du Bois through Randolph and
Garvey accepted the Great Powers' definition of the nationalist agenda and
its stated rationale—the difference between an exploitative German and a
progressive Allied imperialism. The only question on the table at Versailles
and in black Harlem was who would rule German Africa.[29]

28. A. Philip Randolph, speech, May 30, 1919, file 10218-311, MID, in RG 165; *Messenger*, II (July, 1918), 8. One significant difference between the "race first" radicals and
the Socialists was the latter's opposition to the war. Randolph and Owen were arrested in
Cleveland in August, 1918, for speaking out against the war.

29. Arno J. Mayer, *Politics and Diplomacy of Peacemaking* (New York, 1967), 35–41, 395;
Levin, *Woodrow Wilson and World Politics*, 31, 162, 245–61; Woodrow Wilson, "Address De-

Although Afro-Americans did not speak with one voice, a series of conferences called by leading organizations—the Tuskegee-dominated Circle of Negro War Relief in November, the National Equal Rights League in December, the NAACP in January—revealed a consensus that Afro-Americans should have some role, official or advisory, in determining the subsequent governing structure of the former German colonies. In November, 1918, Garvey staged a forum of his own at Palace Casino in Harlem, where he, Randolph, and Ida Wells-Barnett addressed the colonial issues. Of the three, Wells-Barnett was the name that attracted most of the three thousand to five thousand people in the audience. Her unrelenting criticism of lynching during the war and her refusal to orchestrate black support for national unity at a time when most racial leaders had soft-pedaled protest and oversold patriotism, made her a drawing card wherever she spoke. Nonetheless, the results of the meeting were ambiguous. The UNIA had selected Wells-Barnett and Randolph to represent it at the Paris Peace Conference, although the pair were without means to travel. Another emissary, a Haitian named Eliezar Cadet, expected to "contribute to the administration of the German colonies."[30] Perhaps these were Garvey's words or the twenty-year-old Cadet's own inflation of his task. The UNIA also sent petitions to the heads of the Allied nations. But Garvey complained, "We never heard one syllable from the lips of Woodrow Wilson, from the lips of Theodore Roosevelt in America, from the lips of Bonar Law or Balfour in England, as touching anything relative to the destinies of the Negroes . . . of the world."[31]

The specific objectives of the petitions might have been unclear, but Garvey's ambition to "draw into one united whole the four hundred million black people of the world" was unmistakable. At the time of the armistice, however, the UNIA in Harlem was small and rent with warring factions; offshoots of it existed in Washington, Baltimore, and Norfolk. Garvey, to be effective, was therefore forced to join with other leaders. In December, he attended a conference of 250 people called together by the National Equal Rights League (NERL), the all-black rival of the NAACP,

livered at a Joint Session of the Two Houses of Congress, January 8, 1918," in Ray S. Baker and William E. Dodd (eds.), *The Public Papers of Woodrow Wilson* (6 vols.; New York, 1925–27), V, 155–62.

30. With a friend from Paris, Cadet intended to set up a cannery business in Haiti. Although the plan never materialized, he returned to Haiti and became a vodun cultist. *The Garvey and UNIA Papers*, I, 308.

31. Ida Wells-Barnett, *Crusader for Justice: The Autobiography of Ida B. Wells*, ed. Alfreda M. Duster (Chicago, 1970), 380–82; MG, "Extracts from Speech," December 18, 1918; "Memorandum Re: Marcus Garvey," n.d. [1919], file 10218-261/33, MID, in RG 165.

which refused to send a representative. The NERL elected eleven persons to go to Paris to present Afro-American grievances. A small group from the conference, including Garvey, Randolph, Adam Clayton Powell, Sr., of the Abyssinian Baptist Church in New York, and George Frazier Miller, a Socialist minister from Brooklyn, met at the home of the millionaire businesswoman Madame C. J. Walker and formed a new group, the International League of Darker Peoples.[32]

The league was set up to promote the new African issue. Initially, it planned to organize all the delegates to the Paris Peace Conference elected from the various racial organizations so that blacks could present a united front. It proposed to advance the interests of "darker peoples," the Third World in present-day language, through "education, organization, and agitation." The league's analysis of imperialism in Africa, probably written by Randolph, was socialist; most of its program was liberal—the ending of discrimination and of trade and immigration barriers and the fostering of self-determination in Africa. Like Wilson, the group concluded that African self-government "cannot be absolute." But unlike the president and many Afro-Americans, it rejected the proposal that the European powers govern the German colonies. Instead, the league sought a ruling group "composed of the educated classes of Negroes from America, the West Indies, Liberia, Hayti, Abyssinia, and the peoples of Japan and China and other enlightened sections of the African and European worlds." The commission would establish a "modern, technical, scientific system of education" to train Africans to develop their resources without "discrimination and exploitation."

The idea of rejecting the European powers as appropriate rulers of the German colonies and substituting a black elite was the most advanced formulation of Pan-Africanism in the aftermath of World War I. But black elites were still closer to one another than to the masses they claimed to speak for and wished to rule but did not address or organize. The politics of their African nationalism was accidental. Having met some friendly members of the Japanese peace delegation, Randolph concluded that Japan, plus the power of other free nations "combined with an international league of workingmen," could effectively pressure the Western powers. Although the league lacked staying power, its refusal to fall in line behind the mandate system revealed new disaffection and potentially new politics. The dissent spanned militant new entrepreneurs like Madame Walker, young churchmen like Powell, and agitators like Garvey and Randolph.[33]

32. *World Forum*, I (January, 1919), copy in file 10218-296/2, MID, in RG 165. This issue appears to be the first and last. The league apparently disappeared shortly afterward.
33. *Ibid.*

Du Bois, who remained apart from the new group, shared their ideas. In December, 1918, he concluded that "the principle of self-determination . . . cannot be wholly applied to semi-civilized peoples." The disposition of "German Africa should be guided by the chiefs and western educated elite . . . of Africa, educated Afro-Americans and the independent Negro governments of Abyssinia, Liberia, and Hayti." A new state should be created in Africa "under the guidance of organized civilization" and "the thinking class of the future Negro world." But Du Bois soon retreated from advanced Afro-American opinion. While in Europe to investigate the conditions among black soldiers, he hastily assembled a Pan-African Congress in Paris in February, 1919. Tempered by the conservative French colonial elite, the congress concluded only that Africans "should be permitted to participate [in government] as soon as their level of development enabled them to do so. Participation should be extended until at some future time 'Africa is ruled by consent of the Africans.'" Words like *independence, self-government*, and even *Pan-African participation* were conspicuously absent. Africans in the British colonies did not dissent from their French colonial brothers. Casely Hayford's *Gold Coast Leader* summarized the thinking of leading Africans up and down the east and west coasts when he asserted: "We cannot at present rule ourselves. . . . Every other race has had to be under the tutelage of another nation more advanced in the Science of Government until such time as they were sufficiently advanced to manage their own affairs." [34]

Despite these differences, propelled by various ideas and by geography, all leaders advocated modifications of colonial rule to enhance the role of the educated racial elites, who they believed would uplift the masses in the modern way without exploitation or discrimination. In calling for immediate black participation, Afro-Americans were more militant than the delegates at the Pan-African Congress in Paris and the elites of Africa. Nevertheless, their substantive program went no further than the ideas of progress and development enunciated by the African elites. Although inspired by the new mass assertions and aware of the need for organization, they saw no active role for the people.

Blunting the African focus of Afro-American politics was the inevitable priority of black domestic protest. The NERL assembly of December, 1918, had proposed to send a Negro delegation to Paris to add a Fifteenth Point—

34. Charles Kellogg, *NAACP: A History of the National Association for the Advancement of Colored People* (Baltimore, 1967), 280; *Crisis*, XVII (December, 1918–January, 1919), 119–20; Imanuel Geiss, *The Pan-African Movement* (London, 1974), 234–40; W. E. B. Du Bois, "Memorandum on the Future of Africa," n.d. [1918], Box C-385, in NAACP Papers; *Gold Coast Leader*, May 13, 1916; J. Ayodele Langley, *Pan-Africanism and Nationalism in West Africa, 1900–1945* (Oxford, 1973), 63–68; *World Forum*, I (January, 1919).

the "elimination of civil, political, and judicial distinctions based on race or color in all nations for the new era of freedom everywhere"—to Wilson's Fourteen. Monroe Trotter, denied a passport, assumed an alias and took a job as a cook on a trans-Atlantic vessel to get across the ocean to present Afro-American claims. Hubert Harrison shared Trotter's priorities but then found his idea of presenting petitions to the Paris conference as a "sublimely silly" political gesture: "Lynching, disfranchisement and segregation are evils HERE, and the place in which we must fight them is HERE."[35]

Another new organization, the African Blood Brotherhood (ABB) joined the debate on racial goals. Its founder was Cyril Briggs, who came to New York from the West Indian island of Nevis in 1905, when he was eighteen years old. During the war Briggs, a reporter and editor of the new *Amsterdam News*, urged blacks to patronize racial enterprises in Harlem and boycott white businesses that did not hire blacks. He was forced to resign in 1918 for his militant nationalism, which opposed the newspaper's undiluted patriotism. SECURITY OF LIFE FOR POLES AND SERBS—WHY NOT FOR COLORED NATIONS? was the headline of the offending article. In September, 1918, he began a new monthly, the *Crusader*, which became the organ of the ABB, "a revolutionary secret order" Briggs founded in 1919.[36]

Like Frederick Douglass, Briggs asserted that blacks were "a nation within a nation." But, reflecting the new nationalist ideology, he demanded "a square deal or failing that, a separate political existence." His contingent formulation reflected the difficulties in Pan-African politics. He first advocated an independent state in the western United States but then urged a Negro state in Africa. He claimed that Afro-Americans could not be free unless Africans possessed sovereignty but implied that Afro-Americans could free Africa by playing the role that Irish-Americans played in Ireland. Like those of other radicals, the objectives of the ABB in 1919 and 1920 were vague and shifting. In October, 1919, the *Crusader* urged blacks to vote the Socialist ticket. However, though there were some Socialists in the ABB, the *Crusader's* argument was rooted in traditional black protest: to divide the black vote would force the Republican party "to sit up and take notice."[37]

Initially, the ABB was conceived as a tight-knit, semiclandestine, paramilitary group. It announced that it was open to "membership by enlistment. No dues, fees or assessments. Those only need apply who are willing to go to the limit . . . willing to make any sacrifice for the liberation of

35. Stephen R. Fox, *The Guardian of Boston: William Monroe Trotter* (New York, 1971), 180–81; Harrison, *When Africa Awakes*, 30–32.
36. Theodore Draper, *American Communism and Soviet Russia* (New York, 1960), 323–25.
37. *Crusader*, November, 1921, October, 1919.

the Fatherland and the Glory of the Great Negro Race."[38] The ABB resembled the classic revolutionary societies that flourished after the French Revolution. These societies had relied on their own revolutionary activity, forged by oaths, to lead an inert but sympathetic mass. Some awaited popular insurrection, others engaged in individual acts of terrorism. The contemporary organization most relevant to ABB ambition was the Fenian Irish Republican Brotherhood. The likely model for its activities was the Easter Rebellion of 1916. Many of the new militants were inspired by Ireland's resistance.[39]

ABB members were young and intellectual. Their politics corresponded to their impatience with and distance from existing politics—moderate or radical. Most lived in Harlem but aimed to liberate the masses in the American South and Africa. They wanted to rally "Africans in the hinterlands" to a "great Pan-African army" that would "attack colonial plantations." Closer to home, in the United States, the ABB advocated racial self-defense. But the ABB was isolated from the South and from the cities where riots erupted. Its rhetoric was more martial than its actions, and despite its awareness of the wide variety of politics available to oppressed people, the ABB shared the common weakness of the new agitators. All functioned as critics of government policy and racial leadership.

Despite the depth of their analysis, international awareness, and racial consciousness, the protest led by the new agitators carried the traditional weaknesses of Afro-American dissent in that period. Born of issue-related agitation, black protest had rarely been stable. To mature, it required a mass constituency. The majority of blacks, however, were only momentarily caught up by these issues, which spoke of racial discrimination but not to their own conditions. However much the mass of blacks were outraged by racial injustices and atrocities such as lynching, discrimination in the United States Army, race riots in other cities, and imperialism in Africa, these phenomena were not directly connected with their daily lives.

38. *Ibid.*, October, 1919; "Race Catechism," *Crusader*, November, 1918, reprinted in Monroe N. Work, *Negro Year Book, 1918–1919* (Tuskegee, Ala., 1919), 100. In an editorial, "Race First," the *Crusader* argued that "white men give their first loyalty not to their country, but to their race." Copy in "Bulletin of Radical Activities, no. 8," March 1–13, 1920, in Record Group 60, Records of the Department of Justice, National Archives.

39. The August, 1919, *Crusader* featured an article, "Approaching Irish Success." It proclaimed: "When you fight, fight! and he who would be free, himself must strike the blow. There is no middle course when dealing with the oppressor." The ABB was not alone in its Irish inspiration. The MID found "all the Colored speakers in Harlem . . . using the Irish question in their discussions." "Negro Agitation," August, 1919, file 10218-364/1, MID, in RG 165. It cannot be mere coincidence that the UNIA newspaper was called the *Negro World* (after the *Irish World*?), that UNIA headquarters was named Liberty Hall (after Liberty Hall in Dublin?), and that "Race First" and "Ourselves First" are translations of "Sinn Fein."

Like most working people, the majority of blacks were consumed with the tasks of work and family. Organizations unconnected with these necessities had a meager basis for continuous support. The ABB's failure to recruit on the basis of the revolutionary slogans may be inferred from its new appeal in early 1920: "If, because of having others dependent upon you for support or for any other legitimate reason you cannot enlist in the Brotherhood, there are many other ways you can help. You can interest others in it and you can help financially."[40]

The new leaders were not forced to address the question of mass organization or the underlying social issues, because the opportunity and progress realized during the war, as measured in new jobs, higher wages, and increased farm income, confirmed the virtues, not the inadequacies, of industrial society. On the other hand, though the new agitators were more militant and impatient than the racial leaders they excoriated, their own racial agenda, priorities, and organizational forms were modeled after those of the elite. They tried to win the attention of northern blacks by recounting the litany of southern evils and the menace of race riots. But they could not transfer the anger they elicited and shape it to do battle with the South or closer racial targets. The campaign for more racial representation in the GOP, for instance, was incapable of rallying the masses because it ignored the social questions of black working-class life. And without organization in the North, a serious assault on southern racism was out of the question.

The issues of jobs, wages, rent, and food prices were forced on the new agitators only after the end of the war when the inevitability of racial progress in industrial society, in the North as well as in the South and in Africa, was called into question. The two years succeeding the armistice were among the bitterest periods of social conflict in American history. While there had been many local strikes during the war, peace made them larger and national in scope and direction. One of five workers struck during 1919.[41]

Workers usually demanded permanent collective bargaining and wages to approximate the cost of living, which soared in 1919 and 1920, and sometimes urged nationalization and workers' control of aspects of production. The labor offensive was part of the broad, democratic challenge to the ruling hierarchies of modern society. The *Nation* characterized the events of 1919 as a "world-wide movement. . . . The common man, forgetting the old sanctions, and losing faith in the old leadership, has experienced a

40. "Negro Agitation," February 10, 1920, file 10218-364/21, MID, in RG 165; "Program of the African Blood Brotherhood," *Communist Review* (London), April, 1922, pp. 449–54.
41. John Hicks, *Rehearsal for Disaster* (Gainesville, Fla., 1961), 59, 37–40.

new sense of self-confidence, or at least a new recklessness, a readiness to take chances on his own account."[42]

American business and political leaders struck back legally and extra-legally to re-create the unionless, prewar social order. Their actions demonstrated class power, not the class conciliation of the war years. They viewed the diverse movements for racial change through the prism of the national insurgency. Even when men remained sympathetic to the black cause, they were more intent on combatting radicalism than racial injustice. In addition, incentives to accommodate black demands weakened in 1919 and 1920. Returning soldiers and new immigration ended the active recruitment of southern black labor.[43]

The leading forces of racial counterrevolution were southern. The racial fever was registered in the rise of lynchings from thirty-six in 1917 to seventy-six in 1919. But intimidation did not prevent the growth of collective initiatives. In Elaine, Arkansas, sharecroppers who were unwilling to rely upon planter bookkeeping to determine their income for the year formed the Progressive Farmers and Household Union to demand itemized statements of their accounts. The landowners had canceled the effects of the spring and summer rise in cotton prices by enlarging the debt their tenants had incurred during the year. The union's action challenged a central mechanism of political control and method of siphoning off profit from the laborer to the planter. A clash between local law enforcement officers (the instruments of planter power) and black unionists resulted in the death of one white deputy. This skirmish was the basis of the planters' charge that the Elaine blacks planned to massacre the white population. It rationalized an ensuing reign of terror, in which at least twenty-five black men were killed.[44]

Interracial organization of southern workers met equally violent reprisals by local southern authorities. In Bogalusa, Louisiana, AFL carpenters organized a union at the Great Southern Lumber Company, the largest lumber and paper mill producer in the United States. Three-quarters of the members were black. The corporation created the Self-Preservation and Loyalty League, which went through the town promising to shoot any black who remained with the union. The union's black vice-president hid in Louisiana's swamps, but when he emerged, guarded by white unionists, four of his protectors were gunned down on November 22, 1919. Like the

42. Quoted in Jeremy Brechner, *Strike!* (San Francisco, 1972), 101.

43. Haggi Huvitz, "Ideology and Industrial Conflict: President Wilson's First Industrial Conference of October, 1919," *Labor History*, XVIII (1977), 509–24; Robert K. Murray, *Red Scare: A Study in National Hysteria, 1919–1920* (Minneapolis, 1955), 201–205.

44. The best account of the massacre is O. A. Rogers, Jr., "The Elaine Race Riots of 1919," *Arkansas Historical Quarterly*, XX (1960), 142–50.

Elaine posse, the league claimed that the workers were gathering firearms for a battle. As was true of the Elaine killings, no one was indicted for the murder of the unionists.[45]

Popular success in Elaine and Bogalusa would have altered critical southern institutions. In the language of the contemporary northern struggles, both were battles for industrial democracy. Planters and timbermen used all their resources to retain control of a work force that had begun to assert some of the power of organized labor. Although unions did not survive the tyranny of the plantation and company town, some workers in the industrial sector of the southern economy maintained permanent organization. Skilled and unskilled railroad workers sustained unions until government operation ended in 1920. Black longshoremen up and down the southern coast organized, and frequently struck, sometimes successfully. Even black teachers in Baltimore created a union. Inspired by such successes and determined to organize other unions, black unionists from twelve states formed the National Brotherhood Workers of America (NBWA) in 1919.[46]

Organized workers altered the racial agenda. Class and race ideals mingled as black longshoremen in Key West, Florida, fought "for our rights as honest workmen"—"a noble principle in defense of our Race." The question of racial organization received new definition when the blacks of Okmulgee County, Oklahoma, concluded that the "only weapon [they possessed] is in uniting into labor organization," because "the clash of these interests [labor and capital] creates the race struggle." Political issues often emerged out of the economic struggles and the unions. During a strike of construction laborers in St. Petersburg, Florida, the men demanded higher wages and also equal rights with white people and the right to vote.[47]

Most southern whites considered the ballot as subversive as the militant union. The *Mississippi Daily News* warned that "if the Negro seeks the ballot . . . such ambition will inevitably lead to trouble; the door to hope is

45. Philip S. Foner, *Organized Labor and the Black Worker, 1619–1973* (New York, 1974), 149–50; Frank Morrison to Mary Ovington, February 4, 1920, and President, Louisiana State Federation of Labor, "Situation at Bogalusa, La.," Box C-319, both in NAACP Papers.
46. Baltimore *Afro-American*, April 20, July 4, October 10, 1919. The Justice Department's weekly "Bulletin of Radical Activities," compiled in 1919 and 1920, documents numerous strikes involving blacks and is an indispensable source because black newspapers rarely reported successful interracial or even racial unionism, only racial discrimination in unions. See Horace Cayton and George S. Mitchell, *Black Workers and the New Unions* (Chapel Hill, 1939), 393–98.
47. L. A. Gabriel to James Weldon Johnson, January 26, 1919, "Open Letter," January 18, 1919, Box C-319, in NAACP Papers; Working People's Civil and Equal Rights Federation of Okmulgee County, Oklahoma, "Statement ot Demands," in "Bulletin ot Radical Activities, no. 10," March 27, 1920, in RG 60.

forever closed to the Negro insofar as participation in politics is concerned, and there is no appeal from that decree." R. R. Moton was privately told by a leading white southern educator that "it may be perfectly logical and reasonable that Negroes should have the right to vote, to hold office, serve on juries, etc., but these things cannot be in the South."[48]

The racial elite was caught in the middle of escalating black demands and southern efforts to restore the prewar social order. During the war, Negro Welfare Advisory Committees met regularly with the Councils of National Defense. In Mississippi, two hundred whites and seventy-five blacks met publicly in Gulfport. By 1921, the new southern Interracial Commission, composed of churchmen, college presidents and teachers, and social workers, advised that interracial contacts should be private. Du Bois' wartime optimism vanished. In May, 1919, he declared, "We are cowards and jackasses if . . . we do not marshal every ounce of our brain and brawn to fight . . . the forces of hell in our own land." Tuskegee's Albion Holsey said, "So many things have happened that were positively of such a discouraging nature that one feels like saying, 'What's the use.'" The Negro "feels both hopeless and helpless," he added. Fred Moore stated that he had come to

> recognize that the real rights of our people in the South are live subjects and ought to be met in a courageous way. For instance the Jim Crow proposition and the disfranchisement proposition are questions that will not down, whether we are at fault in some respect in not performing our duty as a voter is a question. Whether we comply with all of the requirements is a question. I would like to talk over with you some of these features. We cannot afford to join in with hot-headed, impulsive people who are simply yelling without first having given serious thought to the fundamentals.

Whatever their particular response, race leaders discovered that their hegemony dissolved as former white allies withdrew and the masses adopted new agendas and methods.[49] Often disciples rebelled against former mentors. A former war correspondent selected by Emmett Scott now criticized his politics: "I appreciate that the country—and the world, as you state, is in a chaotic state, but to my mind that is no reason why we, as a race, must lay down, and become submissive forever; no reason why we should be-

---

48. [Jackson] *Mississippi Daily News*, June 20, 1919, Box C-3, in NAACP Papers; T. H. Harris to William Anthony Aery, February 4, 1920. Moton agreed "that the question ought not to be brought to the front now." R. R. Moton to Aery, March 7, 1920 (marked "Very Confidential"), in Moton Papers.

49. Wilma Dykeman and James Stokely, *Seeds of Southern Change: The Life of Will Alexander* (Chicago, 1962), 64; *Crisis*, XVI (May, 1919), 111; Albion Holsey to Garet Garrett, editor, New York *Tribune*, October 14, 1919, and Fred Moore to R. R. Moton, November 18, 1919, both in Moton Papers.

come hypnotized by promises for the future, which like the past may be broken." Indicting the entire Tuskegee philosophy, he said that "ever since we have been chasing this will-o-wisp money, we have been losing rights and privileges in city after city."[50]

The NAACP, founded on principles of agitation and financed by blacks, had more latitude than Tuskegee in responding to the crisis of 1919. It approached unions, black and white workers, and radicals in hopes of forming what might be called an antiestablishment coalition. This loose alliance was different from the wartime collaboration between R. R. Moton and Samuel Gompers of the AFL—limited attempts by the black leader and labor chief to work together so that they both might serve the government. Critical of the nation's political and economic institutions, officials of the NAACP now moved ideologically to the left, toward working-class methods of protest.

The NAACP was pushed from below into its new position. A Fisk professor observed that "the negro leaders are really now being led by the masses in this spirit of bitterness and unrest." Working-class blacks flooded headquarters with requests for aid and charters. From January through May, 1919, the organization added 9,300 members, a number that equaled its entire membership before the beginning of the upsurge in 1918. During 1919, the NAACP gained 85 new branches and nearly 35,000 members. Prior to 1919 the organization had been composed principally of members of northern black elites, but the new growth drew large numbers of black workers from Deep South towns and cities. In 1919, for the first time in its history, the majority of members were southern.[51]

Overwhelmed with evidence of initiatives by black workers, James Weldon Johnson, the first black field secretary of the NAACP, declared in December, 1919, that the "mightiest weapon colored people have in their hands is the strike" and urged its use to demand "abolition of jim crow conditions." He appeared on platforms with white radicals like Elizabeth Gurley Flynn and Harlem's black Socialists in defense of the Elaine, Arkansas, victims. He castigated the "pussyfooters . . . and spineless men who are relying on 'good white friends' to give them citizenship rights." A not-so-veiled attack on R. R. Moton, Johnson's speech revealed that the wartime truce between northern and southern black leaders had rested on black gains. But neither Johnson nor the NAACP was committed to mass action or to a conflict model of social change. The NAACP vacillated and

50. Ralph Tyler to Emmett Scott, March 29, 1919, in Scott Papers.
51. Paul F. Mowbray, "9th Meeting of University Committee on Southern Race Questions," April 25, 26, 1919, p. 4, copy in Phelps-Stokes Fund Papers, Schomburg Center for Research in Black Culture, New York Public Library; Kellogg, *NAACP*, 225–91.

finally opted for lobbying over striking. But in contrast to Tuskegee's view that racial progress was a by-product of economic development, requiring only racial harmony and adjustments, and in contrast to its own earlier, elite advocacy of justice for American blacks, the new NAACP was franker in its pursuit of racial power.[52]

Although southern conditions continued to dominate the black agenda, the outbreak of race riots in northern cities extended concern to areas once considered havens. Southern racial conflict grew out of black challenges to critical institutions forged to control black labor or out of black violations of prewar racial etiquette. The northern warfare stemmed from rifts within the working class. Blacks were challenging and defending ethnic territory. The riots typically began when aggressive whites, urged on by rumors that confirmed existing fears and tensions within communities, entered and attacked within the ghetto. The black response was diverse. Some people fought back; others were intimidated. Politically, race riots yielded various responses ranging from palliatives to racial defense to socialism. Businessman E. C. Brown believed that the urban warfare proved that "it is really essential that some place of amusement, some diversion be provided for our people." Therefore, the completion of his theater, the Dunbar Amusement Company, was imperative. The Reverend M. A. N. Shaw of the National Equal Rights League found the violence to be the emblem of "the most vicious and abominable plutocracy that encumbers the face of the earth today." He urged a campaign to obtain one dollar from each of the fifteen million blacks in the United States for a legal defense fund for riot victims. The new agitators believed that the northern warfare would convince blacks that, despite their progress in the North, they required racial organization.[53]

The riots and other forms of racial violence produced a new urgency and perhaps a new opportunity that had not existed during the war, but they pointed to no single course of action. Three types of modern, mass organization were visible in the new crisis. With varying degrees of consciousness, each incorporated criticisms of industrial society that had been absent before the war. The first, which took the working-class approach, grew out of the new power labor demonstrated nationally and internationally during and after the war. Although infused by the racial con-

52. James Weldon Johnson, speech with cover letter from Betty Thompson, November 30, 1919, pp. 22, 26, in Records of the Joint Legislative Committee Against Seditious Activities, New York State Archives, Albany (hereinafter cited as Records of the Lusk Committee); "Negro Agitation," December 10, 1919, file 10218-364/16, MID, in RG 165; Baltimore *Afro-American*, December 5, 1919.
53. E. C. Brown to Emmett Scott, August, 10, 1918, Scott Papers; Boston *Guardian*, July 14, 1918.

sciousness of the new black working class, it was not defined by it. Its leading expression was the labor unions. The other political instruments, as Hubert Harrison observed, had been fostered by the "Great War" and its "advertising campaign for democracy." The second type of organization focused on the battle against Jim Crow, conservative race leaders, and "educational starvation." Its leading expression was the NAACP, which had grown in numbers and militancy, erasing many of the gaps between its leaders and the masses of blacks. A new enterprise founded by Garvey was the best expression of the third type of organization, which had as its goal "racial independence in business." Harrison wrote, "One of the most striking enterprises at present is the Black Star Line, a steamship enterprise being floated by Marcus Garvey of New York." This was Garvey's bold attempt to move from agitation to organization. But although he had been inspired and encouraged by popular struggles, Garvey's politics would be modeled on the symbols and institutions of large nations.[54]

54. "Negro Activities," October 20, 1919, file 10218-364/12, MID, in RG 165.

4 / The Black Star Line
Business as Pan-African Politics

Throughout most of 1919, the UNIA was a small organization centered in New York, with satellites in a few cities along the Eastern Seaboard. At meetings, Garvey's indictment of racial injustice and imperialism in Africa and his delineation of a prosperous and powerful alternative for blacks earned the cheers of enthusiastic audiences. Garvey's hopes were raised in what he called "the revolutionary world" of 1919. Typically, he celebrated the Russian Revolution and the short-lived one in Hungary. He welcomed revolutions for the "breathing space" they might give blacks. But he added, "We are not very much concerned as partakers in these revolutions." He urged blacks to prepare and to develop leadership for the future, for "whenever the world again becomes disrupted." He sensed the opportunities brought by war and revolution, but he also was aware of the absence of black programs and organizations to effect change. For the moment, despite his militant rhetoric, Garvey was cautious.[1]

Advocates of numerous political causes joined him on the stage at Liberty Hall, the UNIA's new headquarters, formerly the Metropolitan Baptist Church on 138th Street. In August, for instance, the association held a debate on Bolshevism. Most of the audience was in sympathy with the new Communist victory in Russia and cheered its defender, the Reverend M. A. N. Shaw of Boston. Leading Garveyites were generally sympathetic to the socialist, union, and other popular movements, but few were active in them. One exception was W. A. Domingo, the Jamaican-born editor of the UNIA's newspaper, the *Negro World*.[2]

Domingo had known Garvey in Kingston, where they worked briefly together in the National Club. At the time that Garvey went to Central America in 1910, his comrade went to Boston and then New York, where he continued to advocate the democratization of Jamaican politics. He also advocated socialism, becoming a leader in the young black Socialist group of

1. *NW*, March 26, November 30, 1919.
2. "Negro Agitation," August 29, 1919, file 10218-364/3, MID, in RG 165; *NW*, August 2, 1919.

Harlem. When Garvey reached New York, he contacted Domingo, whose journalistic experience with the Socialists' New York *Call* served him well as editor of the new UNIA paper. The socialist editorials and reprints from the *Call*, which appeared regularly in the early *Negro World*, were the work of Domingo. He lectured on Negro radicalism at the Socialists' Rand School, championed the IWW, and supported many of the period's popular campaigns in New York—strikes and demonstrations against wage reductions, rent profiteering, and high food prices.[3]

Because of the UNIA's weak links to the menacing radicalism of 1919, it was barely touched by the hysteria of the Red Scare. Garvey's agitation had been observed because the government feared the possible merging of the UNIA and other black organizations with the Socialist party. But UNIA offices were not raided in June by agents of the Lusk committee of the New York State Legislature in search of the Red blueprint for conspiracy. But in one incursion at the Rand School, fifty policemen and committee agents seized a memorandum written by Domingo on the importance of blacks to the radical movement. The discovery brought Garvey and the UNIA within the net of surveillance. District Attorney Edwin Kilroe questioned him on August 5 about Wobblies, Socialists, and anarchists, and the Washington race riot. Previously, on the basis of an investigation made after dissidents had complained about Garvey's use of UNIA funds, Kilroe had judged Garvey to be a skillful charlatan. But in the turmoil of the summer, Garvey appeared to be connected with the larger events. After the Chicago race riot in July, most black organizations were monitored. The theory was that all groups "be they Socialist, revolutionary, nationalist, communist and anarchist have dropped their differences of opinion on detail for the common purpose of securing a change of Government in the United States."[4] Fearing the worst, Archibald Stevenson of the Lusk committee attended Garvey's August 25 meeting at Carnegie Hall with members of the city's bomb squad.[5]

In the real world, the UNIA was associated with the popular politics of 1919 only through individuals like Domingo. Garvey spoke of preparation

3. A brief biography of Domingo, *The Case of Domingo* (Kingston, Jamaica, 1941) is in the Schomburg Center, New York Public Library.

4. "Radicalism and Sedition Among the Negroes as Reflected in Their Publications," in *Investigation Activities of the Department of Justice*, Senate Documents, 66th Cong., 1st Sess., XII, 163–87; "Office Memorandum," October 16, 1919, Box C-4, in NAACP Papers.

5. Julian F. Jaffee, *Crusade Against Radicalism: New York During the Red Scare, 1914–1924* (Port Washington, N.Y., 1972), 120–41; Special Agent to R. L. Stevenson, June 14, 1919, in Records of the Lusk Committee; Richard Warner and Edgar Grey, "Statement in Relation to Black Star Line Inc. and Marcus Garvey," July 18, 1919, file 10218-373/4, MID, in RG 165; *NW*, June 14, 21, 28, 1919; New York *Times*, June 30, 1919.

"for the next war, twenty, thirty, or forty years hence," but the association did not officially engage in or engineer popular actions against the numerous injustices itemized by UNIA speakers. As in Jamaica, the UNIA staged elocution and speaking contests, enlisting prominent New York City judges and educators to preside over the verbal battles. Moreover, the radicalism of 1919 began to create deeper divisions among the popular forces in America. In July the NAACP convention declared its opposition to such "attractive programs as Bolshevism." Meanwhile the opponents of socialism and bolshevism exercised increasing influence in the UNIA. After a trial at which Domingo's socialist editorials were attacked by the UNIA executive committee, he resigned as editor of the newspaper in July.[6] In a debate in September, the writer Claude McKay argued for affiliations with radical groups, while William Ferris opposed them. Ferris, as literary editor of the *Negro World*, had much more influence in the UNIA.[7]

Garvey had charted the organization's course earlier in July when he announced that the UNIA "has absolutely no association with any political party. . . . Republicans, Democrats, and Socialists are the same to us— they are all white men to us and all of them join together and lynch and burn negroes." Garvey's disavowal was not a tactical shield to protect the UNIA from government attack but the ideological expression of his current practices and larger plans.[8]

Garvey had never been merely an agitator. On July 2, 1918, he had incorporated the UNIA in New York as a fraternal and the African Communities League as a business corporation. The ACL, whose stock was owned by the New York UNIA, launched a restaurant and also the UNIA newspaper. Fraternals—social institutions popular among the Afro-American middle class—were sometimes nuclei for successful businesses and political careers. There was much talk about the new economic opportunities at UNIA meetings. In October, Mary Church Terrell, a wealthy and politically prominent civil rights activist, had reminded an audience "that the war was giving the Negro a larger economic and industrial freedom." The Reverend Dr. W. W. Brown of Metropolitan Baptist Church, also a successful businessman, preached a gospel of enterprise. He told a UNIA audience

6. The few surviving copies of the *NW* for 1919 reveal a tension between the ideas of Domingo and Garvey before the July confrontation. Garvey's editorial of June 28 in support of black business suggested that he favored a passive role for the black working class, which contrasted strongly with the editorials penned by Domingo.

7. *NW*, September 20, 1919; Robert A. Bowen to Solicitor William H. Lamar, September 22, 1919, in Office of Solicitor, Correspondence Unarranged, Mail Violations, 1917 Espionage Act, 1917–21, in Record Group 28, Records of the Post Office Department, National Archives.

8. *NW*, July 19, 1919.

that "Harlem has a fine opportunity to develop into business." Throughout 1918, there was much talk about beginning businesses, but it was not until February, 1919, that the UNIA opened its first one, the restaurant.[9]

Garvey's improvised combination of business and agitation did not appear promising. Because UNIA members viewed the local chapter as an instrument for their own economic self-improvement, they were suspicious of Garvey's use of funds and came to meetings armed with embarrassing questions. Deft parliamentary maneuvers aided by the police quieted dissenters, but the petty squabbling led Harlem journalist John Bruce to resign his position as chairman of the UNIA executive committee. He announced in March that Garvey was "impractical, utopian, and Jackassical." Bruce seemed to object more to Garvey's failures than to his rhetoric and ambitions. He advised Garvey in print that "a good military strategist, wise statesman, and shrewd politician always conceal more than they reveal when talking of their plans. But Garvey *tells all.* . . . You wont do Mr. Garvey, too *muchee talkee.*"[10] A more likely source of weakness was Garvey's joining of ambitious rhetoric with meager resources. The UNIA's restaurant and most of the other proposed racial businesses were not likely instruments to effect the "redemption and regeneration of Africa."

Garvey was thinking of bigger things. He told a group in Baltimore that blacks must prepare for the "titanic industrial and commercial struggle" that he predicted. "If we are . . . to become a great national force, we must start business enterprises of our own; we must build ships and start trading with ourselves between America, the West Indies, and Africa." The basis of "racial greatness" was becoming a "commercial and industrial people." But it was not until May, 1919, when Garvey announced plans to create the Black Star Line, that the UNIA possessed a project that could carry the weight of its goals.[11]

Ships were preeminent symbols of national power. The creation of an American merchant marine and navy, previously a satellite to the British fleet, had received the highest priority in the nation's mobilization. Most American men and matériel went to war on foreign ships, but the establishment of the U.S. Shipping Board and a shipbuilding auxiliary in 1916

9. *Constitution and Book of Laws of the Universal Negro Improvement Association and African Communities League* (New York, 1918); Ida Wells-Barnett, *Crusade for Justice: The Autobiography of Ida B. Wells,* ed. Alfreda M. Duster (Chicago, 1970), 391; A. A. Garvey, "Marcus Garvey," 11–12; *Home News,* October 10, December 23, 1917, reprinted in Robert A. Hill (ed.), *The Marcus Garvey and Universal Negro Improvement Association Papers,* (10 vols. projected; Berkeley, 1983–), I, 224, 229–30; *NW,* March 1, 1919.

10. A. A. Garvey, "Marcus Garvey," 32, 50–65; John Bruce to Major W. H. Loving, March 13, 1919, file 10210-261/39, MID, in RG 165; editorial, n.d. [1918], file B-3-19, in Bruce Papers.

11. *NW,* February 1, 1919.

revealed the government's commitment to commercial expansion and naval power. At the time of the armistice, the U.S. Shipping Board owned, managed, or chartered 1,300 vessels, which it had commissioned or commandeered from Germany during the war.[12]

The new fleet was to be the core of a string of American shipping lines capable of retaining and expanding the foreign markets American businessmen had captured from Europeans during the war. While the greatest prizes were in Latin America, the African continent also assumed a new significance in postwar plans. American trade with Africa had increased from $47 million in 1914 to $325 million in 1920. Although the 1920 level would not be reached again until 1941, the Shipping Board mapped an ambitious future: "The exchange of manufactured goods for the rich and necessary cargoes of the great continent of Africa opens up unlimited possibilities of trade." A boom in African commodities in 1919 and 1920 encouraged Americans to begin thinking of Africa in terms of raw materials, not big game. And the Shipping Board concluded that successful commerce depended upon sending American ships to Africa. Prewar German and British shipping companies had effectively excluded their few American competitors in West Africa through a combination of deferred rebates to American merchants, long experience on the coast, and low rates on American goods. To penetrate the British monopoly after the war, the Shipping Board authorized A. H. Bull and Company of New York to operate vessels to the west coast of Africa.[13]

American ambitions were applauded by native African merchants who wanted alternatives to Britain's Elder Dempster line. Competitive shipping facilities were part of the merchants' plans to compete with European trading companies, whose dominance, they believed, was maintained by the favored treatment they obtained from Dempster. Cognizant of the boom for African products, many Africans looked to black and white Americans. During the war, Dusé Mohamed Ali's *African Times* had resurrected the Pan-African solution. It appealed to Afro-Americans to turn their attention to the "Racial Motherland" to aid native shippers and merchants with "capital, industry, and commerce." Other Africans brought the mes-

12. Paul Zeis, *American Shipping Policy* (Princeton, 1938), 81–114; Burl Noggle, *Into the Twenties: The United States from Armistice to Normalcy* (Urbana, Ill., 1974), 58–59.

13. Joan Huff Wilson, *American Business and Foreign Policy, 1920–1925* (Lexington, Ky., 1971), 7; "Commercial Outlook in West Africa," *Review of Reviews*, July, 1920, pp. 102–103, December 1920, p. 663; David Killingray, "Repercussions of World War I in the Gold Coast," *Journal of African History*, XIX (1978), 43; Charlotte Leubuscher, *The West African Shipping Trade, 1909–1959* (Leyden, Holland, 1963), ch. 1; U.S. Shipping Board, *Bulletin*, V (June, 1921), 4; U.S. Shipping Board, *Trade and Shipping in West Africa* (Washington, D.C., 1920), 17.

sage directly to the United States. Some of the travelers were frauds, peddling fool's gold. T. Ras Makonnen, a Guianese Pan-Africanist, explained: "The temptation in the American scene was to play upon the average American's ignorance of Africa. You would therefore try pretending yourself as a prince or a chieftain—the Nigerians were the worst offenders here. Or you would set up some African institute in New York with the object of starting business links between America and Africa." Many combined the appeal for capital with an uplift project. The Reverend Prince U. Kaba Rega of Uganda combined missionary work with appeals for money for a steamship company linking the United States and Africa during his whirlwind tour in 1918 and 1919.[14]

If the African market was potentially vast, the absence of African-American commercial structures and information made the African presence only occasional, not sustained. West Indian commercial affairs were publicized more regularly because of the large expatriate communities in the cities of the United States and Canada. Big foreign firms dominated the transportation and selling of West Indian products. The marginal seller of cash crops in the Caribbean, like the producers in Africa, lacked sufficient shipping facilities and often faced monopolies. Bananas, requiring specially equipped steamers for the transportation of perishables, were carried on ships owned by the United Fruit Company and its foreign subsidiaries. Because United Fruit produced as well as transported bananas, it discriminated against competitors. In 1919, a committee of the British Parliament found that the company did "not carry fruit on behalf of independent shippers." Moreover, steamship companies stopped less frequently at, or even abandoned, many West Indian ports that did not generate enough traffic to make them profitable. The same economic forces that reduced service increased the numbers who needed transportation to find work off the impoverished islands. Seasonal, interisland, migratory labor was usually transported in steamers owned by sugar and banana planters. But for those with only hopes, and no work contracts, obtaining passage was difficult. The problem was acute on the smaller islands. After Garvey created the Black Star Line, inhabitants of Christiansted, St. Croix, petitioned its offices to call regularly because the steamship companies often refused them berths. West Indian migrants crowded UNIA offices to try to buy passage for their families who had remained in their native lands.[15]

14. Anthony G. Hopkins, "Economic Aspects of Political Movements in Nigeria and the Gold Coast, 1918–1939," *Journal of African History*, VII (1966), 133–34; M. J. Hughes, "An Appeal to Afro-Americans," *African Times and Orient Review*, IV (March, 1917), 56–57; T. Ras Makonnen, *Pan-Africanism from Within* (Nairobi, Kenya, 1973), 94, 153; Prince Rega to R. R. Moton, April 23, 1918, in Moton Papers.
15. Gisela Eisner, *Jamaica, 1830–1930: A Study in Economic Growth* (Manchester, En-

The diminishing number of available passenger places on the ships exacerbated racism. The American consul in Trinidad found that "many persons who are now going first class . . . are practically paupers, and their expenses are being paid by collections raised by persons anxious to get rid of them. It is such a class of people that is evidently taking up much accommodation." Responding to the complaints of businessmen, he began to deny visas to all "who are not going for business purposes, returning to their homes in America, Canada or England, or who do not belong to classes such as really are first class, according to what is expected by the usual term, 'first class passengers.'" The alternative was deck passage—crowded, dirty, and subject to the whims of Caribbean weather.[16]

First-class facilities were often denied middle-class blacks because of their color. Some leaders, therefore, began to delineate more sharply the class distinctions within the race. R. R. Moton was once allowed to pay the first-class fare on a ship of the intercoastal Chesapeake Steamship Company, but he was denied the saloon privileges that usually went with it. Asking a white friend to intercede with the company's president, Moton acknowledged the right of the company to exclude even when the passenger paid first-class fare: "The steamboat company has police rights as the Pullman Company has, that is, if any people are not well dressed, if men are in working clothes and are not the right type they are not permitted to go in the Pullman cars." But if dress, the badge of class, was not a sufficient criterion, Moton suggested setting off a special part of the saloon for black use—segregation. On the other hand, racial militants offered racial enterprise as a solution. The editor of the Baltimore *Afro-American* urged blacks to patronize boats "owned and operated by our own people." His solution, however, was only practical for the smaller popular excursion boats, some of which were operated by blacks.[17]

gland, 1961), 180–86; Sir Sydney Olivier, *White Capital, Coloured Labour* (London, 1929), 380–81; "Report of the West Indian Shipping Committee," August 15, 1919, Colonial Office (Great Britain), pp. 3–4, 11, copy in file 12395/B-6-C, in Record Group 38, Records of the Chief of Naval Operations, Office of Naval Intelligence, National Archives; Baltimore *Afro-American*, July 30, 1920; Louis LeMoth, "Interview," May 6, 1922, Garvey file, in Record Group 65, Records of the Federal Bureau of Investigation, National Archives.

16. "Report of the West Indian Shipping Committee," 4–8, 14; Henry L. Baker to Secretary of State, April 2, 1919, file 844g.111/1, in Record Group 59, Records of the Department of State, National Archives.

17. R. R. Moton to R. E. Blackwell, July 8, August 1, 1921, Blackwell to Moton, September 9, 1921, in Moton Papers. Liberians, too, complained that "deck passage has become the only possible means of travel for our citizens. . . . Steamship agents . . . in nine cases out of ten refuse to sell anything but deck tickets, thus leaving the passenger at the mercy of the captain and crew, and subject to all kinds of deck exposure, humiliation, and hunger in travel." *Liberian Methodist*, n.d., cited in *Age*, July 23, 1921. Even Thomas Jesse Jones, traveling through West Africa for the Phelps-Stokes Fund, had to obtain the inter-

Although the need for more shipping facilities existed throughout the black world, only in the United States was it economically and politically feasible for blacks to establish shipping companies. Elder Dempster's political power in London ensured that the British colonies in Africa would not incubate rivals. In the West Indies, most lines, unable to maintain their profits, were cutting down services. The British subsidized the existing lines for political, not economic, reasons. Blacks in the United States found conditions more favorable. The American policy of expanding the merchant marine for routes to Latin America and Africa meant that new companies enjoyed government support.

It is possible, however, that Garvey's initial interest in shipping had political objectives. Despite its failures, Henry Ford's peace ship offered an example of how modern vehicles could be used for political propaganda. Ida Wells-Barnett recalled that Garvey spoke to her in December, 1918, about his plans to obtain a ship. Although she did not elaborate, his likely purpose was to transport the UNIA delegates to the Paris Peace Conference. At that time, all of the Afro-American representatives had been denied passports. He might have toyed with the idea of obtaining a ship, sailing to Europe, and then presenting the UNIA petitions. He was probably aware of Monroe Trotter's clever ruse of disguising himself as a ship's cook to avoid the government prohibition and attend the Paris meetings. Garvey certainly knew of the impressive popular welcome that greeted Trotter on his return in July, when Garvey picked up the idea again. Indeed, the *Yarmouth*, the ship that brought Trotter home, was purchased that fall as the first vessel of the Black Star Line.[18]

Potential political dividends only encouraged Garvey in his idea to respond to the continuing call for additional shipping to serve Africa, the West Indies, and the United States. The chorus of approval of the plan for the Black Star Line appeared to guarantee economic success. One merchant, J. T. Bishop, president of the West Indian Trading Association of Canada, founded in 1918, was a tireless advocate who met frequently with Garvey in New York and Canada during the summer and fall of 1919. Bishop summarily dismissed the internal dissension and exhorted Garveyites to "Organize, Cooperate. . . . That's the keynote of success, that's

vention of a colonial governor to get an Elder Dempster ship to stop at Monrovia to avoid a three-week delay in his plans. "Thomas Jesse Jones Diary," September 28–October 1, 1920, p. 21, in Phelps-Stokes Fund Papers; Baltimore *Afro-American*, September 22, 1919.

18. Wells-Barnett, *Crusader for Justice*, 381; Stephen R. Fox, *The Guardian of Boston: William Monroe Trotter* (New York, 1971), 232–33; New York *Times*, July 28, 1919; "Negro Agitation," August 1919, file 10218-364/1, MID, in RG 165.

the secret of Anglo-Saxons." Bishop's encouragement was not commitment. Although a UNIA shipping line could facilitate his own mercantile aspirations, Bishop appealed to the *Messenger* group, too, and offered similar advice to other would-be entrepreneurs. There is no evidence that he gave Garvey much more than counsel and enthusiasm. Mutual needs and hopes reinforced each other, but they were pursued singly.[19]

Suitable ships cost from $150,000 to $500,000. Once purchased, they had to be tailored to the kind of cargo carried. Refurbishing and repair added between $10,000 and $25,000 to the purchase price. Individual blacks lacked sufficient capital or access to credit, and black entrepreneurs required capital for their own enterprises. Garvey had wanted the BSL to be owned and controlled by the UNIA, but since he lacked sufficient funds, he was forced to appeal to the public.

A new potential source of funds was the enlarged black working class. The idea of accumulating wealth through stocks and bonds had been widely publicized during the war. Many new wage-workers first entered the world of paper wealth through the purchase of Liberty Bonds, which black leaders often encouraged during the war. Holders of securities among all Americans increased from half a million before the war to seventeen million by 1918, and the potential market was even greater. War workers and returning soldiers possessed savings readily targeted by capital-starved marginal businessmen and promoters, both legitimate and fraudulent.[20]

Like other Americans, blacks were often intrigued by the prospect of the new wealth. Some took up the new game, the "numbers"; others gambled on new enterprises. In January, 1920, the New York *Age* warned blacks that "in this era of get-rich-quick enterprises, which promise the gullible investor all sorts of interest on a small investment, it behooves the capitalist to look well before he leaps." In mid-1921 the editors reported that "the craze for buying stocks . . . has become almost epidemic in Harlem. Individuals who have laid aside a comfortable nest egg in the savings bank or in the now despised but always secure Liberty bonds, have exchanged the certainty of four per cent for the hopeful anticipation of at

19. New York *Amsterdam News*, July 13, 1940; "Negro Agitation," October 17, 1919, file 10218-364/11, MID, in RG 165; *NW*, August 23, 1919. For other black interest, see W. E. C. to R. R. Moton, March 8, 1918, in Moton Papers.

20. "Minutes of the Board of Directors," September 11, 1919, in *Marcus Garvey v. United States of America*, 267 U.S. 607 (1924), 2559; Cedric B. Cowing, *Populists, Plungers, and Progressives: A Social History of Stock and Commodity Speculation, 1890-1936* (Princeton, 1965), 95; Baltimore *Afro-American*, October 13, 27, 1917; *World's Work*, XXXVII (January, 1919), 314, (February, 1919), 393–98, (March, 1919), 509; *Saturday Evening Post*, CXCIII (February 26, 1921), 9.

least ten or perhaps twenty per cent. dividends from some unproved oil well or doubtful industrial enterprise."[21] One group even planned a Harlem Stock Exchange in 1920.[22]

While the *Age* warned, it also contributed to the speculative mentality by telling readers that "the gold mine still exists in Harlem and paying ore awaits the efforts of the earnest and industrious pioneers." Similarly, the crusading, proper Boston *Guardian* urged the purchase of shares in the Colored American Theatres Corporation. An editorial promised "net earning of 50% on its capital," while pointing out that "depositors in savings banks earned 4 or 5% only." The favored corporation was steered by many prominent race leaders, including New York realtor John Nail and Washington politician James Cobb, both affiliated with the NAACP. Many well-known blacks were taken in by this new enterprise and by others, white and black. Professionals appear to have been the dominant class of new black investors, and Cedric Cowing's observation about the new American investing public applies well to blacks: "Lacking businesses of their own to invest in, [they] disposed of their surplus funds in the market to simulate the thrills of real proprietorship."[23]

Steamship corporations were at the forefront of enterprises soliciting black and white dollars. Military intelligence reported that New Orleans alone spawned twenty-three "fake steamship companies." Shipowners had reaped huge profits during the war because rates for ocean transportation rose as high as 1250 percent. The American-Hawaiian Steamship Company made net profits of 236.2 percent in 1916; the Luckenback Steamship Company earned 66.9 percent in 1917; the Atlantic, Cuba and West Indies Company's profits exceeded its capital investment from 1915 through 1920. The boom continued after the armistice because of heavy exports to Europe. One postwar shipment of coal to Europe grossed $250,000— three-quarters of the prewar purchase price of the vessel. A shipping executive told a Senate investigating committee in 1922 that in those days "anybody experienced or inexperienced in the shipping trade could make

21. *Age*, January 10, 1920, May 28, 1921. On the fleecing of southern Negroes, see Pittsburgh *Leader*, August 1, 1918. The *NW* of June 28, 1919, also spoke of swindlers urging black workers in the cotton mills of Texas to sell their Liberty Bonds to buy oil stocks. An article, probably written by Domingo, concluded that the social forces that led workers to pursue promised dividends would produce bolshevism. At the time, Liberty Bonds were selling below par, and numerous people were selling them to purchase speculative stock.

22. An emissary of the Phelps-Stokes group thought, wrongly, that Garvey was behind it. Ida A. Tourtellot to Anson Phelps Stokes, February 4, 1921, in Phelps-Stokes Fund Papers.

23. *Age*, December 20, 1919; Boston *Guardian*, January 3, 1920; Cowing, *Populists, Plungers, and Progressives*, 95.

money." Some promoters appealed to the ethnicity and patriotism of potential shareholders, as well as to their self-interest. Common in Afro-American history and prevalent in beginning businesses, use of the appeal to ethnicity and patriotism is not limited to small capitalists. American oil companies in the mid-1970s appealed to American nationalism. Southern promoters used regional nationalism to accumulate capital for cotton mills after the Civil War. During and just after World War I, the Shipping Board's sales campaigns urged Americans to buy ships for wealth and patriotism. Other ethnic groups set up shipping lines by appealing to group solidarity. Irish businessmen created the Green Star Line; Polish businessmen, the Polish Navigation Steamship Company.[24]

The ethnic promoters addressed a population that had recent experiences with the patriotic appeal for money. In April, 1919, blacks in New York were told: "When one becomes the owner of a bond of the United States, he becomes a stockholder in the country. As a stockholder, he will feel a greater degree of interest in the welfare of the country and is entitled to greater consideration in its affairs. Invest in the stocks of Uncle Sam." It was not very difficult to replace the patriotism of race for that of nation. Blacks had historically contributed generously to racial causes. Both the NAACP and NERL were soliciting contributions to defend riot victims. The *Messenger* urged blacks to buy five-dollar Liberty Bonds for the magazine. The defenders of imprisoned black IWW leader Ben Fletcher sold five-dollar Liberty Bonds to free him. Now Garvey's Black Star Line promised racial advance and immediate returns for a five-dollar share. Initially, Garvey had promised neither dividends nor profit. By July, 1919, he was forced to sweeten his package. The Black Star Line presented "to every Black Man, Woman, and Child the opportunity to climb the great ladder of industrial and commercial progress" and pledged "large profits and dividends to stockholders." The president of the UNIA division in Norfolk, Virginia, informed his audience that he "had been chairman of all Liberty and Victory Loan drives [in Norfolk] so now let's buy loans for this purpose [the Black Star Line]."[25]

The Black Star Line closed the gap in Garvey's politics, as his first appeals on its behalf clearly revealed. In June, 1919, as he had done earlier, he urged blacks to prepare "for the future racial struggle which the next war

24. Morris R. Werner, *Privileged Characters* (New York, 1935), 320–21; Zeis, *American Shipping Policy*, 85–86; U.S. Shipping Board, *Fifth Annual Report* (Washington, D.C., 1921), 266–69.

25. *Age*, April 19, 1919; *NW*, June 7, 1919; Norfolk *Journal and Guide*, February 5, 1921; A. Philip Randolph, speech at John Wesley A.M.E. Zion Church, May 30, 1919, file 19218-361, MID, in RG 165.

would open up." But now he offered them the means of preparation. He announced the formation of the BSL and promised financial success. He then stated, "Our race is in no mood to be tampered with," thus immediately investing the BSL with the rhetoric and urgency of the militant temper of racial politics.[26]

Until the Black Star Line unveiled its first ship in October, 1919, there was little to distinguish its promoters from others. Garvey's aspirations were infused with broad goals but were without racial significance. Even when the ship appeared, Garvey's financial appeal was only a variation on common ways businessmen used ethnicity to accumulate capital. The Black Star Line's appeal reflected marketplace values, and its creators aimed to succeed as a business. But Garvey's ultimate aspirations were political. Some businessmen use politics to gain the licenses, tax abatements, and other advantages parties in power confer on the loyal. Garvey occasionally pursued these relationships with the local Democratic party in New York. Many black businessmen appealed for black patronage by claiming an identity of interest between their own aspirations and those of the race. Garvey made these claims, too. But these characteristics of Garvey's activities cannot essentially capture the politics of the creation of the BSL because they do not take into account the unusual social environment of 1919. His particular aims and the uninnovative character of the methods he employed are not especially important. What is significant is that in order to promote the Black Star Line, man his new ships, and create UNIA locals, he required something more than merely an economic environment favorable to a shipping line. He required numerous men of talent and ability who were politically committed. And it was the crisis of 1919 that led his associates to join their own personal aims with Garvey's in the Black Star Line and launch what they believed was a new mass politics.

The men who joined with Garvey were not sentimentalists. They joined the UNIA, becoming nationalists, for practical reasons. The first directors of the Black Star Line conceived of the new line as a business venture of the New York UNIA. The creation of a shipping line was their politics in 1919. Initially, however, the same reasons that eventually drew them to the Black Star Line caused them to oppose it. The decision to begin the line was not unanimous. In May, 1919, some members objected to the use of funds for a shipping line while the UNIA still owed them money for its restaurant, which had opened in February. Others, surmising that Garvey was pilfering funds, demanded an accounting. Whatever the truth of the suspicions,

26. NW, June 28, 1919; "Minutes of the Board of Directors," September 11, 1919, in *Garvey* v. *U.S.A.*, 2559.

the culture out of which small business ventures emerged did not encourage generous appraisals of human motives. Until the first ship appeared in October, mistrust and skepticism threatened to overwhelm hopes and ambition. Both sides engaged in newspaper warfare. Four of Garvey's opponents enlisted the pen of William Bridges, a young gadfly who spoke nightly on Lenox Avenue on race riots, the IWW, Indian freedom, and other timely subjects. Bridges edited a new Harlem newspaper, the *Challenge*, which aired the charges of the dissidents. They also complained to District Attorney Kilroe, who summoned Garvey three times in June.[27]

On June 21, the *Negro World* announced that the "traitors" had been routed. Garvey explained to his readers that Edwin Kilroe "was very much against the idea of a Black Star Line. I was forced to tell him that even as there was a White Star Line owned by white men, there is going to be a Black Star Line owned by black men." He promised that he would take the case to state and national authorities. The final action, if necessary, would take place on the "African battle field for which the Negroes of the world are preparing." Garvey had taken a local dispute, related it to the fact of racial discrimination, identified the controversy with the fate of all Negroes, and vowed unrelenting battle, perhaps violent struggle. As he threatened war, he followed the advice of the district attorney and his lawyer to incorporate the Black Star Line. He even discovered that incorporation bestowed useful legitimacy and dividends because numerous people misconstrued the Black Star Line's authorized capitalization of $500,000 for its assets.[28]

In order to raise money for the Black Star Line, organizers fanned out all over the country. Garvey wove the social battles of 1919 into his appeals for funds and managers. Earlier he had asked blacks to prepare for action; he called them now to act by buying stocks. The coupling of legal squabbling with martial rhetoric, and of appeals to conventional authority with charges of official conspiracy was a source of confusion to the government and UNIA members, alike. By reading one side of the page, they found that Garvey urged violence. This made the UNIA attractive to some blacks who were impatient or frustrated, and ignorant of the legal tactics that Garvey used most of the time. Conversely, his verbal extravagance was a liability in Garvey's search for acceptance and respectability, qualities personally necessary and essential to beginning businessmen. The intensity of Garvey's rhetoric demonstrated that he felt that he was engaged in a

27. Edgar Grey, testimony, *Garvey* v. *U.S.A.*, 61–69; A. A. Garvey, "Marcus Garvey," 63–74; *NW*, March 1, 1919; "Negro Agitation," mid-August, 1919, 10218–364/1 MID, in RG 165.
28. *NW*, June 21, 28, 1919; Baltimore *Afro-American*, July 4, 1919; Major W. H. Loving to J. E. Cutler, June 28, 1919, 10218–317/7, MID, in RG 165.

battle for his life and career. American political rhetoric of 1919 heightened the do-or-die politics of the petit bourgeois world, where there were few places but many aspirants.

Garvey alternated between wooing and castigating black leaders. He accused William Bridges of making "it a custom to attack prominent public men and institutions on the avenue to impugn things against them, thereby catering to those who take delight in scandalizing the reputation of others. All last summer his men succeeded in abusing some of the noblest members of the race and was able 'to get away with it.'" All the while, Garvey himself attacked the "Old Crowd," including Booker T. Washington.[29]

One new and frequent claim to legitimacy was the UNIA's assertion of racial independence. Edgar M. Grey proclaimed that the UNIA was the "first organization entirely composed of Negroes for which leadership had not been chosen by white people; its leadership is not only chosen by the led but was controlled and dictated to by its entire membership." Grey's statement, if exaggerated, was not merely rhetorical. Reigning black leaders grew powerful during the war through white philanthropy and the network of Negro advisory councils created by the "better whites." The assertion of racial independence was simultaneously a substantive criticism of leadership and a democratic defense of the new popular politics.[30]

Grey's celebration of racial autonomy was modified in July when he asked the district attorney to help him control Garvey's use of UNIA funds. The rift between Grey and Garvey began when Grey, secretary of the Black Star Line, refused to sign blank certificates for a stock-selling campaign in the Hampton Roads area of Virginia.[31] Garvey satisfied Grey's objections by agreeing to bring along BSL treasurer George Tobias. But Garvey lost a stock book in Virginia, issued shares without paying the federal revenue tax, failed to keep records of his expenditures, and used some of the proceeds to pay off the debt against the UNIA restaurant. Grey and Richard Warner, another BSL officer, now filed formal affidavits with the district attorney accusing Garvey of misappropriating funds. Garvey responded as he had answered attacks in the past. His public response was headlines in the *Negro World* reading TWO NEGRO CROOKS USE OFFICE OF DEPUTY DISTRICT ATTORNEY KILROE TO SAVE THEMSELVES FROM JAIL. Privately, Garvey told the

29. *NW*, June 21, September 27, 1919.
30. *NW*, June 21, 1919.
31. Grey, testimony, *Garvey* v. *U.S.A.*, 6370; Edwin Kilroe, testimony, *Garvey* v. *U.S.A.*, 120–25; New York *Amsterdam News*, July 13, 1940; Melvin J. McKenna to Captain W. L. Moffat, Jr., October 8, 1919, file 10218-373/5, MID, in RG 165. On Garvey's early successes in Virginia see H. Vinton Plummer, "The Universal Negro Improvement Association as I See It—Then—Now," (New York) *Spokesman*, May 27, 1927, pp. 10ff.

officers of the Black Star Line that the stock-selling campaign had to be better organized.[32]

The controversy triggered the first of many reorganizations of the Black Star Line's management. Warner and Grey were replaced by Fred Powell and Edward Smith-Green. In September, Amy Ashwood (Garvey's old comrade and future wife), Cyril Henry, John G. Baynes, and D. D. Shirley were placed on the board. Despite the controversies and disputes, both the old and the new officers emerged out of similar social backgrounds. Many had professional aspirations, which, given the social relations of black work, made them dependent upon black patronage. They were politically ambitious, but none had a political following, though all had ties to local black institutions—fraternals, newspapers, businesses, and churches.[33]

Richard Warner, a member of the Odd Fellows, had been a reporter for the New York *News*, a black paper that was the noisy rival to the *Age*. He had met Garvey through Edgar Grey. Born in Sierra Leone of West Indian descent, Grey had served in the American army. He met Garvey in 1917 but joined the UNIA later, in May, 1919, after his own Foreign-Born Citizens Political Alliance had disbanded. After Grey left the UNIA, he worked as a postal clerk and then as a messenger for a construction company.[34]

BSL Treasurer George Tobias, a Grenadian, had worked as a clerk in the Canal Zone. He came to the United States in 1913 and was employed as a

32. A copy of Grey's affidavit, and a similar one by Richard E. Warner, July 18, 1919, may be found in file 10218-373/4, MID, in RG 165. See also *NW*, August 2, 1919. Kilroe sued Garvey for criminal libel. He was found guilty, fined one dollar, and made to apologize in print; Baltimore *Afro-American*, September 12, 1919. Amy Ashwood's version of the dispute is slightly different but still basically consistent with that of the others. She claimed that the New York UNIA had loaned money to Garvey for the restaurant. Instead of returning the funds, Garvey suggested that investors be issued BSL shares. George Tobias accepted, but Warner refused to go along and went to the district attorney. She claimed that two-thirds of the money from the first stock sales were spent on old debt repayments. A. A. Garvey, "Marcus Garvey," 66–69.

33. "Minutes of the Black Star Line," October 27, 1919, in Garvey file, RG 65. All of the officers lived in the United States. D. D. Shirley was the newcomer with the most ambitious Pan-African plans. While an official of both the UNIA and BSL, he also had a trading company, Shirley and Foreman. Maintaining these commitments, he joined with S. G. Kpakpa-Quartery, a merchant from Accra, to form the African International Traders, which planned to sell stock in the United States. Shirley reasoned that "we Negroes ought to be the richest factors in the world if with the untold wealth of Africa the Africans and the American Negroes could combine in trade." He added: "The ocean transport problem had been solved by Marcus Garvey. . . . It now remains for the Negro banks . . . to assist struggling Negro enterprises." It is unlikely that either Shirley and Foreman or the African International Traders flourished. "Special Report from New York," January 6, 1920, in Foreign Office, 371/4567, Public Record Office, London; Baltimore *Afro-American*, September 17, 1920.

34. Warner, "Affidavit," file 10218-373/4, MID, in RG 165; Warner, testimony, *Garvey* v. *U.S.A.*, 144–45, 163; Baltimore *Afro-American*, January 7, 1921.

clerk in the shipping department of the Pennsylvania Railroad when he met Garvey in New York in 1918. Secretary Edward Smith-Green, a civil servant in his native British Guiana, came to the United States and worked in an ammunition factory in New Jersey during the war before joining the new enterprise. He poured his heart into the enterprise and often worked without pay when the BSL was short of cash. The Black Star Line also tapped the world of small business. Jeremiah Certain, vice-president of the Black Star Line, had temporarily left his cigar manufacturing business. More typical of the businessmen attracted to the Black Star Line was John G. Baynes, who had an employment agency and real estate company—two small businesses whose activities increased as a result of the migration.[35]

Henrietta Vinton Davis was typical of the cultural wing of the petite bourgeoisie attracted to the UNIA. Born in Baltimore, Davis was an actress and elocutionist. Dramatic recitations, pageants, and other theatrical spectacles were popular entertainment for middle-class fraternal organizations and churches. The performer had a place in popular culture but lacked secure employment. Dependent upon black organizations for patronage, Davis supported many efforts for racial organization and unity. Her personal successes and failures took on racial significance to her. After an engagement in Yonkers in 1916, Davis explained the poor attendance by honing the standard middle-class ideology: "I am well acquainted with *my* people. I know their lack of cohesiveness—and it is that very lack that the white man takes advantage of. He knows the weakness of the Negro better than the Negro knows it himself."[36]

Davis made her UNIA debut at a meeting on June 15 at Palace Casino. Like others, she probably was paid from the collection gathered at the end of the meeting. That day, she recited one of Lawrence Dunbar's poems and illustrated it with a large colored doll manufactured by a new black company created during the war, Berry and Ross, which produced dolls and clothing. Davis, probably paid by the company, too, made "a strong appeal for support for the factory that was doing so much to inculcate a spirit of race pride in the Negro race." Between that time and the next meeting of the UNIA on June 22, she joined the organization and started using her talents to promote Garvey and the Black Star Line. Subsequently, she was appointed to the first Board of Directors of the corporation. An indefati-

35. George Tobias, testimony, *Garvey* v. *U.S.A.*, 2123; Jeremiah Certain, testimony, *Garvey* v. *U.S.A.*, 1310–11; Hill (ed.), *The Garvey and UNIA Papers*, I, 227; George Tobias, "Interview," in Garvey file, RG 65, A. A. Garvey, "Marcus Garvey," 349.

36. A. A. Garvey, "Marcus Garvey," 341; Henrietta Vinton Davis to John Bruce, April 30, 1916, in Bruce Papers.

gable speaker and loyal friend, she traveled throughout the United States and Caribbean publicizing the UNIA.[37]

Younger recruits like Wesley McD. Holder, Fred Powell, and Cyril Henry answered the UNIA's call to 10,000 INTELLIGENT YOUNG NEGRO MEN AND WOMEN OF AMBITION. Holder's biography fit the appeal perfectly. Later he recalled that ambition, not poverty, drove him from Guiana to the United States and the UNIA: "We [young school teachers] were stimulated and interested in what was happening in America. . . . We had almost anything we wanted [in Guiana but we were] not satisfied and decided to strike out." Holder organized several divisions of the UNIA in the Midwest. His ambitions were not fulfilled by the UNIA, and he became a Democratic politico in Brooklyn in the 1930s and godfather of the political career of Congresswoman Shirley Chisholm. Fred Powell also was well educated. He had been a notary public in Philadelphia and was studying law. His tour with the Black Star Line was brief. In February, 1922, he joined a rival shipping company begun by other Black Star Line dissidents. Cyril Henry was born in Jamaica but graduated from Boston's English High School. As a student at the Ontario Agricultural College in 1913, he had hoped to be able to go to Africa one day to speed its "settlement and development." He was the only one of the original group of directors who possessed skills useful to the African goals of the UNIA. But Powell resigned in December, 1920, to accept charge of an industrial school in Liberia run by the white Methodist Episcopal Church.[38]

Pursuing various careers, Garvey's associates were physically mobile and ambitious. Many belonged to racial organizations, but since they frequently moved about in search of professional security and advancement, their loyalties were brief. They were persons at the margins of the professional and business world or young persons just embarking on careers. None was from a rural area; none was an industrial worker. Many possessed skills useful in an organization—writing, speaking, the law, bookkeeping. They spent most of their time arranging meetings to sell stock—at Carnegie Hall in New

37. *Age*, March 29, 1919; Henrietta Vinton Davis, testimony, *Garvey* v. *U.S.A.*, 1085, 1092, 1191; *NW*, June 21, 1919, August 23, 1921; William Seraile, "Henrietta Vinton Davis and the Garvey Movement," *Afro-Americans in New York Life and History*, VII (July, 1983), 7–25. The history of Berry and Ross may be followed in *Crisis*, XXIII (December, 1921), 83, XXI (November, 1920), 34; Norfolk *Journal and Guide*, January 22, March 26, 1921; *Age*, April 19, 1919; Baltimore *Afro-American*, December 12, 1919.

38. *NW*, August 2, 1919; Fred Powell, testimony, *Garvey* v. *U.S.A.*, 971, 1026–27; Cyril Henry to Henry Slemun, November 14, 1918, in American Colonization Society Papers, Library of Congress; *Age*, December 25, 1920; "Reminiscences of Wesley McD. Holder," 3, Oral History Project, Columbia University.

York, at Fanueil Hall in Boston, and in the theaters and churches of Philadelphia. Because none of the directors had any shipping experience, they depended upon the advice and judgment of outsiders. They permitted one man, Joshua Cockburn, to purchase their first ship.[39]

Cockburn was born on the island of Nassau. Starting out as a lighthouse tender in the Royal Navy, he later piloted the vessels of Elder Dempster and, from 1908 through 1918, traded for himself in Nigerian waters. Then, after a short visit home, he came to New York, where he read of Garvey's feud with District Attorney Kilroe over BSL incorporation. Captain Cockburn immediately offered his services. Adept at self-promotion, he told Garvey that he was the only Negro possessing a captain's license and that "the prospects were great out there in Africa; plenty of wealth there."[40]

Cockburn arranged the purchase of the SS *Yarmouth*, a steel ship, built in Scotland in 1887. Its owner, W. L. Harriss, was a cotton broker who had purchased the vessel for $350,000 during the war. Like other exporters, he bought his own ships only because the heavy traffic and German submarines made it difficult to obtain adequate transportation to Europe. Harriss had already recovered his purchase price from the profits of several trips during the war and no longer needed the ship. His eagerness to sell was matched by the eagerness of Cockburn and four others, who eyed their commissions. All had reasons to ignore the inexperience of the men of the Black Star Line and the inadequate finances of the company, which. led other shipowners to reject BSL bids.[41]

At the end of September, the company's books showed 5,383 shares sold at $5 a share. Paying $16,500 on September 15, the Black Star Line had at the maximum $10,000 left to complete the $165,000 purchase, operate the ship, and pay the salaries of the Black Star Line officers. Garvey's instincts and experience led him to try first to resolve his financial problems in the political arena. He went to Philadelphia, Pittsburgh, and Chicago. The purchase of the *Yarmouth* had the effect that Garvey had anticipated. Feeling triumphant, he laughed at the "old time Negroes" who had declared that he would never obtain a ship. The Chicago *Defender* was forced to shift its attack from questioning his intentions and ability to buy to enumerating

---

39. "Minutes of the Black Star Line," September 11, 1919, *Garvey* v. *U.S.A.*, 2559.

40. See the testimony by the following persons in *Garvey* v. *U.S.A.*: Joshua Cockburn, 322, 343, 347–49, 368–82, MG, 2211–19, Fred Powell, 971, 996, and Orlando Thompson, 1894, 1903. The best narrative of the transactions was the summary of M. J. Davis, the Justice Department agent who worked on the government prosecution, written on January 20, 1922, in Garvey file, RG 65.

41. Leo Healey, testimony, *Garvey* v. *U.S.A.*, 196, 291; MG, testimony, *Garvey* v. *U.S.A.*, 2211–19.

the travails of operating shipping lines. Engaging his enemy directly, Garvey presented his case to black Chicago. But Robert Abbott, editor of the *Defender*, hired Sheridan A. Brusseaux of the Keystone National Detective Agency, a company of black sleuths that investigated radicals and common criminals for racial leaders and the government, to trap Garvey. Soon after, the Chicago police arrested him for violating the state's "blue-sky laws," legislation to prevent swindlers from selling worthless securities to the uninformed. Garvey was fined and freed.[42]

After Garvey returned to New York, the war resumed in print. The *Defender*'s headlines announced that the Black Star Line's ship had sunk. People in New York rushed to Liberty Hall on Sunday night to discover whether it was true. In Philadelphia the story had convinced so many people that Garvey traveled there to announce that even "if the ship does go down," the people would make a profit from the insurance, a statement as specious as the *Defender*'s charges. Taking a cue from Henry Ford's recent successful libel suit against the Chicago *Tribune*, Garvey announced that he would sue the *Defender* for $200,000.[43]

Garvey relied upon the class and racial conflicts during that autumn to raise money to complete the payments on the *Yarmouth*. After a race riot in Omaha, Nebraska, he said that racial warfare would continue until the Negroes organized the Black Star Line. Speaking in Pittsburgh, he asked his audience to "remember the 31st of October," which "will be the day of triumph or defeat for the Negro." October 31 was the day when the BSL was to take possession of the *Yarmouth*, subject to the raising of the $83,500 balance.[44] On October 14, Garvey was shot by George Tyler, who had loaned Garvey money for the UNIA restaurant. On the streets people whispered that important men wanted Garvey killed. The rumors were strengthened when Tyler fractured his skull and died after he attempted to escape or commit suicide. The publicity gave Garvey a larger hearing and

42. "Negro Agitation," October 3, 17, 1919, file 10218–364/5 and 11, MID, in RG 165; Chicago *Defender*, September 6, 1919; Amy Jacques Garvey (ed.), *Philosophy and Opinions of Marcus Garvey* (2 vols.; 1926; rpr. New York, 1969), II, 321–23; "Memorandum of Payments on Contract Prices of S/S Yarmouth . . ." *Garvey* v. *U.S.A.*, 2637. On the Keystone Detective Agency, see Baltimore *Afro-American*, January 23, 1919.

43. "Negro Agitation," October 17, 1919, file 10218–364/11, MID, in RG 165; "Minutes of Black Star Line, October 13, 1919," in Garvey file, RG 65; MG, testimony, *Garvey* v. *U.S.A.*, 2208. The Black Star Line was awarded a token six cents in damages, when it had requested $200,000, in the libel suit. R. R. Moton solicited the aid of New York politicians Charles Roberts and Charles Anderson on behalf of Abbott. See Robert Abbott to R. R. Moton, November 13, 1919, William White to Moton, November 17, 1919, Moton to Abbott, December 3, 1919, Moton to Charles Roberts, December 3, 20, 1919, in Moton Papers.

44. "Negro Agitation," October 17, file 10218-364/11, and November 7, 1919, file 10218-261/50, MID, in RG 165.

new legitimacy. The violence that accompanied many of the conflicts of 1919 lent credence to Garvey's assertion that the attempt on his life was part of a larger battle plan.[45]

The Tyler incident revealed one way in which Garvey's opponents brought the Black Star Line new support. Attacks by the government and by established black leaders also drew followers because many of Garvey's critics had little currency with black people, who heard the strictures in the context of the officials' other politics, actions, or inaction. Garvey claimed that the *Defender*'s attacks "sent up the stock sales 2000 per cent." Black Star Line records revealed that 11,182 shares were sold in October, compared to 5,530 in September. Although it is impossible to weigh the effects of the *Defender* skirmish, the controversy converted its journalistic competitor, the Chicago *Whip*, to Garveyism. Rivalries among preachers won other adherents. In this way, Garvey convinced the talented Reverend James Eason of Philadelphia to join with him and bring along his People's Church. Eason had led a faction out of the Varrick A.M.E. Church in 1918 and formed his own church. One likely purpose of his initial affiliation with the UNIA was to solidify his ministerial authority.[46]

After the appearance of the *Yarmouth*, Garvey won vital support from well-connected men. Although Garvey's rhetoric alternately wooed and castigated black elites, he consistently sought their wealth and talents. Returning from Chicago in September, he boasted to New York Garveyites that he had attracted "bankers and publishers." Until the appearance of his first ship, he had engaged only aspiring ones. Now men prominent in black life from both North and South joined with Garvey. Like the initial group, their attraction to the UNIA was closely related to their social and professional lives.[47]

William Ferris, a writer and graduate of Yale, was literary editor of the *Negro World* and held the posts of chancellor and assistant president-general of the UNIA between 1919 and 1923. His *African Abroad*, a two-volume history of blacks in the New World, published in 1913, promised future greatness for the race, to be brought about by a great leader. Ferris needed work, however, and black intellectuals from Yale were not very employable. He wrote a friend in 1915 that

> I find that I must get hooked on to some kind of job that brings in so much per week, before I lead a fair damsel to the Altar. This letter does not

45. Baltimore *Afro-American*, November 7, 1919.
46. Cockburn, testimony, *Garvey* v. *U.S.A.*, 2929; "Negro Activities," November 7, 1919, file 10218-261/50, MID, in RG 165; *NW*, August 21, 1920; A. A. Garvey, "Marcus Garvey," 79; "Monthly Summary of Shares of Stock Issued . . ." *Garvey* v. *U.S.A.*, 2648.
47. "Negro Activities," October 17, 1919, file 10218-364/11, MID, in RG 165.

smack of the idealistic philosophy of the "African Abroad." But it is reflections upon the fate of a once happily married friend of mine. I have sent out a few letters to some of my caucasian friends and colored debtors saying in substance, "There is a lightening rod in New Haven waiting and praying to be struck by financial lightening."

Yale had given him the ideology and aspirations of a world that refused him a place. Ministering churches in North Carolina and Massachusetts was not much more inspiring than his early teaching positions in the South. Without a strong talent for a particular vocation, Ferris, like Garvey, thirsted for a significant place in modern society and, like Garvey, discovered few opportunities to realize them. In 1916, Ferris became an editor of the new *Champion* magazine in Chicago. He moved to Philadelphia in 1917, where he became literary editor of the *Christian Recorder*, magazine of the A.M.E. Church, and a lecturer.[48]

Ferris said that it was the prospect of profit and excitement that drew him to the BSL and UNIA. When Garvey said, "Let us buy ships to enter the commercial world and trade with our brethren across the seas," Ferris was transformed. It seemed to him that Garvey was the leader he had imagined in *African Abroad*. Shortly before the *Yarmouth* appeared in New York on October 31, Ferris predicted: "The launching of the ship will send a thrill to the Negroes of two hemispheres and will lift the standing of the Negro race throughout the civilized world. Marcus Garvey was an instrument in the hands of Providence for uplifting the Negro peoples of the world." The shipping corporation promised both the financial security that had eluded him and a significant role in history. Ferris' columns in the *Negro World* continued his quasi-metaphysical musings on the meaning of life, character, and leadership—fit concerns for Yale graduates.[49]

Modern black intellectuals shared Ferris' enthusiasms. Although Hubert Harrison had found Ferris' academic framework archaic, the Black Star Line erased the significance of intellectual differences. Harrison's prophecy that racial enterprise would launch a new black militancy appeared to be fulfilled by the Black Star Line, which thrilled him as it did Ferris.[50] Taking a leaf from Admiral Mahan and the U.S. Shipping Board, Harrison explained at Rush Memorial Church that "nations and people never rose to power without ships." In the world of 1919, in which govern-

48. William Ferris, *African Abroad; or, His Evolution in Western Civilization, Tracing His Development Under Caucasian Milieu* (2 vols.; New Haven, 1913), I, 268; William Ferris to Arthur Schomburg, February 19, 1915, in Arthur A. Schomburg Papers, Schomburg Center for Research in Black Culture, New York Public Library. For more on *African Abroad*, see Ch. 3, n.19 above.

49. New York *Amsterdam News*, February 11, 1925; NW, October 4, 1919.

50. "Negro Activities," October 20, 1919, file 10218-364/12, MID, in RG 165.

ments routinely banned newspapers and denied radicals passports and visas, the Black Star Line could solve the communication problems of black militants. "Ships . . . could carry passengers and men to other countries. They could be passed through as working men," a possible reference to Monroe Trotter's recent feat. "They could get their literature through," he continued. At the very least, the popular enthusiasm generated income for intellectual and political work. In January, 1920, after his own newspaper had failed, Harrison became an associate editor of the *Negro World*. Later that year, he was scheduled to go to Liberia with other UNIA members to begin the work of African colonization.[51]

John Bruce, who had introduced Garvey to other blacks when he first arrived in New York, also became enthusiastic after the purchase of the *Yarmouth*. Earlier, in January, 1919, when questioned about his relationship to Garvey, Bruce had told Major Walter H. Loving, the black intelligence officer in the Army, "not to insult [me] by linking my name with any movement, plan, scheme, plot or enterprise with which Marcus Garvey is identified." But after the purchase of the first ship, in a volte-face, he recalled his mistake and explained his conversion from heathen to apostle: "I did not then thoroughly understand. They [Garvey's plans] seemed to be wild, chimerical, impossible of accomplishment. . . . The things he proposed were easy of accomplishment under a leader as full of his subject as he and why not? From that cold night in October I ceased writing and talking against Garvey." Linking social need with business profit, Bruce advanced the truism that the "more business can be transacted by the company [the BSL] the more dividends will accrue to its stockholders." Perhaps his long, fruitless record of investing in transoceanic black business, including a steamship company, explained his initial suspicion and also his premature judgment of success.[52]

Bruce belonged to numerous professional and fraternal organizations. He had told his fellow Masons earlier in 1919 that "Masonry [was] the medium through which to give the right direction to the thought and policy which is to govern and control the race." He urged them to organize, as

51. Harrison, "Statement," January 16, 1922, in Garvey file, RG 65.

52. John Bruce to Major W. H. Loving, January 13, 1919, Loving to Director, MID, January 25, 1919, file 10218-261/39 and 40, MID, in RG 165; John Bruce, editorial, n.d. [September or October, 1919], file B-3-13, in Bruce Papers. Numerous examples of Bruce's interest in Pan-African businesses appear in his correspondence. He imported coffee from Liberia. He had been interested in investing in gold in the Gold Coast during the boom early in the century. He had been enthusiastic about the New York and Liberia Co., founded in 1904, a venture that was short-lived. George Ellis to John Bruce, April 27, 1907, and "Prospectus," MS 117, both in Bruce Papers.

the white race has done, into "One people, with One purpose, One destiny." Bruce now transferred these hopes to the UNIA. He became an editor and writer for the *Negro World* and a popular speaker at UNIA meetings at Liberty Hall. His wife was employed in the clerical department of the Black Star Line.[53]

Men like Bruce, with good connections in the black world, were useful to Garvey. In 1920, Bruce introduced Garveyites to members of the Liberian elite. But he was an intermediary for other blacks as well, including a conservative young African who toured Africa with the Phelps-Stokes Educational Mission in 1921. Similarly, Hubert Harrison, while propagandizing for the Black Star Line in late 1919, also met with other Harlem blacks to raise money to start a bank organized by an old enemy of Garvey, Augustus Duncan. For his part, William Ferris, moving toward the black Republican clique, sought the nomination for the New York Assembly in 1922.[54]

The common insecurities of status and fortune made the black petite bourgeoisie a group of joiners. They scattered their prestige and skills across the board of black associations. In 1919 and 1920, the Black Star Line appeared to be promising, but they always hedged their bets. A Liberian, unnecessarily, advised Bruce, "Let's not put all our eggs in one basket." The war had made them simultaneously more race-conscious and optimistic of the opportunities available to them. In 1929, a black study of racial business concluded that black businessmen and blacks who aspired to become businessmen "learned that if they could raise money to fight a war," they could do "the same for their race. The experience of the race riots drove them together." Their conception of words like *organize* and *cooperate* was shaped by their personal ambitions. Older men, like Ferris and Bruce, with the experience of blocked opportunities and younger men, like Holder and Powell, with the hopes of future success were equally drawn to the UNIA and BSL in 1919 and 1920. The chance for independence, adventure, and achievement blurred distinctions between young and old, individual and racial.[55]

53. "Significance of Brotherhood," 1919, and John Bruce to Florence Bruce, September 4, 1923, both in Bruce Papers.
54. John Bruce to C. D. B. King, April 3, 1920, Bruce to James E. K. Aggrey, July 4, 1921, in Bruce Papers. In 1920 Garvey wanted Bruce to become president of the "American section" of the UNIA, the position that the Reverend James Eason eventually assumed. Bruce begged off, claiming that a younger man should hold the post. Bruce to Garvey, August 17, 1920, in Bruce Papers. Boston *Guardian*, January 3, 1920; *Age*, September 22, 1922; Baltimore *Afro-American*, November 18, 1919; Amy Jacques Garvey, *Garvey and Garveyism* (Kingston, Jamaica, 1963), 43.
55. C. Logenoh to John Bruce, June 15, 1922, in Bruce Papers; John Harmon, Arnett G. Lindsay, and Carter G. Woodson, *The Negro as a Businessman* (Washington, D.C., 1929), 24; "Reminiscences of Holder," 3.

Other black leaders who never joined the UNIA contributed to the chorus of approval that greeted the Black Star Line. W. E. B. Du Bois, often identified as a critic of Garvey's because of his subsequent opposition, added his voice in December, 1920: "What he [Garvey] is trying to say and do is this: American Negroes can be accumulating and ministering their own capital, organize industry, join the black centers of the South Atlantic by commercial enterprise and in this way ultimately redeem Africa as a fit and free home for black men. This is true. . . . It is feasible. . . . The plan is not original with Garvey but he has popularized it." William Pickens, Yale graduate and field secretary of the NAACP, was less measured: "The creation of a steamship line even in embryo is one of the greatest achievements of the twentieth century Negro." Socialist George Frazier Miller said Garvey made "practical that which had seemed preposterous."[56]

In the turmoil of 1919, many black intellectuals, professionals, journalists, and small businessmen, pressed by the militance of the black masses and scrutinized by the government, joined in support of Garvey's Black Star Line with varying degrees of commitment. Convinced that the war had opened up new opportunities, they attempted to anchor the new racial consciousness in the steamship line. Ideologically, Garvey tried to distinguish between a militant racialism, which he hoped could mobilize the masses, and a subversive radicalism, which he opposed both theoretically and opportunistically. The distinction appeared to buy Garvey significant space in the political environment of 1919. The Justice Department concluded in January, 1920, that Garvey was the "foremost pro-negro agitator in New York. It is apparent, however, that his pro-negroism is secondary to his scheme for the solicitation of subscriptions for stock in the Black Star Line." While the judgment incorrectly made Garvey essentially a simple stock promoter, it also revealed that so long as Garvey channeled "pro-negroism" into businesses, he would be viewed as a secondary problem by the government.[57]

56. W. E. B. Du Bois, "Marcus Garvey," *Crisis*, XXI (December, 1920), 58–60, (January, 1921), 112–15; William Pickens, "Africa for the Africans: The Garvey Movement," *Nation*, December 28, 1921, p. 113. In September, 1922, even after the BSL was formally suspended, Du Bois reiterated his praise of Garvey: "A definite plan to unite Negrodom by a line of steamships was a brilliant suggestion and Garvey's only original contribution to the race problem." *Crisis*, XXIV (September, 1922), 210. Du Bois himself investigated the possibility of beginning a company in January, 1921, in view of the large number of surplus government ships available. See W. E. B. Du Bois to Charles Evans Hughes, January 5, 1923, W. E. B. Du Bois Papers, University of Massachusetts Library, Amherst. See W. A. Domingo's subsequent criticism in answer to Du Bois' continuing enthusiasm: Domingo to Du Bois, August 24, 1922, Box C-304, in NAACP Papers.

57. "Bulletin of Radical Activities," January 20, February 26, 1920, in RG 60; H. A.

Garvey's translation of "pro-negroism" reflected the ideology of the racial stratum he knew best. The Black Star Line was created to aid men like himself. He promised that it would "make it possible for the youth of the race to find respectable employment . . . and remove the need of our high school and college graduates seeking jobs among the whites." This definition of the racial problem placed the discriminations confronting the black elite, not the poverty or other social problems of the black working class and farmers, at the forefront of black concern. Garvey's objectives and ordering of racial priorities were the same as those of the black elite, even when the solutions varied. For instance, Director of Negro Economics George Haynes in the Labor Department also tried to package racial consciousness to produce employment for black college graduates. But he tried to sell it to white capitalists. Haynes argued that just as "the Italian working gang is more readily led by the Italian padrone," black workers would be best led by "Negro leaders." R. R. Moton promoted his National Negro Business League as a movement that would provide opportunity for educated youth. He even accepted the validity of comparisons "between Mr. Garvey's statements and my own, and also of the two movements, the Business League and Mr. Garvey's movement." To Moton, the differences between the UNIA and the NNBL were social, not ideological. Moton saw his own followers as "the most thoughtful and intelligent group of colored people," code words for blacks with property, businesses, and social connections. Over time, and after the failure of the Black Star Line, Moton's distinctions became valid. But the social boundaries were fluid in 1919 and 1920, especially among younger men and women who traversed the worlds of Moton, Haynes, and Garvey easily because no path was certain. The relations among leaders were less harmonious because they were competitors. But, even when the black elite doubted Garvey's achievements and questioned his honesty and methods, they did not criticize his view of racial progress, which was their own. And Garvey frequently criticized their behavior and their lack of financial support of the BSL, but not the significance of their achievements. In 1920, Garvey proclaimed that "the greatest enemy to the Negro race is the successful business and professional man who is satisfied," a mild definition of racial treason.[58]

Strauss to Director, August 27, 1920, file 10218-261/58, MID, in RG 165; *NW*, December 9, 1919. Government surveillance of UNIA meetings concluded that they were dominated by BSL business. Typically, an agent's report of the September 1 meeting concluded: "Nothing of importance occurred [meaning no radicalism]. The object was to sell stock in the proposed steamship line. About $3500.00 was subscribed." September 6, 1919, file 10218-367/1, MID, in RG 165.

58. *NW*, June 12, September 11, 1920; R. R. Moton to Ida A. Tourtellot, October 4,

The financial requirements of the Black Star Line forced UNIA leaders to mine a broader base of black support than elite blacks. Appeals to the masses were necessary. But the masses were potentially disruptive and difficult to contain. And government complacency vanished when the problem became mass Garveyism. Garvey was a threat not because of what he did but because of what he might inspire. The Black Star Line, which possessed three ships, financed and drew thousands to Garvey's first UNIA convention in August, 1920. Throughout the month, international delegates met to formulate racial strategies. Twenty-five thousand people gathered at Madison Square Garden and elected Garvey "Provisional President of Africa" and president-general of the UNIA. Other elected officials from each part of the historic black triangle—Africa, the United States, and the Caribbean—composed a supreme executive council. Garvey's opening speech captured his own and the delegates' sense of hope and determination: "We are here this morning as a free people, claiming equal rights with the rest of mankind. We are here because this is the age when all peoples are striking out for freedom, for liberty, for democracy." The statement was one of generous nationalism. The mainly Irish policemen assigned to the UNIA parade were praised and the struggle of their kinsmen in Ireland applauded.

The delegates published a Declaration of Negro Rights, an eloquent bill of racial complaint that ranged from protesting discrimination in public hotels to decrying the treatment of Africans under imperialist rule. The UNIA demanded equal justice and equal participation for blacks in all institutions that were important in blacks' lives. In short, "the Negro like any other race, should be governed by the ethics of civilization." The convention also empowered a commission to go to Liberia to investigate the possibility of modernizing the only black republic in West Africa.[59]

The declaration was vague about methods and priorities. Its item 12 sanctioned "every means to protect . . . against barbarous practices inflicted . . . because of . . . color." On the floor of the convention, a delegate from Virginia celebrated the progress of blacks in his community and concluded that the racial struggle required only continuation of past practices. The Reverend Thomas Harten, however, stated that blacks should use force to improve their condition in the United States.[60]

1920, in Phelps-Stokes Fund Papers; George Haynes, "Speech Before Annual Conference of National Urban League," October 22, 1920, Division of Negro Economics, in RG 174; See also Baltimore *Afro-American*, February 27, 1920; *Age*, September 4, 1920.

59. *NW*, September 11, 1920; New York *World*, August 4, 7, 1920; *Age*, September 4, 1920; New York *Times*, August 4, 18, 1920.

60. A. J. Garvey (ed.), *Philosophy and Opinions of Garvey*, II, 135–43; *NW*, August 20, 1920.

The convention offered very little that was new in substance. It restated historic black demands and routes to racial progress. The assertion of UNIA hegemony in the black world was the primary novelty: "We hereby demand that the governments of the world recognize our leader and his representatives chosen by the race to look after the welfare of our people under such governments." The assertion was repeated in several contexts. The declaration's item 47 announced that blacks would not do battle "for an alien race" without "first obtaining the consent of the leader of the Negro people of the world," meaning the leader of the UNIA. (But national self-defense was exempted from the necessary assent.) The convention's self-confidence reflected the apparent strength of the UNIA in 1920. The delegates had been enthusiastic and optimistic. But the ability to represent all black people depended upon the growth of the UNIA and its skill in forging strategies that would justify its international structure, vanguard position, and growing mass base.[61]

Since the UNIA lacked a unified political strategy, increasing its membership depended upon Garvey's ability to conquer in the marketplace. The Baltimore *Afro-American* asked the question, "Can Garvey Win?" meaning, Can the Black Star Line succeed? The editor of the Norfolk *Journal and Guide* perceived a conflict between Garvey's militant anticolonialism and the operation of a shipping business. The acquisition of the *Yarmouth* had silenced some scoffers. But the directors of the BSL raised money for its operation and repairs more often through stock sales than through cargo and passenger receipts. To retain credibility, Garvey would not be able to ignore the balance sheet. One well-paid black construction foreman, supervising the building of a new Ford plant in Detroit, was asked by a friend to purchase stock in the line. He bought ten shares out of personal and racial loyalty, but added with skepticism, "If the company is still in business in three months, I'll buy ten more."[62]

Garvey's problem transcended the shipping business. For the Detroit foreman, who already had an excellent career, the Black Star Line was potentially satisfying and profitable, but also marginal. Others demanded more from racial organization. The initial enthusiasm for the Black Star Line cannot be measured by the goals of Garvey or his new associates or the apparent fervor of the many people attracted to it. Even with the cheering crowds and publicity of the convention, Garvey sounded a note of caution. He told an audience at the beginning of the second week's meetings

61. A. J. Garvey (ed.), *Philosophy and Opinions of Garvey*, II, 140.
62. Baltimore *Afro-American*, September 20, 1920; *Age*, August 14, 1920; author's interview with Rupert Jemmott, June 6, 1976.

that "the importance of this convention seems to be more realized by others outside our race than our race itself."

Many blacks were skeptical. Cyril Briggs's *Crusader*, a supporter of the Black Star Line, applauded Garvey's "genius for organization" but questioned "whether he can keep his organization together and make it function." The New York *Age* also defined the UNIA's problem as one of unifying divergent elements. Its editor did not share the New York *Evening Post's* judgment that Garvey was "a dangerous Negro" or the New York *Tribune's* fear that Garvey would accept Soviet aid. It concluded that Garvey's praise of the Bolsheviks was only "a rhetorical flourish to impress . . . his hearers." The anti-Communist *Age* acknowledged, but denigrated, the widespread encouragement that the masses read into the revolution. Not Garvey, but his "deluded followers," took bolshevism seriously, the *Age* thought, sensing a conflict between Garvey and his followers but not identifying it accurately. The question posed by Garveyism was whether Garvey, while continuing his necessary pursuit of market success, could maintain the popular enthusiasm and unity that his movement had shown in 1920. Put another way, could Garvey and his associates continue to rally black workers without addressing their immediate social and economic situations?[63]

63. *NW*, August 14, 1920; New York *Evening Post*, August 18, 1920; New York *Tribune*, August 20, 1920; Baltimore *Afro-American*, September 20, 1920; *Age*, September 4, 1920.

5 / Black Ships, Black Workers
A Sea of Troubles

The Black Star Line transformed Garvey into an international leader of black communities on three continents. The public Garvey was impressive. Although he and Hubert Harrison often vied for the title of ugliest black man, Garvey's intelligence and vitality made his short, stocky frame seem graceful. His energy often overflowed his ceremonial uniform, which was crisscrossed with gold braids and topped with a white-plumed hat—a combination of the latest fraternal costumes. Garvey more often was seen in a three-piece suit, which revealed more accurately his purposes and aims. He employed pageantry and ceremony and bestowed titles and honors because "he believed in their efficacy." But Garvey invested most of his energy in accumulating capital to buy three ships and assemble a New York staff to manage and operate the Black Star Line.[1]

Garvey and his associates organized their first locals in areas populated by the new working class, likely sources of black dollars for the Black Star Line. They tapped high-wage, industrial areas of Virginia, Pennsylvania, Ohio, Indiana, and Illinois. Possession of the *Yarmouth* opened up the islands of the Caribbean to stock-selling. On November 20, 1919, Cyril Henry and Henrietta Vinton Davis brought the promises of BSL propaganda to the West Indies, Central America, and South America.[2] By the end of the year, the Black Star Line had issued stock worth $188,470.87. Its expenses escalated, too, and ate into its capital. The $6,333.26 earnings from passenger and freight were overwhelmed by $30,589.42 operating expenses. Money from stock sales was siphoned off to subsidize the deficit. This fiscal pattern of the first voyage became a regular feature of BSL budget balancing.[3]

1. A. A. Garvey, "Marcus Garvey," 104, *passim*.
2. On the first voyage, the ship transported gasoline drums, cement, and twenty-three passengers, some not paying, to Colon and Jamaica. Louis LeMoth, "Statement," March 6, 1922, in Garvey file, RG 65.
3. *Marcus Garvey* v. *United States of America*, 267 U.S. 607 (1924), 2648; Thomas Merrilees, "Summary Report of Investigation of Books and Records of THE BLACK STAR LINE, INC., and THE UNIVERSAL NEGRO IMPROVEMENT ASSOCIATION . . ." October 26, 1922, pp. 16–17,

Nevertheless, the BSL directors' optimism was fueled by continuing reports of popular enthusiasm. On December 22, the board of directors increased the company's capital stock to ten million dollars, a signal for intensified sales campaigns to purchase more ships, despite the escalating losses incurred by the *Yarmouth*.[4]

Business judgment was sacrificed to the political need to own and operate ships, but political goals were often subordinated to business calculations. To raise money to pay for ships required an appeal to race loyalty. The *Yarmouth* was to be renamed the *Frederick Douglass*, after the abolitionist leader. Earning income once the ships were obtained required less attention to color and racial tradition. Because there were few black exporters, the BSL was forced to do business with white shippers.

The *Yarmouth* returned from her maiden voyage on January 13, 1920, in need of repairs. Nevertheless, Garvey ordered her to sail immediately to Havana with a valuable cargo of liquor. The Green River Distilling Company was anxious to load a $4,000,000 whiskey cargo before Prohibition went into effect on January 17. Captain Cockburn protested that the ship was not constructed to transport liquor but finally agreed to cooperate. When Garvey informed him that he had negotiated a price of $9.50 per ton for the 800-ton cargo, Cockburn's skepticism turned to anger. Not only was the price too low for the valuable cargo, the revenue would not even meet the ship's coal bill. Attempting to pacify his only captain, Garvey told Cockburn to "try his best" and to take the ship "because of the publicity" the line would gain from it. The two quarreled again over Garvey's decision to allow the Irvine Engineering Company to repair the *Yarmouth* for $11,000, which immediately consumed the income from the whiskey.[5]

Garvey drew political lessons from the *Yarmouth*'s recent history. He told an audience at Liberty Hall that he had

> to fight men from two directions—men within the ranks and men without the ranks—white men on the outside and black men on the inside. . . .
> Work was given out to some of the very people who were plotting to over-

in Garvey file, RG 65. This document, prepared by a government accountant for the prosecution, is the best history of the finances of the BSL and UNIA. The original documents on which this report was based have been destroyed. Where other sources were available for verification, the data was checked and found to be accurate. Interpretation, of course, is another question.

4. Merrilees, "Summary Report," 4, 16; "Negro Agitation," January 13, 1920, file 10218-364/18, MID, in RG 165.

5. Joshua Cockburn, testimony, *Garvey* v. *U.S.A.*, 385–91; Leo Healey, testimony, *Garvey* v. *U.S.A.*, 266–74; Fred Powell, testimony, *Garvey* v. *U.S.A.*, 1022–24; "Negro Agitation," February 10, 1920, file 10218-364/21, MID, in RG 165; Hugh Mulzac, *A Star to Steer By* (New York, 1963), 78.

throw us. . . . Because of lack of real business training of some of our leaders, even though they had the best intentions, they gave out work and never asked how much the work would cost before the work was performed and thus played into the hands of the men who were laying a trap for us. Hence a job that was not worth more than $1,000 just a few hours before the "Frederick Douglass" was scheduled to sail, they present a bill charging and demanding . . . $11,000 for the work. . . . They thought that having such a big balance against the Black Star Line they would make a public announcement of it and all of our creditors would pounce down upon us at the same time, and they would tear the Black Star Line to shreds.

At most, Irvine Engineering overcharged Garvey, as others would do when Garvey's impatience overcame his cunning and his simulated affluence overshadowed the BSL's meager resources. But Irvine had no interest in destroying the Black Star Line. Moreover, it was Garvey, not his associates, who had arranged for the repairs, which Cockburn testified were worth only $3,400.[6]

Garvey's desire for success and power blinded him to alternative options at any moment. Fear of failure and suspicions of competitors directed his attention to exposing the real and imagined misdeeds of others rather than pursuing blueprints that required time and work and withheld immediate reward. Associates with qualities Garvey lacked were overruled or summarily dismissed when they offered sound but contrary advice.

The ship sailed with the whiskey cargo, thirty-five passengers, and a libel from the Irvine Company because the BSL did not pay the repair bill. The *Yarmouth-Douglass*'s problems continued on the seas. She was disabled in a storm off Cape May, New Jersey. After the Coast Guard towed her back to port, the shippers, frantic about the safety of their cargo, gave Cockburn two thousand dollars to protect the delivery, untouched by the ocean and crew. While such payments were not uncommon in the shipping business, Cockburn's acceptance of the money at a time when the line was encumbered with debt raises questions about the way employees meshed their own interests with those of the enterprise. Cockburn subsequently claimed that he accepted the money because the BSL had not been paying his salary. But Garvey recalled that the captain had agreed to waive immediate remuneration until after the trip, "to show [his] good interests and especially a feeling for the UNIA and the Black Star Line and the efforts to help

6. "Negro Agitation," February 10, 1920, file 10218-364/21, MID, in RG 165; Cockburn, testimony, *Garvey* v. *U.S.A.*, 385–440; Powell, testimony, *Garvey* v. *U.S.A.*, 222–25. At the time, Cockburn blamed the crew and unnamed "nasty plotters." Cockburn to MG, December 2, 1919, in Marcus Garvey case file of exhibits, C-33-688, FRC 539-440, Federal Archives and Records Center, Bayonne, N.J. (hereinafter cited as Garvey case file of exhibits).

Negro people to own a ship." Cockburn rebutted Garvey's history with the assertion that Garvey drew his own salary during this period.[7]

Whatever the truth concerning this specific controversy, the willingness of employees to sacrifice for the enterprise disappeared when Garvey and other leading officials gave the appearance of living well. Indeed, for many BSL directors and UNIA organizers the trappings of personal success became a surrogate for genuine achievement. In this atmosphere, employees who were denied compensation became embittered. Cockburn obtained money from the shippers. The stevedores who loaded the whiskey, the first of many BSL workers, were forced to sue in court for their wages.[8]

A mirror of the larger world, the Black Star Line demanded more sacrifice from its blue-collar workers—sailors and stevedores—than the line's managers and salesmen. Like other small businesses, the BSL needed cheap labor even more than the larger companies and attempted whenever possible to hire seamen at the lowest wages. When pressed, managers suspended wage payments before other obligations. The appeal to race loyalty did not sustain indefinitely the financial burdens of unpaid labor.

Although the Black Star Line's labor relations were traditional, its resolution of business problems in the political arena were more exceptional. But the use of publicity was becoming more common in this era in which modern advertising was born. The carrying of the famous whiskey cargo, even at a loss, for publicity was not outside the boundaries of accepted business practice. But costly publicity schemes wedded to the financial means and experiences of a small shipping company was a disastrous combination.

Was the Black Star Line economically viable, without the publicity and fanfare? The *Yarmouth* could have sailed as a tramp steamer. Tramps picked up cargoes and passengers where they could because they were not bound by the regular schedules of the established lines. The *Yarmouth* crew demonstrated some of the requisite spirit and ingenuity of this business. After the whiskey cargo was unloaded to Havana, the ship hastily departed for Kingston and the Panama Canal Zone, where, unexpectedly, it picked up five hundred passengers. Thousands of West Indians, unemployed by the cutting of American operations on the Canal Zone and demoralized by an unsuccessful strike, needed transportation to Cuba, where they hoped to find work on the sugar plantations. The crew quickly improvised accommodations for the grateful laborers. Again, on her third and last voyage,

7. See testimony by the following persons in *Garvey* v. *U.S.A.*: Cockburn, 302–16; Healey, 268; MG, 2220–21.

8. Valentine Chaddick, "Interview," June 22, 1922, in Garvey file, RG 65; Fred Powell, testimony, 979–80, in *Garvey* v. *U.S.A.*

the *Yarmouth* rescued a Japanese vessel that had gone aground five hundred miles south of Jamaica. Led by a Captain Dixon, a white Canadian, and Hugh Mulzac, a black deck officer, the plucky crew successfully salvaged the ship and cargo.[9]

Neither the Canal Zone passengers nor the ship rescue yielded profits. Despite the overcrowding and the problem of feeding the five hundred passengers, the *Yarmouth*, at Garvey's insistence, stopped at Bocas del Toro and Almirante in Panama, and at Puerto Limón, Costa Rica, where agents sold shares and signed up hundreds of new UNIA members. The ship discharged some passengers at Santiago de Cuba and sailed for Kingston, Jamaica, to repair her boilers and pick up a seven-hundred-ton cargo of coconuts. Garvey ordered the ship to stop at Philadelphia and Boston before delivering the cargo to New York. These two stops brought the enrollment of more new UNIA members. But by the time the ship was unloaded in New York, the coconuts were rotten. The consigners sued the Black Star Line for over three thousand dollars. Eager to mine political and commercial opportunities simultaneously, Garvey's impatience undercut the BSL's performance as a carrier.[10]

Inexperienced management apparently explained the financial loss in the rescue of the Japanese ship. Hugh Mulzac said that he had asked the BSL agent in Kingston to draw up a contract for $45,000 to save the ship. "The owners of the cargo, and Lloyds of London would willingly have paid this sum, for this was salvage cargo with a freight value from three to five times the value of ordinary cargo," he said. The agent, a building contractor, drew up a contract for only $12,000, barely enough to pay expenses. For the year ending June 30, 1920, the BSL had paid $171,500 to buy the *Yarmouth*. It had spent an additional $138,469.55 for repairs, wages, fuel, and other operating expenses. Earning $44,779.71 from freight and passengers, the vessel's operating loss was $93,689.84.[11]

BSL deficits and missed opportunities led some critics to conclude that better management would have yielded a profit. Mulzac had submitted a plan to reorganize the BSL's commercial operations, but he said the directors were not interested, eyeing only the "booming" membership and cheering crowds. His assertion that he could have run the BSL profitably must be weighed with his own and others' failures to operate profitable shipping lines during this period. The source of Black Star Line insolvency

9. Mulzac, *A Star to Steer By*, 80–83.
10. *Ibid.* Louis LeMoth, a sailor on the ship, agreed that the Boston stop was made for propaganda reasons. He said that the one in Philadelphia was made to discharge passengers. "Statement," March 6, 1922, in Garvey file, RG 65.
11. Mulzac, *A Star to Steer By*, 83; Merrilees, "Summary Report," 31–32.

was more basic than Garvey's business ability. Each problem examined in isolation appeared to have a solution. But the problems that plagued the Black Star Line plagued the industry. The managers' instincts to use the political arena were inadequate responses to genuine market problems. The company could not depend upon salvaging shipwrecked cargo. And in most instances, the big planters in Cuba used their own ships to transport workers from other islands, which meant a smaller market for the BSL.[12]

During the war and the brief postwar boom, the severe and abnormal shortage of shipping permitted small firms with relatively primitive ships to enter the trade, but permanent contracts required more than the BSL could offer. When the *Yarmouth* landed in Havana in February, 1920, her crew and passengers were welcomed by President Mario García Menocal, accompanied by Cuban businessmen and politicians who pledged cooperation and purchased stock. One senator, a large sugar-cane grower who had been shipping on the United Fruit Company steamers, promised to switch if the BSL offered good services. But transporting sugar demanded special boats, financing, and trade connections—all beyond the experience and resources of novices.[13]

The BSL's second ship was purchased to serve the more secure market of popular river excursions. The *Shadyside* was delivered to the Black Star Line on April 10 for $35,000. Its owner convinced Garvey that the steamer, built in 1873, could make trips up the Hudson in the summer to produce profits and "good propaganda for . . . stock salesmen." The boat made several trips during the summer of 1920 but operated with a deficit of $10,952.43. During the winter of 1920–1921, she was damaged in a storm and moored at Fort Lee, New Jersey. She did not sail again.[14]

Garvey's politics were hostage to the economic trouble of the BSL. The more difficult it was to operate a profitable business, the more frantically he turned to the political arena to gain capital and explain the line's problems. If he could not influence the market, he could accumulate money through the sale of stock. The *Yarmouth*'s publicity stops in Central Amer-

12. Mulzac, *A Star to Steer By*, 84–85. A typical advertisement for laborers read, "Free Transportation to Port Limon, Costa Rica." (Canal Zone) *Workman*, September 4, 1920.

13. Hobart S. Perry, *Ship Management and Operation* (London, 1931), 5; Mulzac, *A Star to Steer By*, 80; Robert F. Smith, *The United States and Cuba: Business and Diplomacy, 1917–1960* (New York, 1960), 21–29, 38; U.S. Shipping Board agent, Havana, to H. Y. Saint, June 24, 1921, file 417.1, in Record Group 151, Records of the Department of Commerce, National Archives; Boaz Long to Norman Davis, October 8, 1920, file 850.4, in Record Group 84, Records of the Foreign Service Posts of the Department of State: Embassy and Legation, National Archives.

14. Merrilees, "Summary Report," 32–33. The BSL paid $2,000 at the time it signed the contract, $8,000 at the delivery of the bill of sale, after which it owed twelve monthly notes of $2,000 at 6 percent interest. All but four of the notes were subsequently paid.

ica, Philadelphia, and Boston were necessary to increase stock sales. The rotten coconuts were an unfortunate consequence of that need.

The public arena was not without limits. Stock sales were declining in the spring of 1920, even before widespread public knowledge of the BSL's economic problems. The peak number of shares sold in one month, 11,182, occurred in October, 1919, when the *Yarmouth* first appeared in New York. After that date, monthly sales through April, 1920, hovered between 8,000 and 10,000 shares. In May, they dropped to 6,856, in June to 5,146. In July they rose slightly to 5,690. During December only 2,971 shares were bought.[15]

Garvey attributed these declines to the propaganda of his opponents, fed by the stream of dissenters who abandoned ship. Fred Powell had resigned from the Black Star Line in February and revealed in the New York *News* that the *Yarmouth* was owned by a Canadian steamship company. Technically, he was right. The Canadian government would not transfer registry to the Black Star Line until it was convinced of the company's financial solvency. Meanwhile, the Black Star Line had chartered the *Yarmouth* from its owners in October, 1919, in order to display and use it. Although the BSL held the bill of sale and had paid all but $49,000 by January 17, 1920, the corporation legally did not own the vessel, because it was not registered in its name. Therefore, the *Crusader* magazine safely offered $500 to anyone who could prove that the Black Star Line owned the *Yarmouth*.[16]

Garvey responded to the revelations at a rally at Manhattan Casino on April 21. He reminded his followers that the Black Star Line already had two ships and promised that within a week it would have a third. "This is the kind of answer we give to our critics," he concluded.[17] The latest acquisition, the SS *Kanawha*, was smaller than the *Yarmouth* and classified as a yacht. Vice-President Orlando Thompson attempted to inoculate BSL agents against the inevitable disappointment. He explained, "You will perhaps think the *Kanawha* is nothing compared to the *Yarmouth*," although "in my opinion she is a better and more attractive boat." Garvey also made a virtue of necessity. He told the board on April 23 that "there was a great demand for a ship of small tonnage for the Inter-Colonial trade and as the

15. *Garvey* v. *U.S.A.*, 2448; "Bulletin of Radical Activities," March 1–13, 1920," in RG 60.

16. Dissident New York papers, generally unavailable today, were cited in the Baltimore *Afro-American*, February 20, April 2, 9, 1920. The controversy over registry was narrated in the thirty-one-page "Summary Report" by government agent Mortimer J. Davis in November, 1922, pp. 3–4, in Garvey file, RG 65.

17. Davis, "Summary Report," 9–11; *NW*, May 1, 1920; Merrilees, "Summary Report," 11. Some dissident BSL directors and officers joined L. G. Jordan's African Steamship and Sawmill Co. Another line, the Intercolonial Steamship and Trading Co., purchased a ship in June, 1920, from the U.S. Shipping Board. Baltimore *Afro-American*, June 11, 1920.

Yarmouth was not fitted for long voyages, it would be advisable that such a ship be acquired to take passengers and collect freight between the islands, so that the Yarmouth would be able to make short and payable trips to Jamaica via Cuba and back to New York." Garvey probably intended to use the *Kanawha* for the irregular trips to small islands in search of freight and passengers while the more impressive *Yarmouth* made regular runs from Jamaica and Cuba to New York. Convinced of Garvey's logic, the board agreed to pay $60,000—$5,000 the next day when the contract was to be signed, $10,000 on the day of delivery (May 25), and the balance in six monthly payments of $7,500 each.[18]

Garvey had been given strong advice against making the purchase. Captain Adrian Richardson, a friend of the head of the Boston UNIA, came to New York to inspect the boat. A port captain for a Boston-based shipping company, Richardson had checked its listing with Lloyds of London. Having assumed that the *Kanawha* was the 9,000-ton ship listed, he was incredulous when he discovered that Garvey was about to buy a 375-ton yacht of the same name. He warned that the operating expenses would exceed the purchase price. Garvey responded that "the same as she could run for her former owners and the Government she could run for us." When Richardson protested that the yacht had been owned and subsidized first by oil millionaire H. H. Rogers and then by the federal government during the war, Garvey replied that the BSL traffic manager in New York "said she was all right and she was fit for the sea." Richardson pointed out the yacht's defective boilers and auxiliaries. But Garvey would not be bridled.[19]

Richardson's criticism did not prevent Garvey from offering him the job of captain of the *Kanawha*. Garvey frequently won acquiescence by offering jobs and glory and appealing to race patriotism. Although Richardson refused, he agreed to stay in New York as port captain in charge of the three ships. His differences with Garvey increased. Pressed with numerous debts, Garvey did not repair the *Kanawha* at a shipyard but brought in "a green crew . . . from the office" staff. Richardson supervised their work, but he found that they "knew nothing about seafaring at all and they knew

18. Davis, "Summary Report," 11, 15; Merrilees, "Summary Report," 34–35; Orlando Thompson to Louis LeMoth, August 23, 1920, in Garvey case file of exhibits. At the time of Thompson's statement, it appeared that the West Indian trade would continue to grow. In fact, it reached its peak in February. U.S. Shipping Board, *Fourth Annual Report* (Washington, D.C., 1920), 56, 59–60, 143.

19. Adrian Richardson, testimony, *Garvey* v. *U.S.A.*, 433–37, 441. Richardson testified that he had heard that the ship had been previously offered to a buyer for $10,000 but was turned down because of the costs of operating the ship. Charles Harris, first engineer of the *Kanawha*, also opposed the purchase. Charles Harris, "Interview," July 6, 1922, in Garvey file, RG 65.

less than that of any kind of shipwork." Without consulting Richardson, Garvey advertised a Hudson River sailing for $1.25 round trip. The captain refused to take the disabled and uninspected ship up the river. Jacob Wise, the white captain of the *Shadyside*, agreed to pilot the ship. Sailing as far as 206th Street, the boat returned when a boiler blew out, killing one man. After the completion of additional repairs, which took three more weeks, the ship left port in August under the command of Captain Leon R. Swift, the white broker who had sold the BSL the *Shadyside* and *Kanawha*.[20]

When the boilers blew again a little south of Delaware, the crew rigged the vessel with sails made from the ship's awnings while Swift hired a tug-boat to tow the *Kanawha* to Norfolk for repairs. He resigned his position in Norfolk, and Richardson agreed to take command. The ship's boilers began to leak again a little below Cape Hatteras, and it was towed back to Norfolk. On the way to Havana, Richardson concluded that the ship required thorough overhauling. When the Bethlehem Steel Steam Ship Company could not perform the necessary repairs in Wilmington, Delaware, the ship returned to New York under sails because the boilers would not function at all. Orlando Thompson authorized the reputable National Dry Dock and Repair Company in Staten Island to restore the yacht for an estimated $15,000, even though he now admitted that the *Kanawha* had been "a bad purchase."[21]

Thompson decided to incur large expenses on the ship because BSL managers believed that only a functioning ship could maintain their legitimacy and stay criticism. From the founding of the UNIA, Garveyites had inhabited a world of mortgages, debts, and twelfth-hour loans. But the company was now in danger of losing its only means of resurrection, its ships. Angry passengers expecting to sail were "making it unpleasant" for the officers of the line. Thompson had contracted a shipment of 2,500 tons, and his Cuban agent had arranged for a sugar consignment on the return. And despite her handicaps, the *Kanawha* appeared to be a better investment than the two other ships. After the excursion season, the *Shadyside* had no function. Thompson still hoped to repair the *Yarmouth*, but she had returned from her third and, as it turned out, last voyage in late August carrying libels of $200,000 and repairs estimated at $75,000. At the same time, Thompson tried unsuccessfully to purchase a fourth ship. The managers incorporated a new line, the Black Star Steamship Company of New Jersey, to avoid the financial liens of the BSL ships. In this context of

20. Richardson, testimony, *Garvey* v. *U.S.A.*, 734–42.

21. *Ibid.*, 441–47; Orlando Thompson to Louis LeMoth, October 1, 1920, in Garvey case file of exhibits; Orlando Thompson, testimony, *Garvey* v. *U.S.A.*, 1786, 1858, 1862–68, 1896–1904.

urgency, the $15,000 to be spent on the *Kanawha* appeared to be reasonable. Upon examination, however, the National Dry Dock Company discovered additional damage that raised its estimate to $45,000.[22]

Throughout the summer and fall of 1920, even as Garvey held his first large convention in August, few people knew how critical the situation was. Favorable publicity and popular enthusiasm answered some critics but did not prevent the resignation of men essential to BSL operations. Captain Hugh Mulzac had been willing to accept Black Star Line notes instead of wages to help the cash-short line. But the need to support his family, along with accelerating frustrations over the operation of the line, forced him to resign. Mulzac's career demonstrated the appeal of black nationalism to skilled black workers but also revealed its inability to satisfy them.[23]

The young Mulzac had fallen in love with the sea on forty-mile-long Union Island, part of the British Grenadines. He learned about ship construction and sailing while working with his father and older brother in the family business. However, his desire for travel and experience could not be satisfied by his father's enterprise. So he signed on an oceangoing ship, beginning seven years on the seas and in foreign ports in Europe, North Africa, and South and North America. Despite his British second-mate's license, he could not obtain a deck position in the United States, where most blacks were limited to the steward's department on the major lines. A youthful and unemployed Mulzac accepted a position as cook, for which he had no experience, on board a United Fruit banana boat sailing between Baltimore and Jamaica.[24]

The racial restrictions on ships eased with the outbreak of World War I. The demand for experienced seamen removed the old barriers, and Mulzac obtained the temporary officer's license awarded to aliens. After completing a training course run by the U.S. Shipping Board, he sailed as a deck officer on four vessels from 1914 through 1918. Receiving a perfect

22. Merrilees, "Summary Report," 23–25; Thompson, testimony, *Garvey* v. *U.S.A.*, 1905–1906, 1862–69; MG, testimony, *Garvey* v. *U.S.A.*, 2303–11; Orlando Thompson to Louis LeMoth, August 3, 1920, in Garvey case file of exhibits. It is difficult to ascertain whether the repair costs charged to the BSL were excessive. Other shipowners made similar complaints. Indeed, so great was the problem that a campaign was waged to reduce the rates. Although rates were reduced effective January 13, 1921, it was too late for the Black Star Line. U.S. Shipping Board, *Fifth Annual Report* (Washington, D.C., 1921), 141.

23. Mulzac, *A Star to Steer By*, 84–85. On August 2, 1919, Richard E. Warner and Edgar Grey were expelled. Fred Powell resigned on February 14. John Bayne was dismissed on June 3. James Curley (a former Howard University professor), Elie Garcia, Fred Toote (a minister), William Ferris, and Cyril Henry were added to the board at this time.

24. Mulzac, *A Star to Steer By*, 1–61.

score, he was the first black man in Baltimore's history to pass the master seaman's exam. Despite his skill, Mulzac could not obtain a bridge position after the war. The labor surplus permitted a return to the old prejudices of the hiring personnel. Shippers were once again in control, and conditions for sailors deteriorated. Those seeking employment gladly accepted long hours and low pay.[25]

Unable to find suitable work at sea, Mulzac, recently married, was working as a paperhanger in Baltimore when an old friend informed him one day that the Black Star Line was seeking colored officers. He was excited at the prospect of sailing again. His friend contacted Garvey, who immediately invited Mulzac to come to New York. Entering UNIA headquarters on 135th Street in his master's uniform, he found himself among many "job seekers and supplicants, stock-owners-to-be and a few hero-worshippers." The gallant captain was immediately shepherded to Garvey's third-floor offices. Like others whose current needs harmonized with Garvey's purposes, Mulzac easily became transfixed by the Pan-African vision. Promised the position of chief officer of the *Yarmouth*, and future commands on speedy ships to Africa, Mulzac left with the job and as owner of five shares of Black Star Line stock, which he had purchased.[26]

For Mulzac, the UNIA proved to be only a brief phase in a long search for appropriate work. The racial progress accompanying World War I had advanced him in a career he was later forced to abandon. But armed with the confidence he had gained from his wartime position, he quit his paper-hanging job and joined the BSL in 1920. Mulzac's experiences on the *Yarmouth*, however, soured his faith in the Black Star Line and Marcus Garvey, though not in the viability of a black shipping line. He resigned in 1921, and striking out on his own, he started his own company and sold six thousand dollars worth of stock but eventually concluded that he could not raise sufficient capital. Still believing that blacks had a role to play on the seas, he opened Mulzac's Nautical Academy in New York to teach navigation, engineering, and the wireless. The school closed in 1922. During the rest of the twenties, Mulzac, like most seamen, was happy to find any work at sea.[27] When unions became stronger in the larger society and at sea in the thirties, he found a solution to his problems when he became an

25. *Ibid.*, 69–74.
26. *Ibid.*, 74–75.
27. For Mulzac's appeals for aid to other racial groups, including the NAACP, see Hugh Mulzac to Kelly Miller, January 11, 1924, Miller to James W. Johnson, January 15, 1924, Walter White to Mulzac, January 21, 1924, Mulzac to Admiral Palmer, February 12, 1924, Mulzac to White, February 14, 1924, White to Carl Murphy, February 16, 1925, all in Box C-13, NAACP Papers.

organizer for the National Maritime Union. Another war gave him an opportunity to command a ship. He became captain of the Liberty ship *Booker T. Washington*.[28]

Mulzac's experiences of barriers and opportunities in work had much in common with those of other educated and trained men who were attracted to the UNIA because it promised the opportunity to pursue careers. In turn, the BSL depended upon the skilled men to obtain and operate ships, which won the UNIA the initial tangible achievements that were so critical in attracting its mass constituency. Cyril A. Critchlow's response was typical. A college graduate with two years of additional study at a black medical school, Critchlow had been a writer and editor on several black newspapers and magazines. Possessing typing and stenographic skills, too, he was co-owner of the Critchlow-Braithwaite Shorthand School in Harlem. When the black 92nd Division was created by the U.S. Army, he became a sergeant employed as a clerk, a position that would have been difficult to obtain in civilian life outside of black institutions. The number of black bookkeepers, accountants, clerks, copyists, stenographers, and typewriters expanded between 1900 and 1920 because of the growth of black business and education. In the early twentieth century secretarial skills were still associated with managerial functions. Rarely did blacks, or foreign-born workers for that matter, find employment in the offices of American corporations, which were Anglo-Saxon preserves.[29]

Critchlow became the official stenographer and reporter of the UNIA and traveled with Garvey, recording his speeches for publication in the *Negro World*. Imbibing the optimism surrounding racial enterprise, Critchlow decided to go to Liberia and begin a school like the one he ran in Harlem. Other active organizers—agricultural expert Cyril Henry, accountant Orlando Thompson, and bookkeeper Elie Garcia—shared similar wartime experiences and postwar aspirations. The occasional success of such men nourished the ideology of black business enterprise and blinded many to the visible problems of the Black Star Line and undertakings like it.[30]

28. Mulzac, *A Star to Steer By*, 86–88, 104–107. Mulzac's first engineer, Charles Harris, had similar wartime experiences before he joined the BSL. Harris, "Interview," July 6, 1922, in Garvey file, RG 65.

29. Charles A. J. McPherson to W. E. B. Du Bois, n.d. [received May 4, 1918], Box C-1, in NAACP Papers; John Harmon, Arnett G. Lindsay, and Carter G. Woodson, *The Negro as a Businessman* (Washington, D.C., 1929), 26.

30. The Critchlow-Braithwaite school, which employed four teachers, continued after the war. I. Newton Braithwaite, whose brother Fred headed a UNIA branch in Brooklyn, passed the examination to become a court stenographer. The Braithwaite family and the shorthand school could not afford to support only a single organization. Whereas Critchlow and Fred Braithwaite worked with the UNIA, I. Newton Braithwaite was the official stenographer at the NAACP convention in 1920. New York *Amsterdam News*, Janu-

Of course, all men whose opportunities were enhanced during the war did not migrate to the UNIA. One Edmund B. Trotman sought employment from the NAACP: "I am a young man, colored, a graduate of Virginia Union University, and also of Morgan College. I came here [Bethlehem Steel plant at Sparrow Point, Maryland] to take charge of the Testing Department. . . . The mission is now ended and I thought I would write asking if there is any possibility of being able to secure a position in the service of the National Association." But the NAACP could not offer him a job. Most men in this situation did not go so far as to seek employment from racial organizations like the UNIA or NAACP. But the experiences and needs of men like Mulzac, Critchlow, and Trotman were central to the creation of the BSL and to its appeal.[31]

The ordinary investor had different motivations from men who sought careers in black business enterprise. The common denominator of each stock purchase was the profit motive. Novices often plagued Garvey with questions and demanded refunds when their anxieties outweighed their hopes. Many thought that the purchase of stock was like the deposit of funds in savings banks and could be withdrawn on demand. Garvey's reversion to soliciting direct contributions and loans for the line in 1921 was a response to the "mental trauma" he felt as a result of selling to men and women of small means.[32]

Middle-class blacks absorbed losses more easily. Alice McKane, a doctor in Boston, said, "Colored people do not always think in dimes and dollars. . . . If Garvey fails and we all loose [sic] our money it is our business." But A. W. Bennett of Boley, Oklahoma, inquired of the NAACP:

> I am writing you in the defence of my race now we have men goin around repersenting marcos garvin and getting 5 dollars from each pupil and they say they will make you become a member of the African government and a stockholder of the black star line and I want you to rite me a letter and tell me is that so or a lye. . . . Now I trys to live a christain life and I work hard for a living and every body else am when I put my money in a concern I want someone that nows of it to repersent it to me [sic].[33]

Some investors were like the Boston doctor and others like Bennett. While Dr. McKane might accept her losses for a time, it was unlikely that

---

ary 14, 1921; *Age*, February 12, 1921; author's interview with Marion Alexander, daughter of Fred Braithwaite, July 18, 1976.

31. Edmund B. Trotman to James W. Johnson, May 13, 1919, Box C-3, in NAACP Papers.

32. New York *World*, August 21, 1921. The variety of personal stories on purchases was endless. See reports by James Amos, March 14, 21, 1922, and by Young O. Wilson, March 14, 1922, in Garvey file, RG 65.

33. Alice McKane to Herbert Seligmann, December 27, 1921, A. W. Bennett to NAACP, February 14, 1922, in NAACP Papers.

she would continue to invest her money in a project that showed few signs of success.

In theory the Black Star Line could be incorporated into more collectivist routes to black prosperity. In a letter to R. R. Moton, George Goodwyn, a black organizer for the American Federation of Labor, asked the principal to help oppose the open shop movement in American industry. Goodwyn portrayed the human and family security resulting from dignified union organization. Appealing to Moton's known support of black business and possibly unaware of the divisions in racial politics, he added that blacks earning high wages could "float ships for Mr. Marcus Garvey and Dr. Jordan's African lines [another black shipping company], if found worthy."[34]

This compatibility existed only on paper. To Goodwyn, the prosperity of labor was the prerequisite to racial enterprise, prosperity, and progress. In practice, Garvey's ability to accumulate capital depended upon the earnings of black workers. But to Garvey, progress emerged not from them but from racial leaders who would accumulate and use the surplus to create institutions capable of uplifting the masses. To Garvey, black entrepreneurs would enlighten the race; to Goodwyn, the organization of black workers would be the means for their self-improvement. The new mass upsurge that Garvey had observed in the United States did not essentially change his theology of progress but only modified it somewhat. In Jamaica, he had appealed to leading whites for money to create institutions of uplift. When he first arrived in the United States, he solicited leading blacks. The growth of a militant black working class in the United States freed Garvey from depending upon whites and elite blacks but did not alter his fundamental conception of racial advance.

Socially rebellious, Garvey was ideologically conservative. His gestures defied the powerful, white and black, but the consequences of his actions confirmed their position at the top. This paradox was caught succinctly in John Bruce's favorable comparison between Garvey and Charles Ponzi, before the Boston swindler's arrest. Bruce found "that the 'smart guys' cannot fathom [Garvey and Ponzi], cannot enmesh them in the coils of the law, nor check them in their efforts to help the underdog to enjoy some of the sweets of life. The bankers of Wall St. are excited over Ponzi's activities, and the steamship companies are wondering what Garvey has up his sleeve."

Ponzi contrasted the opportunities for business investment available to the rich and the mere 4 percent return on savings accounts, the common

34. George Goodwyn to R. R. Moton, August 19, 1920, Box C-304, in Moton Papers.

source of investment for workers. By offering 50 percent for investing in his vaguely stated scam, Ponzi provided equal opportunity for the poor. But his message carried conservative ideological baggage. He assumed that wage labor would never allow men to achieve well-being, and certainly not wealth. Collective working-class progress was impossible. "The fat cats will stay fat, and the fools will stay fools," he concluded. Therefore, the sole road for smart men was the capitalist road. He not only hated the poverty of his early life but scorned men who remained poor.[35] Ponzi and other stock promoters sold the hegemony of elite institutions and values along with their financial schemes. After hearing an unnamed black stock salesman who was on tour, Prentiss R. Johnson protested the views of the working class portrayed in the Ponzi-like pitch.

> One of the means adopted by some [promoters] is to attempt to make persons engaged in the lowlier occupations ashamed of their callings, they call it giving them higher ideals . . . by painting a glowing picture of bloated bond holders, drawing miraculous dividends, looking down on their less fortunate brothers or sisters, who still continue to walk in the less exalted avenues. . . . Are these saviors of the race acting with the best judgment possible, when they argue to an audience that may be one-tenth high and mighty, and nine-tenths plain everyday colored folks that these latter are fools to continue to labor in the humbler, yet no less honorable capacities, when with a single wave of the hand, or what these racial benefactors prefer, two or three genuine good old fashioned waves of the pocketbook they can become managers, superintendents, presidents, and I don't know what not?

Garvey's assumptions about progress and his ambiguous attitudes toward rich and poor were similar to Ponzi's and to those of other promoters, even though his was a genuine productive effort. (But Ponzi, too, spoke of beginning industrial enterprises, a steamship line, and even mines in Africa.) Garvey's rhetoric approached Ponzi's when he urged blacks to "help yourself to make money and become prosperous by purchasing BSL stock." More typical, however, was Garvey's merging of the individual and the collective, the self-interested and the idealistic. He claimed that the Black Star Line was an instrument of the people. Faced with criticism from rivals who were creating new steamship lines, Garvey urged the people to stay with the original. "The Black Star Line . ʻ. . is owned by the people and is a

35. The most accessible study of Ponzi is a fictionalized treatment, Donald H. Dunn's *Ponzi: The Boston Swindler* (New York, 1975), based upon Ponzi's privately published autobiography. Because Bruce's comparison between Ponzi and Garvey was positive, I assumed that the undated column was written before the swindler's indictment in August, 1920. John Bruce, "Bruce Grits," n.d., in Bruce Papers. In December, the headline BLACK PONZI GOES TO JAIL appeared over an article about a man caught selling the stock of a mythical corporation. Baltimore *Afro-American*, December 24, 1920.

movement for the people, which tends to their ultimate betterment," he said. Other racial enterprises were led by "selfish capitalistic Negroes."[36]

In the end, whatever corporations they invested in, men battled to protect their jobs and incomes in the dominant economy. Shareholders abandoned the BSL and kept on the working-class route to progress because there was no other. They attended to the social relations of the outside world, the world of work, wages, and prices, out of necessity, not preference. The behavior of Havana's black longshoremen demonstrated how Garvey's conception of progress first intersected with, but then diverged from, the popular one. On the maiden voyage of the *Yarmouth*, Captain Cockburn described the mass enthusiasm that greeted the ship in Havana: "The stevedore's gang containing just a handful of men bought up two hundred and fifty dollars' worth of shares just in a twinkle; we were compelled to say a few words to them from the ship since they were so willing to respond. . . . The people at Havana are mustering in thousands to see the ship and I have no doubt that it would be the means of collecting a Hundred Thousand of Dollars in quick time from them because wherever you go it seems to be the same cry for freedom as in New York." There were many reasons why the stevedores found the Black Star Line an appealing proposition. To begin with, they were promised wealth as owners of a company. Furthermore, many Havana longshoremen were blacks, and perhaps a black-owned and -operated shipping company was attractive to men battling the large, white, principally foreign owners. Cuban political culture, like American, taught workers to identify national enterprise in shipping with their own freedoms. In early 1918, a number of leading Cubans had organized the Cuban Star Line to free the nation from the tyranny of the United Fruit fleet.[37] Conceivably, the Black Star Line, rival to the big companies, could deliver working-class objectives—jobs, superior labor relations—as well as the individual profits. But when workers were in conflict with shipowners, when class consciousness was high, the compatibilities between the Black Star Line and working-class organization vanished. On the *Yarmouth*'s second voyage a month and a half later, the ship was struck along with others docked in the harbor. UNIA leaders then spoke of the warm support of Cuban businessmen, not longshoremen.[38]

36. New York *Sun*, August 4, 6, 1920; *NW*, November 9, 1919; "Negro Agitation," December 10, 1919, file 10218-364/16, MID, in RG 165; "The Negro in the Realm of Commerce," n.d. [1919], in Records of the Lusk Committee; Baltimore *Afro-American*, May 28, 1920.

37. Joshua Cockburn to MG, December 5, 1919, in Garvey case file of exhibits; Boaz Long to Secretary of State, May 12, 1920, W. W. Guerra to Pino Guerra, May 4, 1920, file 850.4, in RG 84.

38. Although the strike was lost, another occurred in June, 1920. A combination of the

And black business ownership proved to be no solution to the problem of high rents. Throughout the United States, the entrance of new workers into cities created housing shortages and soaring rents. Black and white realtors, both experienced ones and those new to the business, reaped huge profits from Harlem property. Insofar as the black elite confronted the housing crisis, it was to protect its own interests. John Nail, a leading Harlem realtor, tried to win an appointment to a new mayor's committee on the housing crisis by drawing attention to the "165,000 colored people owning and controlling millions of real property" in Harlem. But racial representation by a black landlord on a mayor's committee was not a popular issue among the black masses in 1920 when tenant leagues and rent strikes sprang up all over the city, including Harlem. In March, A. Philip Randolph and Chandler Owen created the Harlem Tenants and Lodgers League to obtain legislation to make it criminal for landlords to raise rents above 5 percent a year. The league, begun by Socialists, was citywide and used strikes or strike threats to keep down rents.[39]

Garvey did not address the housing issue directly in 1920. Leading members of the UNIA, including Garvey, purchased homes. Collectively, the UNIA in New York was raising money to pay for its headquarters, Liberty Hall. At least one Garveyite in New York urged Garvey to purchase apartment houses, not ships, in order to take advantage of the opportunity for profit. Applying Garveyism to real estate, however, the Philadelphia UNIA formed the Universal Housing Corporation, proposing to sell stock at eight dollars a share. Like Garvey, the leaders of the Philadelphia UNIA attempted to distinguish between selfish and unselfish capitalism. The directors stated that their corporation was "purely a democratic one" to resolve the problem of high rents by buying buildings and ousting white tenants "by the very methods employed on colored tenants." Ironically, though they promised lower rents, their tactic was the one used by both black and white realtors to raise rents—removing white tenants to extract more rent from blacks. Despite the faulty economic logic, Universal Housing announced plans to expand to other parts of the United States, as well as to the West Indies and South America. Its president, Thomas Cadegan, hoped

<hr/>

deportation of alien strike leaders and economic depression ended labor militancy by 1922. Harold Williamson to Secretary of State, June 25, 1920, file 850.4, in RG 84; report, February 2, 1922, file 2655-Q-53, MID, in RG 165.

39. "Bulletin of Radical Activities," March 10–13, 1920, in RG 60; Gilbert Osofsky, *Harlem: The Making of a Ghetto: Negro New York, 1890–1930* (New York, 1963), 235; *Age*, July 3, November 20, 1920; John Nail to Ferdinand Morton, May 6, 1920, in John Hylan Papers, Municipal Archives and Records Center, New York, New York; "Negroes and Radicalism," January 21, 1921, file 10110-2271/1, MID, in RG 165; *Harlem Magazine*, VIII (February, 1920),

for financial assistance from Garvey. Both Cadegan's appeal and the plans for expansion implied a lack of popular financial support in Philadelphia. Cadegan hoped to attract working-class people—colored tenants, not homeowners. However, his elitist methods, dependent upon business ownership, accumulation of capital, and removal of white tenants, were outside the compass of the black working class. Unlike in New York, the black population in Philadelphia did not organize rent strikes. But the quick disappearance of the Universal Housing Corporation revealed that the methods of the elite did not attract black workers even when they lacked alternatives, because entrepreneurial solutions to racial problems were irrelevant to black working-class life.[40]

UNIA leaders continued to associate racial progress with business ownership. But the informal racial barriers to work in industrial society were falling, though the pace was too slow for black workers. Nevertheless, most of them saw their future as being in the modern economic sector. This was as true for the skilled worker and the professional as for the laborer. Although discrimination was more of a problem in the skilled lines of work, especially white-collar jobs, white firms continued to be the principal employers of trained blacks. But the idea of the special virtues of racial enterprise was not manufactured by the UNIA. A graduate of Tuskegee employed in an American shipyard reported to R. R. Moton that "all men are treated alike and I have worked to the top as mechanick [sic]. . . . Considering we had not stock in the company we were treated very satisfactory."[41] The identity of ownership and freedom, in this case with a racial twist, was an idea deeply rooted in the culture of small businessmen, farmers, and artisans. The tradition awarded Garvey's ideology a certificate of approval from the masses, but it fit uncomfortably with the logic of industrial society and the new mass assertions and solutions that erupted during the war. So long as the majority of blacks were farmers and sharecroppers, the desire for improvement was identical with the desire for landownership. As wage labor and urban migration became more com-

---

18, X (November, 1920), 6; New York *Times*, January 18, 1920; Baltimore *Afro-American*, February 20, 1920.

40. *Age*, July 3, 1920; "Negroes and Radicalism," January 21, 1921, MID, in RG 165; "Rent Profiteering," July 13, 1921, D. Wallerstein to James Ford, August 14, 1918, Ford to J. Wilson Smith, February 26, 1919, H. L. Beach, "Memorandum on Philadelphia Housing Conditions," May 20, 1919, all in Boxes 312–13, Record Group 3, Records of the United States Housing Corporation, National Archives. Records of complaints show that blacks confronted the problem of high rents more than that of removal. The problem of exclusion was more common among homeowners than renters. See Box 318, in RG 3.

41. Felix Washington to R. R. Moton, July 9, 1921, in Moton Papers.

mon, the old aspirations for independence through ownership mingled with new desires for modern life-styles, wealth, and financial security. Many of the resulting conflicts punctuated the stormy history of the Black Star Line. Unnamed, they were at the root of the declining stock purchases in 1920 and the escalating dissatisfactions threatening to overwhelm the BSL and thus the UNIA. But prewar black nationalism had not been dependent only upon the interclass harmonies within each particular region. Pan-Africanism had attempted to unify the elites of the various areas peopled by Africans. To understand the bonds created across oceans, one must examine the UNIA's African plans.

6 / Garveyism in Africa
Improving Liberia

A recurrent problem faced by Pan-Africanists was to define and implement the role that Afro-Americans would play in Africa. In 1920, many journalists resolved the dilemma for the broad public by translating Garvey's assertion that "Africa should be for the black people of the world" into a black Zionism whose goal was the return of Afro-Americans to the land of their ancestors.[1]

The back-to-Africa movement was one expression of Pan-Africanism. Throughout the nineteenth century, individuals, men of relatively high status in the black community, migrated to take advantage of economic and political opportunities in the independent black republic of Liberia or in Britain's African colonies. Many hoped at the same time to uplift Africans to Western standards and culture. But when the Afro-American masses caught "African fever," the causes were rural hopelessness and land hunger. They were drawn by the material conditions of poverty that animate mass movements whatever their ideology. Mass emigration projects were organized by black elites who possessed the necessary intercontinental political and economic associations. They were born when elite aspirations coincided with mass distress. Because the desire for land and independence underlay the mass impulse, however, the largest black exodus in nineteenth-century America was to Kansas, not Africa.[2]

1. New York *World*, August 5, 6, 1920; New York *Sun*, August 3, 1920; New York *Times*, August 29, 1920. The idea of Garveyism as a back-to-Africa movement persisted despite excellent coverage of the 1920 UNIA convention. T. H. Talley's piece in *World's Work*, XLI (December, 1920), 268, explicitly stated that the BSL was created for "commerce . . . not exodus." An article in the New York *Sun*, August 11, 1920, reported that the dominant talk was about commercial opportunity in Africa and the necessity for the Negro "to take his place in commerce." Black leaders like Charles Anderson, who wished to denigrate the movement, chose to call it an exodus. See *Age*, August 21, 1920. Cultural assumptions were another source of misinterpretation. In 1920, the words *Africa* and *Negro* were linked in Western culture. The New York *Times* indexed the word *Africa* under *Negro*. Another source of confusion was the existence of a few genuine emigration movements. See William York to Paul Slemun, July 8, 1920, in American Colonization Society Papers.

2. The leading study of African emigration is Edwin Redkey's *Black Exodus: Black Nationalism and Back-to-Africa Movements, 1890–1910* (New Haven, 1969). See also the impres-

Garvey's Pan-Africanism stemmed from the elite tradition of ambition and uplift, not the mass desire for land. His idea of African freedom was modern, not mythic or utopian. The UNIA plans promised careers for individual Afro-Americans and up-to-date tools of Western civilization for Africans. Although Garvey did not forgo the dividends of ambiguity, his message to blacks in Gary, Indiana, was a typical injunction to "work here and help build up the city in which you live. . . . In the future we will build large and promising Garys in our own beloved land of Africa." Vice-President William Sherrill tried to rectify any misunderstandings directly. "The UNIA is not a 'Back to Africa' movement, it is a movement to redeem Africa," he asserted. "The Negro in America has had a better opportunity than any other Negro."[3]

Garvey's proposed methods in Africa were like the ones he pursued in the United States, though his rhetoric convinced reporters and some colonial officials that he intended to liberate Africa with arms. Garvey proclaimed that "there is absolutely no reason why the 400,000,000 Negroes of the world should not make a desperate effort to re-conquer our Motherland from the white man." But the sentence that followed was more typical of his politics: "If native Africans are unable to appreciate the value of their own country from the standard of Western civilization, then it is for us, their brothers, to take to them the knowledge and information that they need to help to develop the country for the common good." The first statement asserted Pan-African legitimacy, the racial right to rule Africa, while the second revealed the methods of Garvey's nationalism, which he had learned in London, enunciated in Jamaica, and practiced in the United States. Garvey's argument was a racial variant of the ideas of England's new imperial critics, like J. A. Hobson. He implicitly rejected the older, nineteenth-century indictment of imperialism, which had been rooted in liberal individualism and national rights and had simply asserted that native peoples owned their land. Garvey said that Africa must be governed in the "interest of civilization as a whole." The statement accepted the newer, organic view of the world and its resources that assumed the social, international connections of humankind and the values of social efficiency. Like Hobson, Garvey rejected the idea that the "great powers"—white nations—could perform this mission. But where the British critics advocated an international body to oversee the development of resources and "backward peoples," Garvey claimed that it was the responsibility of blacks to govern and develop Africa. His use of the word *Negro* sometimes obscured

---

sionistic but useful David Jenkins, *Black Zion: Africa Imagined and Real as Seen by Contemporary Blacks* (New York, 1975).

3. *NW*, March 15, 1924, May 28, 1922.

the critical social differences among the race, which were crucial in his conception of development. The most important roles would be in the hands of the modern Afro-Americans. The increase of racial power in both Africa and the United States required identical social processes—the accumulation of economic power. Pan-African associations were the critical ingredients in his recipe.[4]

Garvey's plan had been foreshadowed, if not fully developed, earlier. Economic Pan-Africanism had flourished in the worldwide revival of economic investment and trade of the early twentieth century. The boom in African commodities spawned numerous trading corporations and shipping lines to exchange African raw materials and food for Western manufactured products. One of these, the Akim Trading Company, was initiated by an African dubbed Chief Sam, who came to the United States in 1912 to connect the new American buyers of Gold Coast products with African sellers. Sam's project was both a prelude to Garveyite modernism and the last expression of nineteenth-century mass emigration.

Sam told potential Afro-American investors that "the civilized Negro is responsible to develop Africa" with "industrial corporations . . . a college of agriculture and industry . . . hotels, restaurants, bathhouses, theatres." He tried to attract capital in the modern way, offering "at least 100% profit." It was only when this ambitious scenario failed to attract investors that Sam followed the lure of local promoters and organized several hundred Oklahoma blacks, who had been suffering from a cotton depression and a grayer version of southern Jim Crow politics, to leave the United States for Africa.[5]

The African response to Sam's exodus exposed the rough spots in Pan-African relationships. At first suspicious when they feared that Sam was shepherding thousands of penniless farmers, Africans warmed to the voyagers when the ship stops demonstrated the quality of the passengers. Sam had chosen the wealthiest for the first trip. Africans unanimously applauded the steamship line Sam had begun. An African bishop, James Johnson, saw "in it [the shipping Line] . . . great possibilities for West Africa and our Race. It is evidently calculated to promote for us a large measure of commercial and other independence. With steamships of our own, traversing the ocean to and fro between West Africa, America and England, in the interest of commerce, we shall in respect of carrying power,

---

4. Amy Jacques Garvey (ed.), *Philosophy and Opinions of Marcus Garvey* (2 vols.; 1926; rpr. New York, 1969), I, 67; Bernard Porter, *Critics of Empire: British Radical Attitudes to Colonialism in Africa, 1895–1914* (London, 1968), esp. 156–206.

5. William Bittle and Gilbert Geis, *The Longest Way Home: Chief Alfred C. Sam's Back-to-Africa Movement* (Detroit, 1964).

be in a great measure commercially independent." When the ship arrived at its destination on the Gold Coast in January, 1915, local leaders became more enthusiastic: "If we . . . let the Blacks in America unite with those in West Africa as one people, this would evoke a force which nothing can resist."[6]

Afro-Americans were less satisfied. The pioneers did not find the promised land and riches. Sam himself disappeared. A few Americans remained, some died, and the majority returned to the United States. But Sam's failure did not destroy the idea that Africa housed vast resources and that Afro-Americans, if skilled and well organized, were unique agents of African development.[7]

One of Sam's original Afro-American partners, Charles W. Chappelle, a civil engineer and architect, assumed that his professional skill was a passport to inaugurating an African lumber industry. His African Union Company attracted the elites of the African and Afro-American community, not the marginal teachers, churchmen, and local politicians drawn to Sam. Despite the excitement on both sides of the Atlantic, the enterprise lacked the huge capital necessary to transport mahogany from the interior to the coast. Afro-Americans often exaggerated the role of their expertise and underestimated the costs and prerequisites of production in underdeveloped parts of the world.[8] Chappelle turned to the corporate philanthropists—William Jay Schliefflin and William M. Baldwin (active backers of the Urban League and Tuskegee), the Rockefeller-financed General Education Board, and the Phelps-Stokes Fund—that had dabbled in West African development projects as adjuncts to social and educational work. Because their purposes were charitable, however, they lacked the economic motive necessary for success. In the end, white and black Americans rated business opportunities in the United States higher than those of Africa. And African merchants and professionals discovered Europeans more promising partners than Americans, black or white. Economic Pan-Africanism was occasional and rhetorical before World War I. It transmitted modern values and goals along the racial triangle but lacked the convincing logic of successful enterprise.[9]

During World War I, a new vulnerability caused the West African elite to reassert its links to blacks in the Americas. Trade fluctuations and cur-

6. J. Ayodele Langley, *Pan-Africanism and Nationalism in West Africa, 1900–1945* (Oxford, 1973), 52–53.

7. *Ibid.*, 55–57; Bittle and Geis, *The Longest Way Home*, 302–307.

8. Bittle and Geis, *The Longest Way Home*, 71; Durant Ladd, *Trade and Shipping in West Africa* (Washington, D.C., 1920), 48, 51.

9. See the files on the African Union Co. in the Scott Papers and the Washington Papers.

rency and shipping shortages revealed the greater strength of foreign firms and the dependence of colonial economies. The international market determined the prosperity of African farmers who had switched from food production to cash crops during the war. Urban workers found that the inflated prices of food and other necessities diluted their wages. The ending of the war unleashed some of the pent-up opposition. The year 1919 was a banner year of popular protest in Africa as well as America. In Sierra Leone, angry mobs, believing that Lebanese traders profited from the food shortages, attacked the foreigners. Other African workers struck and formed unions to confront the new power.[10]

Capturing the turmoil, the *Africa and Orient Review* produced a scenario of change.

> The small Native trader is pushed out: his class disappears. The big combine, the "billion-dollar trust," on the one hand is opposed to the millions of propertyless wage slaves on the other. A class of intelligentsia is thrown up from below by the struggle, and they lead a revolt against conditions which are growingly intolerable. They confer and petition; they agitate and threaten. Under economic stress the political education of the masses makes great leaps. . . . Then one of two things happens. Evolution makes a violent move forward (and is called revolution for its pains), or Government concedes an inch . . . and remarks how easily fools are pacified.[11]

Britain eventually conceded an inch by accepting limited elective representation in the colonial councils beginning in Nigeria in 1923. Despite the widespread and passionately held grievances, West African politics remained the politics of its merchant class. Like the Afro-American elite in 1919, the West Africans lacked both the ideology and motivation to link up with mass discontent that took the form of strikes and riots. Although they spoke of an "instinctive racial solidarity," their new organization, the National Congress of British West Africa (NCBWA) included only the elites of four British West African colonies—Sierra Leone, Gold Coast, Nigeria, and Gambia. One delegate announced proudly that the congress was not impelled by the "rebellious spirit of Bolshevism or that of Sinn Fenianism."[12]

The NCBWA agitated for political representation and economic organization to combat new imperial economic plans and recent and prospective consolidations in London-based shipping and banking. The new pressure group was financed by and represented the interests of the merchants.

10. Jide Osuntokun, "Lagos Press and the Development of Nigerian Nationalism During the First World War," *Canadian Review of Studies in Nationalism*, II (1975), 272; David Killingray, "Repercussions of World War I in the Gold Coast," *Journal of African History*, XIX (1978), 40, 44–47, 52–58; Langley, *Pan-Africanism and Nationalism*, 199–215.
11. "West African Problem," *Africa and Orient Review*, I (December, 1920), 39–42.
12. Osuntokun, "Lagos Press," 270; Langley, *Pan-Africanism and Nationalism*, 126–27.

Tribal leaders were conspicuously absent. Prewar racial nationalism, embodied in the dying Aborigines Rights Protection Society, had attempted to unite the chiefs with the modern elite by championing native institutions and culture and opposing colonial taxation and land regulation. The new protest reflected the power of the urban men of wealth within colonial society. Its principal concerns were the maintenance and growth of their economic role within the British Empire. Its political objective—elective representation in colonial councils, not independence—registered the continuing reality that the elite's interests were protected by the foreign rulers against whom they were agitating.[13]

At the same time, West Africans looked across the ocean to Afro-Americans for the capital and economic enterprise to protect their interests.[14] The *Africa and Orient Review* reasoned that "this being an age of combinations of one kind or another, it behoves the coloured people of the world to show a solid front." Initial reports of the success of the Black Star Line thrilled Africans, especially those traders subject to the 15 percent increase in shipping rates imposed by Parliament. The Reverend Patrick Campbell of Lagos told the NCBWA delegates meeting in 1920 that "in view of the difficulties hereto experienced in the matter of space on British bottoms by legitimate African Traders and Shippers, this Conference welcomes competition in the shipping line with particular reference to the 'Black Star Line.'" He urged Africans to buy shares in the line, and went on to say: "There ought to be some substantial combination amongst the Educated Africans. Individual efforts can do but very little in the face of combined efforts of the Europeans." Campbell urged the congress to eschew Garvey's agitation but to patronize the line because it was "a Negro undertaking . . . solely for the purpose of facilitating and giving us more and brighter prospects as Africans in our commercial transactions."[15]

The conservative *Times of Nigeria* thought that "the idea of establishing a line of steamers owned and controlled by Africans is a great and even sublime conception for which everybody of African origin will bless the name of Marcus Garvey." The American Charles Young, the highest-ranking black officer in the United States Army and head of the Liberian Frontier Force, found "interest in his [Garvey's] scheme all along the West Coast. . . . Any all-black proposition well financed . . . cannot fail of success in Af-

13. Osuntokun summed up the demands of the Nigerians as the "call of 'careers open to talent.'" Osuntokun, "Lagos Press," 270.

14. Killingray, "World War I in the Gold Coast," 53, 57–58; Osuntokun, "Lagos Press," 274–75.

15. Langley, *Pan-Africanism and Nationalism*, 91, 127, 129. Campbell founded a UNIA branch in Lagos. See G. O. Olusanya, "Notes on the Lagos Branch of the Universal Negro Improvement Association," *Journal of Business and Social Studies* (Lagos), I (1970), 133–43.

rica. Race Consciousness is just that strong. But it must be prepared to fight the machinations and commercial supremacy of the White man. All Africa is in the throes of the World's Unrest. Only God knows whither it leads, but it must be betterment. But one thing is certain and that is it will never be simple pickings for the white man alone, while the African who does the work goes half-fed and half-clothed."[16]

The African commitment, however, was contingent. One Gold Coast businessman welcomed "the influx of the money of capitalists of our own race in America and the West Indies in order that we may ourselves compete with the gigantic combinations that are being formed in England for the undisguisable purpose of establishing a sort of legal or legalised monopoly of trade." But he added: "We [Africans] should be the architects, and . . . our brethren in America and those in the West Indies should be among the builders of the structure of racial oneness. . . . We admit that we are behind in steady acquaintance with the mechanical devices of the Western world . . . but we contend that we have the controlling forces in our hands, and we in Africa alone understand these forces and can direct them aright for the good of the whole Negro race."[17]

Africans' understanding of Pan-Africanism produced a chorus of voices welcoming Afro-American investment. They saw the Black Star Line as one weapon with which to fight the economic power of Europeans. But Africans would not take risks to create it. Transoceanic relations were not their only, or even their principal, instrument to gain economic independence.[18] Appeals to the British for political representation ranked first in 1919 and 1920. In short, Pan-African sentiments did not alter Africans' appraisal of their interests.

Afro-Americans were just as devoted to their own situation as the Africans were to theirs. Leading black Americans responded to the opportunity in Africa, and their response was amplified by the domestic sources of racial consciousness and by the American government's postwar trade ambitions. Most black businessmen lacked the capital to pursue Pan-African enterprise. The directors of Chappelle's African Union Company included several black bankers, but they did not invest their capital. Their meager resources were mostly committed, by law, to real estate and unavailable as venture capital. Even if Afro-Americans had been more adven-

16. Langley, *Pan-Africanism and Nationalism*, 91; Charles Young to Carter Woodson, May 15, 1920, in Box 12, Carter G. Woodson Papers, Library of Congress.

17. Langley, *Pan-Africanism and Nationalism*, 100–103.

18. Ian Duffield, "The Business Activities of Duse Mohamed Ali: An Example of the Economic Dimensions of Pan-Africanism, 1912–1945," *Journal of the Historical Society of Nigeria*, IV (1969), 571–600.

turous and speculative with available funds, the British domination of West African economic life still would have made success unlikely. Despite the brief excitement generated by the postwar commodity boom, the United States government and American business acknowledged the insurmountable walls of British power in her African colonies. Afro-Americans who retained an interest in Africa abandoned colonial West Africa for the independent black republic of Liberia. One man, inspired by Chief Sam's program for the Gold Coast, asked, "Why should not such an industrial organization be the perfect way to assist Liberia?" Garvey followed Afro-American opinion, transferring to Liberia the focus of his ambitions to tap the riches of Africa.[19]

Modeled after the British colony Sierra Leone, Liberia had been created by the American Colonization Society in 1822 to improve the condition of free blacks by transporting them to Africa. Although emigration was a divisive issue within the Afro-American community, the colony provided one alternative for free blacks in the antebellum period, especially after Liberia became an independent and prosperous republic in 1847.[20] The growth of the Liberian economy in the first two decades of independence coincided with the midcentury expansion of world capitalism. Middlemen between interior producers and the Europeans, Liberians took advantage of the new demand for the products of Africa that cheap steamship transportation created. Supplementing indigenous producers, some Liberians set up coffee and sugar plantations, worked by recaptives—Africans freed by the British slave patrols—and poorer settlers from the United States. This golden age of Liberian history ended in the worldwide economic depression of the last quarter of the century.[21]

The increased European presence on the coast and the entrance of improved steamships hurt Liberian merchants and destroyed Liberian shipping. The rise of the coffee industry in Brazil and the beet-sugar industry in Europe eliminated the other economic pillars of elite rule. Although the Americo-Liberians retained their political and social power, they searched in vain for prosperity until exports of rubber and iron provided an economic base after World War II. The Liberian elite financed its rule through internal taxation and the export of laborers to African colonies. The burdens of underdevelopment were placed on the indigenous people, who were voteless until 1944. In 1920, five thousand Americo-Liberians, who lived and traded in the capital city of Monrovia and other towns along the

19. A. S. Connelly to Emmett Scott, July 8, 1925, in Washington Papers.
20. P. J. Staudenraus, *The African Colonization Movement, 1816–1865* (New York, 1961).
21. M. B. Akpan, "Black Imperialism: Americo-Liberian Rule over the African Peoples of Liberia, 1841–1964," *Canadian Review of African Studies*, VII (1973), esp. 221–22, 227–35.

coast, governed almost 500,000 indigenous Africans populating the hinterlands behind the thin strip of settlement. The corruption, extortion, and brutality of Liberian administrators provoked frequent popular rebellions. On the other hand, the weakness of elite authority and the poverty of its military arsenal precluded the successful, permanent pacification achieved by colonial states.[22]

Liberia faced external dangers, too. Although its boundaries were pressed by encroaching British and French imperialism, the principal Western weapons threatening Liberian sovereignty were the loans extended by bankers in 1871, 1906, and 1912 to be used in paying Liberia's mounting debts. Then, World War I, which demonstrated the dependency of all colonial economies in West Africa, menaced Liberia's delicately balanced political independence. The expulsion of the Germans, who had controlled three-quarters of Liberia's foreign trade, and the common shipping shortage made it difficult to market Liberia's agricultural products. The reduced customs receipts could not cover the interest owed on the 1912 loan. Internal revenues did not cover government salaries or the costs of essential services. Even the hut tax imposed on native peoples in 1916 did not help. The Bank of British West Africa, the sole bank in Liberia after the German exodus, agreed to pay government obligations in return for the deposit of internal revenue collections with the bank. When the bank attempted to use its financial leverage to gain political control over the government, Liberian leaders balked and appealed to the United States government for a five-million-dollar loan on January 11, 1918.[23]

Despite Liberia's American parentage and despite the U.S. Navy's protection of the country, American economic influence in Liberia began only with the 1912 loan of nearly two million dollars, funded principally by New York bankers and administered after 1918 by a receivership controlled entirely by Americans. If granted, the new government loan promised to extend the American role in Liberian affairs.[24] The American black elite and whites with a philanthropic interest in Liberia were jubilant. A meeting of the heads of organized black and white missions, foundations, and black politicians endorsed a stronger American presence in Liberia. They

22. Gus J. Liebenow, *Liberia: The Evolution of Privilege* (Ithaca, N.Y., 1969), 1–25; Tom W. Schick, *Behold the Promised Land: A History of Afro-American Settler Society in Nineteenth Century Liberia* (Baltimore, 1980), 115–21; George W. Brown, *The Economic History of Liberia* (Washington, D.C., 1941), 140–42.

23. Brown, *Economic History of Liberia*, 167–74; Raymond L. Buell, *The Native Problem in Africa* (2 vols; New York, 1928), II, 769–70.

24. William Roger Louis, "The United States and the African Peace Settlement of 1919: The Pilgrimage of George Louis Beer," *Journal of African History*, IV (1963), 422–23.

urged President Wilson to reform the nearly bankrupt Liberian government and oversee the nation's "development . . . industrially, economically
and educationally. The United States Government should have a free and
untrammeled hand in the financial affairs of Liberia."[25]

The motives of the Americans were both benevolent and self-interested.
Black and white churchmen looked forward to advancing their influence.
Black politicians, traditionally mediators between the United States government and Liberia, promoted the loan to enhance their power.[26] State Department bureaucrats, especially the current American receiver in Liberia, H. F.
Worley, assumed the loan would increase their leverage and control over
the Liberian government. The Commerce Department, a new voice, had a
historic and functional interest in Liberia. The withdrawal of German
traders had created a vacuum that it hoped to fill with American businessmen. Realizing the disadvantages Americans faced in the Liberian trade, the
Commerce Department, like the U.S. Shipping Board, believed that a
"well-operated American steamship line" was desirable. Finally, State Department officials felt partly responsible for Liberia's current financial
problems because they had encouraged her to declare war against Germany, the act that had severed her major artery of commerce. The combined forces of advocacy prevailed. Liberia was granted the five-million-
dollar loan on September 12, 1918, under the president's emergency loan
powers.[27]

Garvey took up the Liberian issue after Afro-American politicians had
made it a racial priority and after the announcement of the loan. In 1918 he
had followed the vanguard of black opinion when he spoke out on the future
of Germany's former African territories after other leaders had made colonialism a political issue. Then he had joined with other blacks to map out a
political response. In 1919, however, the successes of the Black Star Line
gave him the confidence to act alone. He declared, "We of the UNIA at this
moment have a solemn duty to perform and that is to free Liberia of any
debt that she owes to any white government." Like other Afro-Americans,
Garvey believed that the principal danger to Liberia was the designs of European powers. But he refused to welcome the American presence as a
counter to the old imperialists, because the United States would always

25. "Minutes," December 19, 1918, in Phelps-Stokes Fund Papers; Baltimore *Afro-
American*, January 3, September 12, October 24, 1919.
26. Buell, *The Native Problem*, II, 575; Richard Bundy to Secretary of State, October 25,
1920, file 882.51/1196, in RG 59; R. R. Moton to Ernest Lyon, December 10, 1919, in Moton
Papers.
27. G. M. Jones to H. C. Maclean, January 15, 1919, Maclean to Jones, January 23,
1919, file 480.9, in RG 151.

support "England and France to crush any rising colored race." Instead, the UNIA would raise the five-million-dollar loan to free Liberia.[28]

The differences between Garvey and other leaders were not ideological. All were committed in principle to advance the racial frontier, and all accommodated to "white power" in areas beyond their reach and in the interest of immediate objectives. Thus, black churchmen and politicians advocated an infusion of "white" capital into Liberia to increase black institutional and personal influence. Later, in 1921, Garvey himself would support an American loan to Liberia for similar reasons. Although the UNIA's future financial resources had seemed to be both abundant and growing in 1919 and 1920, Garvey in 1921 had to acknowledge that his organization lacked the necessary means to aid Liberia. As he yielded racial terrain, he also made the appropriate distinctions among white nations to justify the retreat. In 1923, he praised "philanthropic and liberal America, whose honesty in international politics should be better trusted than the ravenous white nations of Europe." But in 1919 and 1920, at the height of his power and full of self-confidence, Garvey extended the boundaries of black occupation farther than other black leaders did. Moreover, he promised that, after its August, 1920, convention, the headquarters of the UNIA would be transferred to Monrovia, a prelude to ambitious plans.[29]

Garvey asked three associates, Hubert Harrison, the Reverend James Eason, and Elie Garcia, to go to Liberia to investigate the prospects of developing the country. John Bruce, an old hand at Liberian-American commercial schemes, gave the trio letters of introduction to the chief justice of the Liberian Supreme Court. But Eason decided not to go, and Harrison bowed out at the last moment because of his health. One Garveyite, Garcia, arrived in Monrovia in May, 1920.[30]

Garcia was a Haitian who had come to New York "on some business proposition" involving the trade in logwood. Unable to succeed in business, he worked at a government laboratory in Nitro, West Virginia, during the war. He met Garvey in Philadelphia in July, 1919. At the time, he claimed to be in partnership with a friend in a company called the United Development Corporation. After a little haggling over the size of his commission, Garcia agreed to represent the Black Star Line in Philadelphia. He

28. "Negro Agitation," December 10, 1919, file 10218-364/16, MID, in RG 165. Other racial militants approved of the loan but criticized the appointment of whites to administer it. Baltimore *Afro-American*, November 18, 1919.

29. *NW*, August 14, 21, 28, 1920, May 20, 1923; New York *World*, August 3, 1920; New York *Times*, August 2, 3, 1920.

30. John Bruce to J. J. Dossen, April 3, 1920, in Bruce Papers; Elie Garcia, "Confidential Report," August, 1920, in A. J. Garvey (ed.), *Philosophy and Opinions of Garvey*, II, 402–403.

became assistant secretary of the local UNIA, too, and was active in some of its local business ventures.[31]

Garcia had feared that the American loan and the resulting American economic and political influence in Liberia would be "a great inconvenience to the UNIA." Under the provisions of the loan, at least thirteen American officials, all designated by the American government, would monitor Liberia's internal finances and customs receipts. The administrators would have, in effect, a veto power over internal taxation and expenditures and over the granting of concessions. Fortunately, Garcia arrived in Liberia at the time when the stringent terms of the American loan had produced a "great consternation among the elite" and a strong movement to reject the loan.[32]

However, the crisis did not foster a Liberian-UNIA entente. Garcia later informed Garvey confidentially that he found the Liberian elite to be "degenerated and weak morally" and suspicious of "American and West Indian Negroes," especially those with "brains, energy, and experience." He claimed they perpetuated slavery and practiced polygamy, "highly detrimental to the improvement of morality among the natives as well as to social development among themselves." In short, Garcia shared the judgments of many white and black Americans that the Liberians were devious, unreliable, and parasitic. He recommended that the UNIA retain control of the money disbursed. "Otherwise it will be only fattening the purses of a few individuals." Garcia's analysis demonstrated the inevitable political thrust of investment in underdeveloped countries. He advised Garvey to disguise and conceal the UNIA's political objectives—the same methods used by other foreigners in Liberia, who required official sanction to operate but also political changes to succeed. Using the methods of alien businessmen, however, did not augur well for an organization claiming racial brotherhood.[33]

Garcia returned to the United States to attend the UNIA's convention of August, 1920. He left behind a local chapter of the UNIA and took with him Liberian Secretary of State Edwin Barclay's promise to extend "every facility legally possible" to foster "its [the UNIA's] industrial, agricultural and business projects." Gabriel Johnson, the local head of the Liberian UNIA and mayor of Monrovia, also came to the convention, and Barclay secretly empowered him to evaluate the UNIA's financial resources. Johnson told a Harlem black that he intended "to get all the internal improve-

31. Elie Garcia, "Statement," January 13, 1922, in Garvey file, RG 65.
32. Buell, *The Native Problem*, II, 813; Edwin Barclay to Lyon, February 23, 1920, in Scott Papers.
33. Garcia, "Confidential Report," 399–400, 403–404.

ments [for Liberia] he could get off of Garvey." While in the United States he met with numerous other blacks to create "good will for the African country." In Baltimore he stayed at the home of Ernest Lyons, a former American minister to Liberia who was hostile to Garvey and the UNIA. Simultaneously, the Liberians pursued the promises of British capitalists and worked to alter the terms of the American loan. Liberians retained other options to extricate the country from debt and poverty. Afro-Americans proceeded cautiously, too. Garcia warned Garvey that the Liberians "fear only political domination from their helpers—blacks or whites." They worried about UNIA claims to represent all black people. Therefore, at the 1920 convention Garvey had Gabriel Johnson run unopposed for potentate, the supreme power in the UNIA, according to its constitution. Aware of Garvey's real power, Johnson was probably not fooled by his own legal supremacy.[34]

Ignoring the problems, Garvey set out to implement Garcia's plans, beginning with an infrastructure—a small railroad of thirty or forty miles, a line of steamers to connect the several ports along the coast and free Liberia from reliance on Elder Dempster, and about a hundred miles of good roads. Garvey planned to send a ship of the Black Star Line to Liberia with goods to trade and machinery to begin the projects, which would be supervised by the UNIA's own experts. The convention had voted a two-million-dollar construction loan for this work. The decision, like others, only empowered. The money would have to be raised.[35]

Despite the enthusiasm of the 1920 UNIA convention, the UNIA was desperately short of money. It was feverishly trying to purchase another ship because the three it owned were unsuitable for an African voyage. Without assimilating the implications of the financial difficulties, Garvey decided to send a small group to Liberia before the Black Star Line purchased a ship and before the construction loan had been raised. He chose hard-working and trustworthy Cyril Critchlow to head the delegation. One might have expected Garcia to lead it. Perhaps he had concluded that the project could not succeed. Whatever his reasons, Garcia did not intervene.[36]

34. M. B. Akpan, "Liberia and the Universal Negro Improvement Association: The Background to the Abortion of Garvey's Scheme for African Colonization," *Journal of African History*, XIV (1973), 116–17; Edwin Barclay to Elie Garcia, June 14, 1920, in A. J. Garvey (ed.), *Philosophy and Opinions of Garvey*, II, 36.

35. Garcia, "Confidential Report," 403–404; Ida Tourtellot to Jesse Jones, March 11, 1921, in Phelps-Stokes Fund Papers; Baltimore *Afro-American*, October 27, 1922.

36. MG, "To Whom It May Concern," February 1, 1921; MG to Gabriel Johnson, February 1, 1921. These letters and the full correspondence and record of UNIA experiences in Liberia are in file 882.00/705, RG 59. When Critchlow sought the aid of the American minister to Liberia, J. L. Johnson, he provided full documentation of the UNIA's activities, which Johnson transmitted to his superiors on July 16, 1921.

Amy Ashwood Garvey
Courtesy Lionel Yard

Amy Jacques Garvey
From Amy Jacques Garvey (ed.),
Philosophy and Opinions of Marcus Garvey,
courtesy Charles Scribner's Sons

The Two Wives of Marcus Garvey

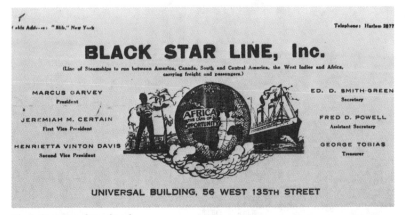

Black Star Line letterhead
Courtesy Federal Archives and Records Center, Bayonne, New Jersey

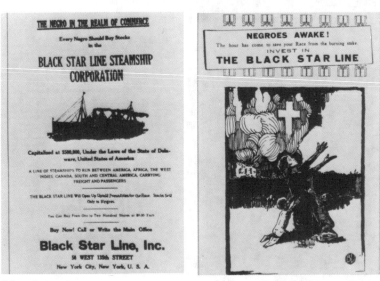

Advertisements
Courtesy New York State Archives, State Education Department, Albany, N.Y. 12230

Appeals of the Black Star Line

Yarmouth
(*Frederick Douglass*)

Shadyside

Kanawha

General Goethals
(*Booker T. Washington*)

Black Star Line Ships

Photographs from Amy Jacques Garvey (ed.), *Philosophy and Opinions of Marcus Garvey*, courtesy Charles Scribner's Sons

Jeremiah Certain, first vice president

Edward Smith-Green, secretary

George Tobias, treasurer

Fred D. Powell, assistant secretary
and assistant treasurer

Captain Joshua Cockburn

Officers of the Black Star Line

Photographs courtesy New York State Archives,
State Education Department, Albany, N.Y. 12230

The UNIA's team of experts sent to Liberia in 1921. *Seated, left to right:* G. O. Marke, supreme deputy of the UNIA; Cyril Critchlow, resident secretary. *Standing, left to right:* Rupert Jemmott, builder; J. Laurence, pharmacist; Cyril Henry, agriculturalist; Israel McLeod, surveyor.

From Amy Jacques Garvey (ed.), *Philosophy and Opinions of Marcus Garvey,* courtesy Charles Scribner's Sons

Garvey in his UNIA ceremonial regalia

Courtesy Schomburg Center for Research in Black
Culture, The New York Public Library, Astor,
Lenox and Tilden Foundations

Scene in front of Liberty Hall during the UNIA convention of 1921

From *The Independent*, February 26, 1921

UNIA Conventions and Parades

UNIA officials reviewing a parade during the 1922
convention. Gabriel Johnson is in the light-colored
cape. Garvey is to his immediate left.

From Amy Jacques Garvey (ed.), *Philosophy and Opinions of Marcus
Garvey*, courtesy Charles Scribner's Sons

UNIA parade in 1925. The sign reads, GARVEY IS IN PRISON, GARVEYISM IS AT LARGE.
From *Philosophy and Opinions of Marcus Garvey*, courtesy Charles Scribner's Sons

On board the SS *Saramacca* before Garvey's deportation from New Orleans in 1927.
Left to right: J. A. Craigen, Detroit UNIA; S. V. Robertson, Cleveland UNIA; Garvey;
E. B. Knox, Chicago UNIA; William Ware, Cincinnati UNIA; J. J. Peters, New
Orleans UNIA.

Photograph by A. P. Bedou, reproduced courtesy Xavier University of Louisiana.

Critchlow, a director of the Black Star Line and official stenographer of the UNIA, was planning to go to Liberia to begin a business school like the one he ran in Harlem. His appointment revealed that Garvey trusted neither Gabriel Johnson nor George O. Marke, a former civil servant from Sierra Leone who had been elected supreme deputy of the UNIA. A carpenter, a pharmacist, a surveyor, and an agricultural expert completed the UNIA group. The carpenter was told to construct housing for the UNIA delegation "as cheaply as possible"; the pharmacist was to open a drugstore "to sell medicine to the local public"; the agriculturist was to start farming immediately. Materials unavailable in Liberia would be sent on the ship Garvey expected to buy, which was to sail in March or April, 1921.[37]

The delegation sailed on January 20 and arrived in Liberia in March. Gabriel Johnson easily arranged a meeting with the Liberian cabinet because he was part of Liberia's ruling family network. President Charles D. E. King had married his niece, and former president Arthur Barclay had married his sister. His brother was a justice on the Supreme Court, and his son-in-law was a member of the cabinet.[38]

Because President King was in the United States attempting to renegotiate the American loan, Edwin Barclay, the secretary of state, presided. The Liberians' response was correct and helpful, but cautious. Acting upon a Liberian nationalism unmodified by Pan-Africanism, the cabinet welcomed foreign resources but restricted their use. The UNIA could work in established settlements, which meant that the undeveloped hinterlands would be closed to them and their operations would be scrutinized where Liberian authority was effective. Ships flying Liberian flags would have to be owned and manned by Liberians. By law only Liberians could own real property in the country. Therefore, the Parent Body of the UNIA in New York would not own the land they intended to use and develop. Legal claims to assets would be uncertain because Johnson was the constitutional head of the UNIA and the Liberian chapter of the UNIA was the official sponsor of the project. In the end, any dispute would be settled in Liberian courts, where the UNIA held no greater advantage than other non-Liberian litigants making claims against Liberians.[39]

At the cabinet meeting, Johnson, explaining the purpose and projects of the UNIA to the other Liberian officials, underscored the point that the

37. MG to Gabriel Johnson, February 1, 1921, H. F. Worsley to Joseph Johnson, July 9, 1921, in RG 59.

38. J. L. Johnson to Secretary of State, July 16, 1921, Cyril Critchlow to MG, June 24, 1921, Consul, Monrovia, to Secretary of State, June 25, 1921, in RG 59; author's interview with Rupert Jemmott, June 6, 1976.

39. Critchlow to MG, June 24, 1921, in RG 59.

UNIA's anti-imperialism was "only propaganda." Barclay did not need that reassurance. He informed the delegation that

> the British and French have enquired from our representatives in America about it and have asked definite questions on the attitude of the Liberian Government towards the UNIA. I will say this among ourselves. There isn't a Negro in the world who, if given the opportunity and the power to do certain things, will not do them. But it is not always advisable nor politic to openly expose our secret intentions—our secret thoughts. That is the way we do—or rather don't do—in Liberia. We don't tell them what we think; we only tell them what we like them to hear—what, in fact, they like to hear.[40]

Liberian habits, so carefully cultivated in their dealings with white nations, were not without use in their dealings with black Americans. The productive partnership that Johnson had promised UNIA delegates in New York became in reality a one-sided relationship. Marke told Critchlow that "the American and West Indian Negroes could control things on their side of the water; we Africans will run things over here. We hold the trump cards." Indeed they did. Critchlow could not execute the impossible task of controlling the African members of the UNIA. Relations between Johnson and Critchlow were poor. Johnson's son Hilary, installed in the UNIA office, proceeded to usurp Critchlow's authority. An architect and builder by training, Hilary Johnson had attended a college in the United States and believed himself superior to most of the Afro-American Garveyites in Liberia. Gabriel Johnson let it be known that he planned to replace Critchlow with Hilary, who was about to be married and needed "a good job by which he can support a wife."[41]

Garvey had hoped that Critchlow could prevent Johnson from engaging in any "other line of business outside of what his position as Potentate calls for." This assignment was hopeless. The Johnson family was involved in numerous interrelated small businesses. Gabriel ran a motor launch boat for travel on the St. Paul River. His wife had a dress shop in Monrovia. His son-in-law Momalu Massaquoi, an assimilated Vai, headed his own development corporation. Massaquoi financed the newspaper, the *Liberian Patriot*, edited by Hilary. The potentate spent more time on his private interests than on UNIA matters and apparently thought the UNIA was a means to advance them. He planned to lease an old building he owned to the association for its drugstore. He arranged to have the UNIA rent land, later discovered to be poor and worn out, from a woman to whom he owed a

40. Edwin Barclay, "Minutes of Meeting," March 22, 1921, in RG 59.
41. *Ibid.*

favor. Although this behavior was not a good omen for UNIA success, it was not unusual. The constitutional provision that only Liberians could own land was supposed to protect the nation from foreign control, but in practice it functioned more to enhance the income of the Liberian elite.[42]

Dual allegiance was neither unique to Liberians nor the cause of the rupture within the UNIA delegation. The Reverend Francis W. Ellegor, high commissioner of the UNIA and a member of its executive council, hoped that the UNIA association with Gabriel Johnson would help his own export-import business. Garvey himself had asked Critchlow to investigate the possibility of obtaining land for his own personal use. For his part, Critchlow planned to set up his business school while working for the UNIA, as he had in New York.[43]

Meager UNIA resources terminated the first UNIA initiative in Liberia after only a few weeks. By April 18 funds had run out, and work surveying land and constructing houses came to a halt. Garvey was in desperate financial difficulties. In March, without fanfare, he had endorsed the United States government's loan to Liberia. His wide financial commitments could not be met. Most money collected in 1921 had to be used to pay salaries and debts in America and deposits on ships.[44]

Johnson appropriated for himself most of the £123 that arrived from the Parent Body on May 31, and departed for New York. Confident that Johnson could convince Garvey to get rid of Critchlow, Marke seized control of the Liberian organization and its finances. While Marke plotted, Critchlow was ill with blackwater fever. He asked for the aid of the American minister to reverse Marke's coup. Writing to Garvey, he excused this appeal to the American government by citing the precedent of Garvey's own behavior: "I did neither more nor less than Your Excellency [Garvey] has done on several occasions in the attempt to secure justice for himself and his cause in the Federal Courts. [The American legation] is an arm of the Government whose functions, *inter alia*, are to protect the oppressed and see that justice is done alike to all." Counseling the techniques that the Liberians excelled in, Critchlow urged Garvey to support Gabriel Johnson "in all things calling for diplomacy; otherwise the clannishness and sensitiveness of Liberians will be their trump card to make or break, which will but lead to irrevocable disaster and failure. This would be unfortunate from any angle. Liberia must be developed and the world of Negroes must accomplish it. It would be regrettable if the Association could not be the means to ac-

42. Critchlow to MG, June 24, 1921, in RG 59; Liebenow, *Liberia*, 136.
43. Cyril Critchlow to MG, July 21, 1921, in RG 59.
44. *Ibid.*; NW, March 26, 1921.

complish this glorious result. I can afford to overlook any personal differences for the larger welfare of the race and the UNIA."[45]

Ex-Garveyite Cyril Henry expanded upon Critchlow's criticism of the Liberians. Henry had left the UNIA to go to Liberia as an agricultural expert with the white Methodist Episcopal Church, the largest missionary presence in the country. Although not officially with the UNIA party, he had offered his services to Gabriel Johnson, who rejected them. Nevertheless, Henry accompanied Critchlow and others of the American group on a search for coal, gold, and diamond deposits. Because he was the only member of the group with knowledge of geology, his presence was valuable even though the search for riches was unsuccessful. Henry maintained a warm interest in the UNIA and periodically offered friendly advice and criticism to his friend Orlando Thompson, vice-president of the Black Star Line. In line with Mulzac's criticism of the operation of the Black Star Line, Henry found that the UNIA tried to do too many things for its slender resources. "The ponderous official salary list" and the rewards allotted to influential newcomers demoralized older members.[46]

Liberian sins, however, were more serious because they made genuine Pan-Africanism impossible. According to Henry, the Liberians welcomed Afro-Americans, but they were quick to warn that "your [Afro-American] numbers, your influence and combined power should not be sufficient to supplant our political preferments; i.e., the presidency, the secretaryship, consulships abroad, customs service, etc. You must adopt our ways, be scattered amongst us, not combined, be not ever-zealous about the welfare of the aborigines—us first. And do not place us at odds with the white governments from whom we expect favors."[47]

Garvey, who privately indicted the Liberians even as he wooed them publicly, and Henry both believed that the Liberian elite deliberately sacrificed the development of their country, and implicitly the power of the black world, to the preservation of its own power. On the other hand, they believed that the UNIA and Afro-Americans were idealistic and capable practitioners of Pan-Africanism. While their judgments stemmed from subjectively experienced points of conflict, they did not address the heart of the problem. Africans in the British colonies and Liberia wanted capital and skilled men from black America. Liberians had tried to extract resources from their own producers—the indigenous peoples—with little

45. J. W. Johnson to Secretary of State, June 25, 1921, Critchlow to MG, July 21, 1921, Critchlow to Secretary of State, September 21, 1921, in RG 59.
46. Cyril Henry to Orlando Thompson, July 1, 1921, in RG 59.
47. *Ibid.*

success.[48] Primitive methods of production could not yield the surplus necessary for development. Even if the elite had been more frugal and hard-working, Liberians could not have modernized the nation independently. Therefore, they sought foreign capital, the results of the accumulations from the expanded production of industrial capitalism.

Liberians tried but failed to obtain foreign investments for roads, railroads, and harbors—an infrastructure. A British corporation concluded in 1924 that "no scheme of development will pay in a country which is too small and still too undeveloped." So Liberians, hoping to discover a profitable resource that would justify further investment, feverishly granted concessions to alien capitalists. With cheaper alternatives, foreigners invested in other places.[49]

The UNIA appeared to offer capital and the rhetoric of alternative development. But capital was generated by a social process with power relations. The UNIA demanded separate settlements, just as the funders of Liberia's loans demanded political changes in Liberia's government, in order to control the resources and labor of the nation. Capitalist values and competition were the determinants of relations between Afro-Americans and the Liberian elite.[50] Moreover, Afro-Americans would not have been able to avoid the logic of settlement in its relations with the indigenous Africans. The UNIA plans were never tested, because the organization lacked the capital to embark upon them. But the history of the Black Star Line and other UNIA businesses infused with similar ideology and rhetoric does not support the view that Garveyism offered Liberia a realistic or harmonious road to development.

Differences between the Liberian elite and UNIA leaders were overt. The divergent interests of the Afro-American working class and Liberia were covert but fundamental within the UNIA conception of development. Garvey possessed even less control of productive processes than the Liberian elite. His capital came from voluntary contributions from the Afro-American working class. Cyril Henry recalled his experiences "upon the voyages of the 'Yarmouth' and sojourn in Panama. But for my ready sales of stock to liquidate debts, we would have met disaster on more than one occasion. Here [in Liberia] there is neither enthusiasm nor the money to raise

48. The Liberians also stepped up the collection of internal taxes. A new hut tax in 1916 was a major cause of internal rebellion but represented one-third of all government revenue in 1922. Akpan, "Liberia and the UNIA," 111.

49. Robert R. Durrant, *Liberia: A Report by the Special Commissioner in West Africa for the African International Corporation* (London, 1925), 70.

50. For an example of the competitiveness of the African and Afro-American elites see the Reverend A. Agbebi to John Bruce, June 25, 1920, in Bruce Papers.

by the sale of stocks." The UNIA's temporary ability to convince American blacks to invest in the Black Star Line and Liberia produced the possibility of a trans-Atlantic alliance. But Afro-Americans would not sacrifice their own future for the benefit of Liberians. Pan-African assertions and feelings unsupported by mutual advantage quickly dissolved.[51]

Individual ambitions that initially fed Pan-Africanism in Liberia soon were in conflict with racial solidarity. Rupert Jemmott's story is significant. A carpenter born in Barbados, he was one of the experts Garvey sent to Liberia. He had worked on the Panama Canal, rising to a position of foreman. After its completion he supervised construction in Havana and the United States, where he obtained an engineering degree at Chicago Technical Institute. While he was a foreman, supervising the building of a Ford plant in Detroit in 1920, a friend informed him that a fellow islander was selling stock in the Black Star Line. His feeling of Barbadian solidarity overcame his suspicions, and he purchased twenty shares. At the time, Jemmott was earning over a hundred dollars a week.[52]

In early 1921, he was living in Harlem and working in the New York area. He had heard that the UNIA needed skilled men for a development project in Liberia. Personal reasons, such as the chance to travel to Africa, were as tempting as anything else to him. Garvey promptly signed him to a six-month contract to survey land for the UNIA. After the suspension of UNIA plans, Jemmott decided to stay in Liberia. Its government promised him the post of superintendent of construction if it obtained the five-million-dollar loan it sought from the United States in 1922. But the loan did not come through, and sixteen months after Jemmott arrived in Liberia, he returned to the United States. There he continued his successful career, working on bridges and factories. In 1933, he went into business for himself and became a prosperous building contractor.[53]

Men like Jemmott were as critical as Captain Mulzac to the establishment of the legitimacy of UNIA enterprise and ideology. But for most of these men, the UNIA served no function. Jemmott was never a member. He was too busy at work that gave him money, status, and adventure. His decisions were dictated by his career, not by ideology. He went to Liberia for personal, not UNIA, purposes, and to realize his ambitions, he needed Liberian, not UNIA, support. In turn, to become a construction chief, he required the United States loan along with all of the related social and political baggage that conflicted with racial independence. When the United States Senate rejected the loan in 1922, Jemmott immediately obtained a

51. Cyril Henry to Orlando Thompson, July 1, 1921, in RG 59.
52. *Ibid.*; interview with Jemmott.
53. Interview with Jemmott.

new job surveying land in Rio de Janeiro. Neither the UNIA nor Liberia offered skilled black men as much opportunity as the wider world. Racial appeals were attractive, but they were insufficient to encourage collective behavior. And mere exhortation could not impose the disciplined purpose and effort necessary to pursue seriously, not to mention achieve the success of, the UNIA's plans in Liberia. Garveyism in Liberia ran into the same kinds of dissension and conflict that it did in the United States. And neither in Africa nor in America could the UNIA resolve the problems that resulted.

7 / The Twenties
Political Poverty and Economic Progress

The halting of the Liberian work was one result of the UNIA's acute financial crisis in 1921. Membership fees for the year yielded less than four thousand dollars. Various special drives raised income to ninety thousand dollars, but more than half of the revenue was earmarked for the salaries of UNIA officials. Money problems were signs of the deeper crisis. "Of the 480 chartered divisions, only a few made reports," Garvey acknowledged àt the second UNIA convention in August. Many members lost their jobs or suffered wage cuts, and abandoned the UNIA at the same time that its leaders were asking for funds to resurrect the organization's failing enterprises. Precipitated by reduced government spending and declining demand for American exports, the depression of 1920–1921 was sharpest in the Tidewater area and in midwestern cities, which had attracted many blacks during the war. Nationwide unemployment hovered above 20 percent, and over 100,000 marginal businessmen went bankrupt. The depression showed that the UNIA had been built on black prosperity, despite its leaders' claim that they had created it. The true relationship between the UNIA and the economy can be seen in the story of Thomas Cort, an independent artisan and BSL investor from Galveston, Texas.[1]

Cort had done repair work for the U.S. Shipping Board on a contract basis during the war. In 1919 he purchased BSL stock with an eye to his retirement. Before he invested his money, however, he traveled to New York, where company officers convinced him that the corporation would "pay from 40 to 50 cents a share within the next year." Cort paid two hundred dollars for forty shares of stock and returned to Galveston. The anxious investor sent a steady stream of letters to New York to obtain information about the company's prospects. In 1921, Cort went out of business, a victim of the depression in shipping. Now he needed employment, not future income. The BSL offered him a position as a ship repairer in June, but

1. Thomas Merrilees, "Summary Report of Investigation of Books and Records of THE BLACK STAR LINE, INC., AND THE UNIVERSAL NEGRO IMPROVEMENT ASSOCIATION . . ." October 26, 1922, p. 14, in Garvey file, RG 65. The BSL bank balance was only $638.91 in May, 1921, according to the *NW*, October 1, 1921.

when Cort and his wife arrived in New York in July, the line was no longer operating ships. Like Hugh Mulzac, Cort tried to create a business independent of the UNIA. But ship repair work was no more viable in New York than in Galveston. His subsequent effort to start a laundry was no more successful. Black entrepreneurial ambitions required a more favorable economic climate.[2]

Despite the disaffections, debts, and poor prospects for racial enterprise, Garvey decided to replay the script of 1919 and 1920 by obtaining a new and better ship. Big enough to sail to Africa, the new ship would simultaneously revive the BSL, the UNIA, and the plans to colonize Liberia. The decision was partly shaped by Garvey's personality and past success. His brief triumph had come after a long period of fruitless effort, anonymity, and occasional ridicule. Garvey explained accurately that the BSL had "brought into the fold of the UNIA hundreds of thousands of Negro men and women who could never have been reached otherwise. . . . It elevated the Negro from the state of indifference and nonrecognition to a position of recognition."[3] It also elevated Garvey. His failure to assess accurately the current prospects for a shipping line or the divisive aspects of BSL history suggests not only that Garvey was seeking to remain in the limelight but also that there was no obvious alternative to the methods that had brought him glory. His difficulties, if not his solutions, were shared by most racial leaders of the time. The black militancy during the war was nurtured by the era of revolutionary assertion. The stagnation of racial politics during the 1920s was rooted in a global reconstruction that muted dissent, paralyzed popular politics, and ended the gains extracted from nations at war.

Like the different dreams and fears of 1919, the new order was worldwide. The political benchmarks were victories of right-wing parties—Mussolini's Fascists in 1922, the South African Nationalists and British Conservatives in 1924—and the defeats of left-wing movements—the huge French strikes in the spring of 1920, the American strikes of 1922, the state governments of the left in Germany in 1923. The chorus of dissent was softer now. A police observer of Pan-African organizations on the West Coast of Africa noted that "the tone of their meetings has been much more moderate. . . . I am glad to say that there is now an entire absence of 'Africa for the Africans only and as early as possible.'"[4] The forces of the left were in retreat throughout the world. Bourgeois society was stronger than its attackers

2. Thomas Cort, "Interview," February 3, 1922, in Garvey file, RG 65.
3. *NW*, August 6, 1921, August 26, 1922.
4. J. Ayodele Langley, *Pan-Africanism and Nationalism in West Africa, 1900–1945* (Oxford, 1973), 149.

had imagined. A mixture of repression, payoffs, and fatigue produced a new political stability. The Great Depression would reveal that the new reconstruction was weaker than its prophets proclaimed, but that still lay ahead.

All popular leaders commented on the change. In 1924 Garvey concluded that "1914 and 1919 up to 1922 presented the one glorious time and opportunity for the Negro. . . . The world has practically returned to its normal attitude." At the 1921 Comintern meetings, Leon Trotsky had said: "Now we see . . . that we are not so near the goal of the conquest of power, of the world revolution. We formerly believed in 1919, that it was only a question of months and now we say it is perhaps a question of years." Popular leaders were forced to rethink the question of organization and tactics in the new period, which socialists called one of "capitalist stabilization" and which capitalists termed a time of "reorganization."[5]

Although the new economic order was literally mortgaged to American prosperity, the United States appeared to be a firm anchor. Its young automobile, chemical, and electrical industries nourished a construction boom and new consumer goods, the playthings of the Roaring Twenties. The "new capitalism" was also at the root of more durable items. A sweeping application of mass-production techniques and new machinery increased American output 13 percent but reduced the work force 8 percent. The 29 percent rise in worker productivity yielded an increase of only 4½ percent in real wages. Profits soared.[6]

The weakness of unions and popular politics during the 1920s not only facilitated the increase in power of American capitalists but was a prerequisite to it. The number of workers in the trade union movement declined from 5 million in 1920 to 3.4 million in 1929. By 1923, when the economic boom began, about 90 percent of the losses had already taken place. A series of bitter, unsuccessful strikes from 1919 through 1922 decimated unions. Rationalization, new machinery, the speedup, and unemployment came in the wake of defeat. Political organizations of the working class had been early casualties. The effects of repression on the Socialist party were already visible in the last year of the war. The ensuing Red Scare put Socialist leaders on the defensive at a time when the Bolshevik triumph in Russia had challenged their gradualist practices. Socialists counted 110,000 members in 1919; in 1923, they numbered 12,000. The party vanished from

5. *NW*, August 23, 1924; Theodore Draper, *The Roots of American Communism* (New York, 1957), 275; Charles S. Maier, *Recasting Bourgeois Europe: Stabilization in France, Germany, Italy in the Decade After World War I* (Princeton, 1976), 193–99.

6. Solomon Fabricant, *Employment in Manufacturing, 1899–1939* (New York, 1942), 142; Harry Jerome, *Mechanization in Industry* (New York, 1934), 218–25.

whole areas in the Southwest and the Middle West. The accumulated political knowledge and self-confidence of the prewar period disappeared as individuals scattered. Where the party survived, it was too weak to apply what it remembered. The new Communist party, formed out of the Socialist split, was incapacitated because most of its leaders were underground or under indictment. When it emerged publicly in 1923, its small size, 15,000 members, precluded serious efforts to initiate its ambitious agenda. The class conflicts it hoped to politicize were in decline. Born in the atmosphere of revolutionary possibility, the Communist party was incubated in the period of conservative reaction.[7]

Organized blacks suffered the same kinds of defeats as other workers on the docks and railroads and in packinghouses and coal mines. The National Brotherhood Workers, the ambitious black trade union created in 1919, did not survive the retreat.[8] Racial strategies dependent upon popular power came to seem utopian, as the allies that had spearheaded the movement—the IWW, the Socialist party, and the unions—vanished from the political landscape. A few black militants like A. Philip Randolph continued to act on the belief that working-class organization was the prerequisite of racial progress. After several false starts, Randolph eventually found a vehicle in the Brotherhood of Sleeping Car Porters in 1925. However, success—a union contract—was not achieved until 1937. Along the way, Randolph's militant comrade Chandler Owen exchanged the frustrations of working-class organization for the more certain dividends of the real estate business. Independent black militance was as short-lived as black unionism. Cyril Briggs flirted briefly with Garveyism before abandoning his African Blood Brotherhood for a home in the Communist party. Lacking victories until the 1930s, communism and unionism were no rivals to the faltering but remembered success of the BSL and racial enterprise.[9]

Although not so tied to the fate of popular politics and organization, the objectives of the Urban League and the NAACP were slowed by the postwar economic crisis. The leaders of both groups accommodated to the new climate. The Urban League negotiated with businesses for relief and

7. Leo Wolman, *The Growth of American Trade Unions, 1880–1923* (New York, 1924), 26, 33–37; James Weinstein, *The Decline of Socialism in America, 1912–1925* (New York, 1967), 272–89; Draper, *The Roots of American Communism*, 38–39; James Green, *Grass-Roots Socialism* (Baton Rouge, 1978), 396–97.

8. "Negroes and Radicalism," January 21, 1921, file 10110-2271/1, MID, in RG 165; Horace Cayton and George Mitchell, *Black Workers and the New Unions* (Chapel Hill, 1939), 251–56; Philip Foner, *Organized Labor and the Black Worker, 1619–1973* (New York, 1974), 161; George Haynes to Vernon Kellogg, March 15, 1921, in NAACP Papers.

9. Author's interview with A. Philip Randolph, July 19, 1978; William Harris, *Keeping the Faith: A. Philip Randolph, Milton P. Webster and the Brotherhood of Sleeping Car Porters, 1925–1937* (Urbana, 1977).

jobs. Without challenging the prerogatives of management, the league possessed only the Tuskegee-created stereotype of black docility and its modern successor, "Americanism," to combat unemployment. It reminded corporate executives that black workers, "although in desperate circumstances . . . are not given to radical or Bolshevistic attitudes, accepting their lot with an admirable fortitude." The Urban League's orthodoxy ensured its survival and expansion to seventeen new cities after 1923. Institutional growth, however, was not identical to racial power.[10]

Although the NAACP delegated economic issues to the Urban League, its ability to fight for racial equality was impaired by the sharp falloff of black contributions because of the depression.[11] As the search for work subsumed other goals, most blacks found the agenda of the NAACP even more remote, though if asked, they probably would have applauded its principal objective from 1919 through 1923, the passage of antilynching legislation. Although briefly attracted to mass politics and actions during 1919 and 1920, the NAACP returned without regret to prewar practices of appealing to businessmen and the Republican party. The tactics aborted local initiatives and implicitly denied the role of black organizations in altering public opinion. Predisposed by education, social position, and expediency to a concept of gradual change, NAACP leaders retreated still further from popular action to pursue individual cases of injustice in the courts after the antilynching bill failed to pass the Senate in 1923.[12]

The toll the depression took on the UNIA was potentially greater than on its rivals. Black militants like Randolph and Briggs suffered frustration but lacked substantial organization vulnerable to the new conditions. Leaders of the NAACP and Urban League absorbed setbacks because their goal, the improvement of race relations, and their method, lobbying, were viable under any balance of power. But Garvey had pioneered a new method of racial advance—the mass organization of urban communities behind black business enterprise. The UNIA promised that its own economic

10. Forrester Washington to James Weldon Johnson, June 3, 1921, Box C-320, in NAACP Papers; T. F. Woofter to R. R. Moton, February 18, 1921, in Moton Papers; Pittsburgh chapter, National Association of Corporate Training, "Minutes of Meeting 'Unskilled Labor and America,'" February, 1922, Ser. 4, and Eugene Jones to Executive Board, March 18, 1921, both in National Urban League Papers.

11. Like Garvey, NAACP leaders discovered numerous weak or "defunct branches" of their organization beginning in 1921. Some attributed the decline to the "general economic depression." Others attributed NAACP problems to its strategy and leadership. Frank Bell to Walter White, December 21, 1924, Box C-320, David Pierce to Herbert J. Seligmann, October 25, 1930, Box G-158, "Report of A. W. Hunton," October 18–December 6, 1921, "Branch Bulletin," n.d. [1921], 38, Box C-8, in NAACP Papers.

12. George Harris to James W. Johnson, December 3, 1923, Box G-65, Walter White to Carter Woodson, January 27, 1921, Box C-8, White to Johnson, December 4, 1923, Box C-389, in NAACP Papers.

power would improve the status of the race. Without enterprise, the UNIA risked destruction. Therefore, Garvey attempted to restore the BSL by buying another ship, even though he lacked sufficient capital and a favorable market. He adjusted his earlier exuberance and scaled down some of his pledges. He did not dangle the promise of profit but emphasized the grim reminder that blacks lacked alternatives. He advised a New York audience to remain and work for the UNIA because "there were no jobs elsewhere. I have been travelling for the last couple of months and in all of the western states I have seen Negroes out of work in centers like Pittsburgh, Detroit, Cleveland, Columbus, Youngstown, and Chicago. So you might as well stay where you are and face the situation." Garvey's tour of the Midwest had sometimes attracted crowds, but it rarely brought in sufficient money to pay for his expenses. Assistant Vice-President William Ferris was equally unsuccessful in New England. He found that people "do not invest money in extraneous business propositions."[13]

Garvey appealed once again to the black middle class. He asked "the men of the Negro race who have $1000 to invest at least $500 in the Black Star Line so that we can transport the unemployed from this Western Hemisphere to Africa." Unanswered, Garvey turned to his existing constituency. He asked the presidents of the fourteen largest UNIA divisions to raise twenty-five thousand dollars, and he sailed to the West Indies on February 23 to try to raise more money. Garvey also empowered BSL Vice-President Orlando M. Thompson and UNIA Counsel-General Wilfred Smith to purchase a ship.[14]

The new maritime conditions made it easier to purchase ships at the same time they made it harder to profit from them. Ocean rates had plummeted, and the volume of world trade contracted quickly at the onset of the depression in late 1920. Between September, 1920, and June, 1921, the *Yarmouth*'s freight income was only $8,644, compared to $32,210 for the preceding year; passenger receipts had declined from $12,578 to $4,696. The BSL owed money on its past purchases, for repairs on the *Kanawha*, and to creditors and employees who had successfully sued the company. But the contraction also lowered the price of ships. Vice-President Thompson obtained the services of an optimistic broker, Anton Silverstone, who promised to obtain an African ship for the BSL.[15]

13. *NW*, February 19, 26, 1921. While the new advertisements urged purchases to provide black jobs, the old promise of dividends continued, too. See *NW*, February 12, April 2, 1921.

14. Mortimer J. Davis, "Summary Report," November, 1922, p. 23, in Garvey file, RG 65; *NW*, February 12, 1921.

15. Merrilees, "Summary Report," 11, 32; Orlando Thompson, "Interview," January 13, 1922, in Garvey file, RG 65.

Silverstone agreed to purchase a ship for $350,000, which included the costs of necessary repairs and his commission. He placed bids on two ships offered by the U.S. Shipping Board, mandated by the Merchant Marine Act of June, 1920, to sell the more than one thousand ships it still operated. The board's original goal of promoting American shipping and markets competed with a new mission of selling the government fleet quickly, a boon to private carriers and private enterprise. Nevertheless, the board concluded that Silverstone's $190,000 offer for the SS *Orion* was too low. The former German steel ship had been valued at $675,000 in late 1920, and officials thought $400,000 a fair price in the depressed market of 1921. Silverstone then bid $225,000 for the smaller *Porto Rico*. The ship, in a Brooklyn dry dock, was inspected by several directors and Hugh Mulzac. Chosen the future captain of the vessel, Mulzac recruited a black crew and came to New York to help raise money for the ship. But the Shipping Board rejected the bid on June 28 because the "company of Negroes . . . had never operated a ship" and proposed to use it for the African trade, not the "Puerto Rican trade," for which it was built. "It would be against the spirit of the Merchant Marine Act, 1920, to take the vessel out of the trade for which she is equipped and needed," the board concluded. Although the board was ignorant of the Black Star Line's experience in the field, accurate information obviously would not have yielded a favorable decision.[16]

Silverstone turned again to the *Orion*. He increased the bid on the larger ship from $190,000 to $225,000. The board looked more favorably on the offer because the ship's charterer had canceled its contract when the vessel was not delivered on time. The commander now believed that $200,000 in cash was "a fair price given the age, the length of time on the hands of the Board, its cost of maintenance if in dry dock, and the newly passed Immigration Restriction Act." The board still did not think there was enough trade between the United States and Liberia "to warrant putting steamers in that trade," but it accepted the bid on July 19 "on condition that the ship remained under American flag and pending a report of the financial condition of the company."[17]

The UNIA's urgency exceeded the pace of bureaucratic decision making,

16. For the changes in the terms of sale, see Darrell H. Smith and Paul V. Betters, *The United States Shipping Board* (Washington, D.C., 1931), 48–56. Under the new policy, the down payment was reduced from 25 percent to 10 percent. J. Harry Philbin, "Memoranda," October 25, 1920, May 11, 1921, no. 796.2 Orion, June 22, 28, 1921, and no. 796.2 M71, Porto Rico, all in file 605-1-653, RG 32.

17. In June, 1921, after the installation of a new board, officials reevaluated pricing policy in view of the depression. U.S. Shipping Board, *Sixth Annual Report* (Washington, D.C., 1922), 80; Philbin, "Memorandum," July 6, 1921, "Minutes" of board meeting, June 22, 28, July 19, 1921, file 605-1-653, in RG 32.

which was slowed by the appointment of new personnel on the board. Garvey hoped to use the ship at the convention of August, 1921, to answer growing criticism. Earlier, on the strength of Thompson's promises that the *Porto Rico* sale was certain and imminent, the BSL directors had designed celebrations in Norfolk, Philadelphia, and New York. Memory of the *Yarmouth* festivities informed plans to sell stock and charge an admission price of a dollar to view the ship. They planned to invite the most important black leaders in the country to a luncheon on July 4 to secure their moral and financial support. Thompson told local leaders to "spread the good news along, sell all the stock you can so that we might be able to put on the fuel, stores, and linen that is necessary to send her out to sea." But the Shipping Board's rejection of the bid on the *Porto Rico* dampened spirits and set off another round of recriminations. Then things reversed themselves again, as a decision to revoke Silverstone's legal authority was rescinded when the Shipping Board accepted the UNIA's bid for the *Orion* on August 2.[18]

The board's decision did not quiet Black Star Line investors. One angry group demanded an accounting at the August convention. Garvey legalistically dismissed their complaints by distinguishing the UNIA from the BSL. He appealed to the loyalty of the delegates. When persuasion failed, the African Legion, positioned at strategic places about the hall, intimidated dissidents. Garvey blamed the delays on unnamed traitors who had sabotaged the affairs of the line when he was attempting to raise money in the West Indies. But he retained his negotiating team of Thompson, Garcia, Silverstone, and Wilfred Smith. Along with them he continued to work through the month of the convention to obtain the *Orion*. Explanations to stockholders by Garvey and other leaders prevented wholesale disaffection but failed to win their confidence, much less their enthusiasm, prerequisites for raising the necessary sums of money for the new ship.[19]

The Shipping Board required, first, a $22,500 deposit (10 percent of the $225,000 purchase price); second, another 10 percent in cash and a performance bond for the unpaid balance on delivery; and finally, payments of 10 percent a month, plus a small interest charge, until the purchase was completed. The initial hurdle was the deposit. Although Silverstone had re-

18. Merrilees, "Summary Report," 11–12; Orlando Thompson to William Ware, June 24, 1921, *Marcus Garvey* v. *United States of America*, 267 U.S. 607 (1924), 2722. Final acceptance upon completion of a financial report was routine. The board had rejected a bid from the Polish-American Navigation Co. because a credit report revealed it was not a "good business risk." "Minutes" of board meeting, November 8, 1920, file 605-1-653, in RG 32.

19. For the variety of complaints see Edward Brennan to William Burns, May 24, 1922, and V. Rider, report, June 14, 1922, in Garvey file, RG 65.

ceived $25,000 from the Black Star Line, he placed only $12,500 of the required $22,500 with the Shipping Board. He told the directors that he had spent the difference on attending expenses. Undoubtedly, he had used some of the funds traveling to and from Washington. Money, no doubt, was passed around to officials, lawyers, and other brokers and agents to facilitate business. These "costs of doing business" were to be drawn from his commission. Had Silverstone been part of a well-established firm, some of the expenses would have been unnecessary and others could have been absorbed until the final contract was signed. Had the Black Star Line been a solvent corporation, additional money would have been available. Neither of these conditions existed. Silverstone's honesty was certainly questioned and questionable, but in a world where success, which all desired and needed, was just around the corner, it was not the decisive issue. Despite the escalating acrimony and mistrust, no one dared to sever a relationship whose success, it seemed, would resolve all problems.[20]

The BSL directors concluded that they could not raise the $10,000 needed to complete the deposit on the *Orion*. Therefore, Silverstone and the BSL's marine advisor and lawyer, Lloyd Nolan, borrowed the money from the Massachusetts Bonding Company, controlled by Charles Harriss, the seller of the *Yarmouth*.[21] The company refused, however, to issue the equally necessary performance bond. In late October, Nolan told associates that no bonding company would issue surety under current shipping conditions. The delays increased the doubts of the Shipping Board, and it contemplated canceling the contract. In December, it doubled the size of the performance bond to $400,000. The directors made a last desperate effort to raise cash to pay for the ship, which would eliminate the need for credit. Nolan made a novel proposition to two new brokers. The UNIA would sell $202,500 in bonds to its members in return for a cash advance of $135,000, plus commission. He agreed to the condition that the *Orion* would be managed by a shipping company named by the brokers, who would be paid from the sale of bonds and from freight and passenger profits. In short, to obtain a ship the BSL managers were prepared to accept only the symbol of ownership, yielding the substance.[22]

20. Merrilees, "Summary Report," 26; Philbin, "Memorandum," July 6, 1921, in RG 32; Anton Silverstone to BSL, June 16, 1921, *Garvey* v. *U.S.A.*, 2663. In his "Statement" to Agent Mortimer Davis in November, 1921, Silverstone alluded to friends on the Shipping Board who had facilitated the transaction. Garvey file, RG 65.

21. Davis, report, April 20, 1922, in Garvey file, RG 65. Nolan was brought into BSL negotiations by UNIA lawyer James Watson. *Garvey* v. *U.S.A.*, 2702–11.

22. Harry Philbin to Shipping Board, September 6, 1921, G.P.L. to Ship Sales Division, October 5, 1921, Shipping Board to General Counsel, October 8, 1921, file 605-1-653, in RG 32; Lloyd Nolan to Julius Wolff, December 28, 1922, in Garvey file, RG 65.

The prospective large profits attracted the brokers. One of them, Julius Wolff, was told that the shipping company had sold $600,000 in stock in 1921, that the UNIA had several million members, and that the funds of the UNIA could be used to pay off the BSL debt, if necessary. Impressed, Wolff later stated that he was not concerned about how the company had spent its money in the past; he was concerned only with its ability to raise the funds, because he would control the ship. Indeed, he and his partner withdrew their offer only when Garvey was arrested for mail fraud in January, 1922. Desperate, UNIA leaders turned again to the members. But knowing that in the past they had been promised ships that never appeared, Nolan asked the Shipping Board to sail the ship to New York so that UNIA members could view it. When the board refused on February 7, Nolan asked the government to return the BSL's deposit on the *Orion*. The search for a ship was suspended as the preparations for the trial of Garvey and three associates assumed priority.[23]

The timing of the board's decision to reject the BSL request and the Justice Department's indictment of BSL officers has led historians to conclude that the two were related. E. David Cronon and Tony Martin, disagreeing on many other issues, both believed that the acts of the Shipping Board were hurdles thrown up by government officials eager to rid the nation of a leading black radical. Both weighed heavily a letter that William Burns, director of the Bureau of Investigation of the Justice Department, sent to the Shipping Board on August 31, 1921. Burns informed Frank Burke of the board's Bureau of Investigation that Marcus Garvey was "negotiating at the present time for the purchase of a boat from the U.S. Shipping Board." Forwarding the information, Burke identified Garvey as the president of the UNIA, a "ratical [sic] agitator" and member of "the communist party" who "advocates and teaches the overthrow of the United States by force and violence." Cronon and Martin attributed the board's delays and the doubling of the performance bond to the Justice Department's intervention, though no other evidence supports their conclusion. The board's actual deliberations and the timing of critical decisions suggest that the warning played no role in the negotiations. It is very likely that the decision makers on the board never saw Burns's letter.[24]

23. Lloyd Nolan to Clinchfield Navigation Co., February 3, 1922, Nolan to Ship Sales Division, February 7, 1922, Ship Sales to Quartermaster Corps, February 3, 1922, file 605-1-653, in RG 32.

24. E. David Cronon, *Black Moses: The Story of Marcus Garvey and the Universal Negro Improvement Association* (Madison, 1955), 98–99; Tony Martin, *Race First: The Ideological and Organizational Struggles of Marcus Garvey and the Universal Negro Improvement Association* (Westport, Conn., 1976), 161; William Burns to Frank Burke, August 31, 1921, Burke to A. J. Frey, September 1, 1921, file 605-1-653, in RG 32.

On September 1, Burke transmitted the Burns letter to A. J. Frey, a new vice-president of the Shipping Board under the reorganization of June, 1921. But Frey was vice-president in charge of operations, not ship sales. If he thought the matter merited further attention, he would have forwarded the report to E. P. Farley, the vice-president for ship sales. The board's records reveal no evidence that Frey sent or that Farley received the information. In addition, over a month later Farley himself instructed his personnel to extend extra time to the Black Star Line. At the beginning of October the board directed its legal bureau to prepare the forms necessary to complete the transaction. There were delays in the forwarding of the papers because the new board had altered the form of its contracts. Nonetheless, the proceedings continued. All officials and agents of the Shipping Board acted as if the sale were imminent. On February 3, *after* the Justice Department's indictment, the army, which also wanted the *Orion*, was informed that the ship had been sold pending the completion of the performance bond. At no time in this process was there any hint that the Burns memo or the January indictment entered the board's judgments.[25]

The board was ignorant of the BSL and the indictment even after the sale was canceled. It planned to return the BSL deposit because its lawyers acknowledged that the board was dilatory in forwarding forms, though it was legally without fault. Counsel weighed, too, the equity of the stockholders. He said: "There is some indication . . . that the number of stockholders of the Black Star Line runs into the thousands. It is probable that they are for the most part negroes and largely ignorant of business transactions. If the matter comes to their attention they will feel that the Board is taking their money and that they have not received their ship, and thus a prejudice may be created among a large number of citizens in a matter in which the Board may not be entirely without fault." His knowledge of the Black Star Line was imperfect, but his purposes were benign, etched with paternalism, not repression. Moreover, even this limited knowledge of the racial character of the BSL was obtained from UNIA counsel Nolan, not from a government intelligence agency, on February 3, when the lawyer requested the board to sail the *Orion* to New York.[26]

The board learned of the indictment later in March when it was trying to evaluate the numerous claims to the deposit money. The manager of sales asked Frank Burke to investigate because "rumor has it that some of

25. E. P. Farley to Ship Sales Division, October 5, 1921, Ship Sales to General Counsel, October 8, 1921, Shipping Board to General Counsel, October 8, 1921, Farley to General Counsel, December 2, 1921, Ship Sales to Treasurer, January 5, 1922, Ship Sales to Quartermaster Corps, February 3, 1922, file 605-1-653, in RG 32.

26. E. Power Jones to Sanford H. E. Freund, March 6, 1922, file 605-1-653, in RG 32.

their officers are under indictment and it occurred to me possibly that the company may be in the hands of a receiver." The same Frank Burke who had been warned of Garvey in August, 1921, now asked J. Edgar Hoover whether there was "any truth in the information regarding the indictment of any of the officials of that corporation [the Black Star Line] or other legal entanglements." Thus, as late as the spring of 1922, long after the indictment, Burke did not associate Garvey with the Black Star Line. If he had connected the "communist" Marcus Garvey he had been warned about in August, 1921, with the Black Star Line he was asked about in March, 1922, he would not have had to seek information on rumors. And he would not have waited over a month before contacting the Justice Department. On April 26, Hoover confirmed the indictment of all four officers. It is likely that Burke's own interest in pursuing Garvey was not great. He transmitted Burns's August letter routinely but did not follow up on the case.[27]

To fasten on the role of Garvey's indictment in the destruction of the BSL is to ignore its history and overweigh its final act. The indictment immediately affected only the unorthodox Wolff financing. Even assuming that a ship had been obtained through the Wolff plan, it was unlikely that the BSL could have benefited the UNIA if the brokers controlled operations; it was even more unlikely that the UNIA could have repaid the loan, given its usurious terms and the shipping conditions of 1922.

The indictment did not create the ballooning opposition to Garvey's leadership of the UNIA, but it made him more vulnerable to critics. Without public announcement or fanfare, a significant exodus of UNIA leaders had proceeded throughout 1921. Most of the executive council of sixteen left before, during, and after the convention of August, 1921. Many had no motive to fight to change the UNIA, because their differences with Garvey were not ideological. They had participated in associations like the UNIA before. They would no doubt do so again, with or without the mass enthusiasm that the UNIA captured so briefly. Most had social and economic connections that made alternatives promising. A group with special interests in Pan-African economic enterprises—George O. Marke and Dr. D. D. Lewis, both Africans, F. W. Ellegor, a Guianese, and the Reverend J. D. Gordon, an American—left the UNIA when Garvey's Liberian plans faltered. Marke's departure was no more permanent than his initial commitment. He returned to join the UNIA delegation to the League of Nations in 1922.[28]

The departure of two American lawyers on the executive council also

27. H. E. Freund to Harry Philbin, March 9, 1922, in RG 32; Frank Burke to J. Edgar Hoover, April 14, 1922, Hoover to Burke, April 26, 1922, in Garvey file, RG 65.
28. *Age*, December 24, 1921.

lacked finality and ideological motive. William Matthews and Wilfred Smith both joined the UNIA in 1920 and resigned at the end of 1921. Matthews, a Harvard graduate, had worked with Monroe Trotter in Boston. He possessed the appropriate Republican loyalty and racial militance to become an assistant district attorney. UNIA Counsel-General Wilfred Smith had reached Garveyism from the opposite end of the political spectrum. Born in Mississippi in 1863, Smith, the personal lawyer of Booker T. Washington, was one of the creators of the Afro-American Realty Company, which opened up Harlem to blacks. While Garvey was away in the West Indies, Smith had supervised the negotiations for the African ship.[29] Both Matthews and Smith returned to work on preparations for Garvey's trial, which did not mean they had reevaluated the UNIA's prospects. Both of them had political ambitions but lacked a constituency. They joined the UNIA in 1920 when it seemed to have a firm popular base, left in 1921 when the organization was disintegrating, and returned to defend Garvey in 1922 when it appeared that the trial might provide a new basis for mass organization or, at the very least, the kind of career dividends garnered by legal champions of popular figures.[30]

The gradual and casual exit of the well-connected publicists crippled the ability of the UNIA to raise money, a task that would have tried the talents of supersalesmen. Other persons, ideological critics from the right and left, challenged Garvey's politics, his marriage of racial liberation and racial enterprise. Critics from the right like Noah Thompson believed that Garvey's militant rhetoric and irregular methods obstructed the building of black business enterprises, the critical activity for the UNIA. Thompson, president of the Los Angeles division, had attended a business college and in the early 1920s was working, probably as a clerk, in the "money department" of the United States Express Company. Formerly an assistant to the treasurer at Tuskegee Institute under Washington, he retained political ties with R. R. Moton. A founder of the Urban League in Los Angeles, Thompson was already a community leader when he organized the UNIA branch in January, 1921, possibly urged on by two of his college classmates, E. L. Gaines and John D. Gordon, both of whom had been elected to the UNIA executive council in 1920.[31]

29. Norfolk *Journal and Guide*, January 12, October 4, 1924; Gilbert Osofsky, *Harlem: The Making of a Ghetto: Negro New York, 1890–1930* (New York, 1963), 97–98; *Age*, August 14, 1920. Agent James Amos believed Smith should have been indicted with Garvey. Amos, report, May 29, 1922, in Garvey 65.

30. Wilfred Smith to Emmett Scott, October 14, 1914, July 28, October 8, 1921, in Scott Papers.

31. Emory J. Tolbert, *The UNIA and Black Los Angeles* (Los Angeles, 1980), 5, 49–56; H. H. Hopkins, report, November 17, 1921, in Garvey file, RG 65; *California Eagle*, December 6, 1919, November 12, 1921, July 29, 1922, January 27, 1923; *NW*, July 15, 1922.

Garvey's rhetoric and intimidation isolated Thompson's criticism and undercut his demand for an accounting of the ailing BSL at the 1921 convention because his criticism of the UNIA from a businessman's standpoint was incapable of generating political muscle. Thompson's strongest supporters were generally the more affluent and well-connected members, who found other ways to further their careers and businesses. More of them yielded than fought for control. Nonetheless, Garvey knew very well that there were numerous means by which division presidents could go their own way without severing links with the UNIA's Parent Body. Fearing the effective loss of the strong Los Angeles division, he sent Gaines to Los Angeles to oust Thompson and create a new, loyal branch. Because his leadership was not dependent upon Garvey or the UNIA, Thompson immediately created the Pacific Coast Improvement Association, which offered the Garveyite route to racial progress organized on regional lines. The editor of the *California Eagle*, a friend and political associate of Thompson's, explained that the "principal ambition which we have is the salvation of the race along industrial and business lines." Thompson also had a keen desire to invest local money in and around Los Angeles. The new association planned to "pay particular attention to Negro improvement in Los Angeles and Southern California." Thompson urged Los Angeles Garveyites to "do something here on the Pacific Coast and you will do more, yea, ten thousand times more, to redeem Africa than you could by buying shares in Garvey's ships which very truly are ships that pass in the night." [32]

Trying to make the business ideology of the UNIA more explicit exposed the class conflicts within the division. Thompson promised that "the Garvey spirit will be the guiding one [of his new organization] with reservations that ignorance should not be installed over and above intelligence." Under the stated terms, most stockholders followed Thompson into the new organization. The propertyless either stayed with the old local or retained ties with neither organization. [33]

At the same time that Thompson was urging Garveyites at the 1921 convention to become better businessmen, Cyril Briggs of the African Blood Brotherhood was exhorting them to become better radicals. Despite its ambition, the ABB remained a small organization of young intellectuals, workers, and marginal businessmen. During the period of working-class defeats it retained the political style of revolutionary societies, if not the insurrectionary hopes. ABB militance was vocal but floated above popular issues in a vain search for a constituency. To end its isolation, Briggs hoped

32. *California Eagle*, September 10, 24, October 29, December 3, 17, 1921.
33. Thompson's new organization soon fell victim to factionalism and thieving leaders. See *California Eagle*, June 3, July 24, October 14, 1922, December 22, 1923.

to establish the ABB as the vanguard of the UNIA. He thought that Garvey was dominated by "self-glory and aggrandisement; it is not so much the money he cares about as it is the fame and glory of the thing." He considered Garvey's associates to be "intellectual nincompoops" who "would do his [Garvey's] bidding without question and were sufficiently impressed with his greatness so that they would not be dangerous rivals for office or leadership."[34] Still, Briggs thought that a UNIA led by the ABB could become a militant mass movement fighting to protect the Negro's standard of living and to halt lynching and peonage. But his best arguments for the creation of a secret supreme executive council and for use of "underground tactics" came from the recent history of the UNIA in the Caribbean and Central America. He pointed to the suppression of UNIA divisions in Santo Domingo by the United States Marines and the persecution of UNIA divisions in Cuba and Costa Rica by the United Fruit Company.[35]

Briggs believed that the UNIA must respond to the defeat of the popular insurgencies of 1919 and 1920 in the Caribbean region. During the postwar period, strikes and riots broke out throughout the area. As in the United States, the high cost of living, which officials often acknowledged, was at the base of the protest. The mobilizations often escalated into violence and rioting. Although militias and the strategic stationing of warships in the waters of port cities ended the insurgencies, in some places workers were victorious. The Trinidad Workingman's Association, for instance, struck and gained a 25 percent wage increase. But though the seeds of mass trade unionism were planted, the offensive was contained.

To understand the way Garveyism functioned in the Caribbean region, it is useful to distinguish among the impact of the *Negro World*, the effect of local UNIAs, and the influence of Garvey himself. Colonial governments most often objected to the newspaper. The fears of the Costa Rican government were typical. It banned the *Negro World* because "already there occurred several strikes and small riots instigated by negroes. The high officials of the United Fruit Company and the Consul of Great Britain have judged this paper to be pernicious and provocative." In January, 1921, dock workers and government employees formed a union. Workers in the gold mines rioted, and squatters resisted eviction. Faced with working-class militancy, colonial authorities and employers feared further incitement. But the banning of the *Negro World*, published in New York, does not illuminate the role of local UNIA divisions in mass action.[36]

34. *Crusader*, April, 1921; "Memorandum for Lt. Col. Hitt," February 14, 1921, file 10218-417/2, MID, in RG 165; "Negro Activities," October 22, 1921, in Garvey file, RG 65.
35. *Crusader*, November, 1921; Amy Jacques Garvey, *Garvey and Garveyism* (Kingston, Jamaica, 1963), 64–65.
36. [American Consul] Harry D. Baker to Secretary of State, December 6, 8, 9, 11, 19,

The fact that only Spanish trade unionists were deported from Costa Rica during the labor insurgency in that country suggests that if the local UNIA was involved in organizing United Fruit workers at all, it was as a supporter and not an initiator. When the masses were militant, UNIA locals sometimes provided support for the activities of black laborers. Yet trade unions and riots, the models of social organization and behavior that came into play in times of labor militancy, stemmed from the oppressive social conditions of black workers, not from the business enterprises of the UNIA. But governments and workers sometimes possessed blurred images of the various black organizations. The governor of the Windward Islands advocated drastic legislation against the *Negro World* in 1919 because it urged blacks to "turn to Lenin and the Bolsheviks." (The Socialist W. A. Domingo edited the newspaper in that year.) Similarly, in St. Lucia in 1920, local UNIA members contributed three pence a week toward support of the Black Star Line and a future strike fund.

But over time, black politics clarified in the Caribbean as they did in New York. Garvey's immediate interest in the Caribbean and in Central America, as well as everywhere else, was building up the Black Star Line, which conflicted with the creation of a strike fund. Thus, to raise the capital he needed so desperately, Garvey, on his visit to Costa Rica in April, 1921, was conciliatory toward the political and economic establishment. An American official reported that he "did not conduct any radical propaganda" in his address to "the many negro laborers of the United Fruit Company. He was received by President Acosta, who stated he spoke to him only of the African Commonwealth he hopes to establish." Trying to resurrect UNIA businesses, Garvey distanced himself from popular militance.[37]

Therefore, Briggs demanded a new politics and warned Garveyites of the dangers of overemphasizing black business enterprise: "No business enterprise is good enough to base the Liberation Movement and the mo-

---

22, 1919, files 844g.5045/3/2 and 844g.00/–/1/3/4, in RG 59; W. F. Elkins, "Marcus Garvey, the *Negro World*, and the British West Indies: 1919–1920," *Science and Society*, XXXVI (April, 1972), 63–77; E. R. White to Solicitor, January 8, 1920, in Office of the Solicitor, Correspondence Unarranged, Mail Violations, Espionage Act, 1917–21, in RG 28. Elkins exaggerated the significance of the banning of the *NW* by ignoring the fact that most black newspapers from the United States were banned. For instance, in 1919 colonial authorities in Guiana found that the *NW*, the *Crusader*, the Omaha *Monitor*, and the (Philadelphia) *Christian Recorder* were objectionable. Usually, censorship was instituted after a period of insurgency. By 1922 or 1923, bans were lifted in most places.

37. Walter S. Penfield to Robert Lansing, September 25, 1919, H. H. Hibbert to Governor [of Costa Rica], August 5, 1919, E. R. White to Solicitor, January 8, 1920, in Office of the Solicitor, Correspondence Unarranged, Mail Violations, Espionage Act, 1917–21, in RG 28; Elkins, "Marcus Garvey, the *Negro World*, and the British West Indies," 68–69; Walter C. Thurston to Secretary of State, January 22, 1921, Stewart McMillin to Thurston, April 29, 1921, file 840.1, in RG 84. British intelligence added that Garvey's audience in

rale of the Negro masses upon the success or failure of that enterprise. Of course we must have business enterprises, but let's not link them up directly with the Liberation Movement and thereby stake the entire movement upon their chances of success or failure and at the same time invite white aggression to what might be considered a vulnerable spot in our armour." Briggs's analysis made the questionable assumption that the same men who created black business enterprises would also have both the ability and the desire to promote militant politics.[38]

But if blacks could advance through business enterprise without embracing militant politics in their own lives, was it likely that they would promote militant politics elsewhere—in the South, the Caribbean, or Africa? They might support struggles in other parts of the black world in the way Irish-Americans supported the independence of Ireland. Northern blacks already championed the southern struggle through contributions to the NAACP. But Briggs was not content with the legalistic strategy of the NAACP. To follow the Irish example required the development of mass politics in the South, in the Caribbean, in Africa. His criticism of Garveyism assumed that those struggles could be initiated, not merely supported, from New York. He was asking UNIA members to commit themselves to nonexistent, worldwide racial battles when they had joined the UNIA to better their own lives. With little difficulty, Garvey ridiculed the ABB program and retained control of the UNIA. He declared that "a more radical propaganda than the Universal Negro Improvement Association's" was futile.[39]

Garvey also lost the imposing Reverend George Alexander McGuire, chaplain-general of the UNIA. The militant Episcopalian minister had attempted to impose a uniform religious ritual and create a greater role for clergymen in the UNIA. In July, 1921, McGuire had been made a bishop of the Independent Episcopal Church. Then, in September, he was installed as the first bishop of a new African Orthodox Church (AOC) by a prelate of the Russian Orthodox Church. McGuire wanted to make the AOC the official religious body of the UNIA and expand his own base of power. Garvey rejected this move. To institutionalize one religion would close most of the churches of black America to the UNIA. McGuire flirted for a

---

Costa Rica was "disappointed" at Garvey's "lack of answers." A. P. Bennett to Secretary for Foreign Affairs, May 9, 1921, F.O. 371/5684. Similarly, when Garvey visited Belize in early July, 1921, British intelligence reported that his speeches were "moderate in tone, and he stated that his movement was not intended to overthrow any Government." "Monthly Review of Radicalism, no. 34," August, 1921, pp. 48–49, copy in RG 59.

38. *Crusader*, November, 1921.

39. *Ibid.*; *NW*, October 22, 29, 1921; L. B. Weeks to Director, MID, September 3, 1921, file 10218-261/76, MID, in RG 165.

brief moment with Briggs's ABB but eventually returned to the UNIA. His handsome, white-robed figure was prominent at the UNIA's 1924 convention. He obviously needed the UNIA more than it needed the AOC.[40]

After the 1921 convention, the critics from both the left and the right, men like Briggs and Thompson, abandoned the UNIA. The leaders who remained tended to be somewhat rightist—socially mobile men who had business ambitions but lacked entrepreneurial alternatives to the UNIA. They, too, sensed the conflict between business and politics in the UNIA. In 1922, many concluded that UNIA reform was impossible without replacing Garvey, who was vulnerable and floundering after he was indicted in January. Aware of the challenge, Garvey took strong measures against his rivals even before the 1922 convention had opened. He announced a "clean sweep of the personnel of the present cabinet of the UNIA. . . . We do not want irresponsible swell heads who believe that after they are elected to a position they have no other obligation to the people than to make a lot of big noise, to abuse the race and pilfer the pockets of poor Negroes." He pledged that the UNIA would have a new staff when the convention closed on August 30; he called the present officers "crooks" and "thieves."[41]

Garvey's principal challenger was the charismatic Reverend James Eason, elected American Leader of the UNIA in 1920. Like Noah Thompson had, Eason aimed to make the UNIA a more efficient instrument for business enterprise. He told delegates to the 1922 convention that "nothing could be done until the Negro was able to match the white man dollar for dollar dime for dime." He implied that the creation of the Black Star Line had been premature: "If our people cannot compete with other men in running a peanut stand or a cool drink stand in New York or elsewhere they will not be able to compete with others in running a farm or a bank or a mine in Africa." Eason would concentrate UNIA economic activities in the United States, where "our future is brighter . . . than ever before."[42]

Like Garvey's, Eason's blueprint required the accumulation of capital and cast members in the same passive role. If successfully implemented, Eason's plans would threaten the local initiatives and loose associational features that rooted the UNIA at the base even though this cohesion was not translated into capital for the Parent Body. He tried to attract support by proposing new investment projects when most delegates were concerned about the value of their past investments in the Black Star Line. His

40. See Randall K. Burkett, *Garveyism as a Religious Movement: The Institutionalization of a Black Civil Religion* (Metuchen, N.J., 1978), esp. ch. 3. Although my interpretation of the relationship between McGuire and Garvey is not identical to Burkett's, it is consistent with his data.
41. *NW*, April 1, July 5, 1922.
42. *NW*, August 19, 26, 1922.

failure to take a position on the issue of stock redemption deprived him of an issue that might have given his challenge popular support.

Delegates continued to demand an accounting of the BSL failure. Many thought that the UNIA should redeem BSL stock if the company was beyond revitalization.[43] Garvey deflected this criticism by setting up a committee to resolve the question. The group did not report until late in the convention, on August 30, by which time most delegates had departed. After the chairman announced that they had decided that the UNIA should redeem the stock, Garvey ruled that the committee had exceeded its jurisdiction and returned the proposal for more deliberation. At the same time, he appointed its chairman, John Fowler of Oakland, California, minister of industries and labor of the UNIA. The new officer did not pursue the issue of stock redemption. O. A. Williams of Okmulgee, Oklahoma, who had stayed to hear the report, decided to return home and advise members to leave the organization, "as they were merely wasting time."[44]

Both Garvey and Eason skirted the issue because there was no way to satisfy BSL stockholders that was compatible with the survival of the organization. To reimburse stockholders required appealing for funds to the same constituency that had invested. Even if the leaders were able to raise the money, distribution to individuals conflicted with the capital needs of any plan to build UNIA enterprises. To rectify the past imperiled the future despite the political and moral dividends of stock redemption.

Neither Garvey nor Eason offered leadership on other issues. Garveyites expressed a wide range of opinions on lynchings, Liberia, commerce, education, politics, and family life. In the main, their conception of politics was narrow, oscillating without design between the poles of retaliatory violence and individual self-help. A. J. Johnson of New Orleans proclaimed that "the only way to stop lynching in the South is for everyone to get a gun and send every lyncher to Hell." The Committee on Social Conditions concluded that the home was the only medium through which black youth could be taught "courtesy, clean speech, correct manners and good character . . . the hall marks of true leaders and gentlemen." Most recommendations required little active collective implementation because they were exhortations to individuals.[45]

In any event, UNIA structure, tailored after the kinds of loose associations that characterized fraternals, made it difficult to implement collective

---

43. *California Eagle*, December 3, 17, 1921; *NW*, August 26, 1922. They believed it was possible because UNIA officials reported "a substantial balance in hand and also a reserve fund." *NW*, August 26, 1922.

44. Agent Andrew Battle found that one-third of the 338 had already left by August 14. Battle, reports, August 10, 14, 18, September 7, 1922, in Garvey file, RG 65.

45. Battle, report, August 10, 1922, in Garvey file, RG 65.

political action. Most UNIA projects voted at the convention were financed and executed through voluntary contributions and participation. Because decisions did not commit anyone to do anything, it was also difficult to create an effective opposition. At the 1922 convention, delegates vetoed, 135–2, the executive council's decision to send a delegation to the League of Nations to protest the mandates of the German colonies in Africa. Most Garveyites believed that the trip would be a futile gesture. The head of the Chicago division charged "that the petition . . . was doing . . . the very same thing that organizations of Negroes have been doing for 300 years, namely sending resolutions and prayers to white people." Overcoming defeat with a mixture of legalism and threats, Garvey declared that the resolution was not subject to convention approval. Delegates had little incentive to pursue the issue because the commission's expenses were to be financed by a special appeal for funds. Although Garvey announced that each division would be taxed to finance the trip, most members knew that this levy, like other UNIA tithes, was voluntary. Neither Garvey nor his opponents risked testing such plans by requiring active agreement and support. UNIA members and the larger black community voted on the League of Nations initiative with their wallets, the common procedure. But when projects that Garvey favored did not attract enough money, he financed them secretly from the general revenues.[46]

Without effective implementation, there was no analysis of the relative merits of various struggles. The issue of black politics, a potential escape from the miasma of racial business enterprise, was reduced to opportunistic moves by ambitious individuals and the exercise of prejudices by the different ethnic groups within the UNIA. Initially, electoral politics did not play an important role in the UNIA, because its principal goals were to be realized through businesses like the BSL, not through state action. Nonetheless, from its beginnings, the UNIA was involved in political contests. The address of a representative from Mayor Hylan's office on the first day of the 1922 convention was one sign that the UNIA in New York tended toward Tammany Hall. But UNIA locals endorsed a variety of candidates— white and black, Republican and Democratic—in other northern cities, mostly seeking small favors—tax breaks, parade permits, and so forth. UNIA leaders also used the association as a base to launch their own candidacies. Wilfred Smith tried to win the Republican nomination for Congress in 1920; William Ferris chased it in 1922. Running for office, however, required broader affiliations. UNIA officials usually entered politics as individuals, not Garveyites. Ferris, for instance, withdrew his name from

46. *NW*, July 29, August 26, September 2, 1922.

consideration for a high UNIA post because he wanted to broaden his base of support to other groups in Harlem. If he believed that liaisons with other black and white groups were important to the race, he did not so enlighten UNIA members. In practice, UNIA politics were in large part the private arrangements of UNIA leaders with the outside world, not underground militancy or the strategies and debates of popular politics.[47]

The issue of politics became more important at the 1922 convention when the collapse of the UNIA's business enterprises was making alternatives attractive. The issue, however, was used only as a weapon in the leadership fight. Eason criticized West Indians, who thought themselves "too good to vote." The motive behind his attack was transparent—the hope that American blacks would repudiate the UNIA's leading West Indian, Marcus Garvey. Instead of criticizing the excessively high-salaried positions in the organization, Eason attacked West Indian officeholders, charging that Garvey thought West Indians superior to American blacks. Such UNIA nativism was fed by its larger world view. Their conception of human society as an arena of competing and struggling racial groups encouraged leaders to blame the UNIA's problems on rival ethnic groups within the organization.[48]

Group prejudices and alliances were not significant or clear enough to define the issues between Garvey and Eason, which became a personal contest. At one point, the sergeant at arms summoned the police to prevent a physical confrontation between the two men. Garvey demanded and won a "formal trial" of Eason for alleged crimes against the organization. By transforming the issue from Eason's criticism to Eason's behavior, Garvey deflected blame from himself and placed it on a rival.[49]

Garvey charged Eason with using UNIA funds for himself. The UNIA conventions voted salaries ranging from three thousand to six thousand dollars a year for officials of the Parent Body. Because no one ever received his full salary, leaders made up deficits from stock sales and other UNIA revenue. Garvey himself encouraged the practice when he told officials that they, like ministers, would have to work up their own income from appearances before the divisions. But the burdens of the frequent financial appeals—for Liberia, the League of Nations, the Black Star Line, sickness and burial funds, and special assessments for nameless purposes—com-

47. NW, August 5, 12, 19, September 2, 1922.
48. Battle, report, August 18, 1922, in Garvey file, RG 65. Of the fifteen clerks and stenographers working in the president's office, none was American-born. Age, October 21, 1922.
49. NW, September 2, 1922.

bined with the collapse of UNIA enterprises, made the officials of the Parent Body appear to be parasitic.[50]

Garvey, too, was vulnerable. But he had more control over the machinery of the UNIA, and he used its funds to build personal loyalties. This power was greatest at conventions. A month-long convention was costly for most members. Garvey used UNIA funds to subsidize the expenses of individuals he wanted to attend the convention. He presented a woman who was to sing at the opening of the convention with a round-trip ticket between Kansas City and New York. Garvey was trying to convince the woman's husband, a Baptist preacher with a 1,300-member congregation, to become the president of the UNIA there. Similarly, Garvey secretly used four hundred dollars to convince Leroy Bundy to take over the Cleveland UNIA. (Bundy demanded the sum to move from East St. Louis to Cleveland.)[51]

Eason could not overcome Garvey's personal and organizational strength. Lines of loyalty ran from individuals to Garvey himself, not horizontally among the members of the executive council. Eason's vague business program did not rally other dissidents to his candidacy. R. H. Tobbitt, the UNIA's West Indian organizer, hoped Garvey's old employer Dusé Mohamed Ali, in the United States at the time promoting his own Pan-African dreams and writing a weekly foreign affairs column for the *Negro World*, would take over UNIA businesses. Therefore, Tobbitt, unlike Eason, supported the proposed League of Nations delegation because he hoped that the experienced Ali would be on it. Whether Garvey knew of Tobbitt's motive is unclear. But Garvey appointed men loyal to himself, not potential rivals, to a delegation that did not include Ali. Tobbitt and others with similar purposes had supported Garvey's flouting of the convention's opposition to the League of Nations initiative. They could not now appeal to members to support particular individuals over Garvey's choices. Like Eason, Tobbitt and other dissidents masked their intentions because the business solutions at the root of their alternatives to Garvey's program were not compelling. Therefore, they also relied on the appeal of personalities to resurrect the UNIA.[52]

50. James Brooks, "Statement," January, 1922, in Garvey file, RG 65; *NW*, September 2, 9, 1922.

51. Battle, report, August 15, 1922, Effa Bushell to B. Hust, August 11, 1922, in Garvey file, RG 65. With his organization in disarray, Garvey tried to attract established members of the black community, especially those, like ministers, who represented popular constituencies. *NW*, July 15, 1922.

52. James E. Amos, report, June 28, 1922, in Garvey file, RG 65; *NW*, August 19, 1922.

The dissidents' charges against Garvey were blunted by their past testimonials. They had initially acquiesced in Garvey's powers because of UNIA successes in 1919 and 1920. They had furthered the celebration of his leadership in the numerous appeals for sale of Black Star Line stock. Now, Garvey successfully used their past praise to prove that current criticism was motivated only by a desire for position and money. Garvey's confidence at Eason's trial and his summary treatment of dissent at the convention were enhanced by his control of the *Negro World*, the principal instrument of communication with UNIA members all over the world. Although some debate appeared in the newspaper, the knowledge that Garvey's interpretation of events would be the one heard by UNIA members allowed him to absorb some of the more open attacks at the convention.

Eason was found guilty of treason and expelled.[53] New leaders were elected during the final week of the convention, after most delegates had gone home. Garvey was easily reelected president-general along with four assistants: Leroy Bundy, William Sherrill, Rudolph Smith, and Henrietta Vinton Davis. Other positions were to be filled by the leading quintet. Only Garvey and Davis linked the leadership of 1922 with that of 1920. Leroy Bundy was the only new officer who had a national reputation. A dentist and former Republican politician in East St. Louis, he was imprisoned for his alleged role in the city's riots in 1917. Recently released, he was attempting to reestablish a career in Cleveland, where he had lived originally. After the convention, he returned to Cleveland but shortly afterward left the UNIA, later going on to a successful political career.[54]

Rudolph Smith was a journalist, lecturer, minister, and self-styled "world-traveler" from Guiana. William Sherrill, the son of a Methodist preacher from Arkansas, followed another common route to the UNIA. Having attended Northwestern University, he recruited labor for the government and a Chicago corporation during the war. Failing to establish his own employment agency in New York, he worked in a black bank in Baltimore before joining the UNIA in the fall of 1921.[55]

Along with new officers, Garvey acquired a new wife, Amy Jacques, in July, 1922, one month after he divorced Amy Ashwood, the first Mrs.

53. Eason immediately founded the Universal Negro Alliance. *Age*, September 2, 1922.

54. The UNIA constitution was altered to give the president-general, Garvey, the power to appoint the cabinet. The convention could only reject or confirm the choices. All presidents of divisions would be appointed by the Parent Body, with local approval. *Age*, September 23, 1922. On Bundy's later career, see Chapter 12.

55. *NW*, September 15, 1923, May 9, 1925; Battle, report, September 7, 1922, in Garvey file, RG 65.

Garvey. Ashwood had joined him in New York in 1918 to resume their work and romance. They were married in December, 1919, mingling their personal happiness with the first successes of the Black Star Line. Although the precise incidents leading up to the separation were unclear, the clash of two strong wills must have been at the center of the conflict, which had erupted almost immediately after the two returned from their honeymoon. Amy Ashwood had played an active part in UNIA affairs from the beginning. After she and Garvey parted, she began a successful stage career in New York and then ran a popular club and restaurant in London. She was intelligent, vivacious, and liberated, attracting numerous men in the United States, England, and Liberia.

Garvey was drawn to strong women who could help him. Amy Jacques, also from Jamaica, was also very attractive and proved equally useful. Their marriage lasted until Garvey's death because Amy Jacques chose to invest her strength and talents in her husband's career. She defined her role as Garvey's comforter and surrogate, whereas Amy Ashwood had viewed herself more as an equal. According to Ashwood, she left Garvey in the summer of 1921, after a period of separation, when she discovered Garvey and Amy Jacques living together. Amy Jacques said that her romance with Garvey began after he had made the decision to divorce Amy Ashwood. Jacques explained that Garvey would have preferred an American wife, to "please the people." He had contemplated Henrietta Vinton Davis, but she was older than he, and Garvey wanted a son. Other choices were rejected because they lacked the qualities of a comrade. He therefore turned to Jacques because she could be "a stand-in in an emergency." Although Jacques's story strains credulity somewhat, the qualities she claimed Garvey was seeking were certainly ones she displayed as his wife. She played an active role in all the factional fights and was Garvey's surrogate when he was away from New York, when he was in prison, and later, after his death.[56]

But Amy Jacques offered little criticism of Garvey. Acquiescence in Garvey's wishes seemed to be the prerequisite of any long-term relationship with him. He had many admirers and enemies but few friends. U. S. Poston, who had resigned his position as UNIA minister of labor and industries, warned Garvey at the end of the 1922 convention that "in your mad rush to serve your race, in your mad rush to serve humanity, pause long enough to study yourself introspectively." Turning to the new UNIA council, he repeated Napoleon's alleged words when in exile: "Had my

56. A. J. Garvey, *Garvey and Garveyism*, 83–84, 186; New York *Times*, July 23, 1921; A. A. Garvey, "Marcus Garvey," 56–74, 107.

councils advised me, had they opposed me at the time, France would have been supreme."[57]

Neither injunction was followed. The resignations and expulsions hurt the organization by depriving it of able men. Despite Garvey's explanation that the organization had merely expelled traitors, he had won a battle at the cost of losing the war. Without the Black Star Line, the UNIA withered. The history of the Black Star Line was typical of the fate of small enterprises from the boom of the war to the bust of the depression of 1920–1921. The fall in shipping rates and the contraction of trade made the combination of meager capital, inexperience, and the influence of hucksters and misleading brokers a fatal one. The sinking of the Black Star Line was more significant only because of the political and social program it put forward. Created by political calculation and the popularly experienced subjective needs of the black petite bourgeoisie, it was the most ambitious effort to transform racial enterprise into a vehicle for militant politics.

Despite the economic failure of the Black Star Line, Garvey retained control of the UNIA because he did not demand ideological coherence, only personal loyalty. But failing to provide a viable praxis for its international structure and militant rhetoric, the UNIA became a skeleton—the outlines of its reach were visible, but its flesh was nonexistent, its body lifeless. Organizational politics became a surrogate for UNIA politics in the larger world. Garvey's ambitions and determination, which he had displayed as a boy in Jamaica, were projected onto an ever narrowing canvas, unrelated to the lives of the men and women he hoped to lead. In the end, though his transition into the 1920s appeared to be more successful than that of his rivals, it was superficial and short-lived. In the long run, his rivals, who had less immediate success, did better. Racial business enterprise could not be a solution for the problems of blacks in industrial society. Under various umbrellas traditional working-class issues would compose the substance of black politics. This was not so obvious in the 1920s, but the Great Depression of the 1930s would provide elegant and decisive proof.

57. *NW*, September 1, 1922; A. A. Garvey, "Marcus Garvey," 103.

8 / The UNIA Goes South
Garvey and the Ku Klux Klan

The suspension of the operations of the Black Star Line in April, 1922, left the UNIA without a project to unite its members and implement its large goals. Retracing the pioneering selling routes through northern cities and the West Indies in 1921 neither resolved the Parent Body's financial problems nor revitalized local organization. In 1922, Garvey turned to the South, the home of four out of five Afro-Americans. Southern racial mores had erected barriers to UNIA organizing. In small towns and rural areas, where distinctions between radicalism and racial assertion were often academic, Garveyites lacked the political time and space necessary to present the UNIA message. Because so much of the enforcement of Jim Crow and white supremacy was on the plane of symbol and etiquette, the appearance of merely the badges of Garveyism was often considered incendiary. One Alabama black reported the lynching of an organizer selling UNIA stock. Minister of Legions E. L. Gaines was often ordered out of town and warned not to return. Southern cities regularly imposed less rigorous but still effective hurdles. Finding Garveyites parading in military uniform provocative, the police in Chattanooga, Tennessee, arrested them. Leading black ministers and businessmen, fearing outsiders who threatened to disrupt or challenge their precarious power, often convinced mayors to ban UNIA meetings and harass UNIA members. Occasionally, Garveyites billed their meetings as religious services, legitimate racial activity in the southern system, to avoid the political proscriptions. The cities of the Upper South were usually more tolerant than those of the Deep South, but they still demanded obedience to Jim Crow and other open acknowledgments of white supremacy.[1]

Determined to augment his following in the South, Garvey accommodated to regional ways. Incapable of quiet craft, however, he made tactical

1. *NW*, September 16, 1922, December 12, 1923, August 20, 1927; Andrew Battle, report, August 23, 1922, in Garvey file, RG 65; "Negro Agitation," February 5, 1921, file 10218-261/52, MID, in RG 165; New Orleans *Times-Picayune*, February 12, 1923; author's interview with Thomas Harvey, October 15, 1975.

retreat a virtue when he publicly praised Jim Crow and denied the goals of social and political equality. In Raleigh, North Carolina, Garvey thanked the white South for having "lynched race pride into the Negroes." He credited segregation with the building of flourishing racial businesses in the South. On the other hand, manipulating white stereotypes and intraracial humor, he told his Negro audience that, if he had to depend upon blacks, "it would have taken him six months to travel to North Carolina." He reinterpreted the significance of racial indifference to Africa and mimed white clichés when he said that he "did not want all [Negroes] to go over there [Africa]. . . . No there are lots of lazy Negroes who we don't want over there. You just stay here where it suits you." In New Orleans, he went further: "This is a white man's country. He found it, he conquered it and we can't blame him because he wants to keep it. I'm not vexed with the white man of the South for Jim Crowing me because I'm black. I never built any street cars or railroads. The white man built them for your own convenience. And if I don't want to ride where he's willing to let me then I'd better walk." Garvey discarded "social equality" for "our own country and our own land, with our own railroads and 'Booker Washington' cars instead of Pullmans." Even the government agent monitoring Garvey noted that the meeting and speech "was not of a radical nature, was on entirely different lines than the other lectures."[2]

The ambiguous symbol of Garvey's southern strategy was a startling two-hour meeting on June 25, 1922, in Atlanta with Edward Clarke, second-in-command of the Ku Klux Klan. Garvey's politics was the diplomacy of elites. The Klan meeting was a bold attempt to advance the UNIA in the South through political summitry. Garvey had attempted to win the tolerance of mayors, police chiefs, and district attorneys in northern cities, too. But political agreements with southern organizations that openly and explicitly promoted white supremacy and Negrophobia required explicit repudiation of the racial militance that had attracted northern blacks. Nonetheless, with an energy and determination that undercut the surrender, Garvey promoted the new defensive arrangements as he celebrated the UNIA's earlier victories. The politics of accommodation was broadcast as the politics of triumph.

Klan chief Clarke requested the meeting after he read a report of one of Garvey's speeches that praised Jim Crow.[3] Although the Klan leader's particular motives and aims were as opaque as Garvey's, the invitation harmonized with numerous Klan efforts to adjust to the postwar political sta-

2. New Orleans *Times-Picayune*, June 24, 1922; J. T. Tolivar, report, June 23, 1922, in Garvey file, RG 65.
3. *NW*, July 1, 1922.

bilization by substituting politics for its notorious direct action and black consent for black coercion.

The modern Klan was founded in 1915 by Colonel William Simmons, a former Methodist minister, garter salesman, and sometime teacher of southern history. During the war, the Klan was part of the government-affiliated network of voluntary groups that promoted patriotism and combatted dissent. The Klan abducted strike leaders in Birmingham and Mobile, punished "slackers," demanded political action against criminals, and enforced the personal morality of individual Klansmen.[4] Most of the vigilante groups were short-lived. The Klan's history took a different course when Edward Clarke reorganized it in 1920. Conceived in southern nostalgia and nurtured in the antiradicalism of the war, it mushroomed when promoted by modern techniques of salesmanship. Colonel Simmons' Klan was a revival of the Old South of romance and violence, but Edward Clarke's was a modern social organization. Clarke was the brother of the managing editor of the Atlanta *Constitution*, the leading southern newspaper, and his wife came from one of the city's old families. His elite ties were functional as well as personal. Clarke's Southern Publicity Association had packaged financial campaigns for the Red Cross, YMCA, Salvation Army, and Anti-Saloon League during World War I. He marketed the Klan as he had sold the other causes.[5]

The Klan of the 1920s, unlike the original of the Reconstruction period, was urban and national in scope, attracting possibly one million members. Nominally devoted to the preservation of Protestantism, motherhood, morality, patriotism, and education, the Klan's criteria of eligibility—its members had to be white, native-born, and Protestant—revealed its analysis and solutions to America's problems. By organizing only white Protestants, the Klan countered the presumed cohesion of Jews, Catholics, and blacks. Klan leaders tended to be ambitious professionals, politicians, and small businessmen. Although the Klan's resentment against the leading classes was expressed less openly than its white nativism, the *Searchlight*, its national organ, expressed common Klan antagonisms to the "well-organized commercial clubs" and "autocratic chamber of commerce of Atlanta." Klansmen in office, however, followed the blueprint of the elite they castigated—municipal expansion, law and order, and economy in government.[6]

4. Charles O. Jackson, "William J. Simmons: A Career in Ku Kluxism," *Georgia Historical Quarterly*, L (1966), 350–57; Kenneth Jackson, *The Ku Klux Klan in the City, 1915–1930* (New York, 1960), 3–11; *Age*, September 28, 1918.

5. Jackson, *The Ku Klux Klan in the City*, 358–60.

6. Henry Fry, *The Modern Ku Klux Klan* (1922; rpr. New York, 1969), 31–42; Jackson, *The Ku Klux Klan in the City*, 281.

The Klan's methods were as derivative as its ideology. Its early violent period coincided with the elite's overt and covert support of extralegal coercion. Then, former mayor W. F. Dorsey of Atlanta routinely warned that "disloyalists might expect to be branded on the forehead and on either cheek, and the rope would be the end of traitors, in legal process of law or other."[7] But by 1920, the elite returned to the normal institutions of social control. The vigilantism it had unleashed was not so easily contained. The rapid expansion of the Klan had brought with it the spontaneity of mass action. When the price of cotton plummeted in late 1920, night-riding Klansmen attempted to force an increase in price by preventing the ginning and marketing of the white fiber. Rural Klansmen had gone too far for the order's urban leaders. Colonel Simmons won the elite's praise for opposing, denouncing, and ending "rural outlawry."[8]

If direct action in the cotton fields threatened the marketing of Georgia's crops, Klan violence, especially against blacks, threatened to drive the South's black labor force to the North. Earlier, during the crisis of 1919–1920, the white elite, surrounded by "rumors of radical Negro Organizations" and of the "arming of Negroes, and specific evidence of negro aggressiveness in some neighborhoods," had tolerated, if not urged, extralegal violence. As the crisis waned, southerners feared a new black exodus that would "cripple" the "industrial life of the South." As part of a new, conciliatory strategy, leading Georgians invited the NAACP, their prewar nemesis, to hold its 1920 convention in Atlanta. They represented the dominant business wing of the Democratic party—Governor Hugh Dorsey, scion of one of Georgia's leading families; Mayor James Key, a lawyer from Atlanta's leading firm; Eugene Black, head of the chamber of commerce and future chief of the Federal Reserve Board in Atlanta; and John J. Eagan, banker, industrialist, and founder of the Interracial Commission, an elite group created in 1919 to improve race relations. Impressed by, and perhaps fearful of, the growth of the NAACP in the South, the elite believed the invitation could, at the very least, slow the black migration to the North by erasing the southern image of violence.[9]

Eager for the opening among the southern "better whites," the NAACP exuberantly accepted the invitation. The militant Cleveland lawyer Harry Davis predicted the imminent acceptance by the South of the "colored

7. Cited in H. C. Peterson and Gilbert Fite, *Opponents of War, 1917–1918* (Madison, 1957), 223.

8. Gainesville (Ga.) *Tribune*, December 9, 1920; Clement C. Mosely, "The Political Influence of the Ku Klux Klan in Georgia, 1915–1925," *Georgia Historical Quarterly*, LVII (1973), 235–58.

9. Cleveland *Plain Dealer*, June 30, 1919; Pittsburgh *Courier*, March 27, 1920; *Age*, April 2, 1920; R. R. Moton to Max Farrand, December 5, 1919, in Moton Papers.

man's peaceful revolution for political rights." But the Georgians made it clear that they opposed black voting and ruled out an ongoing relationship with the NAACP. The city's elite worked permanently with the Interracial Commission, which employed private negotiations and crisis management—not black politics and agitation—to improve race relations. Nevertheless, the Klan charged that the elite had violated tenets of white supremacy by inviting the NAACP and implied that the two groups had reached secret agreements that promoted black political and economic power.[10]

The hooded order used the same race-baiting tactics against the Democrats that the Democratic elite had used earlier against the Republicans when the GOP made a black, Henry Lincoln Johnson, Georgia's national committeeman. Although the appointment was only a symbolic gesture to placate northern blacks, not a commitment to southern black politics, the Democrats unleashed the racial menace to prevent or limit the predicted Republican resurgence in the fall of 1920.[11]

Once summoned, it was difficult to bottle the genie of race. Although the ideology of white supremacy was an unchallenged principle of southern political life, racial boundaries were mobile and measured by opportunism, not principle. The Democratic business elite of Atlanta appealed to black voters to ratify a local bond issue in 1921 after it had castigated the Republicans' appointment of Johnson as a political deviation, a violation of white supremacy's prohibition of Negro politics. The exceptions and modifications made individuals and factions vulnerable. But all parties played upon fears of Negro domination, validated by the logic of campaign oratory. Because legalized racial discrimination violated the Fourteenth and Fifteenth Amendments and blacks were not sharply differentiated from whites in economic roles, white supremacy lacked the firm boundaries that it had in South Africa or the antebellum South. Without a secure foundation, enforcement was often extralegal and violent but always incomplete. Signs of violations were often symbolic. The Klan had criticized the head of Atlanta's Interracial Commission for meeting with blacks on a basis of equality and addressing them as "mister." Similar issues were ritually dragooned into southern elections. Composed mainly of outsiders ambitious for political power, the Klan played the game. It did not create it.

10. T. K. Gibson to Walter White, May 29, 1920, George A. Towns to Mary Ovington, June 15, 1920, Towns to James W. Johnson, June 30, 1920, Box C-3, in NAACP Papers; Atlanta *Constitution*, June 13, 1920.
11. Walter Ackerman to Warren G. Harding, June 23, 1920, Box 111, in Warren G. Harding Papers, Library of Congress; Richard B. Sherman, *The Republican Party and Black America from McKinley to Hoover, 1896–1933* (Charlottesville, 1973), 135–44.

Klan allegiances and tactics shifted quickly to suit the moment. Its practices had never been uniform, because of its decentralization, secrecy, and
opportunism. But Clarke's meeting with Garvey represented the new style
of the 1920s, securing white supremacy by consent, not violence. Although Klan leaders denied they had ever authorized violence, the order
tried to improve its image after a newspaper exposé and congressional
hearings in 1921 had riveted the nation's attention on the murders, flog-
gings, and tar-and-featherings attributed to Klansmen. The order osten-
tatiously publicized financial grants to black individuals—modest copies
of upper-class philanthropy. The Klan added a thousand dollars to a drive
for a black hospital in Raleigh, North Carolina. It presented an old folks
home for Negroes in Vicksburg, Mississippi, with provisions, flour, meal,
and groceries. In Atlanta, a hundred dollars was donated to a small industrial school for blacks. Just as the Klan claimed it supported the interests of
laboring men but opposed unions, it aided individual blacks or racial institutions that embraced principles of self-help and eschewed black politics, agitation, and racial intermingling. Clarke probably invited Garvey to
determine whether the black Jamaican from New York who had praised
Jim Crow in New Orleans could fit into the new Klan public-relations
initiative.[12]

But Clarke, like the white elite, found it difficult to maneuver within the
straitjacket of white-supremacy politics. Acts necessary to gain elite ac-
ceptability threatened to alienate Klan hard-liners, who denounced the interview with Garvey. Most meetings of black and white elites were conducted privately, without publicity. Clarke broke the rule because he
needed to demonstrate that the Klan was not urging a policy of violence
toward blacks. But the local "Kleagles" in Atlanta openly stated that he had
"played hell" with Klan dogma, making it "impossible to keep the boys of
the South together."[13]

Although rebellion within the ranks may have been one reason why
Clarke pulled back from the association with Garvey, a struggle for control
of the organization was the decisive one. Throughout the summer, Clarke
successfully plotted with Wesley Evans, a dentist from Texas, to retire the
dreamy, inefficient Colonel Simmons from his position as head of the
Klan. But after they staged their successful coup, the two victors imme-

12. R. R. Moton to C. P. J. Mooney, May 17, 1922, in Moton Papers. Another motive for
Clarke's meeting with Garvey may have been a vendetta against the NAACP's Walter
White. See White to E. Y. Clarke, October 1, 1920, and White's "application" for member-
ship in the KKK, September 21, 1920, Box C-3, in NAACP Papers.

13. New York *World*, August 15, 1922; Jackson, *The Ku Klux Klan in the City*, 38–41.

diately quarreled. Evans won and inherited the Invisible Empire. Clarke's expulsion ended whatever agreement he had made with Garvey.[14]

Garvey's motives were also ambiguous and opportunistic. He seized Clarke's invitation as he had used other issues—the industrial school in Jamaica, the African issue during the war, and the Black Star Line. But the earlier politics had capitalized upon black initiatives. The Klan entente, marinated in the escalating UNIA setbacks, was difficult to sell as racial progress. Some of Garvey's associates supposed that the Klan had promised money. Others guessed the alliance was aimed at strengthening the UNIA in the South. Many simply believed that Garvey had some secret purpose. His explanations did not end the speculation.[15]

When Garvey returned to New York, he defensively mouthed Klan sophistry that it was not against blacks but for whites. He minimized the differences between Klansmen and other whites. The order, Garvey declared, represented the "spirit, the feeling, the attitude of every white man in the United States." But it was impossible to transform or even buffer the historic symbol of Negrophobia. In one speech, as soon as Garvey mentioned Clarke's name, his audience began to hiss. Garvey, like other black leaders, had used opposition to the Klan as a unifying device. In November, 1920, he had dared the KKK to come to Harlem or other northern cities, where they would be met by the New York Fifteenth and the Illinois Eighth, two of the black fighting regiments of World War I. As late as February, 1922, Garvey even denied that the Klan opposed other groups—Jews and Catholics. "Their real object is to crush the negro," he stated.[16]

Unable to convince northern blacks that Klansmen were benign or merely like other whites, Garvey fell back on the argument that the KKK could not be opposed because it was too powerful. Using the term popularized by the New York *World* exposé, he declared that the Klan was the "invisible government of America." The proof of Klan power was its continued existence despite campaigns against it. Garvey unintentionally revealed another motive for the Clarke meeting. Entering negotiations with the head of the Klan was personally satisfying. He seemed to delight in telling an audience, "I was speaking to a man who was brutally a white man and I was speaking to him as a man who was brutally a Negro." Garvey used the occasion to parade his triumphs over historic enemies of black people. He boasted of outwitting the New Orleans police, who had

14. Jackson, "William J. Simmons," 359–64; New York *World*, June 27, 1922.
15. *NW*, July 1, 1922; New York *World*, July 19, 1922.
16. *NW*, February 18, July 15, September 24, 1922; Theodore Vincent, *Black Power and the Garvey Movement* (Berkeley, 1972), 19.

tried to prevent his speaking. Now he implied that he had forced the Klan to meet with him personally as an equal.[17]

Garvey's accounts confused at best. The portrait of an all-powerful Klan magnified Garvey's power but, insofar as it was accepted, was a tenuous source of racial unity because it did not point to ways in which other blacks, individually or collectively, could stand up to the Klan. And his analysis of the South seriously misread the actual state of black politics and race relations there. Southern black leaders had shed many of the demeaning rituals that prewar leaders had employed to win influence. R. R. Moton even instructed white journalists on proper terms to use to describe blacks.[18] The editor of the black Norfolk *Journal and Guide* reported the parts of Garvey's southern speeches that urged black unity and self-help but omitted his praise of the southern white elites. Black leaders and editors in the cities of the South did not challenge Jim Crow, but they rarely embraced it.[19]

Garvey's meeting reflected and possibly caused the spread of certain common UNIA practices in the urban South, where local officials were sometimes Klansmen or Klan sympathizers. Garveyites often reported proudly that the mayor or police chief had attended their meetings. The chief of police in Norfolk, Virginia, was a member of the Klan and a frequent visitor at UNIA meetings. Insofar as the UNIA won the tolerance of local governments in the South, there were also explicit or implicit agreements with Klansmen. Insofar as the locals promised to obey the laws, they were endorsing Jim Crow and segregation. The relationships between the Klan and the UNIA probably went no further than the tolerance and perhaps some small favors that UNIA locals extracted from Klansmen in political office.

But accepting the conditions offered by the South implied that blacks could prosper there without altering its leading institutions. That assumption permitted an organizational presence, but existence under such restraint limited the attractiveness of the UNIA. For most southern blacks, Jim Crow, the inequalities of legally segregated schools, the barriers in the search for work, and the burdens of political powerlessness were central to the prospects of the race. Groups that deferred those issues might become social clubs useful to small numbers, but they could not become mass organizations of significant racial power. The nearly four hundred UNIA divi-

17. *NW*, July 15, 22, 1922; New York *Herald*, July 19, 1922.
18. Octavus Roy Cohen to R. R. Moton, February 23, 1922, Moton to Cohen, March 23, 1923, Cohen to Moton, April 12, 1923, in Moton Papers.
19. Compare edited version of the Raleigh speech in the Norfolk *Journal and Guide*, October 28, 1922, with full speech reported in *Age*, November 11, 1922.

sions and chapters of the South testified that Garvey had been there but not much else.

Even the limited gains of the southern foray were offset when Garvey's northern rivals used his meeting with Edward Clarke to unite against him. A headline in A. Philip Randolph's *Messenger* announced: MARCUS GARVEY! THE BLACK IMPERIAL WIZARD BECOMES MESSENGER BOY OF THE WHITE KU KLUX KLEAGLE. It vowed "to drive Garvey and Garveyism in all its sinister viciousness from the American soil." The attack was coordinated by the Friends of Negro Freedom, the umbrella organization begun in 1920 by black trade unionists, civil rights militants, and socialists. The leading actors in the "Garvey Must Go" campaign were A. Philip Randolph and Chandler Owen of the *Messenger* and two NAACP organizers, William Pickens and the Reverend Robert Bagnall. The climax of the campaign coincided with the UNIA's convention in August, 1922. Each critic took his turn on successive Sundays to attack Garvey. Leading off, Pickens told an audience of more than two thousand that Garvey had met with the Klan "so he could go and collect money from Southern Negroes." The next Sunday, Randolph targeted Garvey's despotism: "People now are fighting for the erection of democracies, not of empires." Bagnall likened Garvey to Judas Iscariot. Owen charged that Garvey had become "the worst type of *me-too-boss* and *hat-in-hand* good 'nigger' the race has ever been bedeviled by. . . . A race baiter and a race traitor, Garvey must go. The sooner the better."[20]

Most of the conventional racial leaders did not participate in the fratricide. Because they were not competing with Garvey for a mass constituency, they lacked a motive to pursue the issue, whatever their opinion. R. R. Moton's equanimity was fortified by his belief that the "Garvey movement is, as I predicted, dying out, and rather rapidly." Although the obituary was premature, he was well informed of Garvey's escalating problems from former Tuskegeans working for the UNIA—notably UNIA lawyer Wilfred Smith and *Negro World* editor T. Thomas Fortune.[21]

The four New York radicals were dissatisfied with existing black politics and critical of most race leaders. They fought Garvey because they believed that his appeal, which they judged to be superficial, hampered their own efforts to organize the masses. To Randolph and Owen, the mark of the new radicalism had been the joining of economic issues with issues of civil rights, with the whole being propelled by popular organization. They be-

20. Theodore Kornweibel, Jr., *No Crystal Stair: Black Life and the Messenger, 1917–1928* (Westport, Conn., 1975), 132–75; New York *Times*, August 21, 26, 28, 1922.
21. R. R. Moton to Charles Cox, May 21, 1921, Moton to Newton Baker, July 24, 1922, Emmett Scott to Wilfred Smith, September 15, 1921, in Moton Papers.

lieved that Garvey, too, recognized the importance of economic issues but that his bogus solutions prevented the masses from adopting radical economic remedies and partially explained their own poor showing. Like Cyril Briggs's exposé of the Black Star Line in 1921, their attacks on Garvey aimed to end popular allegiance to what they considered false gods. They believed that "Negroes are the easy marks of the sharpers, having as it were some vague idea that they can make millions like Ford, Rockefeller, and Morgan by buying stocks. . . . As long as a people can be duped by Black Star Line dreams, by the fraudulent Co-operation Society of America and [others like them] . . . there is little hope any substantial economic strides in the very near future." The business route to racial liberation ended in a cul-de-sac, but Randolph and Owen admitted that Harlemites disagreed with them. By revealing Garvey's treachery, they also hoped to tarnish the underlying ideology.[22]

The opposition of Robert Bagnall and William Pickens was not founded on the socialists' belief in the economic basis of racial organization, but it did embrace the conviction that Garvey was misleading a potential constituency. Both men were well positioned to observe the decline in the NAACP's membership from 100,000 in 1919 to 30,000 at the end of the decade. Bagnall was the director of branches; Pickens the field secretary. Nearly 200 of the 449 branches of 1920 were dead or dormant by 1923. Because many of the casualties were in the South, the NAACP was once again forced to rely upon strength in northern communities. But James Weldon Johnson's view that "local support" was "secondary" made it impossible to fortify the northern branches. The centralized structure did, however, mesh with the NAACP's southern-oriented program, which downplayed northern working-class and community issues, and conventional tactics, which rejected mass action for lobbying. Indeed, the politics of the NAACP was one source of the passivity and inaction in the locals that leaders ritually deplored but unwittingly encouraged. The growth of the NAACP in the North, therefore, depended principally upon the prestige of victories it won in the South.[23]

The NAACP's southern objectives were clear and appropriate. Addressing the NAACP's Atlanta convention in 1920, Bagnall named five demands of the Negro: "abolition of lynching, equal education and industrial oppor-

22. *Messenger*, III (September, 1920), 83–84, (October, 1920), 114–15, (December, 1920), 170–72, IV (September, 1921), 248–52, (December, 1922), 537.
23. "Minutes of the Board," November, 1923, "Secretary's Report," March, 1927, March, 1928, Box A-2, David H. Pearce to Herbert J. Seligmann, October 25, 1920, Box G-158, J. P. Clyde Randall to William Pickens, September 24, 1920, Box C-6, all in NAACP Papers.

tunities, the ballot, and abolition of Jim Crow cars and segregation." But the NAACP needed strategy more than it needed goals, a political perspective more than political aspirations. It proclaimed its purposes were harmonious with the progress of the South but at the same time assumed an adversary posture when it began court cases to end voting discrimination, urged reduced southern representation in Congress, and promoted federal antilynching legislation with stiff penalties. The contradictions explained why leading whites from both North and South worked with consistently conciliating organizations—the Urban League in the North and the Interracial Commission in the South—that did not upset harmony by demanding changes in critical southern institutions.[24]

In 1920, Bagnall had been drawn toward the popular alternative to the NAACP's elite lobbying strategy. He attended the joint meetings of the new Chicago Labor party and the Committee of 48, an assemblage of left-wing progressives moving tentatively away from the two major parties. Bagnall was warmly received. He was impressed that both groups were "very much advanced in their attitude on the color line." But a broader racial alliance, at a minimum, would have required a growing radical or progressive movement, which did not exist in the 1920s. Bagnall, caught in the midst of the NAACP's problems, aware of the importance of mass participation but unable to affect it, became susceptible to the view that Garvey's thuggery and demagogism were causes of NAACP problems. He avidly joined the anti-Garvey campaign.

The migration of William Pickens into the opposition was more indirect. Dissatisfied with the NAACP, he had flirted with the UNIA before joining the "Garvey Must Go" campaign. A Yale graduate, Pickens had been a member of the militant Niagara movement. Working as a college teacher in the years before the war, he discarded his youthful radicalism for the orthodox shibboleths of the time—education, alliance with the "better whites," and self-help. Beginning his work at the NAACP during its wartime growth in the South, Pickens became an associate field secretary in 1920 and returned to his earlier advocacy of agitation. As the NAACP experienced setbacks, however, his own personal grievances became less tolerable. Pickens felt slighted by Johnson's assistant, Walter White, and patronized by the aloof Du Bois. Without political victories or personal recognition, his heavy schedules and inadequate salary led him to question the methods of the NAACP. It was not surprising that he became attentive to Garvey's overtures, which had begun in 1920.[25]

24. Atlanta *Constitution*, June 1, 1920; New York *Globe*, June 2, 1920; T. J. Woofter, "Memorandum for Dr. Stokes," n.d. [1921], in Phelps-Stokes Fund Papers.
25. William Pickens to Isaac Casper, April 1, 1925, W. E. B. Du Bois to Pickens, March

Pickens had written publicly and privately in support of UNIA projects. Enthusiastic about the Black Star Line and friendly with many Garveyites, Pickens spoke frequently at Liberty Hall. Garvey had offered him a job in the spring of 1921 at the same time that he had attempted to attract Emmett Scott to the UNIA. Pickens refused but retained warm relations. He continued to defend Garvey even after the mail fraud indictment.

> The Garvey movement is not perfect. No movement is, but Garvey has the right idea that ALL NEGROES of all countries and especially of the Western World, should be in touch and organization with each other. I know Garvey personally, and I do not regard him as a crook. He is something of a visionary; all such men are. He will not FAIL, although he will not see the great success of his plans. The idea he had injected into the Negro masses will stay, even if Garvey should be jailed. . . . The white world . . . [is] more concerned about the "Garvey idea" than over any other move the Negro has ever made for power in the modern world. They know that to effect an international organization is to reach out for REAL power, especially through MASSES of men.

And he warned that "colored Americans will make regrettable mistakes if they help white Americans to fight the 'Garvey idea.' The idea is all right if only Garvey can get rid of some of the crooks that infested his organization and speak plain about the ORGANIZATION of the racial group, and not try to fool anybody about the 'Back to Africa' myth." To Pickens, the UNIA's blemishes were extrinsic to its essential and worthy aspiration, mass racial organization. Nonetheless, Pickens tried to scotch rumors that he was accepting a ten-thousand-dollar position with the UNIA. He reaffirmed his allegiance to the NAACP because of the "EARLIER FRUITION" of its programs.[26]

Garvey's meeting with Edward Clarke decisively altered the balance of contending forces that Pickens saw within Garveyism. The NAACP organizer spurned a UNIA award offered at the 1922 convention. He told Garvey: "You say in effect to the Ku Klux: All right! Give us Africa and we in turn concede you America as a 'white man's country!' In that you make a poor deal; for twelve million people you give up EVERYTHING and in exchange get NOTHING." Privately, and perhaps to prevent a public attack, Garvey told Pickens that he had made no agreement with the Klan. The explanation did not alter Pickens' course. Flaws that had seemed extraneous and

---

28, 1921, Pickens to Board, September 17, 1921, in William Pickens Papers, Schomburg Center for Research in Black Culture, New York Public Library.

26. William Pickens to J. W. Spingarn, September 25, 1921, Pickens to editor of the *Nation*, October 11, 1921, Pickens to Dr. H. Claude Hudson, June 4, 1922, MG to Pickens, July 10, 1922, in Pickens Papers; William Pickens to J. C. McKinney, February 6, 1922, Box C-13, in NAACP Papers; *NW*, February 25, March 11, 1922.

easy to remedy now appeared to be more embedded in the UNIA practice and program. With his new vision, Pickens criticized Garvey, not his subordinates, for dishonest promotions of the Black Star Line.[27]

Initially, Garvey fielded Pickens' turnabout with the appearance of self-confidence with which he had greeted other attacks. "We feel sure," he said, "that Pickens in another few months will be back among Negroes. It is a pity because we had great hope for this young man." Garvey publicized and explicated Pickens' difficulties with the NAACP: "Pickens was too black for the NAACP, which failed to accept the ability of Brother Pickens in its fullest because he is black. Pickens knows this well, and it was for that reason that Pickens was seeking to leave the NAACP not many months ago to join the UNIA." But Garvey's complacency was verbal and momentary. He soon declared that his critics were "paid agents and declared enemies of the cause of racial freedom. And you know what is done to enemies of the cause of freedom." His accusations unleashed a wave of popular violence against his critics.[28]

The potential for coercion had always been present in UNIA ideology, which promised that racial unity would yield racial success and implied, therefore, that racial failure was caused by racial disunity, which easily became racial treason. Racial patriotism was increasingly defined as support of the UNIA. Thus, Garvey told UNIA leaders: "There is no greater way of the Church showing its willingness to expand the functions of the Church than by helping a cause like the UNIA. If a preacher refuses it is evident that he has not been in touch with the proper argument or that he is positively selfish." From the beginning, UNIA activities compelled as well as convinced. One Chicago Garveyite observed that "Negro businessmen, professional men, and politicians who have been hostile to the cause of the UNIA and who are dependent on the mass of Negroes everywhere have begun to line up with the organization to protect themselves, and their business, fearing a boycott." But the line between intimidation and boycott was a slim one in an organization where political principles were vague and often adorned personal ambitions. From the beginning, Garvey used fervent followers to silence opponents within the UNIA. Until the Klan incident and mobilization against Garvey, race leaders outside the UNIA had rarely been affected by the tyrannies within the UNIA. But in 1922 Garvey warned his New York opponents that "the spirit of enthusiasm and friendship for the Association" was so great that "we will not be responsible for

27. William Pickens to MG, July 24, 1922, in Pickens Papers; Andrew Battle, report, August 10, 1922, in Garvey file, RG 65.
28. *NW*, August 12, 26, 1922; Joel Rogers, *World's Great Men of Color* (2 vols.; New York, 1946), II, 602, 608.

what may happen. If you desire your body physically in order, if you desire to keep your limbs as they are, please find some other occupation than to create yourself as stumbling blocks in the war of the UNIA."[29]

Pickens charged that his life was threatened. Then in early September, A. Philip Randolph received a mysterious package sent from "a friend" in New Orleans. Fearing that it contained a bomb, he allowed the police to open the box, which contained the severed left hand of a white man. The accompanying note warned Randolph that if he did not become a paid-up member of the UNIA, his own hand would be sent to someone else. A week later, Randolph received a letter, written in red ink and signed "The Klan," predicting that he "would not live to see the New Year" because "we don't want niggers like you here." There was no proof that Garvey or Garveyites had anything to do with the sending of the hand or the letter.

Randolph's suspicions that the UNIA played some role in the incidents were nurtured in the context of the UNIA strong-arm tactics that had spread from New York to Philadelphia, Cleveland, Pittsburgh, Toronto, Chicago, and Cincinnati. Garveyite threats, actual assaults, and the breaking up of meetings of UNIA critics appeared to confirm the belief that Garvey had made an alliance with the Klan. Even friends of the UNIA spoke out against the increasing thuggery. The Norfolk *Journal and Guide* warned that "threats of suits and dire happenings may occasion serious consequences and be harmful to any movement, for when bulldozing, assassination, thugism, and similar methods are employed to make other people, ignorant and intelligent alike, swallow their ism, then Virginia is not the place for such a colony."[30]

The murder of James Eason, who after his expulsion at the 1922 convention continued to organize against Garvey, on January 1, 1923, was a decisive turning point. The New York opposition suddenly appealed to the government to act quickly on the year-old indictment against Garvey. Two weeks after Eason was shot, Owen, Pickens, and Bagnall, joined by four members of New York's black elite and Garvey's old enemy Robert Abbott of the Chicago *Defender*, wrote a long letter to Attorney General Harry

29. MG, Lesson 21, Five Year Plan of the UNIA, "Intelligence, Education, Universal Knowledge and How to Get It" (Mimeographed, n.d.), 4–5, quoted in Randall Burkett, *Garveyism as a Religious Movement: The Institutionalization of a Black Civil Religion* (Metuchen, N.J., 1978), 112; NW, August 12, September 16, 1922; Norfolk *Journal and Guide*, July 26, September 2, 1922.

30. A. Philip Randolph, in *Messenger*, IV (1922), 499–500; Andrew Battle, report, August 8, 9, 1922, "Negro Activities," September 12, 1922, in Garvey file, RG 65; Chandler Owen to R. R. Moton, September 21, 1922, in Moton Papers; *Age*, September 9, 16, 1922; Baltimore *Afro-American*, September 29, 1922; Norfolk *Journal and Guide*, February 24, 1923.

Daugherty warning of the numerous dangers of Marcus Garvey. (Randolph did not sign it.)[31]

To enlist the government's aid to defeat a rival violated many of the first principles of the new black politics. Appealing to officials who held the southern view of race relations, the petitioners' brief paraded ideas that they had attacked in the past. In former times most of the signers had assailed the dogma that racial affairs were harmonious but for the outside agitator. Now they wrote that Garvey, "like the Ku Klux Klan," was spreading "among Negroes distrust and hatred of all white people." In the past, blacks had protested inadequate and lax police protection in their communities. Now the eight, asserting that blacks opposed all criminals and especially those of their own race, bolstered the southern notion that Afro-Americans had a special responsibility to track down black criminals. Like white southerners, they denied the political nature of the conflict when they called Garvey a criminal. They discounted the political costs of prosecution by characterizing Garveyites as the "most primitive and ignorant element of West Indian and American Negroes. The so-called respectable element . . . are largely ministers without churches, physicians without patients, lawyers without clients, and publishers without readers, who are usually in search of 'easy money.'"

Only after portraying Garvey's danger to whites did the petitioners recite the instances of violence used against black opponents of Garveyism and the frauds against "ignorant and unsuspecting negroes." They exhorted the government to "extirpate this vicious movement," which was "just as objectionable and even more dangerous" than the Klan, in the interest of "civic harmony and inter-racial concord."[32]

Although Chandler Owen had drafted the letter, the signatures of two NAACP officials, Bagnall and Pickens, and of the realtor John Nail, James Weldon Johnson's father-in-law, made the petition appear to be an NAACP brief against Garvey. (Its lawyer Arthur Spingarn had scanned the letter to prevent a possible libel suit.)[33] As a result, Garveyism was catapulted into a national black political controversy. Perry Howard, the GOP national committeeman from Mississippi and holder of the highest black patronage position in the federal government, urged the Justice Department to ignore

31. For the text of the letter see Amy Jacques Garvey (ed.), *Philosophy and Opinions of Marcus Garvey* (2 vols.; 1926; rpr. New York, 1969), II, 294–300.

32. Harry Pace *et al.* to Harry Daugherty, January 15, 1923, in *ibid.*, 294–300.

33. Du Bois, White, and Johnson, though not speaking out publicly, aided, advised, and performed research for the campaign. See A. Philip Randolph to Walter White, August 25, 1922. Both the public and NAACP members, some of whom opposed the campaign, assumed that the NAACP was behind it. "Memorandum," May, 1923, L. M. Hershaw to James W. Johnson, August 31, 1922, Box C-304, in NAACP Papers.

the charges made by "Du Bois, Johnson, and Pickens." In a letter to William Burns, he said that the petition "reduces itself to a cannibalistic scheme of one rival getting rid of the other by annihilation or otherwise." Howard's motives were not quite so Olympian or disinterested. His intervention was part of his long-standing and bitter opposition to the NAACP, which was the leading black challenge to the waning black Republicanism in the South. Howard charged that the NAACP "has done more to create race friction in this country than any other agency I know." The *Crisis* "is about as Bolshevistic as the propaganda by Haywood et al. [of the IWW]." Finally, he accused the rights organization of the ultimate treason: "The NAACP turns up in every campaign in which we engage for the election of Republican candidates, as dyed-in-the-wool Democrats."[34] The NAACP had opposed the reelection of Republicans who had not supported the Dyer antilynching bill, which the Senate had defeated in September, 1922. Because Howard had attempted to amend and, in NAACP eyes, emasculate the bill, the *Crisis* denounced him as a "lick-splittle politician" who "sought to sell us for thirty pieces of silver." He admitted to one of the defeated Republicans, Senator T. Coleman Du Pont of Delaware, a prominent target of the NAACP campaign, that "I had blood in my eyes for the National Association for the Advancement of Colored People. . . . These political bolshevists should be annihilated as the basest of ingrates."[35]

This was not Howard's first intervention on Garvey's behalf. The eight opponents charged that "certain colored politicians have been trying to use their influence to get the indictment . . . quashed." Although the record on that point is mute, Howard had tried to convince Georgia's Republican national committeeman, Henry Lincoln Johnson, to defend Garvey. It would not have been surprising or illegal for Johnson and Howard to urge the dropping of the charges.[36]

Garvey's appeal to the powers that be was not only transmitted by intermediaries. He hammered away at the socialist views of some of his critics and emphasized his own political orthodoxy. He accused the NAACP of fomenting "lynching by always endeavoring to encourage forced companionship between the races." As in the past, Garvey's attempt to maintain and control his constituency undercut his appeal to authority. *Negro World* headlines and handbills branded his critics EIGHT "UNCLE TOM" NEGROES and STOOL PIGEONS. He described one as a "business exploiter" who ap-

34. Perry Howard, "Memorandum for William Burns," February 3, 1923, William Burns, "Memorandum for Perry Howard," February 15, 1923, in Garvey file, RG 65.

35. *Crisis*, XXV (January, 1923), 103–107. See especially p. 104, which has a letter from Perry Howard to T. Coleman Du Pont, November 23, 1922.

36. James Amos, report, March 16, 1925, in Garvey file, RG 65.

pealed to race patriotism while overcharging for his products. Another was "a real estate shark"; a third, a "hair straightener and face bleacher." All were "selfish grafters who have been living off the blood of the race."[37]

Garvey's rebuttal did not change things. Neither the appeal to the classes nor the masses seemed to work. He invited three hundred prominent whites to a big rally at Carnegie Hall. Few appeared, and Garvey was not in good form that night. Although he delivered the anticipated attack on the NAACP and the socialists, he also flayed other UNIA officers, one of his common responses to political setbacks. He had recently accused all of them of dishonesty "in one way or the other." He warned a group of 1,500 at Liberty Hall on February 28 that "any member who starts out with the U.N.I.A. and turns back again should be treated as a soldier is treated, who, in the face of battle, on his own initiative, retreats. As you well know, it is policy for the soldier seeing this condition to immediately shoot the retreating traitor and that will perhaps become necessary in this organization before it can actually become a proven power to its own people, the black race."[38]

The "Garvey Must Go" campaign of 1922 was the final act in the breakup of wartime radical politics. Although the polemics pantomimed real issues, it clarified none of them and brought out the worst characteristics of each contender. Every move stemmed from weakness. Garvey's attempt to penetrate the South had been an act of desperation. The meeting with Clarke was a cartoon symbol of the accommodation his southern strategy required. The resulting "Garvey Must Go" crusade by his opponents was simultaneously an attack on reactionary politics and on a radical rival. It was led by young radicals centered in New York who had hoped to harness the power of the masses behind racial goals. Although they often blamed Garvey's showy but shallow appeal for their failures, he was as much a victim of the intractable limits of racial politics in 1922 as they. Tarnishing Garvey's reputation did not advance the NAACP or the economic radicalism of Randolph and Owen. The radicals had not refuted the racial ideology at the base of the UNIA; they had only wounded its most impatient and militant practitioner.

Despite Garvey's self-promotion, novel methods, and genuine charisma, his underlying social philosophy and goals were shared by the leaders of the Urban League and NAACP. All acted upon (even if they did not acknowledge) the theory that an expanding capitalism provided blacks

37. A. J. Garvey (ed.), *Philosophy and Opinions of Garvey*, II, 294, 300–308; Garvey also red-baited his opponents. See his letter to Attorney General Daugherty, February 4, 1923, file 198940, in RG 60.

38. *NW*, February 10, 1923; Battle, report, February 28, 1923, in Garvey file, RG 65.

with opportunities for bourgeois achievement, which was to them the pre-requisite for black liberation. And migration became the unstated alternative to a more vigorous southern political strategy, especially after the economic upturn of 1923 produced another movement to northern cities. Racial progress had been delayed but not derailed by the postwar depression. In 1929, James Weldon Johnson found that the "Negro's situation in Harlem is without precedent in all his history in New York; never has he been so securely anchored, never before has he owned the land, never before has he had so well established a community life." At the same time, a black investigator in the Department of Labor predicted that "the Negro worker's future, all in all, is roseate and enticing."[39] Young men and women who came to the expanded northern black belts, often militant and racially conscious, did not dissent. One contemporary described them as "young men on the make," who "turn their eyes to the political machine," not radical politics. A conference initiated by Cyril Briggs to create a new politics was captured quickly by conservatives who called it, significantly, the Sanhedrin. The mood of the Chicago conference, in February, 1924, was one of self-congratulation. A reporter observed that "everybody seemed glad to be in great company, but there was a notable lack of things you could remember after you got home." A. Philip Randolph, who did not attend, dismissed the deliberations and the consensus as a "mere repetition of the old programs of the past." The complacency, the emphasis upon racial self-help, and the absence of self-criticism implied that existing methods were adequate and needed only to be extended, deepened, and coordinated.[40]

The economic upturn of 1923 did not rescue Garvey, who required viable black business enterprise, not merely economic prosperity. Moreover, he was hopelessly entangled in his past. Although he survived the "Garvey Must Go" campaign and the internal assault on his power at the UNIA convention in August, 1922, he remained on the defensive. The organization lacked a program and the prestige of success. Worse, the battle tactics that had been used against his New York opponents had unleashed a wave of popular violence that Garvey could not control and that threatened his chances of acquittal in the mail fraud trial.

39. James Weldon Johnson, Black Manhattan (New York, 1930), 159; Charles Hall, "Industrial Trends," n.d. [1930], Oxley-Phillips file, in RG 174; Baltimore Afro-American, December 29, 1922.

40. William Patterson, The Man Who Cried Genocide: An Autobiography (New York, 1971), 60–62; Chicago Broad Ax, February 16, 1924; "Negro Activities," February 14, 1924, in Garvey file, RG 65; Daily Worker, February 14, 1924.

9 / Violence as Racial Politics
The Murder of James Eason

The UNIA's crisis of 1922 produced an epidemic of local violence in New York City. The branches, unable to reconcile and often even comprehend the tortuous strategy and personal rivalries of the Parent Body, were themselves paralyzed by acrimony and disaffection. One response to the setbacks and frustrations was violence against internal and external dissenters. The incidents involving use of strong-arm tactics that Garvey's eight critics cited in their letter to the attorney general were genuine. Some Garveyites interpreted literally the rhetorical violence that punctuated the speeches of UNIA officials. Bellicose oratory often stimulated the violent proclivities of petty criminals and pushed the political consciousness of "respectable" members of the working class toward sanctioning violence as a legitimate response to criticism or "treachery," as the fervid called it. Most of the victims were men named and excoriated by the UNIA leadership—blacks, not whites, and most often former Garveyites. The sin was treason, not racism.

The most important victim of the violence was the Reverend James Eason, the UNIA's former American leader and leading internal critic in 1922. Expelled during the 1922 convention, Eason continued his battle against Garvey by organizing the rival Negro Improvement Alliance. His challenge ended abruptly when he was shot and killed in New Orleans after he spoke at a black church on the evening of January 1, 1923. Before he died in the hospital, Eason described the attack. He initially heard one shot. Unaware that he had been hit, Eason turned around and was shot again in the forehead. He believed he was attacked by three Garveyites to prevent his testifying at the upcoming mail fraud trial. Although Eason could not identify the men, associates with him at the shooting identified two of them as Frederick Dyer and William Shakespeare of New Orleans. The third man was unknown to them. Subsequently, Dyer's wife, Celeste, named Esau Ramus to complete the trio. She told the police that, a few hours after the incident, Ramus had returned to his rented room in her house and admitted shooting Eason. Ramus was apprehended on February 20 in Detroit and indicted for the murder by a grand jury in New Orleans on March 1. Like Dyer and Shakespeare, he denied the charges against him.[1]

The Justice Department had prodded the New Orleans police to pursue Ramus in order to implicate Garvey. Some circumstances supported the government's belief that Garvey was connected to the shooting. He had sent Ramus to New Orleans for undisclosed work. After the murder, Ramus returned to New York and received money from Garvey to go to Detroit. Although Garvey was often indifferent to the legal problems of organizers, he went to great lengths to shield Ramus from prosecution. Garvey traveled to Detroit to devise plans with local UNIA leaders there to keep Ramus out of the hands of the police. When Ramus was arrested despite these efforts, the president of the Detroit UNIA, Alonzo Pettiford, represented him. After Ramus was extradited to New York, Garvey's personal lawyer, Vernal Williams, defended him. The unusual solicitude Ramus received suggested that he possessed information that could implicate Garvey.[2]

Many of Garvey's associates in New York believed that he had ordered Ramus to shoot Eason. Robert Poston, assistant president-general, threatened to resign because Garvey openly bragged about the death. Assistant Secretary-General J. B. Yearwood insisted that he had seen Garvey's letter authorizing the killing. Poston and Sydney de Bourg, the former West Indian organizer, believed that Garvey had sent Thomas Anderson, commissioner of Louisiana and a Parent Body official, to New Orleans to complete Ramus' preparation for the shooting. Both had overheard Anderson tell friends that Eason "got what was coming to him." Implying that he possessed inside information, Anderson informed an undercover agent that Ramus had shot Eason, but was certain that nobody would be able to prove it.[3]

Nevertheless, convincing evidence implicating Garvey does not exist. Because Ramus was never tried, his confession on May 6 that Garvey had authorized the killing, which he then carried out, was never subjected to cross-examination. Despite the urging of the Justice Department, the New Orleans police, short of money, did not request Ramus' extradition from

1. Harry D. Gulley, report, January 16, 1923, George Stanton to William Burns, February 24, March 16, 1923, in Garvey file, RG 65; James Amos, report, September 11, 1922. All reports cited in this chapter, except those otherwise noted, are agents' reports from the Garvey file, RG 65.
2. Andrew Battle, report, February 28, March 1, 2, 1923. Battle worked undercover in New York.
3. Ibid., March 1, 1923. An ex-Garveyite said that she had attended a meeting in June where Garvey promised Anderson a bigger job if he "got rid of" Eason. See also Gulley, report, January 26, 1923.

Detroit to stand trial for murder. Southern police were lax in cases in which the victim was black, and they already held two likely suspects. Dyer and Shakespeare were tried and convicted on March 22, 1923, for manslaughter, a compromise charge, and each sentenced to from eighteen to twenty years in prison. Later, on October 2, the Supreme Court of Louisiana remanded the case for a new trial because it concluded that the judge had improperly excluded defense evidence that Ramus had been indicted but not tried for the crime. Despite the pair's acquittal at a new trial on August 1, 1924, Ramus was not pursued by the New Orleans authorities. By then, he was in a New York prison, serving time for a crime committed in 1921. Garvey himself had been convicted of mail fraud, which ended the Justice Department's interest in Ramus. There was no longer any motive to discover the man responsible for the Eason shooting, which went unsolved and unpunished.[4]

It is likely, however, that Ramus shot Eason. He told the police that he had planned the attack, though he said the actual firing was done by Dyer, aided by Shakespeare. The executive secretary of the New Orleans division disclosed that Ramus told him on December 30, two days before the killing, that Eason's death would be "an easy matter." While Celeste Dyer's report of Ramus' confession might be discounted, Ramus' guilt was implicitly confirmed by a woman friend in New Orleans. In a letter written to him when he was hiding away in Detroit, she chastised him for admitting the deed to Celeste Dyer: "I am surprise of all things that woman [Celeste Dyer] say you told her you was crazy I guess. Now try and change up yourself and see cant you go towards Canada for a while [sic]." There was no suggestion that Dyer's accusation was false, only that Ramus should not have confessed the crime.[5]

Evidence linking Garvey to the murder was more tenuous and improbable. His initial boasting did not mean he actually planned the murder, only that he gloated over it. Garvey had often claimed credit for militant deeds that took place independent of his will or inspiration. Then, too, Ramus' accusations must be heavily discounted by his questionable character and his vulnerability at the time he made them. Convicted of attempted assault, in jail waiting to be sentenced, feeling abandoned by the UNIA, Ramus had every motive to provide the information the government wanted in order to receive a light sentence.

4. Battle, report, March 1, 1923; New Orleans *Times-Picayune*, March 23, 1923, July 30, 31, August 1, 1924.
5. J. W. Jones to William Burns, January 27, 1923, in Garvey file, RG 65. Jones, also known as "800," was the New Orleans undercover agent. Ethel Bruce to Henry Prince (alias of Esau Ramus), February 13, 1923, copy in P. H. Dupuis, report, February 24, 1923.

Existing evidence cannot chart with precision the plotting and carrying out of the Eason murder, but it permits an exploration of the impact of Garvey's militant rhetoric on his diverse followers. Everyone agreed that Dyer, Shakespeare, and Ramus had disrupted Eason's meetings in New Orleans and that Garvey had encouraged them. It is also true that Garvey and many Garveyites approved of the killing. One woman in Chicago explained that it was the duty of any member to protect the organization against men like Eason who betrayed "his oath made to Marcus Garvey. No traitor could live in the Garvey movement."[6]

But middle-class blacks opposed political violence. Many of them joined in the UNIA's military pomp for ceremonial purposes. Minister of African Legions Emmett L. Gaines had been in the black 24th Infantry. During World War I he had led parades of black soldiers. After the war, he staged the military processions for the UNIA. Gaines, who had been a contractor in Cleveland, practiced a symbolic militance, not assassination. The violent Garveyites were men such as Ramus, who were called "ignorant" and "fanatic" by respectable blacks. The Ramuses swaggered, threatened, and bullied. Although they often exceeded their instructions, they did not act without official sanction. As UNIA problems escalated, men like Esau Ramus became very useful to prevent Garvey's critics from organizing against him. At the time Ramus was sent to New Orleans, the city was an important prize in the struggle between Eason and Garvey. Although Eason paraded the democratic procedures and decentralization of his Negro Improvement Alliance before his audiences, his speeches for the most part appealed to and fanned anti-Garvey sentiment, not the virtues of structural reform. He charged that his rival had purchased a $25,000 plantation in the West Indies, that the UNIA treasury contained only $750, and that its businesses were nearly $300,000 in the red. Garvey went to New Orleans in October to try to stop Eason's raids on UNIA membership. Alerted by a group of black Baptist ministers, the police gladly halted a public meeting at Longshoreman's Hall despite the UNIA's permit to hold a "religious meeting." New Orleans police believed that Garvey and Garveyism incited blacks and provoked whites, and they possessed a large arsenal of local laws, ordinances, and powers to keep black militants from public exposure in New Orleans.[7]

The dispatching of Ramus to New Orleans on November 9 was the UNIA's response to the October setback. Garvey informed William Phil-

---

6. Mortimer Davis, report, April 27, 1923; T. L. Jefferson, report, February 27, 1923.

7. *Age*, October 14, 1922; *NW*, October 14, 1922; New Orleans *Times-Picayune*, October 28, 1922; Battle, report, March 1, 1923.

lips, the executive secretary of the division, that Ramus would live in New Orleans and work in the organization. Phillips cooperated. He arranged to have Ramus visit the homes of members to sell UNIA paraphernalia—buttons, anthems, and so forth—on commission. He asked the president of one of the satellite chapters in the area to call a meeting at which "Deputy Esau Ramus" would assist "in arousing more interest" in the association.[8] But Ramus began to organize a UNIA police force, too, despite the opposition of local leaders. The group, composed of about twenty men, was loosely organized. Many did not know one another. But William Phillips was alarmed and asked the Parent Body in New York for information about Ramus' men. Garvey's secretary informed him that Garvey was out of town. She could not authorize the force in his absence but added that Ramus had been very successful organizing police and secret service units in Philadelphia.[9]

Most of Ramus' previous UNIA work had been quasi-military. Born in St. Kitts, Ramus met Garvey and joined the UNIA in New York in 1918. He was active in the mostly ceremonial African Legion. Ramus worked occasionally as a laborer; he sold UNIA memorabilia. Crime and violence promised greater personal rewards. He was indicted in April, 1921, for attempting to rob and assault, with a concealed weapon, a furniture dealer in Harlem. Feigning a dislocated hip suffered at the moment of capture, he was removed to Harlem Hospital, from which he escaped. Ramus, who was also known as John Jeffries, went to Philadelphia, where he obtained a second alias, Henry Prince, a wife named May, and the title of third vice-president of the Philadelphia UNIA. Ramus, forty years old in 1922, was frustrated, angry, and vain. The symbolic militance of the UNIA could not compete with the more tangible rewards of armed robbery. His petty criminality became racial politics only because coercion had a critical role to play in UNIA politics in 1922. Ramus organized the Police and Secret Service Department for the Philadelphia local in July, 1922. The unit was modeled after the recently created group that battled the "Garvey Must Go" forces in New York. Ramus-Prince disrupted Eason's meetings in Philadelphia in September. Attired in his military uniform, he was arrested on September 24 for inciting to riot and carrying a deadly weapon. Garvey provided a lawyer and bail money. Although the Philadelphia case was pending, Ramus-Prince returned to New York under his other alias, John Jeffries. But the New York police had warrants for the arrest of Ramus-

8. MG to William Phillips, November 9, 1922; Phillips to Joseph Martin, December 12, 1922; Gulley, report, January 26, 1923.
9. William Phillips to E. H. Lamos, November 21, 1922, Lamos to Phillips, December 2, 1922, in Garvey file, RG 65.

Jeffries on the old charge of robbing the Harlem furniture store. Garvey urged Ramus to go to New Orleans to elude the police and disrupt Eason's meetings as he had done in Philadelphia. Whether, as Ramus later alleged, Garvey had told him to make sure "Eason did not return to New York alive," is more uncertain and unlikely.[10]

Garvey was informed of the shooting of Eason shortly after the incident occurred. With undisguised delight, he bragged about stopping Eason while he routinely requested UNIA leaders in New Orleans to obtain a hall for January 19 to welcome the delegates returning from the League of Nations mission. Only when Ramus returned to New York and informed UNIA leaders that the police were looking for him did leading Garveyites show signs of concern. It is possible that until then Garvey was even unaware of the identity of Eason's assailants. He acted quickly. On January 12, Thomas Anderson telegrammed William Phillips, the New Orleans local's executive secretary, to retain the law firm of Woodville and Woodville for the two indicted men. The New Orleans leadership had distanced itself from the defense of Dyer and Shakespeare. Acting with a clear conscience and in an attempt to preserve the organization from hostile police, Phillips refused to comply with Anderson's instructions. Nevertheless, the New Orleans police stormed a UNIA meeting on January 19, arrested ten officers, and seized the files. Determined to use the shooting to rid the city of Garveyism, the police hoped to discover evidence to convict Dyer and Shakespeare and prove that the UNIA was planning a race war. Agents of the Department of Justice shared their zeal but were more interested in finding evidence linking Garvey to the shooting. But neither the local nor national police discovered the documents to support their theories and fantasies.[11]

But Garvey's fears of danger had not dissipated. He sent Ramus to Detroit, in the hands of a loyal division, and then visited him personally on January 31. Nevertheless, government agents learned from Sydney de Bourg, the former UNIA organizer, that Ramus was in Detroit.[12] The police located him at a UNIA meeting on February 20. Unlike the New Orleans police, however, the Detroit force did not perceive the UNIA to be a menace to the social order. Instead of raiding headquarters in the manner of their southern colleagues, officers obtained an arrest warrant. They surrounded the building while a federal agent informed President Pettiford of

10. Esau Ramus, "Statement," February 23, 1923, in Garvey file, RG 65; Mortimer Davis, report, February 14, 26, 1923; J. G. Shuey, report, January 31, 1923.

11. New Orleans *Times-Picayune*, January 20, 1923; Gulley, report, January 26, 1923; Thomas Anderson to William Phillips, January 12, 1923, in Garvey file, RG 65.

12. Amos and Davis, report, January 27, 1923; Davis, report, February 14, 1923.

their purpose. Pettiford won a ten-minute delay to finish the business of the meeting, but after only four or five minutes the police stormed the room when they heard a loud noise coming from inside. Entering the adjacent bathroom, they discovered glass scattered on the floor beneath a new hole in a twenty-five-foot skylight. Climbing through to the roof, a bewildered officer could not locate Ramus. Puzzled because there was no contiguous buildings to escape to, he descended to find that another policeman had discovered Ramus on a telephone pole, forty or fifty feet from the building. The acrobatic Ramus had chinned himself along the wire from building to pole.[13]

Conflicting interests nearly freed Ramus at the moment of apprehension. The New Orleans police refused to pay the expenses of extradition. So long as Ramus, or for that matter Garvey, stayed out of New Orleans, they had no interest in pursuing him. Having in custody two men they believed to be guilty, they were reluctant to spend money to track down and return a third man. Only the Justice Department wanted Ramus, for the purpose of linking him with Garvey. J. Edgar Hoover believed that Ramus would "involve Garvey in this case, which would result in Garvey's being included as an accessory before the fact." He was able to convince the New York police to request, and pay for, Ramus' return on the basis of an old charge of assault, attempted larceny, and the possession of a gun. Ramus was brought to the Tombs in New York on April 6.[14]

Perhaps recognizing Ramus' potential for duplicity, Garvey assigned his personal lawyer Vernal Williams to the case. Williams told Ramus that he had no chance of acquittal before a "white Judge, witness, and prosecuting attorney" who were "against Negroes." On April 26, he pleaded guilty to attempted assault. Williams then took forty dollars and left Ramus alone in jail. That afternoon, feeling abandoned, Ramus told one of the detectives working on Garvey's prosecution that he was "through with Garvey" and the UNIA. On May 6, appearing before Assistant U.S. Attorney Maxwell Mattuck, the prosecutor in the mail fraud case, Ramus promised a detailed statement implicating Garvey in the Eason murder if he was given a suspended sentence. Mattuck promised nothing but implied that such cooperation would be rewarded when he delayed Ramus' sentencing until after Garvey's trial.[15]

In return, Ramus told Mattuck that while he was in Philadelphia, he

---

13. Dupuis, report, February 24, 1923.
14. New Orleans *Times-Picayune*, December 28, 1922; J. Edgar Hoover to William Burns, February 13, 1923, George Stanton to Burns, February 21, March 1, 12, 1923, Burns to Edward J. Brennan, February 23, 1923, in Garvey file, RG 65.
15. Davis, report, April 27, May 10, 1923.

had received a letter from Garvey stating that Eason's meetings there "must be broken up or he must not return to New York alive." Shortly afterwards, Garvey told him that Eason "had turned State's evidence against him [Garvey], and must not be allowed to return to New York [from New Orleans] to testify against him." Garvey then gave him a hundred dollars for the trip to New Orleans, where Ramus planned the shooting, which Dyer and Shakespeare carried out. Ramus volunteered to lead agents to UNIA arms caches in New York and Philadelphia. He claimed that guns had been purchased and stored by himself, Vernal Williams, and H. V. Plummer in New York, by Lionel Francis in Philadelphia, and by Levi Lord in Detroit.[16]

Garvey obtained a new lawyer for the fickle Ramus when he discovered that Ramus was cooperating with the government. He also promised to give Ramus' wife two hundred dollars. Simultaneously, Lionel Francis, head of the Philadelphia UNIA, urged Ramus not to testify against Garvey and promised support after he got out of prison. Pressed from both sides, Ramus grew impatient and decided to take his chances for obtaining a suspended sentence immediately, before Garvey's trial. Unsuccessful, he was sentenced to four to eight years in prison. He continued to accuse Garvey, but without a legal conclusion to his own role in the Eason murder, his version of the story lacked persuasiveness.[17]

When it became clear that the New Orleans police would not try Ramus, the Justice Department considered prosecuting him for shooting a government witness. But Eason had voluntarily offered to testify against Garvey. At the time of his death, he had not been a subpoenaed witness, the necessary status to give the federal government standing in the case. It is likely that the Justice Department would have tried to overcome the jurisdictional problem more vigorously had Garvey been freed. Even after Garvey was found guilty and sentenced to prison, Mattuck secured Ramus' promise to testify against Garvey for complicity in the shooting.[18]

If Ramus shot Eason, his previous history of petty crime, violence, and intimidation intermixed with racial consciousness explains why he viewed the murder as a political act. Eager for action, full of self-importance, desiring significance, Ramus was a braggart. He told William Phillips that he had broken his hip in a fight to protect Garvey when in fact he had injured himself while attempting to rob a store. Ramus craved the trappings of power. Instead of crossing the border into Canada, he stayed in Detroit

16. *Ibid.*, May 10, 1923.
17. *Ibid.*, March 9, 1923. The Ramus case was closed in 1926 when he was released on parole after the federal government and state of Louisiana informed New York authorities that they had no interest in pursuing him. C. J. Espinal, report, June 17, 1926.
18. Davis, report, May 25, 19, 21, 1923.

and immediately began ordering the paraphernalia of police forces and se-cret services—badges, cards, insignias, and guns. Ramus required autho-rization, and the approbation of UNIA leaders had given him the freedom to act. When the organization no longer supplied the attention and feeling of importance he needed, he pursued the promises of the government. Ramus' eagerness to track down Eason was fed by private as well as politi-cal ends, which the UNIA often fused and confused. Witnesses testified that the two men had clashed in the past because Eason was "fooling around with Ramus's wife in Philadelphia." [19]

The purposes of Frederick Dyer and William Shakespeare, both mem-bers of the New Orleans UNIA, were more puzzling. Little is known about Shakespeare, a Jamaican longshoreman who worked in South America be-fore he came to the United States in 1918 or 1919. More is known of Dyer's life. A longshoreman, Dyer was thirty-eight years old and had been mar-ried for ten years. Born in Jamaica, he had been in the United States since 1908 except for four years in England during the war. He was a member of the Odd Fellows and Masons as well as the UNIA. Dyer appeared to be stable and rooted. Husband, homeowner, boardinghouse keeper, wage worker, he had numerous social affiliations, the marks of the respectable working and lower-middle class. [20]

Dyer and Shakespeare had been part of Ramus' police force, which met every Wednesday night in Ramus' room. The two had attended the meet-ing where Eason spoke on the night of the shooting. They had been quickly identified as the killers because Eason's friends had recalled their menacing presence at other anti-Garvey meetings. (They would not have known Ramus, a stranger in New Orleans.) Both accused men denied that they had anything to do with the shooting. Even if we accept the court's confirmation of their innocence, the question why a man like Dyer was at-tracted to Ramus remains. Put more abstractly, under what circumstances does the stable working class become attracted to a politics of personal vio-lence and assassination? [21]

Dyer's history suggests that sometimes the break between nonviolent and violent politics is not sharp. He joined Ramus' band in 1922 after a period of turbulence within the UNIA, which, for him, the crime of treason explained and the punishment of violence promised to exorcise. Dyer was one of the founders of the New Orleans UNIA. Although Black Star Line

19. Parish of Orleans, Criminal District Court, *State of Louisiana* v. *William Shakespeare and Constantine Dyer*, "Bill of Exceptions," nos. 25, 30, 49–50, 53–54, in Records of the New Orleans Police Department, New Orleans Public Library.

20. Gulley, report, January 23, 1923.

21. *Ibid.*, January 23, 26, 1923.

stock had been sold in the city in 1919, the division was begun by fifteen men and women, laborers and servants, in October, 1920. Mamie Reason, a domestic and treasurer of the division, stated that the intention of the UNIA was the "uplifting of the negro race, financially, morally, and mentally." UNIA meetings in New Orleans featured inspirational talks by ministers and club officers but also dinners and fashion shows. The only clue that the group was more than another social circle was its ceremonial African Legion for men and its Black Cross Nurse unit for women. Both linked its members symbolically to the more advanced political culture of Garveyism.[22]

The New Orleans division had difficulty transcending the small nucleus that created it. Adrian Johnson, an organizer from New York, attempted to interest other clubs and associations in the UNIA. He urged the West Indian Seamen's Social Benevolent and Library Association "to pay the UNIA a visit to be convinced before turning away from its ideals." He promised that members could join "without ever losing their specific identity." He added, "Whatever we may accomplish in a small way can also be accomplished in a greater, since it only meant greater cooperation, more money, and more faithfulness."[23]

Johnson's appeal was blunted by the numerous questions raised by members and nonmembers about the money already collected for the BSL. In order to find out the true affairs of the company, Mamie Reason attended the UNIA convention in New York in 1921. Garvey attempted to deflect some criticism by alluding to secret aims and projects that could not be publicly proclaimed. He told a group of sixteen, including Reason, that he intended to unite all Negroes and organize an army, navy, and a merchant marine. The Black Cross Nurses and the Juvenile Departments of the locals were preparations for a racial Armaggedon. When blacks were strong enough, they would join with Japan to declare war on the white race and win Africa. Garvey wove current disarmament talks, which featured the rise of Japan, into his portrait of future racial power. He insisted that future victories rested on the unquestioning loyalty they gave to him and the Parent Body.[24]

At the same time, Garvey set up a new civil service system, "which will enable us to guarantee honesty of service to every division of the UNIA by placing trained and disciplined men as Civil Servants in the field. Every branch of the UNIA is to have an Executive Secretary who shall be a Civil Servant." In line with the new plan, Garvey appointed twenty-nine-year-

22. *Ibid.*
23. *NW*, April 2, 1921.
24. Mamie Reason, "Interview," January 26, 1923, in Garvey file, RG 65.

old William Phillips executive secretary of the New Orleans division, with a salary of twenty-two dollars a week. Phillips, a native of Barbados, had been general secretary of the Boston UNIA from September, 1919, through August, 1921, when he accepted the new post in New Orleans. At the same time, Thomas Anderson replaced S. V. Robertson, a porter and the first president of the division, as commissioner of Louisiana. Anderson was born in Virginia and schooled in Bluefield, West Virginia, and Nashville, Tennessee. He had pastored a Baptist church in Adrian, Michigan, until 1919. Active in Republican politics, he was a water inspector in Hamtramck, Michigan, assistant clerk of the village council, deputy sheriff, and president of its NAACP. Like many other UNIA leaders, Anderson was born and educated in the South, moved to the new northern areas, became active in racial politics after the Great Migration, but found the local black population too small and poor to launch a significant political career.[25]

With his new emissaries, Garvey attempted to woo the more substantial members of the black community, which was the organizing strategy pursued in other cities in 1922. Although the New Orleans division had enlisted about three thousand members, it lacked the resources to purchase a building of its own. New Orleans Garveyites met at Longshoremen's Hall, constructed and owned by the local dockers' union, on Thursday nights, the traditional free time for domestics. To break through the wall of ministerial opposition and to attract the more influential members of the city's black community, Garvey sent Eason, the UNIA's American leader, to New Orleans. The *Negro World* explained that Dr. Eason "is a broad-minded diplomat and is the type of what the representatives of the parent body would be if we expect to win over the intelligent as well as the other members of the race."[26]

Despite the agreement on the new recruiting policy, the rivalry between Eason and Garvey, which would lead to the American leader's expulsion in August, threatened Garvey's strategy. Anderson, appointed by Garvey, remained loyal to him. Local leaders Mamie Reason and the division's current president, T. R. Robinson, a longshoreman, supported Eason and other dissidents against Garvey on the basis of their experiences at the New York convention in 1922. Reason and Robinson, charged with treason, resigned. They were replaced with professors from a local Baptist college.[27]

Anderson, now second assistant secretary-general of the Parent Body

25. *Ibid.*; *NW*, August 27, 1921, December 19, 1923.
26. Gulley, report, January 26, 1923; Anderson to Phillips, October 10, 1922, in Garvey file, RG 65; *Age*, January 13, 27, 1923; *NW*, October 2, 14, 1922.
27. *Age*, January 27, 1923; *NW*, October 2, 14, 1922.

as well as commissioner of Louisiana, and Garvey had used the Eason controversy to replace the working-class leaders with the middle-class ones they wanted. But their hopes of extended UNIA influence did not materialize. The Baptist professors who led the division took little interest in the running of the local and failed to stop Eason's progress in the city. Mamie Reason claimed that membership was down to one hundred. Anderson accused Executive Secretary Phillips of secret allegiance to Eason and warned him that "the Parent Body would not tolerate the slightest suspicion of disloyalty. It is your business to see that members do not become dissatisfied with the work and that the division progresses properly." Phillips' rejoinder that the local difficulties stemmed from Parent Body policies, especially the constant appeals for money, fell on deaf ears. Publicly, the *Negro World* told its readers that the division's problems were caused by "those disgruntled elements that belong to the rule or ruin class of members."[28]

Dyer had not joined the Eason forces with Mamie Reason and T. R. Robinson. Possibly, he lacked the personal conflict with Garvey that Reason and Robinson had experienced at the convention of 1922. At that time Robinson had declared: "After spending 31 days with Garvey the New Orleans branch of the UNIA will either quit following Garvey and the outrageous methods he employs in handling the affairs of the association and line up behind some other fairer man who will organize a similar movement in opposition to it, or split up in factions aiming at the same and for the good of the Negro people of the United States. I am sick and disgusted with the pretension of Garvey." Robinson objected to the UNIA's "titles and other tomfooleries" and to the way Garvey overrode "the wishes of the delegates." He concluded, "To follow Garvey any longer one would have to be a rank fool."[29]

Robinson's criticism was not the ideological broadside of Cyril Briggs or A. Philip Randolph, because his expectations of the UNIA were traditional. Robinson was a union officer and delegate to the International Longshoremen's Association Buffalo convention in 1921. Many of the members of that union, once militant and currently on the defensive, were simultaneously members of fraternals. Unlike many of the New York radicals, Robinson measured the value of the UNIA on the scales of the lodge, not the revolutionary vanguard. Although he leaned toward Eason's new organization, he did not invest major efforts in the enterprise. He was not present on the night Eason was shot. His name did not figure in Eason's

28. *NW*, October 14, 1922; Gulley, report, January 26, 1923.
29. *Age*, September 16, 1922.

other New Orleans campaigns. But the *Negro World* accused him of "attempting to deliver the division to Mr. Eason."[30]

Mamie Reason, with Robinson, left the UNIA after the 1922 convention. But she threw her energy behind Eason's new organization. In the audience when he spoke on January 1, Reason was a witness to the shooting. Her political ideas are more available to us than Dyer's because she was more active at UNIA meetings and conventions, where her words were recorded. At the 1922 convention in New York, Reason told delegates, "Negroes were lynched because they were not respected, and not respected because they had no government." Reason employed Garveyite rhetoric and terminology, but the substance of her politics was the practices and goals of the respectable working and lower-middle class of New Orleans. At local UNIA meetings she had urged women to stand behind their husbands and often reminded members to follow the rules of the organization. For her, collective action was not a qualitative change but the accumulation of the nonpolitical, nonagitational individual efforts that she knew in New Orleans. The blueprint of black nationhood was the political economy of the family and local association. To Mamie Reason, the UNIA should help the respectable working class maintain the cohesion of the family, avoid violence, and promote regular habits and hard work. She had returned from the 1922 convention believing that Marcus Garvey was ruining the Negro race with "his radical ideas and intentions." His talk appeared to bolster the violence of southern life, which she had been trying to banish from the black community. Combined with the apparent dishonesty or incompetence of Parent Body leaders and the failure of UNIA projects, the fear that Garveyite militance would only lead to violence and trouble led other New Orleans blacks to withdraw from the UNIA. Whether they were domestics with meager outlets of political expression or longshoremen with more profound associations, many working-class members demanded order, purpose, and regularity from an organization.[31]

Men like Frederick Dyer responded differently to the stimulus and failures of Garveyism. If Mamie Reason had been attracted to Garveyism as a politics of improvement, Dyer was drawn by a politics of justice and vengeance, of racial power and influence, an equally powerful source of the UNIA's attraction.[32] When Dyer was picked up by the police, he had among his papers a picture of the UNIA delegates to the League of Nations at Geneva, the UNIA mission that attempted to win status and power for blacks

30. *NW*, October 7, 28, 1922.

31. Gulley, report, January 26, March 15, 1923; *NW*, August 19, 1922.

32. George Stanton to William Burns, January 13, 1923, in Garvey file, RG 65; Gulley, report, February 23, 1923.

in the wider world. He also possessed a badge with the inscription JUS-TICE—UNIA POLICE 47 and several samples from the same Philadelphia company that Ramus had patronized and probably introduced him to. Possibly Dyer intended to recruit others or simply sell the badges. His loyalties certainly were not exclusive. He possessed a membership card for a Justice Council of another fraternal that recorded his payment of quarterly dues of twenty-five cents three times during 1922 through September. That he did not pay them for the fourth quarter suggests that the purposes that he sought to achieve in the Justice Council were to be realized through the new UNIA police force. He did not possess a regular UNIA card, which indicated that he had not been paying dues or attending meetings regularly.[33]

Stimulated by Garveyism's promise of retribution, Dyer was disappointed by its failures. He had been a member of the African Legion. When Garvey came to New Orleans in October, 1922, its members had been prepared to fire on the police if they had arrested Garvey. The legion had no opportunity to demonstrate its bravery and loyalty because Garvey was not seized. When the police broke up the UNIA meeting at Longshoremen's Hall, only one man resisted and was arrested. The legion had no role to play when the leaders, in this case Garvey himself, chose to obey police orders. After this experience of frustration, several legionnaires readily joined Ramus, who had vague authorization from Garvey to organize a new military force and who claimed a certain amount of success in New York and Philadelphia. Nevertheless, when Ramus first asked him to join, Dyer sought but failed to obtain the approval of the local officers of the UNIA. Dyer's decision to flout local leaders was eased by the large rift within the New Orleans division created by the imposition of the "college men" to replace the laborers who founded the division.[34]

Dyer did not see Garvey's hand in the critical setbacks in UNIA history in New Orleans. Garvey's lieutenants, especially Thomas Anderson, worked hard to retain membership and promote the view that traitors like Eason were the cause of UNIA failings. Eason's promise of a better-run, tidier organization could not have enticed Dyer, as he sought justice, not balanced ledgers, from racial organizations. His frustrations grew at the same time the reporting of the internal conflicts of the UNIA became more inflammatory and UNIA rhetoric more martial. ENEMY ORGANIZATIONS

33. See Randall Burkett's excellent discussion of religious retribution in his *Garveyism as a Religious Movement: The Institutionalization of a Black Civil Religion* (Metuchen, N.J., 1978), 36–37.
34. J. W. Jones to Burns, January 19, 1923, in Garvey file, RG 65; New Orleans *Times-Picayune*, October 28, 1922.

ORGANIZE FORCE AGAINST THE MIGHTY MOVEMENT (*i.e.*, the UNIA), proclaimed one *Negro World* headline. Garvey's prominent reporting of German military plans had the effect of popularizing military solutions to all
racial ills from Jim Crow to Jim Eason. Music director Arnold Ford spoke
of organizing blacks to march and seize territory below the Mason-Dixon
Line. Reporting on an anti-Garvey meeting in Chicago, the *Negro World*
casually informed readers that "several shots fired in an altercation near
the church just after the meeting had adjourned led many to believe that
Eason had paid the price of the traitor, but this line of thought later proved
erroneous." This thinly concealed approval of assassination was a preview
of events in New Orleans.[35]

The new violence also fed other cultural imperatives in the South. The
tradition of vigilantism and the lingering "direct action" practices derived
from the war and its aftermath legitimized force and extended the practices of coercion beyond the criminal, pathological, and passionate into respectable parts of the community. For large parts of the black population,
politics was synonymous with force. Disfranchised working-class blacks
often encountered politics as the power of police authorities. The UNIA in
the South easily incorporated the style of southern politics. In July, 1923, a
group of Garveyites wearing masks flogged a colored woman in New Orleans. The South's disorganized and shifting factional political groups fostered the view that politics was propelled by personality and conspiracy.
Southern Garveyites were especially receptive to the charge that Eason
was the source of UNIA failures. In the desperate world of racial politics in
1922, violence, intimidation, and assassination became the legitimate and
often the only form of politics for men like Frederick Dyer.[36]

35. *NW*, October 7, 14, 1922; *Age*, January 27, 1923.
36. Baltimore *Afro-American*, January 20, 1923.

10 / The Politics of Fraud
J. Edgar Hoover versus Marcus Garvey

Although Garvey was indicted in 1922 for a commercial crime, his prosecutors were driven by the political goal of deporting the leading black alien agitator in the United States. At that time, the hysteria of the war had subsided, which forced bureaucracies to pay more attention to legal forms. The Justice Department fastened upon the crime of mail fraud, accidentally and after a long search for a deportable offense.

Garvey first won notice of the federal government's intelligence apparatus at the time of the Armistice.[1] On November 5, 1918, the British war office requested information on Garvey, Harlem journalist John Bruce, and the UNIA because of their association with Dusé Mohamed Ali, Garvey's old London employer and sometime comrade. The matter was referred to Emmett Scott, the black assistant in the War Department. Scott, who had met Garvey at Tuskegee in 1916, summoned him to Washington on December 9 to warn him that words published in the *Negro World* that disputed the "unity of purposes between the racial groups in America," were provocative. He classified Garvey as "the agitator type," responsive to the "general unrest of Darker peoples," noisy but "harmless"; the UNIA was merely "a paper organization" that "should not be seriously regarded." Major Walter H. Loving, a retired black officer who was a member of the regular Military Intelligence Division (MID) staff, expressed more but still limited concern. He had dispatched agents to attend UNIA meetings. Reporting on one in Washington, D.C., in early January, Loving observed that Garvey's language would have been legally seditious if spoken during the war. He was referring to a statement by Garvey predicting that "the darker races" would aid the side that offered them "freedom and liberty" in the next war. Although individuals in the Justice Department had wanted to take action against Garvey's *Negro World* in early 1919, the assistant attorney general in charge of seditious prosecution saw no basis for action.

1. The Bureau of Investigation was beginning to dominate the federal government's surveillance work. However, much intelligence was still gathered by other branches of government.

He said that "in a democratic form of government like ours the right to agitate to influence governmental policy" is fundamental.[2]

Because Garvey and the other black agitators were generals without troops in early 1919, government agencies monitored their activities but did not consider them a "serious matter." Alien radicals won top billing on the government's wanted list. Among blacks, those who advocated bolshevism were viewed as most troublesome. Behind this concern was the fear that radical forces would unite. Aided by a rash of mysterious bombings in the spring of 1919, Attorney General A. Mitchell Palmer won $500,000 from Congress to create an "investigatory force" to continue their war against radicals in peacetime. J. Edgar Hoover, head of the new General Intelligence Division, unleashed his new manpower and channeled the rising political hysteria in the direction of alien radicals, the most visible and vulnerable of American dissenters. Authorized by laws that made teaching, advocacy, and sympathy with anarchism or anarchists, revolution or revolutionaries deportable offenses, Hoover and a cooperative Immigration Bureau used the dragnet raid and swift deportation to excise the cancer of revolution from the body politic.[3]

Even when the outbreak of race riots in Washington and Chicago in July made black radicalism a government concern, Garvey remained a peripheral problem. On August 9, officials of the MID and the Bureau of Investigation authorized special agents in the field to recruit "reliable negroes" to ascertain the propaganda of the "various negro lodges and associations." The MID operated on the theory that the new black militance had been encouraged by the government itself. The Liberty Loan drives and other patriotic rallies had raised expectations about "a modification, or possible removal, of some of the discrimination of which they complain." The "emphasis which has been laid upon the principles of democracy and the self-determination of racially defined peoples, during . . . the war, has not been without its effect upon the colored people of this country." The army thought that current "tension would be relieved very considerably if proper ways could be found to make the practice of lynching a thing of the past" and to modify "Jim Crow regulations so that their enforcement would strike less harshly those for whom these restrictions are not pri-

2. S. Newby to H. A. Pakenham, November 4, 1918, Emmett Scott to MID, December 11, 1918, Major W. H. Loving to Director, MID, January 5, 1919, file 10218-261/9, 23, and 26, MID, in RG 165; J. Edgar Hoover to Ben A. Matthews, December 3, 1919, file 9-12-725, in RG 60; Alfred Bettman to W. E. Allen, March 17, 1919, in Garvey file, RG 65.
3. Max Lowenthal, *The Federal Bureau of Investigation* (New York, 1950), 270–77; Major W. H. Loving to Director, MID, January 6, 1919, file 10218-261/23, February 17, 1919, file 10218-309/2, MID, in RG 165.

marily intended [the middle class]." Finally, army practices "which were suited to conditions fifty years ago" should be removed. Despite a sophisticated analysis of some of the sources and targets of black protest, the function of the MID was social control, not reform. The army believed that interracial committees and organizations like the Urban League were the proper instruments for racial adjustment. Fighting for Negro rights, especially with arms, would not break down prejudice, which was in its view the cause of racial discrimination.[4]

Alert to the different forms of black protest, the government observed uneasily the growth of racial consciousness, but it feared the merging of the new Negro movement with the nation's "social and industrial unrest." Both the MID and the Justice Department, which showed none of the army's complex analysis of racial questions, investigated blacks in, or advocating work with, the radical groups of 1919—the IWW, the Socialist party, and eventually the Communist party. Groping agents in the field lacked firm knowledge of the ins and outs of black politics. One MID informer imaginatively linked Morris Lewis of the NAACP, Republican Congressman Oscar DePriest, Ida Wells-Barnett, and Garvey together in one socialist bomb-making factory in Chicago. Despite the inaccuracies in the initial period of panicked surveillance, the targets chosen by the government exemplified its theory that the most dangerous black militants were those affiliated with America's radical movements.[5]

In August, 1919, J. Edgar Hoover asked U.S. Attorney Francis Gaffey in New York to indict the editors of the *Messenger* under the Espionage Act. The prosecutor agreed that the September *Messenger* contained "open pleas . . . to Negroes . . . to join the Socialist party and to ally themselves with the I.W.W. . . . and to meet force with force," but he feared that "it would be impossible to secure a conviction given the sentiment in this district." Tactics, not goals, held him back. Gaffey told Hoover: "Unless a successful outcome could reasonably be anticipated, the publicity would further the cause of the I.W.W. elements. . . . These people thrive on publicity, and I am convinced are persistently endeavoring to induce the Government to start court proceedings against them, for the sake of the

4. Henry G. Sebastian, "Memorandum for Colonel A. B. Coxe," August 9, 1919, file 10218-361/3, J. E. Cutler, "Confidential Memorandum," August 15, 1919, M. Churchill to Frank Burke, August 19, 1919, file 10218-361/8, MID, in RG 165.

5. Cutler, "Confidential Memorandum," August 15, 1919, file 10218-361/8, "Memorandum for Colonel A. B. Coxe," July 1, 1919, file 10218-339/2, Chicago operative to Mr. Kenney, October 15, 1919, file 10218-377/1, J. Waller to Military Intelligence Office, September 6, 1919, file 10218-367/1, "Negro Activities," September 27, 1919, file 10218-364/7, MID, in RG 165.

advertisement they would get and also to lend color to their claims of persecution."[6]

Agents of the Bureau of Investigation monitored Garvey along with other blacks. An informant was placed in the office of the *Negro World*. But Garvey's activities in 1919, centered around the building of the Black Star Line, did not trigger indictments, raids, or harassment. In October, 1919, at the height of the government's campaign against radicals, Hoover told complaining Panama Canal officials that he regretted he could not deport Garvey—the UNIA leader had not violated a federal law. Considering that Hoover was currently planning the dragnet raids on alien radicals, this scrupulousness toward the law must have been motivated by his assessment that the danger of Garveyism was low. In January, 1920, the Justice Department acknowledged that Garvey was "still the foremost pro-negro agitator in New York." But it concluded that "his pro-negroism is secondary to his scheme for the solicitation of subscriptions for stock in the Black Star Line, his proposed line of Negro steamships." So long as black sharecroppers were organizing, black Detroiters attending an IWW school, black longshoremen on strike, and middle-class blacks espousing socialism, the government had more pressing problems than Garveyism. But when much of the black militancy dependent upon the larger radicalism of the United States ended, bureaucrats in the Justice Department and Immigration Bureau began to pursue Garvey, who had already won their displeasure and whose alien status made him vulnerable. In July, 1921, immigration agents held Garvey in New Orleans on his return from his West Indian trip. But the popular revulsion against the excesses of the "Red raids" had led to reforms and required minimum due process. Because Garvey possessed a good passport, visa, and lawyer, and was not charged with any crime, eager officials could not prevent his reentry.[7]

6. U.S. Attorney to Attorney General, September 17, 1919, Attorney General to U.S. Attorney, September 30, 1919, file 9-12-72S, in RG 60.

7. A. L. Flint to Bureau [of Investigation], October 9, 1919, J. Edgar Hoover, "Memorandum for Mr. Ridgely," October 11, 1919, file 198940, "Radical Activities Bulletin," January 19–24, 1920, in RG 60; William Matthews to Charles E. Hughes, June 11, 1921, Charles Latham to Secretary of State, April 12, 1921, MG to Hughes, July 13, 1921, file 811.108 G191 29/8/9, in RG 59. Robert Hill believes that Garvey secured his visa after William Matthews, the UNIA's principal lawyer, bribed Alexander McBride, an official of the State Department. Allegedly, Matthews worked through Henry Lincoln Johnson, the leading black politician and wheeler-dealer of the Republican party. Hill's conclusion is based on a suspicion to that effect held by J. Edgar Hoover. Whether or not the visa was obtained this way, the fact that Garvey received it demonstrated that State Department officials did not share Hoover's views of Garvey and that Hoover's freedom to act was bridled by procedures that did not exist during the height of the Red Scare. Robert A. Hill (ed.), *The Mar-*

Patriotic crusaders had less success convincing their countrymen of the existence of the domestic menace in the Age of Normalcy. The new Republican attorney general, Harry Daugherty, was more interested in pursuing personal wealth than Bolsheviks. The failure of most of the strikes of 1919 and 1920, as well as the success of the government's own antiradical program, had diminished the size of the left. Many federal officials resisted the active pursuit of radicals because the states and local governments had reasserted their authority. As William Preston concluded: "The overt delirium had subsided and the techniques of repression had changed. On the other hand, the ideological framework was certainly the same; perhaps it had even become more uncompromisingly anti-radical. Federal officials continued to believe that the best radicals were either dead or deported ones, that the threat from the left was as real as ever, and that it was the duty of public servants to control and isolate this menace."[8]

Therefore, though the hysteria of 1919–1920 was lacking, the ideological signatures of the Red Scare—the emergence of the problem of the "New Negro," the fear of social radicalism and revolution, the targeting of the alien radical—were visible in Garvey's indictment. Justice Department agents pursued him with unceasing diligence but found it difficult to discover a deportable offense. Stymied, William Burns, the new head of the Justice Department's Bureau of Investigation, had warned the Shipping Board of Garvey's menace. Similarly, when Cyril Briggs sued Garvey for libel in October, 1921, a special agent of the Bureau of Investigation briefed an assistant U.S. attorney in New York "on the nature of Garvey's activities and the importance attached to the present proceeding [the Briggs case]." He, too, was uninterested.[9]

Burns looked for income tax violations. Agents pursued the hope of a Mann Act violation by posting an observer outside of Garvey's lodging in Washington. Undercover agent "800" in Harlem found that "Garvey seems to keep just enough within the law and keep out of prison." But the persistent surveillance eventually turned up something. Agent "800" discovered that Cyril Briggs had been attempting to convince the Post Office Department to prosecute Garvey for publishing and sending through the mail a picture of a ship represented as belonging to the BSL but that the BSL did not actually own.[10]

cus Garvey and Universal Negro Improvement Association Papers (10 vols. projected; Berkeley, 1983–), I, lxxix–lxxx.

8. William Preston, Jr., Aliens and Dissenters: Federal Suppression of Radicals, 1903–1933 (Cambridge, Mass., 1963), 240–44, 285.

9. Ibid., 234; William Burns to Frank Burke, August 31, 1921, file 605-1-653, in RG 32; Edward Anderson, report, October 1921, in Garvey file, RG 65.

10. George F. Ruch, "Memorandum for Mr. Hoover," November 5, 1921, William

The Bureau of Investigation dispatched Agent Mortimer Davis to follow up the lead. Briggs assured Davis that the BSL circular had been mailed and promised to provide names and addresses of individuals who had received it. With these pledges, Burns formally approached the chief inspector of the post office in Washington. He wrote: "As you are probably aware, this Bureau for many months past has been investigating MARCUS GARVEY, an alien Negro who, for more than two years has been living lavishly off the meager savings of poor Negroes throughout the United States. The investigation so far discloses violations of several federal statutes not the least in importance being the violation of the Postal laws." The inspector agreed and ordered the New York office to prepare the preliminary case, the basis of Garvey's arrest.[11]

Garvey's indictment was more the result of his past sins than the product of a new theory about Negro radicalism, of the maturation of black protest, or of the effectiveness of the UNIA. At this time, agents found most black organizations and periodicals feeble. One reported, with the breezy air of the *cognescente*, that "the *Crisis* for November [1921] is its usual conservative self"; another, that Chandler Owen's editorial on the Tulsa riot in the *Messenger* lacked "the overt threat of earlier days." Garvey's "affairs and those of his various enterprises" were judged to be "getting into worse financial condition each day. It is reported that he is finding it harder to obtain contributions owing to the lack of employment among the Negroes and the falling off in membership of the U.N.I.A. It is understood that several branches of the latter organization are in open revolt against Garvey and his methods and that recently about 700 members left the Philadelphia organization and more than twice that number left branches in Chicago and other cities." Another agreed with the evaluation of Garveyism published in the Communist *Toiler*: "A shrewd mixture of racialism, religion, and nationalistic fanaticism. . . . It is one of the signs of his [the Negro's] awakening, the noisiest, though not the most effective, challenge to the white world." Mortimer Davis summarized department feeling when he concluded that Garvey "had been giving the Department of Justice endless trouble for years."[12]

Burns to Edward Brennan, November 9, 1921, Mortimer J. Davis, report, November 18, 1921, Burns to David H. Blair, December 12, 1921, in Garvey file, RG 65.

11. William Burns to R. D. Simmons, December 7, 1921, "800" to George Ruch, [November] 1921, W. W. G[rimes], "Memorandum for Files," December 9, 1921, Hoover, "Memorandum for Mr. Ruch," November 17, 1921, in Garvey file, RG 65. Agents searched for a way to indict Briggs, too. Cooperation brought no immunity.

12. Davis, report, January 14, 18, 1922, in Garvey file, RG 65; "Negro Activities," October 29–December 19, 1921, in RG 65; "Report on Radical Press, New York City," October, 1921, in RG 28.

The Justice Department arrested Garvey on January 12, 1922, and a grand jury indicted him and three other officers of the Black Star Line on February 16 for violating Section 215 of the U.S. Criminal Code—using the mails for fraudulent purposes. The other men were Vice-President Orlando Thompson, Treasurer George Tobias, and Secretary Elie Garcia. The government charged that the four had misrepresented the assets and prospects of the BSL at a time when they knew that the company approached bankruptcy. The prosecutor's prize evidence was the propaganda of late 1920 and 1921 implying that the BSL already owned and operated a ship, which the officers referred to as the *Phyllis Wheatley*, that carried passengers and commodities to and from Africa. To prepare its case, the Justice Department deployed two black agents, Mortimer Davis and James Amos, and a white accountant, Thomas Merrilees, to work with Post Office Inspector O. B. Williamson and a bevy of undercover and regular agents in numerous cities. Andrew Battle, the chief secret agent in Harlem, sent a constant stream of tips, leads, and gossip on the broad spectrum of Harlem radicalism as well as about the goings-on in the inner sanctums of Liberty Hall.

Garvey's many and diverse opponents openly or secretly aided the investigation. A witch's brew of principle and opportunism, righteousness and revenge, rationalized the decisions of individual blacks within and outside of the UNIA to cooperate with the prosecution. Cyril Briggs had introduced the agents to ex-members of the UNIA, including its former chaplain-general, the Reverend George McGuire, who told the investigators that he had resigned because Garvey was a "swindler." Cyril Critchlow, who had just returned from Liberia ill and without money, added his bitter experiences to the emerging picture of UNIA practices. A litigant suing for his salary, James Brooks, confirmed the government's *idée fixe* that the *Yarmouth* was "merely a propaganda ship" and that the officers had falsely claimed to own a ship called the *Phyllis Wheatley* when in fact they were still trying to purchase a ship they would have given that name. (As it turned out, the *Phyllis Wheatley* never came into being.)[13]

Gwendolyn Campbell, Garvey's chief stenographer, voluntarily cooperated because she was disgusted with Garvey's attempt to blame Vice-President Orlando Thompson for the BSL's failure to obtain the African ship. After Garvey branded him a traitor, fervent followers threatened Thompson's life, forcing him to leave the BSL and move to another part of the city. Campbell, who thought Thompson was "sincere and honest," disclosed that Garvey regularly drew a hundred dollars a week and additional

13. Thomas P. Merrilees to William Burns, February 11, 1922, Burns to Merrilees, January 22, 1922, W. W. G[rimes], "Memorandum for Mr. Hoover," November 5, 1921, J. E. H[oover], "Memorandum for Mr. Grimes," November 19, 1922, in Garvey file, RG 65.

money for expenses "without giving itemized statements." She hinted that he had stolen money when she said that he and Amy Jacques had deposited only a few hundred dollars in the treasury after raising over twenty-five thousand dollars in the West Indies in 1921.[14]

Hubert Harrison's motivation was less clear. He told agents that he believed that the UNIA had once been, but no longer was, a progressive force. He resigned as an editor of the *Negro World* in November, 1921. He told agents that Garvey had misrepresented the affairs of the Black Star Line to increase stock sales, but he also said that the profits from the *Negro World* were used to subsidize the line's operations.[15] Many people spoke freely to government agents but refused to testify publicly in court because of fear of reprisal, cross-examination, or perhaps guilty consciences. Early in preparation, Davis fingered the weak links in the case. The circular advertising the *Phyllis Wheatley* did not actually state that the ship was owned by the BSL. Even if "the entire effect is to lead one falsely to that impression," the federal crime was not fraud, but mail fraud. Prosecutors attempted to prove that the circular had been sent through the mails to a person who purchased shares on the basis of its claims. The government solicited dissatisfied stockholders by mailing questionnaires to persons listed in the company's records. It was difficult to overcome popular suspicions of government, the consuming affairs of daily life, the inertia of persons surfeited with other disappointments, the continuing allegiance to the UNIA's enterprises, and fears of reprisal from Garvey's supporters. Even after the government located willing complainants, linking a purchase to the mailed promotional literature was a difficult task.[16]

Davis and prosecutor Maxwell Mattuck cloaked the weak parts of their case with copious citations of BSL boosterism and self-promotion. Davis exclaimed, typically, "what could be more fraudulent than the advertisement on March 21, 1921 which called for Passengers and Freight for *** Monrovia, Africa by S/S PHYLLIS WHEATLEY. Sailing on or about April 15th. *** Book your passage now." Both read dishonest intentions into the transferrals of funds among the different parts of the UNIA organization, the sloppy bookkeeping, the technical transgressions, and the misuse of the

14. Davis, report, January 18, 1922, Gwendolyn Campbell, interview, March 6, 1922, in Garvey file, RG 65; Amy Jacques Garvey, testimony, in *Marcus Garvey* v. *United States of America*, 267 U.S. 607 (1924), 1469–71; MG, testimony, *Garvey* v. *U.S.A.*, 227. Garvey testified that most of the money raised was spent on repair and operation of the *Kanawha*.

15. Davis, report, January 21, 1922, in Garvey file, RG 65.

16. Mortimer J. Davis, "Memorandum," January 14, 1922, Davis, report, December 8, 1921, March 8, 1922, in Garvey file, RG 65. Davis received one hundred replies to the five hundred letters sent to stockholders; fifteen said they were not satisfied; of these, seven testified as government witnesses.

UNIA's death fund, which supported its ailing enterprises, not its members. The publication of optimistic and enthusiastic reports at the same time that the Black Star Line approached bankruptcy clinched the case for them.[17]

Garvey's first public reaction to his arrest was to inform the more than one thousand blacks who gathered at Liberty Hall on January 13, the day after the arrest, that he was innocent. But he gave credence to the indictment when he accused other officers of the crime. Garvey told a crowd that he had been raising money in the West Indies while the officers he had left in charge failed to purchase a ship for the African trade and in the process committed whatever illegal acts the government had discovered. Garvey's main defense, however, was an air of invulnerability. Readers of the *Negro World* were informed that "Mr. Garvey, who has up to now given the case very little consideration for the frivolousness of it, is as calm and undisturbed as ever. He will himself be very much amused at the prosecution's endeavor to make a criminal out of a man whose conscience is clear and who has committed no offense against society." At other times, Garvey hinted at more serious dangers. He told a group in Baltimore that he was pursued by "enemies" whom he did not name—"whites who hated him for his efforts in behalf of negroes" and "hypocritical and self-seeking negroes." But he quickly reverted to his posture of invincibility when he told them that "he had been arrested three times before" and would return to Baltimore a "free man."[18]

Garvey's confidence was not feigned. He had overcome numerous legal hurdles in the past. An undercover agent believed that Garvey had successfully bribed the judge in his libel suit against Cyril Briggs in December, 1921. Garvey's lieutenant Emmett Gaines, head of the African Legion, boasted: "We know how to pull the strings with Congressmen, aldermen, Judge, and jurymen. Unless you can pull strings with these men you are no good, and that is what this great man Marcus Garvey can do, with the UNIA behind him." Garvey enlisted the political connections of William Matthews and Henry Lincoln Johnson to get the case dropped. The "old-boy network" fed William Ferris' optimism. He noted that the assistant U.S. attorney, a Harvard classmate of Garvey's lawyer, James McClendon, acted with "unusual courtesy and consideration." The belief that Garvey had inoculated himself against prosecution was widespread. Typically, he reminded audiences at Liberty Hall that the trial had been "put off twenty times" and implied that it might never take place. Shortly before the trial began, Henrietta Vinton Davis told an undercover agent that she had con-

17. Mortimer Davis, "Summary Report," November, 1922, p. 14.
18. "Negro Activities," January 28, 1922, Harold Nathan, report, February 3, 1922, in Garvey file, RG 65; *NW*, November 25, 1922.

tinued to sell stock after the four had been indicted because she "didn't think it would be so serious." Even when it became clear that the case would not be dropped, Garvey did not betray any anxiety to his followers. He told a group in Washington in March, 1923, that he would be happy to have "the opportunity to exonerate himself in a court of Justice."[19] Garvey's strategy of blaming subordinates, feigning access to power, and claiming to have everything under control so muddied the issues that he left no active role for his supporters and defused the anger that might have been constructively mobilized and shaped.

The trial opened on May 21, 1923. It had been delayed fifteen months by the difficulties in preparing the case and by a shortage of judges.[20] The opening statement by prosecutor Maxwell Mattuck attempted to drain the remaining traces of political juice from the case. He told the jury that the trial involved only the question of fraud and that he would prove that the officers of the Black Star Line never intended to make a profit, accumulate a fleet, or serve the Negro race in any way. Then Mattuck led more than thirty witnesses through the details of the untidy history of the Black Star Line. He employed sarcasm and ridicule and feigned disbelief to puncture the defendants' version of events. He scoffed at BSL Treasurer George Tobias, a former shipping clerk in the Pennsylvania Railroad, when he asked, "You were unquestionably fitted by your experience to take the treasureship of a steamship company, weren't you." After Garvey attributed BSL losses to a succession of dishonest officers, Mattuck rhetorically asked him whether he and "George Tobias were the only honest men that held office in that company."[21]

Mattuck elicited overwhelming proof that the officers were poor businessmen and often callous people. Whether the four knowingly used the mails to promote the sale of stock when they knew the BSL was beyond resurrection—the legal question in the trial—was less certain. The common legacy of fraud was nonexistent. Although there was some evidence that Garvey enjoyed a moderate standard of living—he dressed well, traveled by Pullman, and so forth—neither he nor the other defendants had apparently accumulated large amounts of capital or property, though there were numerous rumors about acquisitions in the West Indies and Canada.

19. *NW*, March 11, 1922. On McClendon's political connections, see Andrew Battle, report, July 26, 1922, March 28, May 25, 1923, in Garvey file, RG 65.

20. Burns and Hoover had pressed for "early action." See Hoover, "Memorandum for Mr. Cunningham," August 10, 1922. On the bureaucratic sources of delay see Thomas Merrilees to William Burns, January 9, 1923, in Garvey file, RG 65.

21. George Tobias, testimony, *Garvey v. U.S.A.*, 2150; MG, testimony, *Garvey v. U.S.A.*, 2369; Amy Jacques Garvey (ed.), *Philosophy and Opinions of Marcus Garvey* (2 vols.; 1926; repr. New York, 1969), II, 147.

Proof that the mails were used to effect the scheme, crucial to justify the federal standing in the case, was weak. In the end the existence of the federal offense turned upon the significance of a BSL envelope mailed on December 13, 1920, to a Harlem Negro. The prosecutor claimed that it, and by implication many others, contained the fraudulent circular about the *Phyllis Wheatley*. But the alleged recipient, Benny Dancy, a cleaner at Pennsylvania Station, scarcely recalled its contents. His halting, frightened, and often incoherent testimony was ambiguous at best.[22]

Garvey's defense rested upon an alternative view of BSL history, rooted in the politics of racial advancement. He upheld the virtues of black business enterprise and the BSL and argued that its losses resulted from internal incompetence or corruption. Blaming Thompson for the crime maintained his own credibility with Garveyites, his innocence to jurors, and also the potency of his ideology. When Garvey left for the West Indies to raise money, he empowered Thompson to obtain a ship suitable for travel to Africa. He charged that Thompson and broker Anton Silverstone took twenty-five thousand dollars but failed to obtain the ship. So Garvey unwittingly shifted the question from that of whether a criminal act had taken place at all to that of who was responsible for it. Jurors would have to decide not merely who placed an envelope at the post office or even who authorized the mailing of the letter to Benny Dancy and others, but who made the key corporate decisions. Garvey's line of defense opened a Pandora's box of new troubles. The adversary relations between himself and Thompson disclosed damaging aspects of BSL history, as each of the two major defendants tried to protect himself by incriminating the other.[23]

Although each of the four accused men had his own lawyer, Elie Garcia and George Tobias upheld Garvey's denunciation of Thompson. Garvey testified that Thompson was dishonest, but he did not comment upon Garcia's character, which he had recently impugned when he took him to court for forging checks. Garcia had let it be known that he would testify that Garvey had given Esau Ramus $100 to go to Detroit and would reveal other practices that would "put Garvey in for the rest of his life." Garvey had attempted to silence him by initiating the forgery suit. On March 14, Garcia had been convicted of stealing $47 from the UNIA. He counterattacked by suing the UNIA for loans and notes totaling $1,300 and then contacting Mattuck, who won a postponement of his sentencing until after the mail fraud trial. Garcia apparently flirted with the prosecutor to make

22. MG, testimony, *Garvey* v. *U.S.A.*, 2287, 2351; Benny Dancy, testimony, *Garvey* v. *U.S.A.*, 860–65, 2625. Garvey claimed assets of $60 in the bank, 260 or 270 shares of BSL stock, and a small quantity of UNIA bonds.

23. MG, testimony, *Garvey* v. *U.S.A.*, 2195–2380.

certain that the UNIA's defense fund would pay his legal fees. If Garcia possessed damaging evidence, he did not reveal it. He joined Garvey and the more compliant Tobias to incriminate Thompson. He was restrained and cautious in court. Garcia and Tobias were minor players on Garvey's team. Neither called witnesses of his own. All of the defense witnesses were Garvey's except the three who testified for Thompson.[24]

Thompson's defense was that his actions to acquire the African ship were always controlled by Garvey, who had empowered his personal lawyer, Wilfred Smith, to supervise the purchase and authorize the release of funds. Thompson's course was charted earlier in February, 1922, when Garvey began to blame him for failing to obtain the ship. Thompson decided, therefore, to cooperate with the government as "a matter of self-protection." Nonetheless, his testimony implicitly exonerated all four. He told the jury what he had earlier told BSL directors: the company did not obtain the *Phyllis Wheatley*, because the government delayed sending the appropriate forms for the performance bond. Under cross-examination, however, he admitted that the financial condition of the company was a factor, too.[25] As the principals quarreled over who was guilty, the divisions among them and the open personal animosities that erupted between Garvey and government witnesses—Captains Richardson's and Cockburn's skirmishes with Garvey often aimed at and rarely missed the jugular—revealed mostly the shabby and unsavory, if not illegal, aspects of BSL history.

Garvey struggled to avoid the common identification of the company with himself. He could not shake the impression given by Leo Healey, the agent of the corporation that sold the BSL the *Yarmouth*, that he dominated everyone: "Mr. Garvey, as I said before, was the moving factor in the whole thing. He was the man who talked." Healey had trouble identifying the other principals. With no sense of irony, he gazed about the court room only to conclude that "there are so many folks [who] look so much alike to me here [that] I cannot pick them [the other negotiators] out." In the end, Garvey's behavior in court soon demonstrated that his voice commanded subordinates. If fraud had been committed, he was the likely lawbreaker. The court room became a kind of replica of UNIA offices at Liberty Hall.[26]

24. Battle, report, March 9, 14, 19, 20, 23, 1923, James E. Amos, report, March 15, 1923, Davis, report, April 27, 1923, in Garvey file, RG 65; Orlando Thompson, testimony, *Garvey* v. *U.S.A.*, 2293; Elie Garcia, testimony, *Garvey* v. *U.S.A.*, 2321. After the trial, Garcia won a $1,732 judgment against the UNIA for back salary. New York *Amsterdam News*, July 11, 1923.

25. Davis, report, March 8, 1922, in Garvey file, RG 65; Thompson, testimony, *Garvey* v. *U.S.A.*, 1722–93, 1894–1937, 1960–67.

26. Leo Healey, testimony, *Garvey* v. *U.S.A.*, 226, 276.

Garvey originally had two lawyers, Cornelius McDougald, the chief counsel, a young Harlem lawyer with an excellent reputation, and Vernal Williams. Both had represented Garvey and the UNIA in the past. After the first day in court, however, Garvey fired McDougald and decided to argue his own case. Amy Jacques Garvey later claimed that McDougald was dismissed because he advised Garvey to plead guilty to a "technical charge" that would have resulted only in a fine. She concluded, accurately, that U.S. Attorney Mattuck would not have accepted a guilty plea to a lesser charge. (Mattuck's superiors in Washington, who remained invisible to her, certainly would not have.) If McDougald had made the suggestion, it was partly the result of a bad first day. Edgar Grey, Richard Warner, and District Attorney Edwin Kilroe had portrayed Garvey as a man who reluctantly incorporated the Black Star Line, used the funds collected for the *Negro World* and other purposes, and purchased the first ship only after he was threatened with prosecution. McDougald's cross-examination had made no dent in the testimony.[27]

Garvey tried to obtain another lawyer, a Republican with influence in Washington. Unable to find one at the right price, he championed his own case. The decision ended the personal frustration of sitting silently and passively relying upon lawyers to do verbal battle for him. He was aided by William Matthews, Tobias' lawyer, and by Henry Lincoln Johnson, Garcia's lawyer. Johnson helped Garvey with strategy and legal points in the evenings after the daily court sessions. His examination and cross-examination of witnesses underscored Garvey's version of events and picked up points that he missed. Johnson interjected Thompson's role, and implicit guilt, at every opportunity. After establishing that Thompson had kept Tobias informed about the acquisition of the *Phyllis Wheatley*, Johnson asserted, gratuitously, that the downfall of the Black Star Line was caused by the failure to obtain the ship. Garvey supplemented Johnson's aid and the patient instructions from the judge with Armin Kohn, a white lawyer who examined Garvey when he took the stand on his own behalf.[28]

Garvey's defense was that Thompson had acted autonomously and criminally, and the logic of his proof of this was larded with sarcasm, expressions of disbelief, and hints of conspiracy. Remarks by Garvey to Thompson such as "You are still disposed to maintain the statement that you were only office boy or messenger" and "Didn't you arrange with the

27. Amy Jacques Garvey, *Garvey and Garveyism* (Kingston, Jamaica, 1963), 108. See testimony by the following witnesses in *Garvey* v. *U.S.A.*: Edwin Kilroe, 119–44; Edgar Grey, 61–118; Richard Warner, 144–84. For McDougald's explanation, see 184–86.

28. Battle, report, May 25, 1923, in Garvey file, RG 65; George Tobias, testimony, *Garvey* v. *U.S.A.*, 2136–37.

District Attorney what testimony you were to give?" were typical. But Garvey's courtroom behavior undercut his claim that his associates, especially Thompson, acted on their own initiative. As the *Amsterdam News* said after the trial, though it was "not proven that Marcus Garvey stole money . . . it was proven beyond a reasonable doubt that he was the dominating figure." His aggressiveness certified his control of the organization. He crucified witnesses who disclosed damaging testimony. Sometimes the resulting exchanges were irrelevant, but they always revealed a belligerence undisciplined by the requirements of his defense. He asked Harry R. Watkis, a prosecution witness, if he was married to a white woman. The former BSL salesman retorted that it was "not your business." Not to be deterred, Garvey asserted, "You beat her up often, don't you." The angry Watkis retorted, "I am not divorced though," referring to Garvey's divorce from Amy Ashwood. At other times, Garvey's contentiousness unleashed unexpected and harmful testimony. He demanded to know if a dissatisfied shareholder attended the BSL's meetings. Garvey's purpose was to inform the jury that people had the opportunity to learn about the affairs of the company. The witness answered that she had not questioned management: "You are not allowed to because you would be scared the crowd would be down on you. That was the scheme that you could not very much talk or you would be thrown out." When Addie Still, under Garvey's unrelenting examination, admitted that she could not identify the precise purpose of meetings, she went on to say that she stopped attending them because "they carried on so disgracefully. . . . You used to get to fighting and I had to go out because I was afraid I would get shot. I was afraid to attend the meetings but if you [Garvey] had not asked me I would not have said anything about it." Garvey's tyrannical manner undercut his testimony that he was unaware of many of the financial arrangements of the company. When confronted with damaging evidence, he pleaded ignorance or chanted "I didn't keep the funds." But these explanations were uttered so imperiously that it was hard to conclude that subordinates had carried out any significant action that would displease him.[29]

Elements of UNIA social philosophy sometimes escaped from the volley of charges and denials. Garvey characterized Anton Silverstone, the broker hired by Thompson, as a "man of straw, [who] had no property, had no assets." Garvey's bourgeois calculus combined with nostalgic memories and pride of the early days. Having listened to copious documentation of the BSL's failures, he bitterly responded that "it was not always

29. See testimony by the following witnesses in *Garvey* v. *U.S.A.*: MG, 2335, Thompson, 1896, 1976, 2303, Harry R. Watkis, 795, Addie Still, 848–49. New York *Amsterdam News*, June 27, 1923.

broke." But Garvey's concluding statement, a straightforward and effective narrative of his ambition to build a great Negro steamship line to create self-respect and commercial opportunity for Afro-Americans, was his clearest exposition of purpose. "We had no monetary considerations or reward before us but the good we could do for our race, for this and succeeding generations," he explained. Although idealized and self-serving, it was an accurate portrayal of the ideology of racial liberation through racial enterprise.[30]

Garvey's final speech probably worked against him in the end. The often unsavory if not illegal practices of marginal businessmen that were revealed during the twenty-seven-day trial gave off the odor of a scam precisely because they were joined to the self-sacrificing rhetoric of racial politics. On June 18, the jury found Garvey guilty of the Benny Dancy count. The other officers were exonerated, though two jurors who had believed that Thompson was guilty held out for nearly ten hours. Judge Julian W. Mack sentenced Garvey to five years in prison, fined him one thousand dollars, billed him for court costs, and denied him bail.[31]

The maximum sentence led some to question Mack's role in the case. Before the trial began, Garvey, claiming that Mack was a member of the NAACP, attempted to disqualify the judge. Denying Garvey's motion, Mack acknowledged that he had contributed to the NAACP but denied that his support prejudiced him against the four defendants. After the verdict, Garvey renewed the allegation. However, immediately after the end of the trial the *Negro World* praised Mack's performance and charge to the jury. The judge had told the twelve that the facts had been summed up ably "with most remarkable ability by the layman [Garvey] who addressed you in his own behalf." The astute black journalist and historian Joel Rogers, a friend of Garvey's who attended the trial, observed that Mack was a model of understanding and fairness until Garvey responded to the jury's guilty verdict with expressions like "Damn the Jews." Mack's decision to impose the maximum penalties and deny Garvey bail, Rogers concluded, was his response to Garvey's anti-Semitic remarks.[32]

Julian Mack, a member of the German-Jewish aristocracy in America, was disturbed by the rising fever of anti-Semitism registered by his alma mater Harvard's restrictions on the number of Jewish students at the college, the propaganda of Henry Ford, the party of Adolf Hitler, and the es-

30. MG, testimony, *Garvey* v. *U.S.A.*, 2294, 2303.

31. Davis, report, June 21, 1923, in Garvey file, RG 65; George Featherstone, "Affidavit," January 14, 1927, file 42–793, in RG 204.

32. *NW*, June 13, 1923; Joel Rogers, *World's Great Men of Color* (2 vols.; New York, 1946), II, 599–610.

calating pogroms of Eastern Europe. Nevertheless, Mack's larger social vision offers a more persuasive explanation for the judge's sentence. He instructed the jury to find the principals innocent if it believed they were motivated by a desire to create a profitable business or by racial patriotism, despite the failure of the Black Star Line and the money lost on the venture. On the other hand, if it found the four were motivated by personal ambitions to gain money or power, it was to find them guilty. This absolute division between racial and personal self-interest betrayed the judge's conception of social reform and blinded him to Garvey's.

Mack's social complacency, rooted in his personal success, had been modified first by Jane Addams at Hull House in Chicago. Through her, he began to learn of the world of poor Russian Jews in America, light-years away from Mack's German-Jewish circle. During World War I, he began to appreciate the poverty and pogroms suffered by East European Jews and became a Zionist of the paternalist variety. Mack the American reformer and Mack the Zionist were cut from the same cloth, the politics of uplift, which demanded social efficiency, order, and procedure from reform instruments. He had never lived in the world of humiliation or abuse that diluted idealism with self-interest and drove men to political action to aid themselves.

The world of blacks and black politics was as alien to him as the terrain of East European Jewry and European Zionism. Garvey's mixture of bombast, idealism, and ambition found no echo in his experience or world view. But Mack's sense of fairness, as real as his class biases, controlled his judicial behavior until after the jury returned its verdict. He then explained the maximum sentence on the grounds of the "enormous" misrepresentation of the facts of the BSL and "the financial character of the great mass of people who were induced to put their money into this hopeless undertaking." At the time, most blacks and whites did not find the sentence severe. The prosecution, from the U.S. attorney's office in New York to the Bureau of Investigation in Washington, applauded the judgment and anticipated deporting Garvey because of his agitation, not his alleged deceptions. That Burns and Hoover enlisted the paternalistic instincts of men like Mack revealed how far Garvey had strayed from both conservative and radical racial politics.[33]

Even before the jury had returned, Garvey informed UNIA members at Liberty Hall that he expected a guilty verdict but that he was ready for anything. If he was imprisoned, however, he predicted that "hell will be

---

33. Harry Barnard, *The Forging of an American Jew: The Life and Times of Judge Julian W. Mack* (New York, 1974), esp. 157; Julian Mack, "Charge to Jury," *Garvey v. U.S.A.*, 2412.

turned loose all over the country. The UNIA will never die and the UNIA is ready to play hell if Garvey is put in Jail." UNIA officers had warned that members would rise up in Detroit, Cleveland, Chicago, and Virginia. There was some basis for such predictions. Tension was high in Harlem. Throughout the trial, enraged Garveyites threatened government witnesses and officials. Several hundred had gathered outside the court building to wait for the sentencing. When it was announced, one woman dropped to her knees on the hot June pavement and cried out, "Dear God, Christ died on the cross for the same thing they are punishing Garvey for. Dear God protect him." But she was answered by a chorus of amens, not calls for action. Nevertheless, officers, fearing trouble, removed Garvey through a side door. Mattuck attempted to use the panorama of angry crowds and predictions of violence to deny Garvey bail. He claimed to have "evidence to prove that money is being used in the purchase of guns, arms, and ammunition, and his Legion will stop at nothing to defend him. He is a menace to the community, and at this time, more so than ever, I ask that Marcus Garvey be remanded without bail." He asked Judge Mack to bring Esau Ramus from Sing Sing to confirm the existence of UNIA arms caches. The judge refused and decided independently to deny bail, though he stayed execution of the sentence while Garvey appealed his case.[34]

No disorder occurred. Harlem was not united behind Garvey. The black New York *News*, though it exaggerated, did report the feeling of some parts of the black community when it wrote of the sentence, "People approved and concluded that Harlem would not have been safe if Garvey had been acquitted." Many supporters regretted his fate but blamed him for much of it. The Reverend E. Ethelred Brown of the Harlem Community Church summed up a strong trend of thought when he concluded: "I do not believe Garvey deliberately set out to waste money or to exploit his followers or to enrich himself. He became a victim of a too early and superficial success and gambled both to retain the confidence he had won and to redeem the losses he had incurred. . . . His real sin, as I see it, is lack of courage to admit failure when failure was obvious and his stubbornness in trying to flog back to activity a horse long dead."[35]

Garvey's response to his conviction was a mixture of militance and accommodation. He threatened to "go on a hunger strike as a protest against white injustice and prejudice on which I have been convicted." He dropped that tactic but not his attack on his persecutors. He announced that he was a victim of the NAACP, England, France, and an "international frameup"

34. Davis, report, May 25, June 18, 19, 1923; New York *Times*, June 21, 22, 1923.
35. New York *Times*, June 25, 1923; New York *Amsterdam News*, June 27, 1923; New York *News*, June 22, 1923.

including both blacks and whites. Although he accused many, Garvey did not allow his anger to jeopardize his appeal. He bitterly attacked Mattuck and "his hirelings" but said that the federal "government is not at fault. . . . If he [Mattuck] were a typical representative of our Government then I should have no hope for America but I feel sure that we have men of honor in this Government, and this great country who will jealously guard its fair name." He added that "the peculiar and outstanding feature of the whole case is that I am being punished for the crime of the Jew Silverstone. . . . I was prosecuted in this by Maxwell Mattuck, another Jew, and I am to be sentenced by Judge Julian Mack the eminent Jewish Jurist. Truly I may say 'I was going to Jericho and fell among thieves.'" Relying upon appeals to higher courts, his selective indictment of the three, and the willingness to pander to anti-Semitism reflected a strategy as well as his wrath.[36]

Garvey was in jail throughout the summer until September 10, when Amy Jacques Garvey posted the fifteen-thousand-dollar bail after Garvey's lawyers had convinced U.S. Attorney William Haywood to recommend his release. Soon afterward, in a speech to five thousand cheering men, women, and children at Liberty Hall, Garvey thanked his wife, who he said had worked for him "against the advice of those who said they would stand by him" but did not. He vowed to reverse the guilty verdict on appeal. Garvey told his audience that "if you see some of us talking to white folks . . . don't think anything of it. The UNIA is about to enter politics. I want every one of you to register and those who are not citizens must become naturalized. If Du Bois and James Weldon Johnson with only two hundred thousand followers can send one Negro to jail, the UNIA with two million voters will be able to send that many more." Garvey was preparing for a lobbying effort but did not explain the politics of the case to his audience. Although he exhorted them, he did not mobilize the many who were angered at the verdict. Instead, he implied that he possessed unnamed sources of power that would be effective against an unnamed conspiracy of forces. He appealed for money for a "vacation fund."[37]

Traveling to the West Coast, Garvey and his wife visited the Grand Canyon and then returned through the South stopping off at Tuskegee, where he addressed the student body. The trip, partly a holiday and partly an attempt to revitalize the UNIA, demonstrated that Garvey still attracted crowds. Two thousand came to hear him, and many of them purchased souvenirs or contributed to his defense fund in Pittsburgh. But his evalua-

36. *Negro Times*, June 20, 1923, cited in Garvey file, RG 65.
37. James Dillon, report, September 11, 1923, in Garvey file, RG 65. The reasons for the changed opinion on the granting of bail are not clear. See A. J. Garvey, *Garvey and Garveyism*, 123–28.

tion of his audiences was tough-minded. He told a group in Norfolk, Virginia, that many did not know or care about the UNIA but just "came out tonight out of curiosity to see what I looked like after coming out of jail." UNIA officials estimated that "80% of the divisions were wracked with internal dissension." Returning to New York in November, Garvey set about attempting to rebuild the organization while his lawyers prepared papers for the U.S. Court of Appeals.[38]

Garvey employed the politically influential law firm of Battle, Vandiver, Levy and Van Tine to work with Armin Kohn to prepare his appeal, which challenged Judge Mack's technical instructions to the jury. In essence, Garvey contended that the government had not proved that Benny Dancy received the BSL circular picturing the *Phyllis Wheatley*. The appellate court denied the argument on February 2, 1925. One suspects that the rejection of the appeal's procedural argument rested upon the judge's agreement with the verdict. Judge Charles M. Hough asserted that "stripped of its appeal to the ambitions, emotions, or race consciousness of men of color, it [the BSL] was a simple and familiar device of which object (as of so many others) was to ascertain how it could best unload upon the public its capital stock at the largest possible price." On March 23 the Supreme Court stated that it would not review the decision.[39]

At the time Judge Hough's decision was announced, the Garveys were in Detroit. They boarded a train for New York so that Garvey could surrender to court officials. But he was intercepted by government agents when he arrived at the 125th Street Station and taken immediately to the Tombs. On the next day, he was arraigned before Judge Augustus Hand, who denied bail and ordered the immediate execution of the sentence. On the same day, Garvey was taken away to Atlanta penitentiary.[40]

After two years of legal challenges, the politics of the indictment remained invisible. Friends and opponents had attempted to salvage the ideals of racial consciousness and black business enterprise from the ruins of Garvey's business. At the time of the verdict in 1923, the New York *News* admitted that Garvey had "awakened the race consciousness and pride of thousands." In 1925, William Ferris praised Garvey for teaching Negroes

38. *NW*, November 10, 1923, August 23, 1924; New York *Amsterdam News*, September 12, 1923. Moton agreed to Garvey's request to speak on condition that he did not "discuss his propaganda." Following Moton's guidelines, Garvey discussed "in a general way Mr. Washington, Tuskegee and the importance of Inter-Racial cooperation." MG to R. R. Moton, October 23, 1923, Moton to Fred Moore, November 8, 1923, in Moton Papers.
39. Charles M. Hough, "Opinion of Court of Appeals," *Garvey* v. *U.S.A.*, 7; Amos, report, January 20, February 4, 1925, in Garvey file, RG 65.
40. New York *News*, February 7, 1925; New York *Amsterdam News*, February 11, 1925.

"to think in big terms and to conceive big things." Garvey had not wanted to "fleece blacks," he said, but "he did misrepresent the property of the BSL in selling stock through the U.S. mails and was technically guilty of violating a law." Few looked beyond legal doctrine. The white editor of the Buffalo *Evening Times* thought the sentence harsh and found "something that is not pleasant about this whole business." The New York *Evening Bulletin* concluded that had Garvey had "a fair deal his financial schemes might have been successful and he might have been able to avoid the unfortunate disasters which led him into the courts and brought punishment upon him." None of these doubts was strong or precise enough to go beyond the editorial pages of the newspapers.[41]

Garvey's imprisonment did not end his own efforts for vindication. From his cell he directed a steady stream of visitors and countless correspondents to pressure politicians for a pardon. Shortly after he arrived in Atlanta, he prepared a long and detailed criticism of his conviction, which he claimed rested upon a conspiracy of rival black politicians and organizations, government officials, vengeful former employees, the United Fruit Company, and his former wife, Amy Ashwood, to destroy him and the UNIA. F. E. Shea, the current post office inspector of New York, head of the Garvey prosecution, reviewed his petition for a presidential pardon but dismissed it. He judged that Garvey was "a dangerous race agitator. He is a gifted speaker able to sway his ignorant followers at will and they are fanatically devoted to him." Trial judge, prosecutor, and law enforcement officers—a Greek chorus—concurred that Garvey should not be pardoned or have his sentence commuted.[42]

Loyal Garveyites mounted a huge petition drive and collected thousands of signatures. By 1927, the combined efforts were having effect. And as Garvey's presence ceased to challenge rivals, many former opponents and neutrals began to have second thoughts about the imprisonment, which sometimes masked doubts about Garvey's guilt. William Pickens, a veteran of the "Garvey Must Go" campaign of 1922, had applauded the conviction and incarceration: "If all the rogues are to be sent to the penitentiary, with the sole exception of those who steal from black people, that would be discrimination against black people, indeed!" he had said. But by

41. New York *News*, June 23, 1923; *NW*, March 7, 1925; Buffalo *Evening Times*, February 24, 1925; New York *Evening Bulletin*, February 7, 1925.
42. A. J. Garvey, *Garvey and Garveyism*, 154–55, 179–81; Amos, report, February 6, 1925, E. W. Manson, "Memorandum for Mr. Cunningham," February 24, 1925, Inspector Shea to Inspector in charge, July 14, 1925, in Garvey file, RG 65; *NW*, October 15, December 19, 1925, March 13, December 11, 25, 1926.

August, 1927, Pickens wrote in the *New Republic* that Garvey had served enough time. His conversion was not singular. The campaign for pardon or clemency enlisted Dean Kelly Miller and President Mordecai W. Johnson of Howard University, northern Democratic Congressman Royal Weller from New York, southern Democratic Congressman George Huddleston of Alabama, Republican Senator James Watson of Indiana, liberals like Congressman Emmanuel Celler from Brooklyn, and southern segregationists like Ernest Cox and John Powell of the Anglo-Saxon Clubs of America. The weight of these diverse lobbyists began to affect the opinion of the government bureaucrats monitoring the case.[43]

The attorney general and the pardon attorney had initially accepted Mattuck's brief as an adequate history of Garvey and Garveyism. The prosecution had not rested after its victory in 1923. When Garvey announced that he was appealing his conviction, the Bureau of Investigation instructed agents to "prepare the case based on radical statements so that should Garvey's appeal from his recent conviction on a mail fraud charge be successful the charge of radicalism can be placed against him." An inspector in the Immigration Service asked for preparation of material to bring "the subject within the scope of the alian [*sic*] anarchist provisions of the Immigration Laws."[44] A grand jury indicted Garvey on October 18, 1924, for fraud and perjury in filing income tax returns in 1919 and 1921. Garvey's prosecutors remained vigilant and plied the pardon attorney with their version of events.

Attorney General John G. Sargent's recommendation for commutation was shaped by the new view of the case presented by the "numerous delegations" interviewed by "the Pardon Attorney or myself, and arguments [they] made and briefs [they] presented in an attempt to combat or explain many of the damaging statements made by the United States Attorney in

43. William Pickens, "Garvey's Last Stand," [February, 1925], Associated Negro Press, Box C-304, in NAACP Papers; *New Republic*, LII (August 31, 1927), 46–47; New York *Amsterdam News*, April 29, 1925. Weller had been backed by the UNIA against the black Republican Dr. Charles P. Roberts for Congress. Ernest S. Cox to Calvin Coolidge, March 23, 1927, file 42-793, in Record Group 204, Records of the Office of Pardon Attorney, National Archives. See Pardon Attorney James A. Finch's memorandum recommending commutation and Attorney General John G. Sargent's handwritten comments overruling them on January 23, 1926, file 42-793, in RG 204.

44. The government based its case on the law that permitted the deportation of aliens who committed felonies within five years of their arrival in the country. Davis, report, June 19, 21, September 29, December 15, 1923, Edward J. Brennan to Director, Bureau of Investigation, July 9, 1924, Amos, report, August 7, October 24, 1924, in Garvey file, RG 65. Jan Perry Clark's *Deportation of Aliens from the United States to Europe* (New York, 1931), esp. chs. 5, 9, 10, 11, demonstrates that the procedures used against Garvey were common at that time.

his report upon the case." An effective and detailed rebuttal of the prosecution's case presented by Garvey's lawyer Armin Kohn in March, 1927, was probably critical.[45]

The new information generated by the growing forces convinced Sargent that "none of these people [the alleged victims] apparently believe that they have been defrauded, manifestly retain their entire confidence in Garvey, and, instead of the prosecution and imprisonment of the applicant being an example and warning against a violation of law, it really stands and is regarded by them as a class as an act of oppression of the race in their efforts in the direction of race progress and of discrimination against Garvey as a negro." He was "inclined to think that the facts as reported to the Department [by U.S. Attorney Mattuck] are perhaps somewhat severely stated and are susceptible of modification and explanation in many respects." Like Judge Mack, who supported commuting Garvey's sentence contingent upon deportation after Garvey had served two years, Sargent did not believe that the conviction or punishment was unjust. He also admitted that he would hesitate to recommend commutation if Garvey were to be released in the United States. But the Immigration Bureau had held deportation hearings in March, 1925, in the Atlanta prison, as soon as Garvey had been incarcerated, and determined to deport Garvey on the basis of his conviction after he had served his prison sentence. Therefore, Sargent recommended commutation, which President Coolidge granted on November 18, 1927.[46]

The Justice Department notified the Immigration Bureau immediately and delayed transmitting the order to the warden of Atlanta prison until the arrangements for deportation were completed. Garvey's lawyers tried but failed to stay the ruling, and Garvey was quickly moved from Atlanta to New Orleans. On December 2, he was taken aboard the SS *Saramacca*, sailing to Panama and then Jamaica. Five hundred New Orleans blacks came to see him off, some of them holding banners saying GOD SAVE OUR PRESIDENT. Garvey thanked them for their support and asked them to stay firm and steadfast behind the UNIA. Although there would be numerous attempts by Garveyites to obtain permission for his return to the United States, Garvey had uttered his last words on American soil.[47]

45. Attorney General John G. Sargent to President Calvin Coolidge, November 4, 1927, Armin Kohn, "Supplementary Memorandum in Support of Application for Pardon or Commutation of Sentence of Marcus Garvey," March 1927, file 42-793, in RG 204.
46. Sargent to Coolidge, November 4, 1927, in RG 204.
47. Pardon Attorney Finch, "Memorandum," November 22, 1927, file 42-793, in RG 204; A. J. Garvey, *Garvey and Garveyism*, 176–78; Atlanta *Constitution*, December 3, 1927.

Genuine concern for the black shareholders had motivated some of Garvey's black and white antagonists, but this concern was at best superficial and not significant compared with the underlying motive of sheer antiradicalism. Garvey was indicted because of Hoover's and Burns's political opinions, which sustained and survived the long legal process. But many of the whites who had shared those opinions of black agitators in 1919 no longer did so in 1927. The New York *Herald-Tribune* approved of Garvey's release from prison, because "no man who styled himself 'His Highness the Potentate of the Universal Negro Improvement Association and Provisional President of Africa' could be at heart a cold-blooded fraud. Such exuberance is alien to calculation. It expresses . . . the yearnings of a highly imaginative, child-like people as well as the desire for personal significance at their expense." While the editor did not doubt that Garvey was guilty "according to the standards of white men's justice," he questioned the appropriateness of this standard for judging blacks. To elite whites, Garvey in 1927 was only a "primitive deliverer," a creature of curiosity, not a political menace. Most whites were unaware of Garvey's dramatic exit. He had been indicted when the UNIA was declining. He was deported when the memory of his success was fading, though his oratory of ambition remained the same. The obvious gap between reality and rhetoric was bridged by the racial stereotypes. For black people, Garveyism was more complicated. Nonetheless, most of them would have agreed with the *Negro World* in July, 1927, that "only a negligible minority of the citizenry of the United States would be unwilling to concede that the victim should be set free without further delay." Without a political analysis of Garvey's plight and a campaign to seek justice for him, however, the UNIA in effect freed Garvey only to speed his deportation. It liberated him without uncovering the political motives behind his trial.[48]

48. New York *Herald-Tribune*, November 26, 1927; *NW*, July 2, 1927.

11 / Africa Again
Garvey, Liberia, and the Firestone
Rubber Company

Garvey's failure to obtain a ship for the African trade and the necessary priority of preparing for his mail fraud trial delayed but did not end his plans for Liberia. Despite the political problems in Liberia described by Elie Garcia in 1920 and confirmed by Cyril Critchlow in 1921, and the skepticism of the U.S. Shipping Board and the State Department about economic opportunities there, Garvey embraced colonization again for the same reason he had held onto the BSL in the face of equally poor prospects: success would redeem Garvey as well as Africa.

The Liberian response to Garveyism continued to be determined by the postwar economic crisis. President Charles D. E. King had opted for an American loan to resolve the nation's immediate financial difficulties and to create the American interest in Liberia that could generate private economic investment and protection from British and French encroachment. Although he had marshaled Afro-American support and the backing of the State Department, in September, 1922, the U.S. Senate refused to make Liberia an exception to the new American policy that barred government loans to foreign states.[1] The Senate rejection produced another crisis in Liberian politics. Although some spoke of revolution, the opposition mounted only the People's party, composed of dissident members of the

---

1. Along with most black groups, the UNIA came out in support of the loan in March, 1921. *NW*, March 26, 1921. Senator William Borah, backed by most liberals, led the opposition. In anticipation of the American control of Liberian finances, the price of outstanding Liberian bonds rose from $55 to $102.50. But many Americans were reluctant to "bail out" foreign bankers, the principal holders of Liberia's debt. Except for during World War I, the American government had not loaned money to foreign countries but instead had encouraged private loans. Because no bank or corporation was willing to extend a loan to Liberia, the State Department believed that the government should. But without the interest on the part of business that would have made a public loan unnecessary, the objections of congressional liberals carried the day. Raymond L. Buell, *The Native Problem in Africa* (2 vols.; New York, 1928), II, 816; William Lewis to Emmett Scott, November 24, 1922, in Scott Papers; Charles Hughes to U.S. Minister, December 8, 1922, file 882.51/1575a, in RG 59.

elite, to challenge the ruling True Whig party in 1923. But the power of incumbency overwhelmed the numerous grievances of wide sectors of Liberia's population. King was reelected by a large margin in the most corrupt election in Liberia's history.[2]

Garveyism played no role in King's vision of Liberia. The president's opposition was forged partly out of his conflicts with Liberian Garveyites, especially a personal rivalry with Gabriel Johnson, the potentate of the UNIA. Shortly after Johnson had returned from the UNIA convention in 1920, the two men clashed over the accompanying ceremonial prerogatives of the potentate's UNIA office. After King returned from his lobbying trip to the United States in 1921, he removed Johnson from his appointed position as mayor of Monrovia. The president subsequently named Johnson Liberian consul at Fernando Po, a lucrative but isolated foreign post whose main function was supervising the migration of Liberian laborers who worked the Spanish sugar plantations to the profit of the landowners and Liberian officials. The small size, blood ties, and narrow ideological differences within the ruling stratum—the only political community in the country—produced short-lived factions, easily pacified dissidents, and magnanimous victors.[3]

King's hostility to Garveyism transcended personality and appeared to be rooted in his sense of the potential political challenge of Garveyism—its penchant for stirring up trouble among imperialist powers and native Africans. He interpreted the disputes that poisoned the relations between Americans and Liberians correctly as preliminary skirmishes of a fight for control of the Liberian state. King had shunned Garvey and the UNIA convention when he was in the United States in 1921. Meeting with State Department officials in Washington, he conjured up the specter of Garveyism to help win the loan. When an advance group of three UNIA representatives, Henrietta V. Davis, Robert Poston, and J. Milton Van Lowe, arrived in Monrovia in February, 1924, to discuss the association's plans, neither King nor his equally unfriendly secretary of state, Edwin Barclay, joined the welcoming committee. The friends of the UNIA in 1924 were members of the opposition People's party. Especially prominent were a group of landowners in Maryland County, the proposed site for settlement of the first group of UNIA immigrants.[4]

2. Buell, *The Native Problem*, II, 714; Sydney de la Rue to Solomon Hood, November 17, 1923, file 882.51/1642, in RG 59; Foreign Office to Colonial Office, June 8, 1923, in Colonial Office, 267/602, Public Record Office, London.

3. Amy Jacques Garvey (ed.), *Philosophy and Opinions of Marcus Garvey* (2 vols.; 1926; rpr. New York, 1969), II, 364–66; I. K. Sundiata, "Prelude to Scandal: Liberia and Fernando Po, 1880–1930," *Journal of African History*, XV (1974), 97–112.

4. King's letter in the *Crisis* stating that Liberia was independent and not a natural ref-

Maryland was the southernmost and least developed of Liberia's five coastal counties. Its Americo-Liberian leaders were overwhelmed numerically by indigenous Africans, who rebelled frequently against government tyrannies. Despite Garvey's unchanged ambitions and stated plans, Maryland's leaders no longer believed that the UNIA could supply capital or ships. They expected the UNIA to "increase the civilized population of Liberia," a traditional function of Afro-Americans, and to provide the labor that indigenous Africans failed to supply in sufficient quantity. By 1924, then, the issue of Garveyism in Liberia had been reduced to little more than a dispute over immigration policy. The opponents of the UNIA were families like the Kings, the Barclays, and the Johnsons (Gabriel Johnson left the UNIA in February, 1924), from counties in and about the capital city, Monrovia, which already had sufficient population and labor. The UNIA's supporters were men like Supreme Court Justice J. J. Dossen, a scion of one of Maryland's leading families and a veteran of Liberian campaigns to attract American blacks.[5]

Dossen's scenario required experts, scientific exploration, and capital, as well as population. He hoped that "Rockefeller or Carnegie" would fund industrial schools, too. In 1921 he asked President King and his associates to publicize his dormant Excelsior Mining Company while they were lobbying in the United States. He gave King a gold nugget found on company property to entice prospective American investors. At the same time, he began to bargain with a German company to develop land near the Cape Palmas area of Maryland County for mining. Dossen dabbled, simultaneously, in various development schemes, but increasing the "civilized" portion of the population, Afro-Americans, who would work for wages and consume in the Western manner, was a prerequisite of all of them. Attracting the land-hungry, who would have to supplement subsistence farming with wage labor, was a proven formula to obtain more workers. Given Dossen's objectives, the UNIA was not an alternative but a complement to European or American investment.[6]

Both friends and enemies of Garveyism were represented on the Liber-

---

uge for Negroes or a center of aggression or conspiracy against other states was a scarcely veiled attack on the UNIA. Garveyism continued to plague King. As late as 1929, he feared the U.S. State Department might appoint a "Garvey man" to its diplomatic corps in Liberia. Division of West European Affairs, "Memorandum," April 8, 1921, file 811.4106/55, Clifton R. Wharton to Secretary of State, August 1, 1929, file 882.5048/55, both in RG 59. For Edwin Barclay's opposition see Barclay to Bishop Smith, May 24, 1921, in Executive Mansion Correspondence, 1920–25, Liberian State Archives, Monrovia.

5. I. K. Sundiata, *Black Scandal: America and the Liberian Labor Crisis, 1929–1936* (Philadelphia, 1980), 16–20.

6. J. J. Dossen to John Bruce, August 25, 1909, in Bruce Papers; Sidney de la Rue to Solomon Hood, November 17, 1923, file 882.602/1442, in RG 59.

ian commission created to advise and contain the UNIA. But the commission unanimously opposed offering the UNIA an independent corporate existence. Individuals, not the organization, would live on sites selected by Liberians and take oaths to respect the Liberian government. Determined that the immigrants would be self-supporting, the commissioners advised each family to bring $1,500 and urged the UNIA to send no more than five hundred people initially. To ensure that monies collected in the United States were used for the purpose of colonization, they advised the UNIA to charter, not purchase, a ship to transport the immigrants.[7]

Hoping to gain a foothold in Liberia, Garvey seemed willing to accept the extended terms. He repudiated Garcia, whose damning report had been discovered by the Liberians, and Critchlow. The two men, he said, "did a great deal of harm with their indiscretions, which caused us to have delayed, and in other words, suspended the efforts we started to make in carrying out of our industrial program in Liberia."[8] He agreed to send only four hundred or five hundred people on the first ship. But Garvey's original intentions were unchanged. He announced plans to settle "twenty to thirty thousand families" and begin a new shipping line for trade between Liberia and the United States. He asked for permission to set up five or six townships and use five thousand acres near the settlements "for the exclusive development of the Association agriculturally or industrially, as a source of revenue by which the Association may be able to meet some of its current expenses in its development plans for the good of the country and its citizens." Garvey's request acknowledged his failure to accumulate capital from Afro-Americans. But he did not name a product or market that would justify investments in plantations or mining enterprises.

The specificity of his "modern American plan" for conditions of life in the new towns contrasted sharply with the vaguer plans for production. The UNIA's towns in Liberia would have such facilities and services as courthouses, town halls, police forces, fire departments, and hospitals, theaters, churches, public halls, parks, libraries, public schools, high schools, liberal arts colleges, trade and engineering schools, and modern

7. MG to C. D. E. King, March 31, 1924, file 882.5511/16, in RG 59; A. J. Garvey (ed.), *Philosophy and Opinions of Garvey*, II, 374–75.
8. MG to C. D. E. King, December 5, 1923, file 882.511/16, in RG 59; Francis O'Meara to Secretary of State, February 22, 1924, in F.O. 371/9553; Secretary to Lo Ferguson, September 18, 1922, in Executive Mansion Correspondence, Liberian State Archives. The Liberians learned of the Garcia report as early as March, 1922, when it was published by the London journal *African World Supplement*, in its March 31 issue. The *Liberian News* of August, 1924, refers to the report and states that it "fell into the hands of the Liberian Government." Although the newspaper does not explain how or when the government obtained a copy, from the context of the article it seems very likely that officials had a copy before it was published in London, possibly shortly after Garcia wrote it.

public utilities and transportation facilities. Garvey's promised land was conceived out of his urban social goals and shaped by his knowledge of the aspirations of modern Afro-Americans. He was not appealing to land-hungry blacks, the nineteenth-century masses who were attracted to the idea of being organized into Pan-African utopias peopled by independent farmers.[9]

Despite its undeniable appeal, Garvey's Liberian venture did not attract adequate manpower, because it was obvious that modern ambitions could be satisfied much more easily in the United States than in the Black Republic. The conflict between the goals of Afro-American workers and the real prospects of labor in Liberia was fundamental. Failure was only a question of time. The UNIA's plans could have collapsed in Africa, as Chief Sam's had done, or before the emigrants ever reached Liberia. As it turned out, the chain was snapped by the Liberians, not the Americans. On June 30, 1924, the government banned UNIA members from entering Liberia. A small UNIA party had already left New York to set up camps to house colonists and make the final preparations for an October sailing of emigrant families. When the Americans arrived in July, they were seized, held, and deported.

Garvey subsequently accused his rival W. E. B. Du Bois, who had represented the United States government at the inauguration of President King in January, 1924, of convincing the Liberians to exclude the UNIA.[10] Because the Firestone Rubber Company and the Liberian government had signed a preliminary agreement for a rubber concession in June, 1924, it appeared that the expulsion was related to the new foreign investment. A leading African scholar concludes that the ejection of the UNIA was "a betrayal of the nobler and wider interest of African peoples in favour of the narrow and selfish interest of a corrupt and callous oligarchy" in Liberia.[11]

Although it is impossible to trace the process by which the Liberian decision was made, there is no evidence to support the view that Du Bois convinced a friendly Liberia to expel the UNIA. Du Bois denied that he had spoken to President King about Garvey during his January visit.[12]

9. *NW*, June 28, September 6, 1924; A. J. Garvey (ed.), *Philosophy and Opinions of Garvey*, II, 379.
10. The black politician William Lewis, working for Coolidge's reelection, urged the Du Bois appointment, which he saw as a "good chance to play a little politics at no cost to the government." Lewis to Coolidge, October 4, 1923, Lewis to E. Bascom Slemp, October 20, 1923, File 661, in Calvin Coolidge Papers, Library of Congress.
11. M. B. Akpan, "Liberia and the Universal Negro Improvement Association: Background to the Abortion of Garvey's Scheme for African Colonization," *Journal of African History*, XIV (1973), 126.
12. W. E. B. Du Bois to Editor of the *Daily Worker*, August 28, 1924, Du Bois to B. N. Azikiwe, November 11, 1932, in Du Bois Papers, University of Massachusetts.

There is no reason to doubt him. His position on Garvey was clear and publicly recorded in his *Crisis* editorials before his trip. Du Bois was impressed with Garvey's honesty, leadership, and vision even when he criticized his flamboyance, methods, and tactless behavior. King's judgment of Garvey was more negative than that of Du Bois. To attribute the exclusion to Du Bois ignores the history of the Liberians' relations with Garvey and Garveyites and makes the shrewd Liberians pliant puppets of Afro-American publicists, roles they never played.

The influence of Firestone can be disposed of as easily. Although one of its two proposed sites was on the Cavalla River in Maryland County, there is no evidence in the lengthy correspondence between the rubber company and the Liberians that company officials were even aware of the talks between the UNIA and Liberia that were going on at the same time. If Garvey and some contemporary scholars believed the UNIA was an alternative, a competitor, or a threat to Firestone, the corporation itself did not. At most, the Firestone contract in June was one more factor that allowed the King administration to act on its antipathies without fear of arousing its Liberian critics. Internal reforms King initiated after the defeat of the loan in 1922 plus the upturn in the world economy increased Liberian revenue in late 1923. The Firestone agreement was an additional, if premature, sign that the nation had finally found the export—rubber—that could end her economic stagnation. Under the new conditions, King felt strong enough to risk alienating the Liberian advocates of the UNIA.[13]

The timing of the exclusion suggested that King's tolerance of the protracted negotiations lasted only as long as the UNIA showed no signs of carrying out its plans. As late as May, Dossen, the Liberian most interested in UNIA colonization, appeared to be unaware of the imminent arrival of UNIA immigrants in Liberia. In a letter to UNIA officials, he asked detailed questions about the reception of his pamphlet *Origin, Rise and Destiny of Liberia*, which he thought would serve as "propaganda in your emigration enterprise." His instructions for the number of reprints, price of pamphlets, and remittance of proceeds were meticulous. But his plans for the immigrants were vague. There was no hint that he knew that an expedition from the United States would sail in a little more than one month.[14]

The order of June 30 banning the Garveyite advance party followed a UNIA notice published in the New York *World* on June 26 that combined an elaborate description of its colonization plans, an announcement of the

13. Akpan, "Liberia and the UNIA," 121; Frank Chalk, "The Anatomy of an Investment: Firestone's 1927 Loan to Liberia," *Canadian Journal of African Studies*, I (1967), 12–37.

14. J. J. Dossen to UNIA, May 2, 1924, in A. J. Garvey (ed.), *Philosophy and Opinions of Garvey*, II, 378.

sailing of its first experts, and a financial appeal "to all those who desire to help the Negro." The message unwittingly revealed the UNIA's poverty, but it also boldly announced the UNIA's broad ambitions, which went beyond the Liberian government's instructions. When King and Barclay discovered that UNIA members were actually embarking for Liberia, they acted. J. J. Dossen's death in June removed a potential political obstacle to expulsion. Amy Jacques Garvey's subsequent attribution of UNIA expulsion to Dossen's death inadvertently revealed how slim Liberian support for the UNIA was. The executive order was easily ratified by the legislature in January, 1925.[15]

Although the elimination of Garveyism from Liberia was not engineered out of ideological commitments, the decision illuminated the weak points in Pan-African relationships in the 1920s. Although all parties adopted the Western model of development to achieve African freedom, they disagreed about which roles blacks could and should assume immediately and which whites would perform the necessary functions blacks could not execute. Differences reflected the interests of particular strata in the international racial community, with strong doses of individual opportunism thrown in. American Pan-Africanists, representing blacks who possessed underutilized skills and business ambitions, were more committed than their Liberian cousins to keeping economic development in the hands of the race. In August, 1921, Du Bois had written that the "only way for blacks to succeed was through control of capital by black peoples." Like Garvey, he believed that Liberia needed capital investment, a railroad, a "sound Bank" under Negro control, and "the aid of American Negro capital and colored technical experts" to help develop "agriculture, industry, and commerce." Like Garvey, he believed that the racial brotherhood would remove capitalism's warts. Blacks would avoid the problems of selfishness and exploitation, Du Bois believed, because of the "democratic nature of Negro people."[16]

Du Bois modified the extreme position on black capital, just as Garvey eventually endorsed the United States loan to Liberia, out of necessity, not ideology. Du Bois came to share President King's conclusion that "economic development of the country [Liberia] should be left, for the present moment, to private foreign enterprise under safe and reasonable terms of

15. Edwin Barclay to Elder Dempster & Co., June 30, 1924, Francis O'Meara to Secretary of State, August 8, 23, 1924, in F.O. 371/9553; New York *World*, June 26, 1924; "Minutes of the House of Representatives, 1924–1930," 1st Sess., January 12, 1925, in Liberian State Archives.

16. W. E. B. Du Bois to C. D. E. King, January 21, June 30, 1924, in Du Bois Papers, University of Massachusetts; W. E. B. Du Bois, *Crisis*, XXII (August, 1921), 152.

operations." The judgment was based upon his blind admiration for King, not a theory of development. When King happily announced a "liberal understanding . . . with the Firestone Rubber Company," Du Bois responded warmly and positively despite his earlier opinions, which placed him closer to Garvey's views on foreign white capital.[17]

Du Bois had met with Firestone surveyors when he was in Liberia for King's inauguration. He had informed the Liberian president that American capital could be controlled more easily than European because Afro-Americans "have enough political power to make the government go slowly." *Crisis* would inform Afro-Americans about Liberian affairs so as to protect Liberian sovereignty and prevent a new Congo. Reflecting the current vogue of welfare capitalism, Du Bois thought that experts "trained in anthropology and economics"—whenever possible "colored American citizens"—should be employed to protect the "native races" from exploitation. He had reluctantly acknowledged that the economic and technical aspects of development would probably have to be conducted by whites, but "personnel in sanitation and education could and should be black." The cancer of plantation agriculture would be removed by black managers, just as the wounds of black wage workers were to be treated by black social workers in the United States. Du Bois informed the State Department that he "would push the Firestone project if it gave an opening for colored graduates." Convinced by Firestone's promises, which had been aimed at pacifying potential opposition, Du Bois believed that Firestone was "very enthusiastic about welfare work on a national scale. He is very interested in the idea of establishing schools, hospitals, agricultural training schools, and so forth, for the development of the aborigines. . . . He grasps the idea of developing a model nation from these primitive people." But Du Bois' hopes for Afro-American employment and Liberian development did not materialize.[18]

Garvey and Du Bois tried to replicate the latest achievements of the modern world. They probed beneath the rhetoric of racism but not of capitalism. They eyed problems of caste and administration. Rejecting the political control of an alien race, they did not question the cultural values that instructed that race. Both men assumed that the placing of black men in

17. King to Du Bois, June 30, 1924, Du Bois to King, July 29, 1924, in Du Bois Papers, University of Massachusetts.

18. W. E. B. Du Bois, "Report on Mission to Liberia," March 24, 1924, file 882.00/739, in RG 59; Frank Chalk, "Du Bois and Garvey Confront Liberia: Two Incidents of the Coolidge Years," *Canadian Journal of African Studies*, I (1967), 141; Du Bois to King, July 29, 1924, Du Bois to Harvey S. Firestone, October 26, 1925, Du Bois to Lester Walton, May 26, 1927, in Du Bois Papers, University of Massachusetts; Du Bois, *Crisis*, XXXIV (March, 1927), 24, (October, 1927), 26.

positions of power would avoid the evils of colonialism and capitalism seen in other parts of the continent. But their racial nationalism could not order the process of racial replacement or determine the proper candidates for the new roles. Garveyites, more than the followers of Du Bois, used politics to create jobs and careers, and Garvey was more impatient to fill "white roles" in Liberia and in the United States. Du Bois, speaking for a social stratum that was more established and secure than the one attracted to Garvey, was not so dominated by immediate pressures. The conflicts generated by the different constituencies were aggravated by the vanities of two large egos. Although they rarely competed on the same terrain, each admired, and possibly coveted, the attainments of the other. The aloof and aristocratic Du Bois esteemed Garvey's charisma, which his own politics demanded but his personality precluded. Garvey, for his part, longed for the educational credentials and respectability of the older man.

Incapable of unifying Afro-Americans, Pan-Africanism failed to resolve the regional competitions for racial leadership. Although both the Liberian elite and the Garveyites agreed that Liberia was for black peoples— only Negroes could become Liberian citizens and own land—the answer to the question of which blacks should rule Liberia did not follow logically from Pan-African ideology or Liberian nationalism. The elite jealously guarded its sovereignty from the threats of political participation by "indigenous" Africans and of competition from "alien" Negroes from the Americas. If the Liberian elite's racial nationalism was compromised, its bourgeois legitimacy was weak, too, because the government pursued development fitfully, always evaluating growth on the scales of class preservation. Most objective observers concluded that its first principle was to maintain its political monopoly. The crisis of the postwar period had forced the Liberian elite to draw upon its Pan-African connections. In 1919 and 1920, Liberians interested in Garveyism had hoped to obtain investments, shipping, and skilled labor—to use racial links to construct an incipient national bourgeoisie independent of foreign white capital. Even in these years of Pan-African optimism, Liberians, often the same men who flirted with Garveyism, also tried to attract foreign capital. But when the meagerness of UNIA resources became known, most Liberians lost interest. Only a small circle, mainly from remote Maryland County, found that the UNIA could aid Liberia by transporting people. When the UNIA demonstrated its ability to dispatch emigrants to Liberia and continued to assert its larger ambitions, which threatened to challenge the sovereignty of the Liberian elite, the King administration decided to act on its preferences and permanently ban Garveyism from Liberia.

Because the UNIA vowed to continue despite the Liberian decision,

Ernest Lyon, the republic's consul general, asked the United States government to publicize the official prohibition. After determining that Garveyism was too weak to be a factor in the American elections, the State Department agreed.[19]

At the UNIA convention of August, 1924, Garvey publicly asked the Liberian House and Senate to overturn King's expulsion order. He told his American audience that "if we [the UNIA] had the money, you would at this moment be having everything you want in regard to Liberian development. You cannot blame certain people [*i.e.*, the Liberian government] for their actions because Liberia is obligated to England and France. Liberia owes them one and a half million dollars." The United States government escaped attack because Garvey was simultaneously appealing to the "conscience of white America and to Mr. Firestone." He asked Firestone to "refrain from taking advantage of the opportunity given him of standing in the way of progress of a people."[20]

Some UNIA members opposed Garvey's conciliatory attitude. They attacked the Liberian elite. Garvey warned them to be "careful in their speech, and say nothing they did not mean or which would embarrass the organization." He continued to find it difficult to moderate the militance of his following in the interest of UNIA diplomacy. His own petition to Liberia warned of the "great danger" of the Firestone Rubber concession. He predicted that "the white capitalists" ultimately would seek usurpation of the government, "even as has been done with the black Republic of Haiti after similar white companies entered there under the pretense of developing the country." Firestone's ultimate aim would be to place Liberia "in the hands of the white race." Out of his own frustrations, Garvey had pinpointed the political control required by investors in undeveloped countries. He saw no alternative to it: "Capitalism is necessary to the progress of the world, and those who unreasonably and wantonly oppose or fight against it are enemies to human advancement." Unable to advance racial capitalism and lacking an analysis of the conflicts within capitalism that might yield a substitute route to racial progress, Garvey found no source for a politics of opposition to the exploitation that he warned Firestone would bring to Liberia. Like Du Bois, he appealed to humanity and racial unity, gestures of despair more than hope.[21]

19. Division of West European Affairs to Secretary of State, August 25, 1924, file 811.4016/191, William Castle, "Memorandum," September 6, 1924, file 882.5511/10, in RG 59; A. J. Garvey (ed.), *Philosophy and Opinions of Garvey*, II, 386–93; NW, August 23, 1924.
20. NW, September 6, 1924.
21. A. J. Garvey (ed.), *Philosophy and Opinions of Garvey*, II, 392–93, 72. The final agreement with Firestone, signed in 1926, did not bring the economic changes that advocates predicted and critics feared. Firestone had come to Liberia in search of rubber to avoid the

Outside of Liberia, Garveyism in West Africa was an occasional inspiration for Africans and an irritant to European colonial authorities. UNIA locals in Lagos, Nigeria, and Freetown, Sierra Leone, were short-lived. It was not surprising that the Lagos branch was the largest in colonial West Africa, because the city was the most modern and Westernized area on the coast. It had three hundred members on its books, though only twenty-eight paid their dues. As in Liberia, the clerks, teachers, and aspiring traders of the Lagos branch wanted shipping and capital. An occasional young revolutionary like John Camara of Sierra Leone might take Garvey's rhetoric literally. Camara was reported to be holding meetings in Dakar, Senegal, and "exhorting his hearers to spread the revolutionary movements which would in the end cast the white man out of Africa." But the UNIA in Africa was better characterized by the editor of Lagos *Weekly Record*, who found that local Garveyites were "neither traitorous nor revolutionary, neither fantastic nor visionary," though he did condemn Garvey's "aggressive and militaristic tendencies." Another on-the-scene observer believed that the leaders of the Lagos UNIA were "sincere, but their methods were dictatorial, publicity poor, and internal struggles disastrous." The branch disintegrated at some point after 1922, the combination of the international decline of Garveyism and local problems having been fatal.[22]

Weakly grounded, organized Garveyism in Africa was unstable and ineffective. The message, however, was occasionally heard by the aspiring petite bourgeoisie, the same group that shaped Garveyism in the Americas. Thomas Jesse Jones, touring Africa for the Phelps-Stokes Educational Commission, discovered three UNIA sympathizers in the course of his travels. Two were Americo-Liberians. The third was a "native teacher" who had been a student at Fourah Bay College in Freetown. Jones was distressed to discover that the teacher was determined to send ten pounds to Garvey despite the disapproval of his European colleagues at the school. But it was precisely among the teachers, students, and aspiring young businessmen that the Garveyite appeal to modernism was answered in Af-

---

British domination of production. But the ending of the British policy of restriction and a decline in prices limited Firestone's scale of operations in the 1920s. Structures of dependence appeared immediately, however. Liberia was forced to subscribe to a Firestone loan, similar to the one rejected by the U.S. Senate in 1922. Everyone, including Firestone, agreed that there was no economic need for one. The company insisted on one to eliminate British and French bondholders and thus make Firestone the dominant and only economic power in Liberia. In the end, the nation's future was determined by Firestone and the United States, not by Liberia. Chalk, "Anatomy of an Investment," 12–33.

22. R. L. Okonkwo, "The Garvey Movement in British West Africa," *Journal of African History*, XXI (1980), 105–17; Sir Hugh Clifford, "Report of UNIA Activities in Nigeria," April 12, 1922, in C.O. 583/109/28194; J. Ayodele Langley, *Pan-Africanism and Nationalism in West Africa, 1900–1945* (Oxford, 1973), 93–94.

rica. Neither Garvey nor the men inspired by him attracted other groups—laborers, peasants, or artisans.[23] Nonetheless, Garveyism raised the identical Pan-African issues that disrupted UNIA relations with Liberians. J. J. Dossen's son-in-law, the Reverend Van Richard, told Garveyites at the 1924 UNIA convention, after the association had been expelled from Liberia, that "Africa will redeem herself when the time comes. Not from without but from within." Similarly, Kobina Sekyi, a Gold Coast nationalist and lawyer, developed the idea more fully in 1925 when he said that Garvey

> does not understand how we Africans in Africa feel about such matters as the Colonial Government; neither can he and his set . . . realise that republican ideals in the crude form in which they are maintained in theory, at least, in America go directly against the spirit of Africa, which is the only continent in the whole world peopled by human beings who have in their souls the secret of constitutional monarchy. . . . *The salvation of the Africans in the world cannot but be most materially assisted by the Africans in America but must be controlled and directed from African Africa and thoroughly African Africans.*

Although claiming to represent the "spirit of Africa," Sekyi was expressing the conservative, almost royalist politics of his class. Garveyism threatened, however crudely, to raise the issue of political independence in a time when the West African elite was seeking its role in the British Empire. To Sekyi, even Afro-American immigration would "create new sources of trouble. The most we can allow is to open the way for the influx of the money of capitalists of our own race in America and the West Indies in order that we may ourselves compete with the gigantic combinations that are being formed in England for the undisguisable purpose of establishing a sort of legal or legalised monoply of trade."[24]

Like King, Sekyi feared that Garveyism might inspire other parts of the African population that the West African elite could not practically accommodate in their plans for an African future. Garvey's rhetorical flourishes could be heard as a revolutionary clarion by many ears. Some of the older Ashanti welcomed news of Garveyism, as they had once welcomed Chief Sam, because they hoped Garvey could return their King Prempeh, who had been exiled after the British had defeated them at the turn of the century. The more imaginative believed that Garveyites would come in battleships to drive the British out. In the Transkei, in southern Africa, one

---

23. Thomas Jesse Jones, "Itinerary," diary of African trip, 1920, pp. 21, 72, in Phelps-Stokes Fund Papers.
24. *NW*, September 6, 1924; Langley, *Pan-Africanism and Nationalism*, 39–40, 99–103.

Wellington Butelezi offered his tribesmen membership badges costing 2s. 6d. and promised the resurgence of his people's past glories. He told his following that American blacks would arrive from the air to liberate them from the whites. In Africa, as in the United States, men interpreted Pan-Africanism in terms of their own needs.[25]

In the end, the West African elite chose the opportunities of the British connection over political independence or Pan-Africanism. Colonial Africans were as determined as the independent Liberians to monopolize African politics. Even if their monopoly was only banked for the future, they insisted that their leadership was the sine qua non of success. Confusing their prominence with dominance, they substituted their wishes for historical necessity.

Despite the limited inroads that Garveyism made in Africa, colonial governors, like the Liberian government, acted to keep out nonresident Garveyites. Garvey himself was denied a passport on the grounds that his visit would lead to unrest. Although the Nigerian governor's assessment of Garvey's motives reflected the bias of his class and position, his measure of the danger was accurate: "Marcus Garvey probably has a larger following in the West Indies than he has in West Africa, but it is in Africa that he wanted to institute his Negro State: consequently his object must be to stir up trouble and to incite sedition in Africa. What he wants from the West Indies is money. Probably this is his chief want so far as Africa is concerned as well; but if his movement is ever to achieve anything he must also create a spirit of unrest in Africa."[26]

Although the specter of Garveyism loomed large and occasionally inspired the populace, Garvey was as incapable of producing a political movement to challenge the colonial state as were the West African elites. Because the modern world had only just begun to erode traditional society in Liberia and West Africa, Garvey's appeal to progress met with a narrow response. Garvey's question of why Africa should not give to the world its black Rockefeller, Rothschild, and Henry Ford was not located in African social reality and made sense only to students, teachers, and businessmen seeking capital and transportation for careers and personal advancement. Pan-African enthusiasm was a perishable commodity. Independent economic development, the most Garvey could offer, could not compete with

25. David Jenkins, *Black Zion: Africa Imagined and Real as Seen by Contemporary Blacks* (New York, 1975), 104; Peter Walshe, *The Rise of African Nationalism in South Africa: The African National Congress, 1921–1951* (Berkeley, 1971), 92, 165.
26. R. C. Maughm to Governor of Gambia, June 15, 1922, Confidential No. 384/255/52, and "Nigeria Confidential 'C,'" July 9, 1923, in C.O. 583/118/34197.

the global economic order of the 1920s, despite its various discriminations. And so long as Pan-Africanists sought Rockefellers, not Lenins or Gandhis, the elites of Afro-America and Africa became competitors, both of them divorced from the masses they aspired to speak for.[27]

27. MG, "Africa's Wealth," April 18, 1923, in A. J. Garvey (ed.), *Philosophy and Opinions of Garvey*, II, 68.

12 / Ethnic Politics as Pan-Africanism
The Locals of the UNIA

Even if the BSL and other Pan-African projects of the UNIA had been more successful, good relations between the Parent Body and the numerous locals would have been constantly tested by the association's hierarchical structure. Almost immediately, local people demanded autonomy, information, and sometimes power, demands that were usually dismissed by Garvey and his aides. The secondary role of the divisions of the UNIA was a corollary of Garvey's assumption that racial progress flowed from strong leadership and the concentration of resources. UNIA locals would fund the projects planned by the Parent Body, the directing authority of the UNIA. The heady success of the initial BSL sales confirmed the theory, but the company's ballooning debts soon demonstrated that local financial support was not limitless or unconditional.

Selling Black Star Line stock was a critical activity in all branches in 1919 and 1920. Garveyites were known as "Black Star Liners" in numerous cities, especially in the South, where southern racial ways precluded a strategy of politics and protest. Most locals created in this period were offspring of the stock-selling campaigns. Typically, a UNIA organizer, with the support of community leaders, set up a series of meetings to sell shares and organize a permanent division.[1]

It took a minimum of seven persons to set up a branch. Dues were thirty-five cents a month, ten cents of which was sent to the Parent Body in New York. Most divisions purchased copies of the UNIA constitution, songbooks, photographs, flags, uniforms, and the *Negro World* from New York headquarters. Meetings usually began with prayers and songs—hymns of church and state, not of the old folk or new urban culture. "Onward Christian Soldiers," "Greenland's Icy Mountains," and "The Star Spangled Banner" were staples in the ritual of most UNIA divisions. Then the audience listened to a series of inspirational talks, punctuated by musi-

---

1. Baltimore *Afro-American*, July 20, 1923; author's interview with F. Levi Lord, June 18, 1976; Ralph Watkins, "The Marcus Garvey Movement in Buffalo, New York," *Afro-Americans in New York Life and History*, I (1977), 411–12.

cal entertainment. On one evening, Hartford Garveyites heard discourses entitled "Organization," "Truth," "The Negro Question," "Freedom of Africa," and "A Plea for Womanhood." Larger divisions tapped international black culture. The South African educator Solomon Plaaje addressed the Boston division. Although the details of the speeches were rarely reported, the titles suggested a common ethic stressing purposeful behavior. At Homestead, Pennsylvania, the president asserted that "it takes time for all things." The next speaker urged members to "have an object in view." A new member tackled the topic "Obstacles and How to Surmount Them."[2]

Without unifying projects or collective politics, however, UNIA chapters incorporated the culture of the surrounding local community. Members, who belonged simultaneously to numerous fraternals, churches, clubs, and societies, brought the practices, styles, and expectations of their other associations into the UNIA. Some locals were simply social clubs, surrounded by a thin veneer of racial purpose. A *Negro World* editorial acknowledged that the meetings of the auxiliary Black Cross Nurses were "largely social in character." The division in Waterloo, Iowa, informed fellow Garveyites that "after the business part of the meeting the vice president turned over the meeting to the master of ceremonies," but the business of the branch went unreported. Entertainment took on regional and class characteristics. The New York division preferred elite culture. One of its meetings featured classical music, the sextet from *Lucia di Lammermoor* and the overture to *Rigoletto*, among other selections. Reflecting popular culture, the branch in River Rouge, Michigan, showed moving pictures on Saturday night. New Orleans members once staged an Oriental bazaar and decorated the hall "with streamers of the royal colors—Red, Black, and Green. Booths lined the aisles and each was styled as an estate ruled by dukes, lords, counts, and princes. The most delicious delicacies were served à la Africanna." The UNIA was truly international in New Orleans. The winner of its "style show" wore a "Parisian modelled gown of blue canton crepe trimmed with silver cloth." The Boston group pursued more purposeful recreation. It formed a Literary and Publicity Club to educate its members in literature and oratory: "It will stock books by prominent Negroes and on the life of prominent Negroes, and it has been voted to purchase the 'Encyclopedia Brittanica,' 'The Standard History of the World,' and other such useful works . . . to develop the minds of the members and assist them in rising to a higher plane in life."[3]

2. *NW*, January 6, April 15, 29, 1922; E. David Cronon, *Black Moses: The Story of Marcus Garvey and the Universal Negro Improvement Association* (Madison, 1955), 61; Amy Jacques Garvey, *Garvey and Garveyism* (Kingston, Jamaica, 1963), 103.

3. *NW*, April 23, 1921, March 25, 1922, July 9, 1927.

The frequent reiteration, at division meetings, of the purposes and rules of the UNIA suggests that participation was often casual and occasional and that new members and nonmembers composed a large part of UNIA assemblages. Like ministers, UNIA presidents were often praised for their speaking ability, a powerful asset in attracting money and new members. The Reverend T. V. Glashen, commissioner for the UNIA in Tennessee, "held one meeting" spellbound for a space of an hour and fifteen minutes. "Oh, how our hearts burned. Seven joined the organization," a member reported. Larger recruiting drives were similar to religious revivals and often featured speakers from the Parent Body. Garveyites advertised a series of talks in Cincinnati as "Billy Sunday Meetings." The tone was not otherworldly. Boosters predicted that "no Negro who has one drop of Race Pride and Ambition will miss these meetings." New goals and ambitions were common by-products of Garveyism. One young man exulted that black people now "have hopes of a coming industrial future instead of an all-religious affair. . . . Before the dawn of another century we shall have climbed to the places we are now dreaming of." Having grown up in a culture suffocated by religion, he was overjoyed to find that the UNIA encouraged broad learning and secular aspiration. An important factor in Garvey's appeal was his transference of black redemption from the afterlife to the here and now. Although victory or success was often placed in the future, Garveyite promises inhabited secular, not spiritual, realms in history.[4]

While many were attracted by a good speaker, individual inspiration, or the racial enthusiasm at mass meetings, longer commitments required more tangible services. The typical Garveyite used the model of the fraternal as a measure of UNIA performance. Therefore, the Parent Body accommodated to popular expectations by establishing a system of sickness and death benefits, though few received the promised aid. Garvey argued that the system did not work because local leaders failed to remit the required ten cents. Divisions were frequently delinquent, but the Parent Body did not segregate the collected money, which was used indiscriminately for the most pressing UNIA financial obligations. "Payments of death claims, matters of supplies and non-reception of important communications forwarded to New York" headed the list of grievances submitted by Virginia divisions in 1922. They warned that they "were not prepared to continue affiliation unless Parent Body practices were more responsive."[5]

Garvey's failure to map out regional, national, and international objectives clearly was at the root of many of the conflicts between the locals and

4. *NW*, May 4, 1922, April 11, 1925; leaflet, n.d., Box C-304, in NAACP Papers.
5. *NW*, January 6, 1922, August 23, 1924, July 23, 1927.

the Parent Body. The head of the Pittsburgh UNIA complained that Garvey had refused to help the local purchase property because he was interested in Africa, not the United States. Without a political agenda, words like *independence, freedom,* and *status* conveyed various meanings to Garveyites of different classes and regions. The Parent Body attempted to accumulate capital to compete with big industry, but the most common form of accumulation for rank-and-file UNIA members was the traditional one for working people, home ownership. The Miami division reported that "its members . . . are yet making untold sacrifices for this cause." The Floridians interpreted the "cause" to be ownership of a Liberty Hall and of "houses from which they derive rentals and on which not one penny is owed." To the men and women of the branches, independence was property ownership free of debt, not a black government in Africa, which was a common standard of Garveyite rhetoric.[6]

Garvey's failure to enunciate a principled politics was the source of conflict within locals as well as between locals and the Parent Body. Internal strife was so common that the UNIA possessed an official prayer for the restoration of peace within divisions. Would-be businessmen often took advantage of the UNIA's appearance of collective enterprise to promote their own companies. Members of the board of trustees of a Chicago division were directors of the Elroy Manufacturing Company, a short-lived firm that hoped to manufacture caskets, boxes, and undertaking equipment. Money for it was solicited with other UNIA projects, though the corporation was not the property of the division. Merging individual and racial interest encouraged some local leaders to use the chapter's funds as venture or operating capital. Divisions did not report stealing but the end of stealing. A Philadelphia officer once announced, "Many leakages have been closed up owing to such unrest."[7]

Despite Garvey's castigation of leaders who used the prestige or funds of office for personal benefit, conflicts of interest were embedded in UNIA ideology and practice. William Sherrill confessed his own affiliation in terms of his ambitions. When he began working in a black bank in Baltimore, "as is the custom of men in business, I joined everything in Baltimore, including the Universal Negro Improvement Association," he recalled. "It was good business to be connected with all churches, lodges, and everything else when you are in business."[8]

6. W. C. Francis to Editor of the Pittsburgh *Courier*, n.d., Box 12, in Universal Negro Improvement Association Papers, Schomburg Center for Research in Black Culture, New York Public Library; NW, March 23, 1927, February 28, 1925.
7. NW, June 3, 1922, September 8, August 23, 1924.
8. NW, September 20, 1922, May 9, 1925.

Official descriptions of UNIA officers and activists highlighted their so-cial status and economic assets. One report described the "Hon. Mdm. McGregor," the lady president of a Virginia chapter, as "one of the wealth-iest and most prominent ladies of the race in Suffolk." The Philadelphia division proudly, if inaccurately, reported that "most of the prominent doc-tors, lawyers, and businessmen are active members." These criteria made individual achievement, not racial identity or service, the badge of racial patriotism and eroded the incentive to become or remain active Garveyites when individual opportunities unrelated to the UNIA made affiliation bur-densome. President F. A. Brewster of the Norfolk chapter resigned "owing to his many business interests." The exodus of the prosperous undercut UNIA claims to economic leadership. Only marginal businessmen re-tained the faith.[9]

Class conflict was another source of internal weakness. Leaders of the Kingston, Jamaica, branch forced out its "trouble-makers"—"those who did not pay dues." The substance of the issues in the conflict was not revealed in the *Negro World* report. In most instances, class divisions in the locals were expressed socially, not ideologically in alternative programs and practices. Garvey warned the Denver local: "We must work together. . . . If we hap-pen to be members of the same organization, and the illiterate man tries to embarrass you, do not become disgusted, but remember that he does it be-cause he does not know better, and it is your duty to forbear and forgive, because the end that we serve is not of self, but for the higher development of the entire race." Nevertheless, Garvey expected locals to be led by edu-cated men and women, especially after 1921, when the UNIA was desper-ate for funds and required bridges to more affluent blacks.[10]

The very poor, when attracted to the UNIA, were not active members. A social worker's survey of blacks in Gary, Indiana, discovered a UNIA family from Mississippi who had been in the North for eight years. He found them "living in the vilest place I have ever seen. . . . There were ab-solutely no sanitary facilities. The head of the family was paralyzed, the children were ill. The probation officer arranged that day to send the hus-band to the charity hospital, and the wife and children to a home for the destitute. . . . It appears this family were members of the . . . Universal Negro Improvement Association. One of the children had the distinction of being named Marcus Andrew Henry Garvey Davis." UNIA divisions did not and could not provide services for impoverished blacks. Families like

9. *NW*, May 13, September 20, October 14, December 23, 1922, May 9, 1923, Septem-ber 23, 1925.
10. *NW*, May 27, July 8, 1922. See Chapter 9 for a discussion of conflicts in the New Orleans division.

the Davises coped alone or, if discovered, received aid from state or private social agencies. Their attachment to Garveyism might be fervent, but it did not generate the UNIA's praxis. Active Garveyites were marginal, not desperate, men.[11]

The locals suffered in hard times. Typically, an officer of the Kinston, North Carolina, division reported in 1927 that the membership was down "due to economic conditions." If the UNIA could not offer concrete aid, the unemployed occasionally found some inspiration in the UNIA. A miner reported: "My job ceased for about three months. Of all the newspapers I have read, none refreshes my mind as the *Negro World*. . . . I believe in prayer. As one writer says, 'The prayers of the righteous availeth much,' and we are fighting a righteous cause." An organization that did not seek to improve the world of work or address the problems brought by the accidents, illnesses, and insecurities that went along with industrial society might be useful to some blacks, but workers who participated regularly enjoyed enough economic security to permit associations not immediately functional to their daily lives. Most fraternals in American life grew from and served local communities, whether they provided insurance, death benefits, or capital for homes or business. The most durable were often fortified by bonds of kinship and language. UNIA locals sometimes performed these functions, though usually irregularly. Its original elite goals warred with local needs. The Parent Body tried to compete with elite institutions, not serve the immediate needs of its constituency.[12]

These characteristics of local Garveyism emerge when we see how various UNIA divisions interacted with other urban institutions—corporations, unions, political parties, churches, schools, fraternals, and other racial organizations—in specific communities. I have chosen to examine the four UNIA divisions in Detroit, Cincinnati, Cleveland, and Gary. More data is available on them and their surrounding communities than for many other branches, and each was a local of considerable size that began in 1920 and continued through the decade and into the thirties. Although they were leading centers of Garveyism, they were not dominated by Garvey personally. Combined with the scattered information available on the activities of other UNIA divisions and with the history of the Parent Body, an analysis of these four locals provides a fair view of the impact of

11. Thomas M. Campbell, "Report," November 11–December 15, 1923, p. 25, copy in RG 174.
12. *NW*, July 23, 1927, July 19, 1923. On the economic functions of fraternals see Scott Cummings (ed.), *Self-Help in Urban America: Patterns of Minority Economic Enterprise* (Port Washington, N.Y., 1980).

Garveyism at the community level. Moreover, each of the four sheds some light on significant historical problems posed by Garveyism and twentieth-century black history. The course of the Detroit UNIA illuminates the relationship of black politics in the 1920s with that of the 1930s; the Cincinnati history documents some of the social sources of the UNIA's politics of improvement; the Cleveland experience raises the problem of leadership; and the Gary record measures UNIA influence on an important issue of the 1920s, school segregation.

Many members of the Detroit UNIA were among the area's highest-paid blacks, workers in Ford's River Rouge plant, which employed 10,000 Afro-Americans in 1926. The Houston of the 1920s, Detroit boasted of its efficiency and prosperity, which was rooted in the automobile industry, the magnet drawing thousands to the city. Its black population rose from nearly 6,000 in 1910 to over 40,000 in 1920. And by 1930, its 120,000 blacks composed 7.7 percent of Detroit's citizens.[13]

The political and organizational life of blacks in Detroit flowed from the social relations of the factory. Automakers ruled their plants without challenge by ruthlessly eliminating nascent unions. They monopolized political power with their wealth and election procedures—the citywide constituencies and nonpartisan voting discouraged working-class or ethnic politics. Most residents participated in the new Detroit only with their labor.[14]

Few cultural and civic institutions were independent of capitalist largess. The Detroit Urban League, founded in 1916, was a ward of the employers' association, which financed it directly through the community chest. The city's leading businessmen dominated the NAACP. Branch literature, resembling the Urban League approach to migrant problems, instructed blacks on cleanliness and public deportment. The NAACP president, the Reverend Robert L. Brady, head of the largest Baptist church in the community, worked closely with Henry Ford and other employers of black labor. Brady and the Reverend Everard Daniel of St. Matthew's Episcopal Church screened workers, receiving in return financial contributions from Ford and the patronage of blacks who hoped that membership in one of the two churches would produce a job. The black electorate was orga-

13. U.S. Department of Commerce, Bureau of Census, *Negroes in the United States, 1920–1932*, (Washington, D.C.), 55; Richard Thomas, "From Peasant to Proletarian: The Formation and Organization of the Black Industrial Working Class in Detroit, 1915–1945" (Ph.D. dissertation, University of Michigan, 1976), 7; David Allan Levine, *Internal Combustion: The Races in Detroit, 1915–1926* (Westport, Conn., 1976), 147–48.

14. Levine, *Internal Combustion*, 6, 28–29; Ralph J. Bunche, *The Political Status of the Negro in the Age of FDR*, ed. Dewey W. Grantham (Chicago, 1973), 585.

nized by a GOP club run out of the Ford employment office. No black held a significant elective office during the decade. An axis of black ministers, Ford officials, and Ford goons was the private sector's equivalent of machine rule.[15]

The city, with its impoverished public and political life and its economic opportunities, advertised business solutions to all problems. A young Fisk graduate, William V. Kelley, who went to work in the automobile factories during the war, was advised by Director of Negro Economics George Haynes to "start out in business for yourself. The business field among Negro people is to be one of large development in the future." Building on these sentiments, Garvey traveled to Detroit in the spring of 1919 to meet with black leaders to raise money for the BSL. He was rebuffed by Charles S. Smith, the African Methodist Episcopal bishop of Michigan, a representative of black Detroit's Old Guard. Smith judged Garvey to be "an adventurer and a grafter, bent on exploiting his people to the utmost limit." Writing to Attorney General A. Mitchell Palmer, he said that Garvey "is in every respect a 'Red,' according to the sense in which that term is used in the common parlance of the day. He should either be required to discontinue his present vicious propaganda and fake practices or be deported as an undesirable."[16]

Garvey's spring trip preceded the acquisition of ships. Although he never won the approval of the bishop, a UNIA division was created in Detroit in 1920 after the BSL had captured the imagination of many and after the big New York convention. The BSL appealed to workers who had tasted a new combination of freedom and bondage on the assembly lines, which paid more than men had dreamed of while at the same time producing numerous grievances against the tyrannies of the factory. Although hopes of economic independence were unrealized for most of them, dreams were sustained through participating in the BSL and other UNIA enterprises. The local's able leadership and relatively well-paid membership of about four thousand produced a stable division that generously answered the financial appeals of the Parent Body. Although it bought a building for its meeting place, the local was content to purchase stock in the BSL and

15. August Meier and Elliott Rudwick, *Black Detroit and the Rise of the UAW* (New York, 1979), 6, 21; Levine, *Internal Combustion*, 28–29, 80–81, 202–203; Fred Hart Williams to Secretary of Branch, August 4, 1926, G-94, W. Hayes McKinney to William Pickens, October 13, 1925, both in NAACP Papers; Thomas, "From Peasant to Proletarian," 71–185.

16. George Haynes to William V. Kelley, September 11, 1919, Kelley to Haynes, August 25, 1919, Division of Negro Economics, in RG 174; Bishop C. S. Smith to A. Mitchell Palmer, June 25, 1919, in Robert A. Hill (ed.), *The Marcus Garvey and Universal Negro Improvement Association Papers* (10 vols. projected; Berkeley, 1983–), I, 446–47.

not launch businesses of its own. When it established a restaurant in its Liberty Hall, the purpose was service, not entrepreneurial training. Leaders hired experienced blacks to operate it.[17]

The division's efficient if modest operations can be attributed to F. Levi Lord, its founder and, until 1925, its executive secretary. Lord had been a schoolteacher in Barbados. The wrong religious affiliation denied him advancement, and he left the island to take a six-month tour as a policeman in Nassau, a way station for migration to the United States in 1918. Lord had been trained as a shoemaker—his father's trade—as well as a teacher. He easily found employment in a Brooklyn shoe factory for forty-five dollars a week. At the same time, he traveled to Harlem to hear the new agitators, especially Garvey. Lord, who had taught himself Pittman shorthand, volunteered to transcribe Garvey's speeches, which were then reprinted in the *Negro World*. After the 1920 convention he accepted the assignment of creating a UNIA division in Detroit at a salary of twenty-five dollars a week. He jumped at the opportunity to see the country as well as serve the UNIA. He also studied accountancy by correspondence.[18]

Lord recruited an able leadership of businessmen and professionals. Alonzo Pettiford, a lawyer active in the elite institutions of black Detroit, was president of the division in the early 1920s. J. A. Craigen succeeded Pettiford. Born in British Guiana, he came to the United States during the war as a Spanish interpreter for the Navy Department at Muscle Shoals, Alabama. He migrated to Detroit and worked at Ford. The board of trustees, which managed the division's property, was led by Charles Diggs, an undertaker who came to Detroit in 1913 and established his business in 1922.[19]

The UNIA's public profile was low. Most Garveyites, like most of the city's blacks, were not active in Detroit politics. The division made its political debut in 1925 when it endorsed the maverick Charles Bowles for mayor. Bowles's strength was among disaffected, native-born members of the petite bourgeoisie, the same social strata that nurtured the Klan, which also backed Bowles. The elites of Detroit, black and white, supported the incumbent, Mayor John W. Smith, who was reelected with the ballots of most blacks who voted. Republican politics alone yielded apathy, not political alternatives. Bowles's platform of efficiency, municipal growth, economy, and law and order was no different from the elite's blueprint for good

17. Author's interview with F. Levi Lord, June 18, 1976; Thomas, "From Peasant to Proletarian," 123.
18. Interview with Lord.
19. *Ibid.*; Alonzo Pettiford, "Statement," February 15, 1923, in Garvey file, RG 65.

government. Indeed, when Bowles ran again in 1929, he was elected with blue-ribbon blessing.[20]

Although the circumstances of the UNIA's endorsement of Bowles in 1925 are obscure, the political choice was typical of the pattern of UNIA local politics in the 1920s. The association did not mobilize blacks independent of the old client or newer machine politics. The initiative was usually taken by other white and black organizations. Often, urban dissidents, seeking to construct winning coalitions, approached the UNIA, a relatively independent force in the black community. In turn, the UNIA embraced political issues and candidates opportunistically, occasionally achieving traditional machine largess like cash or, more rarely, the newer form of patronage, racial representation. The commitments were rarely permanent. In 1927, Mayor Smith spoke at Liberty Hall and appealed with other politicians for the release of Marcus Garvey, at the time in federal prison in Atlanta. In 1928, Frank Murphy, the judge of the Sweet case and future mayor, addressed the division. Without a political program, the heightened racial consciousness of the UNIA simply reinforced black ethnic politics, which, as weak as it was in Detroit, was easily dominated by the black elite, which was better able to organize and influence the black community and connect with the larger urban community.[21]

Blacks abandoned the Republican party and participated more vigorously in the political arena when they were offered a politics with new substance. Like blacks in other northern cities, Detroit blacks became Democratic in the election of 1936, most heavily in the slums and working-class districts. Ex-Garveyites J. A. Craigen and Charles Diggs prepared the way. Although no longer associated with the UNIA, the two became the nucleus of the new Democratic group in 1932. Their new partisanship was the sign of a more profound ideological change.[22]

The two leaders had possessed faith in the virtues and efficacy of self-help and individual endeavor in the 1920s, when capitalism was vigorous and hegemonic, and working-class organization weak or nonexistent. Fordism was simultaneously all-powerful and relatively benevolent. The

20. Levine, *Internal Combustion*, 101, 135; *NW*, July 18, December 5, 1925; Bunche, *The Political Status of the Negro*, 587.

21. *NW*, May 21, 1927, August 4, 1928. The defendant in the Sweet case was Ossian Sweet, a doctor who was acquitted in 1926 of murdering a man while protecting his home from a howling mob opposed to blacks' living in the predominantly white neighborhood. Because of Murphy's fairness in conducting the trial, he, as well as Clarence Darrow, Sweet's lawyer, became a popular figure in the black community. Levine, *Internal Combustion*, 153–90.

22. New York *World*, October 29, 31, 1925; Levine, *Internal Combustion*, 171; Nancy J. Weiss, *Farewell to the Party of Lincoln: Black Politics in the Age of FDR* (Princeton, 1983), esp. 205–35, 314.

inspirational ideology of the UNIA accurately encompassed their past lives, current achievements, and future hopes. Racial consciousness took the form of individual endeavor. It dangled the glittering prizes of middle-class status through education or business.

The Great Depression blocked the path of men who had looked forward to entrepreneurial and professional careers. The rise of new social movements challenged the individualism at the root of UNIA ideology and politics, demonstrated the poverty of the ententes with corporations, and created alternatives to the opportunistic alliances of the 1920s. The United Automobile Workers, a member of the new Congress of Industrial Organizations (CIO), confronted the seemingly fixed tyrannies and insecurities of factory labor. A reformed Democratic party addressed the class and racial issues that had been outside the agenda of racial politics in the 1920s. Would-be professionals and businessmen found careers affiliated with the new social movements. Craigen, now a lawyer, became a CIO-endorsed member of the Michigan Workmen's Compensation Commission in 1937. Diggs, a Democratic state senator, was an active link between the CIO and black workers.[23]

Lord followed a similar route in New York. He had returned to take a position with the Parent Body in 1925. But he was forced to leave the UNIA a few years later so that he could support his family. After several small business ventures were aborted by the depression, he took and passed an examination for a white-collar civil service job. Then he threw his considerable energy and talents into the creation of a successful credit union in Brooklyn.[24] He had once worked to create the Black Star Line, an enterprise quite representative of black thought and aspirations of the 1920s, which reflected the overwhelming power of capital in American society and the continuing domination of Afro-American politics by the black petite bourgeoisie and its ideology.

In the 1930s, the balance of class forces within the nation and race changed. The creation of credit unions, labor unions, and new political affiliations were signs of the times. The needs of wage workers became the central issues in black politics. Working-class progress, not the growth of racial enterprise, became the preferred route to racial economic power, which was both an end in itself and the platform for the fight against racial discrimination.

Even before alternatives were created, the UNIA foundered in Detroit. At the 1929 UNIA convention, which Garvey held in Jamaica, the division

23. Henry Lee Moon, *Balance of Power: The Negro Vote* (Garden City, N.Y., 1948), 147–56; Meier and Rudwick, *Black Detroit and the Rise of the UAW*, esp. chs. 3, 4.
24. Interview with Lord.

was dealt a crushing blow when Craigen and other stalwarts resigned because they believed that Garvey was using the association's meager resources to fortify his own personal and political power. Although Craigen attempted to marshal the troops into a new organization, he was unsuccessful. And the faction loyal to Garvey, like those in other cities, broke into fragments, each claiming Garvey's legacy.[25]

Craigen had traveled to Jamaica with William Ware of Cincinnati, who joined Craigen in attempting to create a new UNIA without Garvey. Ware had led the UNIA local in Cincinnati since 1920. In Detroit the UNIA was inspired by the new gods of capitalism. But its program was more old-fashioned in cities like Cincinnati, where an older and less affluent black community worked in the kinds of traditional jobs more typical of southern cities. Nevertheless, only 19 percent of black males in the city remained domestic and service workers in 1920. Between 1910 and 1920 Cincinnati's black population rose from 19,636 to 30,079; by 1930 it was about 48,000—10 percent of the city's total population. Because Cincinnati was a major railroad and steamship nexus between the North and South, large numbers of temporary residents on their way to other northern cities swelled the resident population. Its permanent workers, unlike Detroit's, were scattered and dispersed throughout the city's medium-sized, diverse industries.[26] There were no large employers of black labor such as those who created the Detroit Urban League and its equivalents. This left a social vacuum and created an opportunity for free-lance labor recruiters and adjusters during the war.[27] One bureaucrat observed that workers were being "'welfared' to death. Every little grafter and graftee, every pseudo sociologist and every hypocritical preacher, every angel and every gambler, every orator and every shyster, every good natured simpleton and every sycophant, every bully and every weak-brained pretentious fool and every highwayman and liar are working overtime with an alleged welfare scheme to help(?) the 'man and brother.'"[28]

Unlike the professionals who ran the Urban Leagues, the heads of the community welfare groups, both the genuine and the bogus, often came

25. *NW*, August 24, 31, 1929, February 27, April 5, 1930, January 10, April 4, 11, July 4, 1931, January 9, 23, December 5, 1932.

26. Cincinnati Chamber of Commerce, "The Status of the Negro in Industry and Occupational Opportunities in Cincinnati, 1930" (Mimeographed, n.d.), 1, 3, copy in National Urban League Papers; New York *Herald*, November 14, 1925.

27. Joseph Jones, the head of one of the largest fraternal and regalia manufacturing establishments in black America and one of the promoters of the prewar African Union Company, moved easily into the business of labor recruiting. W. P. Dabney, *Cincinnati's Colored Citizens* (Cincinnati, 1926), 197.

28. Charles Hall to Walter White, November 14, 1919, Box C-319, in NAACP Papers.

from the same social class as their clients. Their activities, however, were modeled on the elite's culture of uplift. In 1917 William Ware, the future UNIA president, founded one of these community-based, social-improvement groups, the Welfare Association for the Colored People of Cincinnati. Representing it, he attended the UNIA convention in 1920, and upon his return to Cincinnati he transformed his group of forty-seven into a UNIA division.[29]

Despite its new Pan-African links, the purposes and activities of the new division were probably unchanged. Its activities can be deduced from the details that Ware included in, and omitted from, a printed biographical sketch of him published in a "who's who" of Cincinnati blacks. He came to the city in 1903 from nearby Lexington, Kentucky, where he had been born in 1872. Ware's work with the UNIA won him the professional title of social worker in the sketch. If the designation was selected by the editor, a member of Cincinnati's old colored upper class, then it revealed the elite's view of the function of the UNIA or, at least, its diagnosis of the needs of most Garveyites. Whatever its origin, the description probably revealed Ware's own view of his UNIA stewardship.

The biography was cluttered with numerous organizational, fraternal, and religious affiliations, but it omitted his occupations and sources of income for all earlier periods of his life. UNIA leaders who were not professionals, businessmen, or white-collar workers rarely disclosed their work. Some UNIA presidents, like Lionel Francis of Philadelphia, even feigned professional credentials—deceptions but also expressions of ambition and expectation. If Ware's deletions were typical of other UNIA leaders, his lack of education was not. Most division presidents in big cities were graduates of high school; some had college experience. It was unlikely, however, that Ware graduated from the grammar school his biography reported he attended. Limited schooling explained his failure to advance up the UNIA hierarchy to a position on the Parent Body, a common destination for successful local leaders. In March, 1926, Garvey, in prison in Atlanta, instructed his wife to fill a vacated top post with an educated man. If one was unavailable, he added, "then Ware or someone should act with arrangement to give way later to a proper person." Rarely did this criterion have to be articulated. Ware's limited opportunity for social mobility within and outside of the UNIA explained, however, his long tenure as president of the Cincinnati UNIA throughout the 1920s.[30]

29. Dabney, *Cincinnati's Colored Citizens*, 213–14.
30. William Ware, testimony, *Marcus Garvey* v. *United States of America*, 267 U.S. 607 (1924), 1665; *NW*, June 5, 1926; MG to Amy Jacques Garvey, March 19, 1926, in Amy Jacques Garvey Papers, Fisk University Library, Nashville. Another possible expla-

The UNIA tried to satisfy working-class aspirations for status outside of the world of wage labor through business, social service, home ownership, and organizational positions. Its ethic of social respectability was strongest in UNIA women like Lizzie Branch, "lady president" of the Cincinnati division. Accomplished in needlework and flower arrangement, a domestic in the home of affluent whites, she and her husband accumulated enough money to purchase a home in the old Negro suburb of Walnut Hills, where she formed a satellite branch of the UNIA. Active in a variety of uplift organizations—the Colored Women's Club, the YWCA, the NAACP—as well as the UNIA, her migration from the West Side ghetto to the suburb reflected her achievement but also separated her from most blacks who continued to live in the central-city district.[31]

The inadequacy of the self-help ethic was implicitly acknowledged by the openness of UNIA locals to urban politics. Like the Detroit division, the Cincinnati UNIA entered politics on invitation from others, not because Garveyites formulated a political strategy. The UNIA's suitor in Cincinnati was the respectable Charter party, a coalition of independent Republicans, Democrats, and progressives who convinced the city to institute nonpartisan elections, proportional representation, and the city manager form of local government to bridle the power of the old Republican machine. Conceivably blacks, labor, and Catholics, all of whom had little access to municipal power under the old system, would benefit equally with the independent businessmen who had initiated the change. The reform group remained together to function as an opposition party. In the first election under the new system in 1925, the Charter party elected six of nine councilmen. But the old machine triumphed in the Negro wards. The black Eighteenth Ward gave white Republican leader Fred Schneller 2,374 votes out of 3,619 cast. Two blacks received only 192 and 128 votes respectively. Two years later, when the Charterites decided to compete more aggressively with the ward heelers for the black vote, they approached the UNIA.[32]

The Republican machine coexisted uneasily with the UNIA in the West

nation of Ware's lengthy tenure and the division's stable membership was the likelihood that Ware and many Garveyites were simultaneously members of the Hod Carriers Union. Ware was very friendly with the union's white lawyer, Nicholas Klein, who spoke frequently at UNIA meetings. The common ties of work and race were a source of stability in other locals, too. Through Ware, Klein became a supporter and admirer of Garvey's and worked hard for his release from prison after 1925. For Klein's role in Cincinnati, see Ralph Straetz, *PR Politics in Cincinnati* (New York, 1958), 128–31.

31. In this period, 83 percent of all black working women were domestics. Bunche, *The Political Status of the Negro*, 3; Dabney, *Cincinnati's Colored Citizens*, 317; *NW*, April 14, 1923.

32. Straetz, *PR Politics in Cincinnati*, xiv–xvii, 102, 109; W. P. Dabney, *Chisum's Pilgrimage and Others* (Cincinnati, 1927), 35.

Side ghetto. The black boss, William Copeland, a funeral director, constructed judicious alliances with bootleggers and compliant black ministers, cemented by city jobs and cash at election time. Clergymen connected with the machine had attempted unsuccessfully to get the mayor to ban a series of UNIA meetings in 1921. For protection, the UNIA had united with the independent and elite Hamilton County Negro Republican League behind a black insurgent running for governor on a platform demanding more patronage. In 1923, Ware tendered the elite solution when he advocated "black representation in city government" as the solution to the migrant problem.[33]

Most black leaders uncorrupted by Republican pork looked favorably to the Charter party. But the coalition of white businessmen, elite blacks, and working-class blacks was not firm. At a meeting held at UNIA headquarters in the heart of the West End, the three groups attempted to rally behind the candidacy of Frank Hall, a retired black police officer. Hall was flanked by two representatives of the black elite—Wilbur Page, minister of the city's leading black Baptist church, and A. L. Dalton, a lawyer who had graduated from Howard and had been active for forty years in Republican politics. The Charter party was represented by Victor Heintz, a former Republican congressman and a dynamic leader of the reform movement, and two leading businessmen, Charles P. Taft and Charles Eisen.

The meeting bared the cultural gulfs separating the three groups. Ware opened the meeting with an attack on the machine and its ministerial retainers: "The Negroes' lamentable condition here is largely caused by sticking to preachers and the Republican party. Many of them go to the Republican campaign managers and get about fifty dollars or a suit of clothes and solemnly say, my church is with you. Our white speakers are always talking about Abraham Lincoln . . . and their black mammies. . . . We are tired of that stuff." Taft defended the religious calling and affirmed the existence of Heaven by singing a Negro spiritual, which proved to be very popular with the audience. Returning to politics, A. L. Dalton told the audience simply that it was time to elect a "colored man" to the city council. Also avoiding theology, Page criticized GOP boss Fred Schneller and Jews for the crimes on the West End, a reference to the Republican moonshiner Jack Rubenstein. But he also accused the Charter party of "driving the Negro out of city hall." The instituting of educational requirements for jobs and the efficiency drive to prune city payrolls removed blacks and threatened future appointments.[34]

33. Dabney, *Cincinnati's Colored Citizens*, 306; Dabney, *Chisum's Pilgrimage*, 32, 44; NW, October 23, 1926.

34. Dabney, *Chisum's Pilgrimage*, 22, 44; Dabney, *Cincinnati's Colored Citizens*, 323, 342.

Despite the absence of blacks on the city council, the consensus that a black legislator was desirable, and the existence of proportional representation (which enabled blacks to transcend their geographical dispersal), Frank Hall was not elected. Although the UNIA claimed several thousand members, that strength was not transferred to Hall in 1925 or in 1927, when he ran again. The gulfs between working-class and elite blacks and between blacks and the elite whites of the Charter party were not bridged. Ironically, Hall gained office in 1931 when the Republican machine itself nominated him.[35]

In the 1920s, most blacks either voted for the white machine candidate or did not vote at all. Without challenging the substance of public policy, black politics was a matter of cash and jobs, which the machine dispensed more liberally than the reformers. On the other hand, even though most Afro-Americans lacked a political agenda and ideology independent of the elite, they did not assume that the election of leading blacks would improve their own lives. The rhetoric of racial unity did not bridge the social gap within the black community. Typically, the man who was editor of Cincinnati's black newspaper, head of its NAACP, and a Charterite blamed the rise of residential segregation on the black masses: "Such trouble would hardly exist if the masses moved into neighborhoods in keeping financially and otherwise with their circumstances." Until the "average Negro" learned his place as the white "low class man" knew his, racial conflict would erupt and prejudice would spread, he concluded. After raising class barriers, the elite failed to corral the masses behind their leadership.[36]

Although politically ineffective, the UNIA divisions in Detroit and Cincinnati were large and stable. The stagnation of the UNIA in Cleveland, a city with a sizable and relatively affluent black population, is more problematic. Its black community had also grown during and after World War I. From 1910 to 1930, some 63,000 migrants brought the population up to 71,899—8 percent of the city. In 1915, only one-fifth of all black men labored in industry; in 1920, the proportion was two-thirds.[37] The history of the UNIA in Cleveland suggests that cities possessing racial institutions and organizations visibly independent from white power structures ham-

35. The revival of black Republicanism was temporary. By 1936, the heavily black Sixteenth Ward gave 65.1 percent of its vote to Franklin Roosevelt. Ernest Collins, "Cincinnati Negroes and Presidential Politics," in *The Negro in Depression and War*, ed. Bernard Sternsher (Chicago, 1969), 258–63.

36. Dabney, *Cincinnati's Colored Citizens*, 144–47; Straetz, *PR Politics in Cincinnati*, 256, 109–13; *NW*, October 23, 1926; William Giffin, "Black Insurgency in the Republican Party of Ohio, 1920–32," *Ohio History*, LXXXII (1973), 40.

37. Kenneth Kusmer, *A Ghetto Takes Shape: Black Cleveland, 1870–1930* (Urbana, 1976), 190.

pered the growth of the UNIA by weaning away potential leaders and appropriating militant rhetoric.

The labor and racial organizations of the city were stronger than their equivalents in Cincinnati and Detroit. Black Clevelanders struck with other workers in the 1919 steel strike. The legacy of lingering, if weakened, unionism and socialism produced a political diversity that did not exist in Detroit. In this climate the related tradition of egalitarian black Republicanism was serviceable, if not powerful. Similarly, the NAACP was run by blacks independent of businessmen such as those who dominated Detroit's branch. Unlike Cincinnati's NAACP, black but passive, Cleveland's fought discrimination affecting the working class as well as middle class. In one case, the NAACP successfully worked for the freeing of an ironworker who unknowingly had ignored an extradition waiver that could have led to his being returned to the custody of prison authorities in South Carolina. The NAACP publicized the fact that he was a Garveyite who had not been aided by the UNIA.[38]

Black politics in Cleveland deprived the UNIA of issues and targets. A two-party system and the expansion of the ghetto gave blacks both the numbers and a critical strategic position to increase black representation. Politics began with Cleveland's old black machine, more formidable than Cincinnati's because it was headed by the race-conscious Thomas Fleming, a police court lawyer and city councilman since 1909. He distributed government jobs and services and also gave out money for numerous racial institutions. Unlike the black machine in Cincinnati, which was linked with a Jewish moonshiner, the Fleming organization's most important ally was a black—Starlight Boyd, a leading saloonkeeper and impresario of illegal gambling whose race pride was as ostentatious as Fleming's. After a coalition of the UNIA, NAACP, and other community groups failed to unseat Fleming in 1921, reformers learned to respect his power. Acknowledging his bailiwick in the old ghetto, Claybourne George and other NAACP leaders formed a political club in the new area of black settlement. Electing two of their own in 1927, they joined with Fleming to defeat an organization candidate for county prosecutor who had threatened to end the policy rackets in the primary election of 1930.[39]

38. William Connors to Arnold Hill, July 7, 1925, in National Urban League Papers; Harry Davis to William Baldwin, April 7, 1924, Davis to Walter White, November 15, 1922, Box G-157, in NAACP Papers; C. R. Miller to T. J. Woofter, December 10, 1920, in Moton Papers.

39. Russell H. Davis, *Black Americans in Cleveland* (Washington, D.C., 1972), 230–31; Kusmer, *A Ghetto Takes Shape*, 134, 146–47, 221, 269, 271–73; Charles White to Robert Bagnall, November 15, 1927, Bagnall to White, November 18, 1927, Box G-157, in NAACP Papers.

The Parent Body of the UNIA sent out numerous outsiders to lead the Cleveland division, but none succeeded. When they found a native son, Leroy Bundy, the political opportunity in the city quickly weaned him away from Garveyism.[40] Bundy was the son of a prominent Cleveland minister and the brother of Richard Bundy, an official in the American legation in Liberia. After graduating from Western Reserve University with a degree in dentistry, he left Cleveland and moved first to Detroit and then to Chicago before settling in East St. Louis, Illinois. Like many other black professionals, Bundy combined his dental practice with business and politics. He bought and sold votes like any other party boss in the city. His political prominence and visibility made him a scapegoat for the race riot of 1917. He was charged with murder and conspiracy.[41]

The NAACP took his case initially but withdrew after questioning his use of money raised for his defense. Although convicted, Bundy won his freedom on appeal in 1921. He resumed his dentistry practice in Cleveland. In March, 1922, he became president of the local UNIA and soon won the organization a better hearing in the city.[42]

At this time Bundy was trying to reenter politics, though his ultimate ambitions were unclear. Some UNIA leaders believed that he wanted to succeed Garvey as head of the organization. At the 1922 convention Bundy served up the standard nostrums: success in business such as that achieved by "Jews and Greeks who can hardly speak the English language," and the "redemption of Africa" through "sacrifice and suffering and hard work." But Bundy's willingness to sacrifice was not excessive. Made assistant president-general of the Parent Body, he demanded and won a salary of six thousand dollars a year. He informed hostile delegates that "they should not expect that he would lay aside his business and give up his professional work at a sacrifice and then, probably in two years time, be forced to resume his professional business." The controversy was reminiscent of Bundy's earlier one with the NAACP, though Garvey, unlike the NAACP officialdom, supported Bundy's demands.[43]

40. When Levi Lord was sent to Detroit in 1920, Wesley McD. Holder went to Cleveland but failed to make headway. That it was conditions in Cleveland, not personal inadequacy, which explained his failure can be seen in his subsequent career. A creator of the Brooklyn black Democratic party, Holder engineered the nomination, election, and political organization of Congresswoman Shirley Chisolm and remains a powerful local political influence today. Interview with Lord; "Reminiscences of Wesley McD. Holder," passim, Oral History Project, Columbia University.
41. Elliott Rudwick, *Race Riot at East St. Louis, July 2, 1917* (Carbondale, Ill., 1964), 117–32.
42. *Ibid.*, 122–23; NW, March 18, 1922.
43. "Negro Activities," July 5, 12, 1922, in Garvey file, RG 65; NW, August 30, September 9, 1922.

Returning to Cleveland, Bundy was greeted by angry local Garveyites who charged that he had pilfered money to pay for his trip to New York. They wondered where he had obtained funds for a new Haynes sedan. Bundy seemed more interested in promoting himself and attacking NAACP leaders than in building up the UNIA in Cleveland. Traveling to Detroit, he "flayed Dr. Du Bois and the National Association as 'thieves,' and 'Pink Tea Promoters.'" He undoubtedly discovered quickly that the voting of salaries at UNIA conventions was not equivalent to payment. At some time in the fall, Bundy concluded that the UNIA could not be a launching pad for his personal ambitions. When Garvey spoke in Cleveland later in the year, Bundy was conspicuously absent from the meetings. By 1928, he was elected to one of two new black seats on the city council. Poised between eleven Democrats and eleven Republicans, he and Claybourne George created an effective political machine.[44]

Hedged in by a black-run political machine in the old ghetto and a militant and racially conscious elite in the newer areas of settlement, the UNIA was marginal, its membership small, and its presence insignificant. The UNIA president in the late 1920s was S. V. Robertson, head of garbage collection in Cleveland. The sanitation unit, which was 75 percent black, had been Fleming's plum since 1922. Apparently the boss had incorporated the local UNIA into his powerful machine.[45]

The UNIA was not overcome in Cleveland by the success of its rivals. Neither ethnic politics nor the NAACP in Cleveland represented the interests of most blacks or even won their attention. A NAACP member concluded in 1930 that "if the Cleveland branch [of the NAACP] is typical of other branches, then the NAACP is in bad shape. We hold practically no mass meetings throughout the year. Consciously or otherwise, the Negro leaders take a high-brow attitude toward the Negro masses and no effort is made to interest them in the affairs of the organization. . . . What saves us is that the white people in town do not know how ineffective we really are or how poorly we are qualified to speak for the Negroes of Cleveland."[46]

Nevertheless, Cleveland blacks had carried the politics of racial pride and representation as far as it could be stretched in the 1920s. Fostered by the same forces that fed the UNIA in other cities—the rise of black districts, black businessmen, and black consciousness—Cleveland's tradi-

44. W. Hayes McKinney to Robert Bagnall, November 14, 1922, Box G-157, in NAACP Papers; Kusmer, *A Ghetto Takes Shape*, 227–29, 234, 236; Davis, *Black Americans in Cleveland*, 229; Baltimore *Afro-American*, September 22, 1922; *NW*, February 19, 1921, April 30, 1927.

45. Kusmer, *A Ghetto Takes Shape*, 229.

46. David H. Pearce to Herbert J. Seligmann, October 25, 1920, Box G-157, in NAACP Papers.

tional racial institutions and elite captured the new spirit and reflected its limitations. Constantly drained of leaders and issues, the UNIA in Cleveland remained marginal, ending the decade as a literal appendix to the conventional politics.

In Detroit, Cincinnati, and Cleveland, the UNIA confronted racial politics structured by a tradition of black participation. Because the World War I migration created the black community in Gary, Indiana, the UNIA conceivably should have had more opportunity to dominate racial politics. Nevertheless, it took on the same secondary role, rallying behind the politics and candidates of the black elite.

Gary was founded in 1906 by the United States Steel Corporation to house its new works, at that time the largest and most modern industrial complex in the world. The city's black population was small and marginal to the steel economy until World War I, when the European exodus and conscription produced a shortage of unskilled labor that was soon filled by black migrants. Recruited directly from the Lower South, primarily Mississippi and Alabama, the newcomers increased the black population to 5,200—9.6 percent of Gary's population—by the end of the war. By 1930, the black population rose to nearly 18,000, or 17.8 percent of the city's residents. Throughout the 1920s, blacks composed about 16 percent of the workers in the steel complex.[47]

Despite the rise of the black population and the secure role blacks played in the steel economy, the Gary UNIA rarely exceeded 185 dues-paying members. But it was not isolated from Gary life. Its lively band, the Black Cross Nurses, the Black Legion, and a parade of outside lecturers won the admiration and attention of many who never became members. The friendly editor of the black Gary *Sun* called the movement "the vanguard of a bigger and more powerful revolution in the thought of black people of the world."[48]

The absence of sharp racial separation and conflict in the city contributed to the weakness of all racial organizations. Although segregated from the city's white elite, Gary blacks shared the South Side with the polyglot working class. In 1925, the *Southern Workman*, Hampton Institute's journal, reported that "the lines of color are not very rigidly drawn" in housing, schools, and even professional services. Separation was generally the rule

47. Elizabeth Balanoff, "A History of the Black Community of Gary, Indiana, 1906–1940" (Ph.D. dissertation, University of Chicago, 1974), 14, 33, 184, 461; Powell A. Moore, *The Calumet Region: Indiana's Last Frontier* (Indianapolis, 1959), 383–90; Horace Cayton and George S. Mitchell, *Black Workers and the New Unions* (Chapel Hill, 1939), 390.

48. *NW*, July 23, 1927, May 27, 1922; Neil Betten and Raymond A. Mohl, "The Evolution of Racism in an Industrial City, 1906–1960: A Case Study of Gary, Indiana," *Journal of Negro History*, LIX (1975), 62.

in social and religious life. But in this sheltered market, the UNIA was forced to compete with the numerous churches, fraternals, and clubs that the migrants carried with them from the South and also numerous new ones. In the competition, a series of unpopular outside fund-raisers blunted the appeal of Garveyism. One irate local Garveyite complained, "Some of the men sent from New York treated the members as fools."[49]

However, the main reason for the weakness of racial organization was the dominance of U.S. Steel, which strengthened the power of traditional and often divisive associations, such as the churches, by subsidizing them, and opposed modern, independent institutions, such as unions. The literal economic monopoly of the steel corporation went a long way to ensure its political hegemony. Emmett Gaines, in charge of all of the UNIA's African Legions, told Garveyites in 1924 that "you must support the people who give you work in Gary—the steel people—you can't afford to bite the hand that feeds you." The corporation's supervisory personnel headed the school and park boards and composed five of fifteen members of the city council in the 1920s. When blacks protested their exclusion from a well-equipped park, steel Superintendent William Gleason ordered the firing of any black worker who entered it. Churchmen became corporate mouthpieces. One confessed, "The ministers dare not get up and say anything against the company."[50]

Given the power of steel, the plane of politics was narrow, and its practice opportunistic. For instance, the UNIA backed a Klan-supported slate in a primary fight in May, 1924. When a Garveyite was asked why he was working in the election, he responded that he was being paid. In the fall contest, the UNIA accepted money from both parties. UNIA political behavior was not uniquely venal. The victory of the Klan in the GOP primaries led many black Republicans to retain the petty plums of orthodoxy by endorsing Klan candidates. Although the order had not been very strong in Gary, its state victory in 1925 increased its local currency. The rhetoric of moral revival took on new meaning after numerous politicians including Gary's mayor were convicted of illegal bootlegging and political graft. The three black councilmen swept into office on the victorious Klan slate were rewarded with municipal patronage.[51]

49. Thyra J. Edwards, "The Gary Interracial Program," *Southern Workman*, LIV (December, 1925), 546; Balanoff, "History of the Black Community of Gary," 90, 99; Morris Lewis to Robert Bagnall, July 5, 1923, Lewis Campbell to James Weldon Johnson, June 23, 1921, Box G-63, in NAACP Papers; *NW*, July 15, 1922.

50. *NW*, June 14, 1924; Campbell to Johnson, June 23, 1921, Box G-63, in NAACP Papers. Ministers in Gary, like in Detroit, performed recruitment functions. Paul S. Taylor, *Mexican Labor in the United States: Chicago and the Calumet Region* (Berkeley, 1932), 93.

51. Campbell to Johnson, May 19, 1924, Box C-390, in NAACP Papers; Balanoff, "His-

Despite the presence of the Klan in local politics and the rise of racial prejudice and consciousness, a decisive issue, an opening for new leadership, was absent in Gary until two years later. At that time a school board decision to exclude blacks from the city's leading high school posed the question of segregation clearly and forcefully.

School assignments in Gary resulted from the combined class and racial ideas of the city's steel magnates and mandarins. The Wabash Railroad bisected the city into northern and southern sections, which simultaneously were class divisions. Schools south of the tracks were attended by the children of the working class; upper- and middle-class children went to schools north of the tracks. Racial policy was set early, in 1908, when there were few blacks in the town. The Gary school board, headed by U.S. Steel's William Gleason and Superintendent of Schools William Wirt, chose a segregated system, which was an option under Indiana state law. Even so, the system was not monolithic but a mixture of de facto, de jure, and voluntary segregation and integration.[52]

Black parents and teachers generally protested new moves toward segregation, even though their pressing concerns were most often overly large classes, unsafe physical conditions, and insufficient books and other educational necessities. Black leaders—a small clique of ministers, doctors, lawyers, and realtors—ignored popular complaints and supported the school board's disciplining of dissident teachers. But their complacency ended in 1927 when white students went on strike to remove blacks from Emerson High School. Gary had two comprehensive schools encompassing kindergarten through high school—the racially mixed Froebel School and the white, elite Emerson School. Some high school work was also offered in the primary schools of the city. In 1927, the school board transferred eighteen black pupils out of an overcrowded primary school to Emerson. Although six blacks already attended Emerson, white students boycotted classes. Bowing to the pressure, the school board and city council decided to return the students to their old school and build an all-black high school.[53]

---

tory of the Black Community of Gary," 330–34, 357; Moore, *The Calumet Region*, 557.

52. Betten and Mohl, "The Evolution of Racism in an Industrial City," 54; Balanoff, "History of the Black Community of Gary," 83–87, 278. At the time there was no evidence of conflict between black and white children. The decision to create separate schools expressed the racial mores of the native-born teachers and school officials. See Ronald D. Cohen and Raymond Mohl, *The Paradox of Progressive Education: The Gary Plan and Urban Schooling* (Port Washington, N.Y., 1979), 116, 119.

53. Cohen and Mohl, *The Paradox of Progressive Education*, 125; Lewis Campbell to Robert Bagnall, August 4, 1922, Morris Lewis to Bagnall, February 10, 1923, Box G-63, in NAACP Papers.

So long as the growing black population of Gary could be contained in the schools of the working-class district, pupil assignments in Gary were made with a pragmatism that permitted some integration. But black pressure on elite facilities triggered the full implementation of the racial and class assumptions of the school board, city officials, and their constituencies. The issue of separate education divided the black elite. Some had accepted separation for the children of the black masses but not for their own, who attended or aspired to study at Emerson. The failure to fight segregation earlier, when it principally affected the children of the poor migrants from the South, had licensed its extension. Even now, the three black councilmen did not protest the board's solution until they were faced with escalating protest from black parents and grass-roots leaders. Finally galvanized, the black elite, led by the NAACP, sued but lost in 1931, when the Indiana Supreme Court affirmed racial assignments so long as there were "equal educational opportunities."

The UNIA took a backseat in the controversy until the question of the racial composition of the new high school was raised. Even after the students were excluded from Emerson, some blacks, led by the head of the hod carriers union, fought for the construction of a new integrated high school. The UNIA, led by its new president, Charles James, took the lead in the fight for a black one.[54] Its debut in politics was not impelled by pressure from its mostly working-class constituency but by the immediate interests of two of its leading members, F. C. McFarlane, head of a temporary black school annex and future principal of the new black high school, and William Lowden, a teacher in McFarlane's school.[55]

McFarlane was born in the Virgin Islands and educated in Denmark and at Columbia University. He was an enthusiastic, if solitary, black champion of race separation. "Intelligent Negroes no longer whimper about segregation," he declared. "They have discovered that what they really want is to be free within themselves. . . . They merely want to grow and develop along with the whites, but as a separate group. . . . They no longer seek social equality." The black Gary *American* commented: "It is pitiable to see an otherwise intelligent Negro accept segregation with a lover's kiss. . . .

54. James was from the island of Antigua. His father was a schoolteacher who had purchased a hundred shares of BSL stock. James came to New York in 1922 at the age of fourteen with the shares and the desire for a combination of adventure, opportunity, and racial mission that had attracted so many others. He worked as a clerk at UNIA headquarters while he attended P.S. 89 and City College in New York. Then in 1927 he took charge of the Newark UNIA but was assigned head of the Gary division after one year. By 1931, James had brought the membership up to two thousand. Author's interview with Charles James, August 19, 1980.

55. Balanoff, "History of the Black Community of Gary," 278, 285–86, 418.

The city respects him as an educator, but as a social scientist he seems to be little more than a clearing house for antebellum asinities."[56]

Nevertheless, "antebellum asinities" governed assignments in Gary's schools. Although the UNIA trio believed they had translated racial pride into institutional power, they had merely cheered on and rationalized elite ideas and decision making. Gary's steelmen and functionaries believed that the few blacks who were equal to whites could not be realistically or successfully separated from the inferior majority. For this reason, separate education was appropriate and practical. In Gary's political world, which was shaped by elite racial logic, Garveyite appeals to black pride and advocacy of racial schools were ritualized invocations, incapable of uniting blacks permanently or harmoniously, because they ignored the hierarchy of racial power and rewards that made these invocations hollow. Put another way, in the 1920s, the frontier of black nationalism for most blacks, except the few who stood to gain immediately, stopped well before the construction of a black high school, especially when the political context tarred it with the stigma of exclusion, as it did in Gary.

All UNIA divisions were marriages between the traditions of local racial communities and the advanced culture of New York Garveyism. Given the weakness of the Parent Body, the most salient characteristics of the divisions were those they shared with other organizations in their community. Nonetheless, the effects of Garvey's rhetoric—his call for new leadership, new organization, new power—made the locals magnets for dissenters from the narrow platform of black political life in the 1920s. But the disjuncture between the UNIA's appeal and its bourgeois ideology kept it unstable, often at war with itself, and therefore marginal to black political life. The size and effectiveness of individual divisions were buffeted by the vagaries of personality, leadership, and competition because the UNIA lacked clear goals and functions.

The local leaders of the UNIA were not the elite of the black community but a middling group, an upwardly mobile petite bourgeoisie.[57] During the course of the decade, UNIA leadership became more proletarian, as the successful found affiliation to be a liability while the unsuccessful pursued other avenues of advance. Originally built by the ideology of racial enter-

56. *Ibid.*, 297, 243. McFarlane did not remain in Gary but became principal of a new segregated high school in Dayton, Ohio. In 1945, the president of the Dayton NAACP charged that "the Board [of Education] so far has refused to [remove him] because he preaches the gospel of segregation which fits into their scheme." Marion Smith Williams to W. E. B. Du Bois, August 6, 1945, in Du Bois Papers, University of Massachusetts.

57. Emory J. Tolbert has made the same point in *The UNIA and Black Los Angeles* (Los Angeles, 1980), 94–96, 110.

prise, the UNIA, after the effective collapse of its creations, especially the critical Black Star Line, possessed only its calling card—racial militancy and unity—which was insufficient to produce a mass movement. After the new migration in 1923, the UNIA, like other black groups, turned to local political organization. Garveyites failed to mobilize blacks independent of the old client and the newer machine politics. The goals of politically active blacks in the 1920s were largely defined by other white and black organizations, not by the UNIA. The heightened racial consciousness of the UNIA fed black ethnic politics, which was dominated by black elites, which were better able to organize and influence the black community and connect with the larger urban community. Nevertheless, the Garveyites contributed much to the newer ethnic politics by injecting their determination to use politics to further their own careers. The older black politics had often been dominated by men who already had status through a profession or business. For them, politics was more a sign of their success and community leadership. The newer ethnic politics was franker in its pursuit of local power. It demonstrated a mass appeal, however, only in the 1930s, when it was wedded to a social program that promised and delivered more than the narrowly defined objectives of the 1920s. But, as we shall see, Garveyism proved to be a poor vehicle to transport the new social concerns of the 1930s.

13 / Garvey and Pan-Africanism
The Last Years

From his deportation in 1927 to his death in 1940, Garvey persistently sought to regain the power and influence that he had tasted briefly. His travels from his home in Jamaica through the islands of the Caribbean to London, Geneva, and Paris followed the route he had taken as a young man. Although Garvey spoke about creating enterprises modeled on the old ones, his last years were spent primarily agitating and criticizing the acts of others. He began newspapers and magazines, petitioned the League of Nations, and even ran for office in Jamaica. Hoping to rekindle the American movement, he held UNIA conventions on the Canadian border in Toronto in 1936, 1937, and 1938. In 1935, Garvey moved permanently to London, where he mostly recounted his former days of glory to audiences of the curious at Hyde Park. Nothing worked.

Garvey's fruitless politics was one example of the problems of Pan-Africanism in the era of the Great Depression. The movement had been reduced to a small band who worked, studied, and agitated in London without enough of a following even to hold conferences, much less formulate or achieve concrete objectives. Although based in London, most of the blacks in the movement were sympathetic with, and often involved in, the new mass politics of the 1930s, which erupted in all parts of the black world and provided the muscle—boycotts, strikes, demonstrations—for a new Pan-Africanism after World War II. Garvey's relationship to the new politics was much more ambiguous and problematic.[1]

Until he was deported in 1927, the problem of a new politics did not exist for Marcus Garvey. Whether in prison or out on bail, he chanted old formulas. When he launched his second Liberian venture in 1924, he created another shipping line, the Black Cross Navigation and Trading Company, to transport the first colonizers. Ships continued to rank high as passports to freedom. In July, 1923, the *Amsterdam News* boosted a new

1. On the changes in Pan-Africanism see J. Ayodele Langley, *Pan-Africanism and Nationalism in West Africa, 1900–1945* (Oxford, 1973), esp. ch. 9, and Imanuel Geiss, *The Pan-African Movement* (London, 1974), chs. 19, 20.

shipping line created by Boston blacks, "notwithstanding the amount of shipping that is now lying idle in the harbors and docks of the United States." As if his words were recent discoveries, not pale echoes, a Detroit Garveyite told delegates at the 1924 UNIA convention that a "mercantile marine had contributed to the greatness of nations in obscurity." A Baptist professor from New Orleans thought that the shipping line would "prevent white capitalists from obtaining this produce [cotton] at a ridiculously low figure." E. B. Eaton of Virginia saw ships as the essential ingredient to successful black manufacturing. Garvey's current scenario featured the company's ships transporting the raw materials of Africa to the United States, where blacks would manufacture articles exported back to the continent for sale to African producers.[2]

Garvey told skeptics who recalled the history and propaganda of the Black Star Line that he had learned "from past mistakes." The U.S. Shipping Board disagreed, demanding evidence that the Black Cross Line could pay for the SS *Susquehanna* in cash before it accepted its bid of $140,000. Garveyites had more success with the Panama Railroad Company, the government agency that ruled the Canal Zone. It eagerly sold one of its unprofitable ships, the SS *General Goethals*, for $100,000. Announcement of the purchase on August 13, 1924, while the UNIA delegates were meeting in New York, sent a stream of Garveyites to the Hudson River pier at Thirty-fifth Street, where the ship was moored. They were impressed with the ship, which was renamed the SS *Booker T. Washington* and proved to be the best vessel ever bought by the UNIA. Nevertheless, her history followed the same course as her shabbier predecessors.[3]

The methods used to finance and operate the *Washington* were as irregular as those for the earlier purchases. But this time, the corporation sold bonds, not stock, to members of the big, loyal divisions—New York, Detroit, Chicago, and Cincinnati—and completed payment on January 19, 1925. Like the Black Star Line, the Black Cross faced its greatest challenge operating, not purchasing, ships. The first voyage was billed as a pleasure cruise, costing $350 but adorned with economic dividends: "New associations can be found with your own people, new contacts created such as white travelers have done to their own commercial and industrial interests."[4]

2. New York *Amsterdam News*, July 4, 1923; NW, August 15, 23, 1924, January 31, 1925.

3. NW, March 22, 1924; J. Harry Philbin to President of Fleet Corporation, June 16, 1924, E. L. Archey to Chauncey G. Parker, March 15, 1927, file 605-1-653, in RG 32; Panama Railroad Company, *Seventy-Fourth Annual Report* (Washington, D.C., 1923), 21; *Seventy-Fifth Annual Report* (Washington, D.C., 1924), 21; New York *Times*, August 19, 1925.

4. NW, November 1, 22, 29, 1924, January 24, October 10, 1925.

The *Washington* sailed with great fanfare but also with poor prospects for covering the operating costs of the voyage. Garvey's detailed instructions to the purser for the payment of salaries and receipt of monies from meetings, boat inspections, and collections implied ominously that revenues from freight and passengers would be meager. Garvey had planned to go but could not obtain the court's permission to leave the country. He accompanied the vessel to Philadelphia and Norfolk. There he left Secretary-General G. Emonei Carter, Henrietta Davis, and Mdm. M. L. T. de Mena in charge of the ship, which would sail from Norfolk to Havana, Kingston, Cristóbal, Colón, Puerto Limón, and Bocas del Toro.[5]

The voyage confronted numerous hurdles, which extended the trip from its advertised time of one month to an actual time of five months. In Havana, creditors temporarily libeled the ship for the debts of the Black Star Line. Freed from the past, the ship arrived without funds and with few provisions in Kingston, where it was delayed by new libels placed by her unpaid crew. One sailor claimed that sufficient money had been raised at the numerous meetings held along the way to pay all of the ship's bills, including the crew's wages, but that Garvey and other officials of the company and UNIA had squandered the funds. He said that Carter and Davis rented automobiles, bought expensive clothes, and purchased a Panamanian plantation in their own names instead of obtaining new passengers and cargoes of sugar and coal. Whether the charges were true or not, UNIA officials, as in the past, enjoyed luxuries while the crew went unpaid. Daily operating costs of $650 taxed the financial resources of the company and triggered the internal acrimony of the earlier voyages. The Kingston crisis ended when Carter took the U.S. consul's advice and cabled New York. He soon received money that satisfied the crew and the ship's repairers.[6]

Having disposed of the class issue, the *Booker T. Washington* was nearly grounded by racial conflict. Garvey had hired a Norwegian captain and five white and two black deck officers. Two of the whites were unpopular with some of the black crew and passengers. Carter and Davis competed with the captain and his officers for authority. The chain of command had never gone unchallenged on BSL ships, but on the *Washington*, with the additional factor of race thrown in, the conflicts escalated rapidly. The U.S. consul was called upon frequently to reconcile shifting and often violent disputes between the mainly white officers and the black owners, and also

5. José de Olivares to Secretary of State, March 1, 1925, file 811.109g 191/39, in RG 59; *NW*, March 20, 1926; (Canal Zone) *Workman*, May 23, 1925.
6. Olivares to Secretary of State, March 13, 1925, in RG 59; *Daily Worker*, October 28, 29, 30, November 4, 5, 7, 1930.

among individuals within each group. The day before the ship was to sail to Colón, two white officers refused to continue on board because they feared for their lives. Once again the consul patched up a conflict that threatened to abort the voyage.[7]

Having escaped destruction from internal racial conflict, crew and passengers together faced an attack from the Ku Klux Klan in Jacksonville, Florida. A cycle of unsolved murders had conjured up rumors that a black man would be lynched for the crimes. A group of black ministers stirred up the bubbling racial cauldron by informing the mayor that the SS *Washington* had come to the city to preach racial equality. Someone also alerted the Klan, because white-sheeted men boarded the ship and threatened to throw the captain overboard for "working for niggers." Captain Jacob R. Hiorth argued them down, but later, hooded men carrying dynamite approached the ship. The officers and crew quickly took the ship out of the port and anchored upstream before the mob could attack again.[8]

The lengthy voyage yielded little besides debts and dissension. UNIA resurrection seemed even more distant after the court rejected Garvey's appeal in early February, 1925. He was imprisoned shortly after the *Washington* had sailed. When the ship returned in June, William Sherrill, left in charge in New York, and Garvey agreed that the corporation should charter the ship to experienced operators. Sherrill approached a broker, Anthony Crawford, who was the head of the Overseas Navigation Company. Although never active in the UNIA, Crawford's past history was a mixture of racial consciousness, business ambition, and politics such as that of many Garveyites. He had contributed financially to Cyril Briggs's *Crusader* in 1918. He bought a ship, the *Inter-Colonial*, which sailed the Caribbean in 1921 and encountered the same kinds of problems as the ships of the BSL did. Crawford appealed successfully, if temporarily, to the all-black crew to purchase stock and defer their wages on the grounds of race loyalty. However, in Santiago de Cuba, Jamaica, the crew petitioned the U.S. consul because they lacked food, as well as their promised wages. Crawford pleaded with the consul to allow the ship to sail without paying the crew. Unable to convince him, conciliate his crew, or raise funds, Crawford abandoned the ship, which was quickly robbed of its valuables. It foundered on its moorings in January, 1924.[9]

7. Olivares to Secretary of State, March 13, 1925, in RG 59.

8. *Daily Worker*, June 5, 1925, November 6, 7, 8, 1930. For a laundered version see *NW*, September 5, 19, 1925.

9. Harold Chum to Secretary of State, April 27, May 3, 1921, June 6, 1923, file 196.7/1347 and 1348, Francis Stewart to Secretary of State, April 2, 1924, file 196.7/1349, Santiago de Cuba, in RG 84.

Crawford's maritime ambitions did not end with this loss. Before Garvey was imprisoned, he appointed Crawford freight agent to acquire cargo for the *Booker T. Washington*. Although Crawford failed to deliver any cargo, he libeled the ship when the corporation failed to pay his salary. As president of the newly formed Overseas Navigation Corporation, he offered to charter the Black Cross ship. Although the truth about the charges is buried beneath accusations and unwritten agreements, Crawford appears to have been double-dealing. He claimed agent's fees of $350 a month from the Black Cross Line while he chartered the ship to his own company. The final break was precipitated after Crawford demanded the resignations of Garvey and current officers and the appointment of new ones, whom he presumably could control. Although Crawford claimed to be motivated by racial patriotism, his past and current actions demonstrated only his continued desire to operate ships. Controlling, if not legally owning, the *Booker T. Washington* was an attractive proposition because he would not have to use his own capital.[10]

While Garvey and Crawford fought for possession of the ship, the organization, and the remaining legacy of enthusiasm, twelfth-hour appeals to the big UNIA divisions saved the ship from the auction block until March, 1926, when it was sold for $25,000. The loss of the ship deepened old conflicts and created new ones. From his cell in Atlanta, Garvey declared war against Sherrill and the UNIA local in New York for conspiring with Crawford to lose the ship.[11]

The son of an Arkansas preacher, William Sherrill had worked as a labor recruiter during the war and then attempted but failed to operate his own employment agency after it. He won high office at the UNIA's 1922 convention, which had ousted so many of the original leaders. Garvey placed him in charge of the UNIA when he was incarcerated in Atlanta. Sherrill worked well with George Weston, the leader of the New York division. Weston was born in Antigua in 1885. The eldest of nine children, he, like many other West Indian Garveyites, had escaped insular provincialism by becoming a seaman. Joining the UNIA in Boston in 1919, Weston gave up the sea for selling and ministering, which he combined with his UNIA work. He organized a chapter in his native Antigua and directed the Pittsburgh division before he came to the New York local shortly before Garvey

10. NW, February 20, 1926; Clifford Bourne to MG, in NW, March 20, 1926; Anthony Crawford to MG, October 20, November 19, 1925, February 6, 1926, William Sherrill to MG, November 28, 1925, Mopsie (Amy Jacques Garvey) to MG, November 10, 1925, in Amy Jacques Garvey Papers.

11. NW, April 3, 1926; Sherill to MG, November 6, 1925, in Amy Jacques Garvey Papers.

was imprisoned. He won Garvey's anger, however, when he refused to join the campaign to remove Sherrill.[12]

To circumscribe the influence of Sherrill and the rebellious New York local, Garvey staged and directed, from his Atlanta cell, a convention in Detroit in March, 1926.[13] The tested strategy of isolating weak opponents and reselling old ideas was successfully followed again. Garvey removed Sherrill and installed his own men to retain control of the Parent Body. He had wanted the Reverend George Alexander McGuire, head of the African Orthodox Church, to intervene and perhaps take charge. Although McGuire refused to play an official role in UNIA politics, the new head of the association, Fred Toote, was a clergyman in his church. William A. Wallace of Chicago and Levi Lord of New York completed the ruling triumvirate.[14]

Garvey next moved against the leadership of the New York local. Weston's plans to replace the old, ramshackle Liberty Hall with a modern new building served as the pretext for attack. Garvey charged the plans challenged his leadership, squandered the people's money, and served only to enhance the power and financial gain of Weston and his associates. The New York group countered that Garvey opposed the project only because others had conceived and planned it and presumably would reap the prestige involved. The dissidents called a rump convention in August, 1926, in New York, at which they condemned "the reckless handling of money by the Garvey regime" and voted to drop the title Provisional President of Africa attached to Garvey's name. Wesley McD. Holder, secretary of the local, declared that the designation was an insult to Africans. "We still respect Garvey as the man who gave the idea for the African program, but we admit at the same time that as a businessman he was a failure," he said. "We feel that the Association needs most at this time an economic program which we are not willing to submit to Marcus Garvey."[15]

12. *Age*, August 28, September 4, 18, 1920; Baltimore *Afro-American*, September 3, 1920; Lionel Yard, "George Weston" (Mimeographed study in possession of author); *NW*, February 20, March 6, 1926; Samuel Haynes to MG, November 26, 1925, MG to Norvall Thomas, January 30, 1926, in Amy Jacques Garvey Papers.

13. The *Age*, March 27, 1926, claimed that 90 percent of the New York Garveyites had opposed the Detroit Convention.

14. MG to Convention Speaker, March 18, 1926, MG to William Ware, March 12, 1926, MG to Amy Jacques Garvey, March 4, 18, 19, 1926, Alexander McGuire to MG, n.d. [March, 1926], in Amy Jacques Garvey Papers; Baltimore *Afro-American*, March 6, 1926; *Daily Worker*, March 23, 1926; Randall K. Burkett, *Garveyism as a Religious Movement: The Institutionalization of a Black Civil Religion* (Metuchen, N.J., 1978), 71–99.

15. On January 30, 1926, Garvey ordered the editor of the *NW* to deny Sherrill and Weston access to the newspaper. MG to Chair, Marcus Garvey Committee, February 6, 1926, in Amy Jacques Garvey Papers.

As they broadened the focus of their opposition from Garvey's personal stewardship to UNIA operations and then to the UNIA program, the rebels attempted to end the New York local's isolation from other black militants. They invited A. Philip Randolph, William Pickens, Lovett Fort-Whiteman, and George Schuyler to address their convention. Former Garveyites Edgar Grey, Adrian Johnson, U. S. Poston, and others were reunited. Despite politic assertions to the contrary, the gathering was a declaration of independence from Marcus Garvey. But opposition to him was the only common bond of the group, which covered a political spectrum from black Communists to blacks with simply an intensely iconoclastic attitude toward the existing social order. And although Holder spoke of the need for an economic program, specifics were vague.[16]

Garvey loyalists, in control of the *Negro World*, attacked the dissidents in print. Weston was portrayed as a failure in Pittsburgh and Cleveland; Holder, a "five dollar a month school teacher" from a little village in Guiana, "a henchman first to Bundy, Sherrill, and now to Weston." Ferris was characterized as "an eloquent example of the futility of mere learning, glutted with the philosophy of Kant and stricken with the mentality of a child." At one stormy meeting where Weston was charged with treason, the insurgents were literally driven out of Liberty Hall. But Garvey's stand-ins could not save Liberty Hall or two other buildings that were laden with mortgages from years of financial crises and whose walls and ceilings were crumbling. Casper Holstein, the racially conscious numbers banker of Harlem, bought Liberty Hall to preserve black ownership and rented it to the UNIA.[17]

Garvey's new leadership also failed to revive the New York division. Weston and Sherrill had led a group into a new association, the Pioneer Negroes of the World, which purchased two apartment buildings but lost them in 1931. The orthodox Toote group split, the beginning of numerous breaks that dispersed Garveyites into factions that sometimes seemed like warring feudal entities. Although the rhetoric of secession was seasoned with professions of loyalty and charges of heresy to Garvey and Garveyism, most of the disputes were actually fights over organizational monies, a long-standing source of UNIA fissures.[18]

16. *Spokesman* (June, 1926), 5, (September, 1926), 36; *Age*, September 11, 25, 1926; Baltimore *Afro-American*, August 7, 1926; Yard, "George Weston," 21–29.

17. *NW*, June 26, September 11, 25, October 3, 1926; Amy Ashwood Garvey, "Marcus Garvey: Portrait of a Liberator" (Typescript in possession of Lionel Yard, Brooklyn, N.Y.), 355.

18. Fred Toote to Co-Worker, March 30, 1927, in UNIA Papers, Schomburg Center; *Spokesman* (September, 1926); *NW*, January 1, 8, 15, March 19, May 28, 1927; Yard, "George Weston," 29–30; Fred Toote to MG, December 31, 1926, January 10, 1927, MG to Kohn & Nagler, June 6, 1927, in Amy Jacques Garvey Papers.

The new working-class politics of the depression years created another source of contention. Even "orthodox" UNIA divisions shed much of their entrepreneurial ideology after 1929. Partly a function of the unemployment within UNIA divisions, a new working-class orientation was a response to the popular, often Communist-led or -inspired, politics that won jobs, relief, and tenant protections for numerous blacks. UNIA officials were often defensive about their new alliances and politics. Captain A. L. King, head of one New York division, admitted to Garvey in 1935 that the branch was "deviating from our past politics. Our policy of self-help will continue to be the same, but existing circumstances make it necessary to accept other methods." No matter what King meant by this statement, things would never again really be the same.[19]

The local leadership was tentative and halting because the UNIA needed to change in order to survive, but the new politics often drew away militant Garveyites who discovered that the UNIA was a poor vehicle to pursue the new working-class thrust. St. William Grant's course revealed one variant of the problem. A Jamaican veteran of the West India Regiment of World War I, Grant had helped organize the African Legion in New York. In the 1930s, he headed the Tiger Division, a loyal Garveyite local that shared orthodoxy with the Garvey Club headed by Madame de Mena. A fiery street speaker, Grant participated in the campaign in defense of the Scottsboro boys and other popular protests. Eventually, he returned to Jamaica. Instead of affiliating with Garvey or the UNIA, he became a lieutenant of Alexander Bustamante's new labor organization during the working-class upsurge of 1938. No less race-conscious than before, Grant had nevertheless discovered a better organization than the UNIA to achieve personal and political goals.[20]

The institutional fragility of the UNIA in Jamaica and the United States cannot be separated from the historical experience and fate of the class that created it and produced most of the important UNIA leaders—the black petite bourgeoisie. That section of the black community had mistaken a certain amount of racial progress for verification of its class ideology. But the ranks of black independent professionals and businessmen were decimated by the depression. The hopes of economic independence, as conceived in the 1920s, disappeared for broad sections of the black population

19. A. L. King to MG, December 19, 1935, King to Joseph Stark, November 22, 1927, in UNIA Papers, Schomburg Center; "Minutes of Philadelphia UNIA meeting, February 11, 1934," in Fred Braithwaite Papers, in possession of Marion Alexander, Brooklyn, New York.

20. *Age*, August 13, 27, 1932; Ken Post, *Arise Ye Starvelings: The Jamaican Labour Rebellion of 1938 and Its Aftermath* (The Hague, 1978), 219, 239, 277–79, 288–91, 330, 355, 387, 414.

when black banks, insurance companies, and heavily mortgaged church buildings were lost. Some businessmen continued to sell the ideology of black enterprise. But they tended to be those who already had businesses, not the beginning or aspiring Garveyite types. Even the elite shifted gears when it endorsed the DON'T BUY WHERE YOU CAN'T WORK campaigns, which reflected the new importance of jobs, not economic enterprise.[21]

Former Garveyites like Holder, Diggs, Craigen, Lord, Grant, and numerous others transferred their hopes and talents to building new working-class institutions—left-wing political clubs, trade unions, and credit unions. The UNIA was discarded in the process as an irrelevant association. Similarly, ordinary members migrated to the trade union, the relief line, or the government job. Consistent participation in the UNIA had always required enough economic security to permit associations not immediately functional to work. An explicitly modern, new organization that did not seek to improve the world of work or mitigate the insecurities of urban life had been useful when blacks, too, rode the crest of the economic boom. But in the 1930s, few possessed the necessary economic security. And when persons participated in the new politics, they had less emotional need for fraternals. As the leadership abandoned the UNIA, the rapid disappearance of divisions made the question of working-class affiliation academic. At the far end of the social spectrum, the UNIA lost its poorest, least-educated members to the cults, whose ideology and practice were often more satisfying than the middle-class cultural style of many of the old Garveyite leaders. In 1934, Charles James, head of the Gary UNIA, deplored the fact that "simple-minded Negroes were turning Moors, Arabs, Abyssinians. . . . They were growing beards and refusing to cut their hair . . . and have even gone the length of changing their names." The UNIA was abandoned from all quarters in the 1930s.[22]

The fate of American Garveyism was repeated in Jamaica during the 1930s despite the temporary tonic of Garvey's return in November, 1927. The island had not changed much in his absence. Foreigners and foreign capital continued to dominate Jamaica's economy. Although numerous peasants occupied small holdings, one-half of the land was owned by the 907 proprietors who possessed 500 or more acres. Neither a more liberal policy facilitating credit for small farmers nor nearly 4,000 land grants

---

21. See Abram Harris' *The Negro as Capitalist: A Study of Banking and Business Among American Negroes* (Philadelphia, 1936) for an account of the decline of black business.

22. Lionel Francis to Herbert Hoover, October 1, 1932, file 20-145-2, RG 60; Benjamin Moore to J. B. Keeran, May 21, 1935, file 39-51-821, in RG 60; Kingston *Daily Gleaner*, August 15, 1934.

awarded to returning Jamaican veterans of World War I altered the balance of power between planters and peasants.[23]

Jamaica's prosperity continued to rest upon the international market for sugar and bananas, her major exports. Although prices rose in the middle years of the decade, after their disastrous fall in 1920–1921, laborers discovered that opportunities to escape low wages and unemployment by working abroad were diminishing. Beginning in the 1920s, the numbers returning exceeded those who migrated because of the slowed growth of the world economy and the reduced demand for labor. Then after 1929 the sharp contraction of foreign economic opportunity and the growth of laws and popular sentiment against alien employment unleashed a torrent of repatriation.[24]

The ingredients for rebellion were plentiful. The additional pressures placed on Jamaica's laboring class during the 1930s and the end of the safety valve of migration produced favorable conditions for protest. The presence of returned Jamaicans who had gained knowledge of modern political organizations and ideologies in Cuba and the United States ensured that there would be many effective leaders. Combined, these factors produced the great strike wave of 1938, which brought into being the twin vehicles of modern colonial politics and independence—the trade union and the political party.[25]

When Garvey returned to Jamaica in 1927, he had not charted his own or the island's future. His maiden speech informed his countrymen that he "will be running in and out. Some days I will be in Trinidad, sometimes England, France . . . and sometimes in the United States." He spent most of 1928 in transit. He traveled through the West Indies and then in April went to England, where he hoped to attract the British public to his African plans. A meeting that drew only a small audience to Royal Albert Hall was a typical, if extravagant, failure. Ignoring the poor response, Garvey plunged ahead with characteristic energy. In September, he penned a lengthy appeal to the League of Nations.[26]

An exhaustive and occasionally eloquent catalog of white injustice, the petition repeated some of the proposed solutions of the war period: plac-

23. Post, *Arise Ye Starvelings*, 30–42.

24. *Ibid.*, 95–96, 117, 125–26, 132–33, 187 n49, 153.

25. *Ibid.*, 207–465.

26. Len S. Nembhard, *Trials and Triumphs of Marcus Garvey* (Kingston, Jamaica, 1940), 117; Pittsburgh *Courier*, September 29, 1928; Baltimore *Afro-American*, April 28, 1928; *Age*, June 16, 1928; A. A. Garvey, "Marcus Garvey," 275; MG to Secretary of State, December 20, 1927; U.S. Consul, San José, to Secretary of State, March 5, 1928, "Report of Meeting, London, July 2, 1928," file 811.108g 191/42/46/49, in RG 59.

ing South Africa's mandate in Southwest Africa in the hands of Westernized blacks and creating an independent black state in West Africa. Unlike the petition he sent to the league in 1922, this one was signed by Garvey alone; it did not have the signatures of other UNIA officers. It was sent "on behalf" of the "Hundreds of Millions of Black, Struggling and Oppressed Peoples of the World." The earlier one had claimed to represent them. But the petition's account of Garvey's personal trials towered over its discussion of other racial issues. His own setbacks—the American trial, the Liberian rejection, the bannings of his newspaper, his passport and entry difficulties—formed the bulk of his indictment of the West.[27]

Garvey delivered the petition personally and then traveled from Geneva to Paris before he returned by way of Canada in time to wait out the American presidential election of 1928. Urging American blacks to vote for Al Smith, he hoped that, if Smith won, "my friends will be in and . . . they will say to me, 'Come home.'" After Hoover's victory, Garvey returned to Jamaica and prepared to pursue his ambitions and goals on the narrower stage of insular politics. For the moment, politics in England or the United States was impractical.[28]

Garvey had purchased a large, two-story house with spacious grounds, Edelweiss Park, for his headquarters in Kingston. He constructed a stadium to hold political meetings and to rent to popular entertainers. Assisted by an entourage of secretaries, he began a new weekly newspaper, the *Blackman*, on March 30, 1929. He officially and spectacularly entered Jamaican political life with a grand UNIA convention in August. Jamaicans who had only read of the celebrated month-long meetings in New York were caught up in the excitement. Even the unfriendly *Daily Gleaner* found the first day's parade "truly a red letter day." Its reporter was impressed with its "orderliness" and dazzled with its pageantry. Thousands lined the streets of Kingston to cheer a "mammoth procession . . . the like of which has never been seen here before." Madame de Mena, "in uniform and mounted on a grey charger with drawn sword," led marching bands, uniformed Black Cross Nurses, African Legions, and UNIA officials costumed in the regalia of fraternities down King Street toward the Jamaican Race Course and then to Edelweiss Park. The mayor of Kingston and other local

27. Copy of petition in Amy Jacques Garvey and E. U. Essien-Udom (eds.), *More Philosophy and Opinions of Marcus Garvey* (London, 1977), 200–24; Chicago *Defender*, October 31, 1931.

28. New York *Amsterdam News*, October 31, 1928; *NW*, August 4, September 29, 1928; Baltimore *Afro-American*, April 29, 1928; Nembhard, *Trials and Triumphs of Garvey*, 118; Pittsburgh *Courier*, September 28, 1928; Wesley Front to Secretary of State, November 8, 1928, file 811.1089 181/5, in RG 59.

dignitaries greeted delegates. Official Jamaica might not have been converted, but it gave Garvey the respect it had denied him in the past.[29]

The convention's speeches were mostly inspirational. Charles James of Gary, Indiana, reported tersely that "we can't exactly complain, but we can do much better." A Nigerian disclosed that "natives are flogged if they do not make obeisance to the white man." Delegates served up reheated Garveyite panaceas, plans for economic independence and programs to promote nationalism. One man from Nassau ranked "finance to help cultivation" first on his island's agenda of needs. Henrietta Vinton Davis claimed that land acquisition was a prerequisite to any racial politics. On the surface, UNIA factionalism had remained in the United States. "Tears flowed freely" as Garvey recounted stories of how "the organization was robbed by members of its own race." Although one delegate from Detroit objected to Garvey's portrait of his American associates, he was easily shouted down. But Garvey's American problems were not ended so easily.[30]

The former deputy potentate, George Marke, had won a judgment from a New York court for unpaid salary. Because the New York division and the Parent Body lacked assets to satisfy his claim, Marke carried it to Jamaica, where he hoped to attach UNIA assets. Although Garvey asserted that the property of the UNIA in Jamaica belonged to local people, not the Parent Body, the court ordered him to produce the records of the association's Jamaica branch. Garvey sent inadequate documentation and instructed officials to ignore the court's orders. Fined for contempt and forced to make restitution to Marke, Garvey formally split the organization in November by creating the new "Universal Negro Improvement Association, August, 1929," to terminate the endless demands of former officials and employees on his current and future assets. Old loyalists Henrietta Vinton Davis and Fred Toote stayed on with Garvey initially. Most of the important local leaders of the 1920s had already left the UNIA or, like William Ware of Cincinnati and J. A. Craigen of Detroit, departed at this time. They now concluded that Garvey's escalating financial demands on the American divisions were being used to prop up his personal power in Jamaica, not the UNIA. They had a point. The 1929 convention had been a costly show to stage. Its purpose was to launch Garvey's career in Jamaica, not new international initiatives.[31]

From 1929 through 1935, Garvey flirted with modern instruments of

29. Kingston *Daily Gleaner*, August 2, 1929; Baltimore *Afro-American*, August 10, 1929; *Age*, September 3, 1922; Nembhard, *Trials and Triumphs of Garvey*, 123.

30. Nembhard, *Trials and Triumphs of Garvey*, 133–47.

31. *Ibid.*, 151–66; Post, *Arise Ye Starvelings*, 214.

popular power—the political party and the trade union—in Jamaica. The island's politics were still bridled by its status as a crown colony, which had been imposed after the peasant uprising of 1865 demonstrated that the planters could not govern. The new government, responsible only to the Colonial Office, did not challenge the planters' economic and social power, only their governing authority. The introduction of an elective element in the appointed Legislative Council in 1884 was more a concession to the planters than a road back toward democracy. Combined taxation and property requirements limited the voting rolls to 12 percent of the population. In the 1920s, elected legislators demanded a larger political role to protect their economic position in the imperial system, but most Jamaicans remained on the sidelines in this noisy conflict between oligarchy and monarchy.[32]

Garvey's People's Political party (PPP) appeared to advance Jamaica's politics by replacing individual contests based upon personality with races featuring candidates tied to a party and platform. The fourteen-point PPP program for Jamaican development was progressive, shaped by the visions of the small man of property and other middling elements. It promised to limit the power of large and foreign capitalist agriculture and industry by propping up Jamaica's native businessmen and farmers. In turn, encouragement of industry and opening up crown lands would provide work for the unemployed. Explaining that he was not seeking to redistribute wealth, Garvey agreed that "there must be different classes. But the poor need not be living in misery as they do in Jamaica." Like his Liberian blueprint, the Jamaican one was more specific in portraying the fruits of economic development—schools, opera houses, libraries, and universities—than the machinery of production.[33]

Appealing to those in power, Garvey did not advocate universal suffrage. He argued only that the predominantly black population should be represented by men of like color, which was part of the old ideology of the dark-skinned middle class of Jamaica. Garvey's racial argument was partly vitiated by his bitter attack on two black members of the Legislative Council. One, the planter and lawyer J. A. G. Smith, was as much of a popular hero as any elected official could be in colonial Jamaica. He had defended strikers in 1918 and attacked the United Fruit Company. He had been

32. James Carnegie, *Some Aspects of Jamaica's Politics, 1918–1938* (Kingston, Jamaica, 1973), 62–64; Kingston *Daily Gleaner*, September 10, 1929; *Age*, March 1, 1930; Trevor Munroe, *The Politics of Constitutional Decolonization: Jamaica, 1944–62* (Kingston, Jamaica, 1972), 14.

33. Nembhard, *Trials and Triumphs of Garvey*, 194–99; Carnegie, *Some Aspects of Jamaica's Politics*, 50–51; Amy Jacques Garvey, *Garvey and Garveyism*, (Kingston, Jamaica, 1963), 195–99; Kingston *Daily Gleaner*, January 8, 1930.

Garvey's lawyer in an abortive effort to win an estate of a deceased UNIA member from Honduras. Smith's popularity caused Garvey to drop his criticism, though he did not let up on the other black councillor, Theosophilus Wint. An elementary school teacher and former president of the Jamaica Union of Teachers, Wint was running for reelection from Garvey's native parish.[34]

Despite a vigorous campaign, all but one of the candidates he endorsed were defeated. Garvey himself ran for the Legislative Council and was beaten by George Seymour Seymour, a council member's son and a planter who was director of the elite Jamaica Banana Producers' Association. Garvey lashed out at the electorate in familiar language: "We have constantly begged you to think for yourselves, but it seems to us that your brains just won't function. The common people of Jamaica will sell their mother for a morsel of bread and a drink of rum." His new party and platform were modern veneers covering his old politics. The party did not select candidates but merely approved incumbents and candidates who had already announced. Garvey's disproportionate effort to defeat two black rivals demonstrated that endorsements were triggered by his personal purposes, not by his program. Indeed, the platform was not accepted by the candidates backed by the party, and Garvey himself ignored most of it except for one plank advocating stiff new laws to penalize corrupt judges. And the island's judiciary was not the linchpin of Jamaican poverty but of his own. He used the political campaign to attack court decisions and the judges who had mandated payment of Marke's salary. The denunciation won him an indictment, conviction, and sentence of three months in prison and a fine of a hundred pounds. Garvey's political rhetoric, honed in the American environment, was too extreme for the fragile authority of Jamaica's judiciary. Jamaica's rulers recalled that the rebellion at Morant Bay in 1865 had been preceded by popular criticism of the courts. Although the nineteenth-century challenge had represented the grievances of a class and Garvey's only the pique of a losing litigant, Jamaican officials could not afford to make distinctions or take chances.[35]

Just as Garvey flirted with modern party organization, he created a labor association that possessed some modern trappings. After his defeat in the 1929 election, Garvey briefly took up the labor question. Although throughout his career he always claimed to represent the interests of the

34. Carnegie, *Some Aspects of Jamaica's Politics*, 64–66, 80–81, 100, 119, 206–11; Nembhard, *Trials and Triumphs of Garvey*, 171, 193–94, 199.
35. *Age*, September 10, 1932; Post, *Arise Ye Starvelings*, 129; Nembhard, *Trials and Triumphs of Garvey*, 217. Garvey was released from jail on December 19, before the election. Baltimore *Afro-American*, January 4, 1930; A. A. Garvey, "Marcus Garvey," 120.

black poor, sympathy for labor and even the mass organization of the UNIA were not equivalent to working-class politics. He usually argued that the masses needed to be uplifted "to a higher state of culture," not organized into trade unions or political parties. He often attributed poverty to folly, not class relations. He told a group of Jamaicans that a "man gets rich because there are so many other fools who will hand up their share of what they should have to him." Garvey wanted the opportunity for blacks to "exercise their intelligence," in other words, to leave the laboring class, which in his view would always remain in the same relationship to the owners of capital. Earlier he had believed that blacks could accumulate the capital necessary for their development. He now appealed to an enlightened elite, the colonial government, to usher in the PPP program of economic development. Neither universal suffrage nor trade unions, two necessities for an alternative model of progress based upon class conflict, were part of his program. Occasionally supporting unions, he easily denounced unions when it was personally expedient. In the midst of the militant strikes of oil workers in Trinidad in 1937, Garvey told a reporter that workers have no right to strike and should be content to labor under the Union Jack.[36]

Understanding Garvey's view of progress places his championing of the workers' cause in the proper context. In April, 1930, he led a delegation of workers to the governor to ask for a minimum wage. At the same time, he founded the Jamaica Workers and Labourers Association, the first and only explicitly working-class organization he created. Garvey hoped that the governor would lend his support to the minimum-wage proposal on humanitarian grounds. When he did not, Garvey did not work to advance the power of the workers' association, which did not survive his withdrawal. His next venture, a newspaper named the *New Jamaican*, implicitly resisted class organization or conflict when it attributed Jamaica's stagnation to the sloth and laziness of its laboring class, disclaimed "hostility or ill will toward any one," and promised "to help the Government bring about a better order of things." Accepting the capitalist paradigm for development as natural, necessary, and even desirable was not unusual for him and many others. But in this situation it limited his ability to extend his role beyond that of agitator.[37]

36. Kingston *Daily Gleaner*, August 14, 1929, April 15, June 23, 1930, November 8, 1934; Post, *Arise Ye Starvelings*, 2–3, 240. The president of a UNIA branch in Trinidad responded that Garvey was not welcome there. Pittsburgh *Courier*, October 17, 1937.

37. "Election Manifesto of People's Political Party," *Blackman*, January 2, 1930; Post, *Arise Ye Starvelings*, 255; *New Jamaican*, July 9, 1932; Kingston *Daily Gleaner*, July 13, 17, 1933.

Garvey's attempt to enter politics and champion workers and peasants illuminates the continuity of his politics. Immediately after his election defeat of 1930, he defended his proposal for government banana plantations to provide employment for the jobless. He ignored the economic problems of the plan, which would have worsened an already depressed market. But the fundamental problem with Garvey's politics was that he never grounded his proposals in his organizations. For instance, in 1930 he did not organize the workers or the unemployed, though some probably heard him speak. Ideas cascaded from his lips and pen, but the problem of how to put his ideas into effect and the process of political change rarely won his attention. The defeat of 1930 made him realize the difficulties of waging elections without universal suffrage. He had also observed the ability of employers to dominate the voting of their employees. But instead of working to change these features of Jamaican life, he reverted to a position of conciliation, appealing to the government and to the leading classes he had recently attacked in the election. Because of his political style, Garvey's audiences were often fervent but weak, which increased his own vulnerability to official harassment. Governments were often suspicious or hostile because of the rhetoric he employed, but they were easily able to contain him because of the weakness of his organization.

His time was running out. After his unsuccessful campaign for the Legislative Council, Garvey searched for an issue, a way to regain the limelight and pay off the large debts he had incurred since his return. The birth of his second son, Julius Winston Garvey, named after Caesar and Churchill, added to Garvey's financial and domestic problems. He converted Edelweiss Park into an amusement place and sold shares to raise money. He appealed to his American followers. Begging and borrowing from friends and supporters, he was still forced to suspend the *New Jamaican,* though he began a new monthly magazine, the *Black Man,* in 1933. Its name suggested that he was giving up Jamaican politics and reviving his Pan-African ambitions.[38]

Garvey hoped to retrieve his situation at another UNIA convention in 1934. But the seventh UNIA convention was only a shell of its predecessor of 1929. Only ten Americans joined twenty-five Garveyites from the West Indies and Central America in Kingston. The ranks had been thinned by the depression, which had made the costs of travel prohibitive. But the basic cause was the precipitous decline of the movement. The convention

38. A. J. Garvey, *Garvey and Garveyism,* 207; Pittsburgh *Courier,* June 3, 1933; New York *Amsterdam News,* June 29, 1940.

was largely a Jamaican affair. Its major legacy was the Permanent Jamaica Development Convention, a project of the Kingston UNIA.[39]

Like the American locals, the Jamaican division had been dominated by aspiring capitalists, small businessmen, ambitious artisans and clerks, and allied churchmen. Laboring people had departed voluntarily and had sometimes been thrown out. By 1927, the local acknowledged that the working classes were "neither members nor sympathizers." Class was not the only source of conflict and division within the organization. The petite bourgeoisie itself was united only by its aspirations. Weakened by an epidemic of schisms, the Jamaican UNIA and the class it represented oscillated between programs of enterprise and nativism. In the first flush of Black Star Line success in 1919 and 1920, the division veered toward development. After the collapse of the UNIA businesses and their local equivalents, Jamaican Garveyites moved from nationalism toward nativism by demanding the exclusion of foreigners. The UNIA had occasionally denounced the island's Asian minorities, who competed directly with the Jamaican petite bourgeoisie. The depression and the return of Jamaicans who had been subjected to discrimination in foreign countries increased anti-alien sentiments. In 1930, a group of UNIA dissidents seceded to form a new organization, the Native Defenders Committee.[40]

The Native Defenders' indictment of foreigners was selective. They did not harangue Jamaica's mainly English big capitalists. They did not even object to all Asians. The Indian agricultural workers, who had first come to labor on the plantations in the period after the end of slavery, "fitted well," they declared. But "the case was different with the Chinese and Syrians." In 1936, a total of 172 Syrians and 2,492 Chinese were in business on the island. The chairman of the Native Defenders charged that many Chinese were in the country illegally. Two members of the organization were arrested because of their involvement in incidents of social disorder. Although the Native Defenders did not attack the leading capitalists or planters and pledged allegiance to the Empire and opposition to bolshevism, the elite perceived a "powerful class hatred" that aimed to make Jamaica "like Haiti," the hobgoblin of the white imagination.[41]

With the most militant anti-alien forces siphoned off into the Native Defenders, the UNIA stood firmly behind the strategy of enterprise. Shortly

39. Kingston *Daily Gleaner*, August 15, 22, 1924; Norfolk *Journal and Guide*, September 15, 1934; Post, *Arise Ye Starvelings*, 206–207.

40. Kingston Daily Gleaner, March 17, 22, 1921; Carnegie, *Aspects of Jamaica's Politics*, 99–111; *NW*, July 18, 1922, July 11, August 8, 1925, August 14, September 11, December 11, 1926.

41. Carnegie, *Aspects of Jamaica's Politics*, 101–105; Post, *Arise Ye Starvelings*, 208–209; Kingston *Daily Gleaner*, September 16, 1930, April 25, 29, July 7, November 13, 1931.

after the adjournment of the 1934 UNIA convention, Garvey and other Jamaicans called upon the government to raise a ten-million-pound loan for land settlement, irrigation, roads, model housing for the poor, the tourist trade, an industrial bank, a national shipping line, and a university. Similar to Garvey's 1930 platform, the program was tailored to the man of small property who needed more land and capital, though it was promoted as a "program for all Jamaica," under which both "capitalist and laborer would get his due." In November, 1934, Garvey led a delegation that presented the program to the government, which rejected it. This outcome could not have surprised Garvey. When the committee was first set up, he told the group that he would not head it because there were many capable men to lead them. He had in fact already decided to leave Jamaica for England. His reasons were numerous. Although he was well-known in Jamaica, his success was limited to a seat on the Kingston–St. Andrew municipal corporation. The UNIA faced numerous competitors for the allegiance of Jamaica's petite bourgeoisie and had made no inroads among capitalists or workers. Garvey's political party and labor association had died of inattention. If Garvey was going to be forced to practice the politics of petitioning, he might as well appeal directly to British power, not to its surrogate in Jamaica.[42]

Personal and financial problems reinforced his decision to leave. Excessive borrowing and mortgaging ended his ownership of Edelweiss Park, just as it had Liberty Hall in New York. Garvey was pressed with the expenses of debts, a wife, two young children, a car, secretaries, and expensive clothes—the trappings of happier days. American Garveyites were not sending in contributions as they had done in the first years after his deportation. He appealed, unsuccessfully, to the State Department for permission to reenter the United States for thirty-five days. He claimed that the purpose of the trip was to have his diabetes treated, but it was more likely that he thought he could raise money among his American followers. Although planning to go to England, the dream of returning to the United States remained with him.[43]

Garvey left Jamaica for England in 1935, ironically, only three years before the labor rebellions that created modern politics on the island. Although some Jamaicans predicted that he would return to participate in the new politics, he did not. When he toured the West Indies in 1938, he stopped at other islands but not Jamaica. There was no place for him

42. Post, *Arise Ye Starvelings*, 207; Kingston *Daily Gleaner*, September 10, 14, November 8, 1934.
43. MG to Secretary of State, January 7, 1935, file 811.1089 191/9, in RG 59; A. A. Garvey, "Marcus Garvey," 293.

among the new group of charismatic leaders that the labor rebellion had spawned, and Garvey would never play a supporting role. And even more important, the new working-class politics was alien to his experience, ideology, and personality. While Jamaicans were creating new trade unions and a modern political party, Garvey's politics were mired in appeals to the Empire for economic development that would yield a productive Jamaica and the kinds of "careers open to talent" that had eluded him from his early days.[44]

Garvey's last years in London, from 1935 until his death in 1940, were spent in the same kind of obscurity as his first years there. The remembered successes and dreams of earlier days haunted him as he mimed his past political activity. He traveled to Toronto in 1936, 1937, and 1938 to hold conventions. He vowed to run for Parliament. He continued to publish the *Black Man*. But, mostly, he spoke about the old days to curious but unengaged crowds in Hyde Park. Amy Ashwood, in London at this time, observed sadly that Garvey "could not command the crowd. They heckled him." The Pan-Africanist George Padmore, saw a man "vain, arrogant, and highly sensitive to criticism . . . boasting of his former glory." The Jamaican writer Richard Hart observed a "lonely figure," a man who had once inspired millions, making a "brave attempt to maintain an international front gradually petering out." Both men were correct. They delineated Marcus Garvey's response to failure.[45]

Although Garvey's personal style and isolation were singular, his political frustration in the 1930s was not unique. Pan-African organizations survived the 1920s and disappeared in the 1930s. W. E. B. Du Bois had staged his own Pan-African Congresses in 1919, 1921, 1923, and 1927. He, too, had been unable to create an ongoing association or movement with agreed-upon goals, strategy, and tactics. Each conference was a tribute to his personal will but not much else. Participants changed, but the congresses had not planted Pan-African ideas beyond the elites that had first espoused the ideology in 1900. Du Bois appealed to enlightened world opinion, not so much because of his faith in international justice but because of the absence of any other political agency. In 1921, he petitioned the League of Nations to investigate the condition of native labor in Africa and also to place a black man on its Mandates Commission. (Although a futile gesture, the appeal was possibly the model for Garvey's 1922 petition.)

44. MG to Secretary of State, May 26, 1938, in C.O. 137/827/68868/2, cited in Post, *Arise Ye Starvelings*, 375.
45. George Padmore, *Pan-Africanism or Communism* (London, 1956), 80–81; Richard Hart, "The Life and Resurrection of Marcus Garvey," *Race*, IX (1967), 217; A. A. Garvey, "Marcus Garvey," 117, 293–94, 388.

Du Bois carried on through the 1920s, but the onset of the Great Depression, with its new economic problems, snapped the remaining interest in the congresses. In 1941, he wrote that the Pan-African movement was "only an idea on paper and in the memories of a considerable number of former participants in America, the West Indies, and Africa."[46]

The regional variant of Pan-African politics in West Africa was no more serviceable in the 1930s than equivalents such as the UNIA and the NAACP in the New World. The National Congress of British West Africa (NCBWA), founded in 1920, had steadily declined. Its elite members easily accommodated to constitutional reforms that gave them elected representation in councils similar to Jamaica's but left intact the basic power structure of the colonial political system. Although they sometimes used democratic rhetoric, their definition of representation excluded most Africans. Returning prosperity in the mid-1920s reconciled them to junior partnership in the imperial economy. The NCBWA's fourth meeting, in 1929 in Lagos, was its last.[47]

Imanuel Geiss correctly observed that Communist Pan-Africanism replaced Garveyism and Du Bois' congresses from 1927 until 1934, when Stalin's strategy of collective security against fascism muted support for the revolutionary nationalists in Africa and Asia. Pan-Africanism and communism shared a common opposition to colonialism and imperialism. To Lenin, imperialist rivalry in Africa had been a major cause of World War I. In the next era, the African struggle against imperialism would color world politics. The initial failures of European socialist revolutions made work in colonial areas necessary as well as promising. Lenin's "Theses on the National and Colonial Question" (1920) linked success of revolution in Europe with the struggles of colonial peoples in Asia and Africa. The question of strategy was more of a problem. Neither autonomous Communist activity nor alliance with "bourgeois nationalists" overcame global barriers to radicalism after 1919. The tiny size of the working class in most colonial regions doomed the first; the Kuomintang's massacre of Chinese Communists in 1927 ended the second.[48]

46. Geiss, *Pan-African Movement*, 229–62; W. E. B. Du Bois to George Finch, February 11, 1941, in Du Bois Papers, University of Massachusetts. Like Garvey, Du Bois often concluded that money was the cause of his political problems. He once said, for instance, that "if the Negroes of the world could have maintained in Paris during the entire sitting of the Peace Conference a central headquarters with experts, clerks and helpers they could have settled the future of Africa at a cost of less than $10,000." Quoted in Geiss, *Pan-African Movement*, 240.

47. Geiss, *Pan-African Movement*, 284–93; Langley, *Pan-Africanism and Nationalism*, chs. 3, 4.

48. Geiss, *Pan-African Movement*, 322–39.

To help resolve some of these problems, the Communist International in 1927 brought together at Brussels 180 delegates representing leading intellectual and party leaders of the European left and the colonial world. Although it exceeded the boundaries of Pan-Africanism, the League Against Imperialism (LAI), which was created at the Brussels congress, functioned as a surrogate Pan-African organization. Although the LAI's Negro Commission issued liberal and democratic, not socialist, goals, the designated agency of change—"a mass movement in a united front with other peoples and oppressed classes in a common fight against imperialism"—made the LAI's urgings more radical than previous Pan-African assertions. Black participation in Brussels bridged organizational chasms. William Pickens of the NAACP attended with Richard Moore, formerly a member of the African Blood Brotherhood and in 1927 a Communist. Although it was reported that Moore was also an emissary of the UNIA, the *Negro World*, proclaiming "a great gulf fixed between Communism and Garveyism," repudiated the representation. The LAI held another conference in Frankfurt in 1929 and moved to London after Hitler came to power.[49]

The other major Communist organization of Pan-Africanism was the International Trade Union Committee of Negro Workers, created in 1929 and presided over by Afro-American James Ford. At the time, its journal, the *Negro Worker*, was the leading magazine with Pan-African coverage and ideology. Edited by the militant George Padmore, it was the principal tool for organizing black workers and the first major effort to bring Pan-African ideas to the working class. Although the downgrading of colonial work after 1934 ended the marriage between Pan-Africanism and communism and often produced bitter separations, the alliance had been fruitful. The Communist movement provided a perspective and formidable political instruction for critical figures in the Pan-African movements after World War II—George Padmore, Timeko Kouyaute, Jomo Kenyatta, and I. T. A. Wallace-Johnson. Communism injected the technique of militant struggle and broadened the agenda to include the goals of the working class as well as the elite.[50]

After the divorce, Pan-Africanism floundered. Its headquarters and principal activities were confined to London, where Harold Moody served as a center of moderate Pan-African association and George Padmore led a more militant, formerly Communist circle. Moody, a dark-skinned Ja-

49. *Ibid.*, 325–34; NW, February 19, 1927.
50. Geiss, *Pan-African Movement*, 335–37. Communism was not the only source of working-class consciousness. T. Ras Makonnen's experiences at Brookwood College, the Socialist party's labor education center, were critical in his development. Ras Makonnen, *Pan-Africanism from Within*, ed. Kenneth King (Nairobi, Kenya, 1973), 105–107.

maican doctor married to an English woman, had founded the League of Coloured Peoples in 1931. Most of its work consisted of providing social service and informal gatherings for West Indian and African students in London. A friendly critic characterized the league's politics as "mild protest, or, if you like, harassing the goody-goody elements in Britain." Despite their political differences, relations between the league and the radicals were amiable throughout the interwar years because Moody opened up the league's journal, *Keys*, to them.[51]

George Padmore was the leading radical. Born in Trinidad in 1902, educated in the United States, where he joined the Communist party, Padmore was sent to Moscow in 1930 to head the Negro Bureau of the Profintern. As editor of the *Negro Worker*, he was the heart of a black working-class network reaching into Africa as well as the United States and the West Indies. As it became clear that the Comintern was about to dissolve the International Trade Union Committee of Negro Workers, Padmore resigned from all Communist positions. Then, in February, 1934, the party expelled him for being a "petty-bourgeois nationalist." In 1935 Padmore joined the remnants of other Pan-African movements in London.[52] Later that year he and countrymen C. L. R. James and Sam Manning, T. Ras Makonnen of British Guiana, and I. T. A. Wallace-Johnson from Sierra Leone formed the International African Friends of Abyssinia (IAFA) to marshal support against the Italian invasion. The Ethiopian protest preserved Pan-African organization, ideology, and action. It forged personal associations that in 1937 led to the formation of the new International African Service Bureau, a clearinghouse for information and propaganda. The bureau asserted its independence from Communists, Fabians, and Liberals but was well disposed to the declining Independent Labour party. It did not exclude whites, yet its principals were blacks. It attacked Communism but was oriented toward ideas of the left. Although members had wide political experience and sported radical ideologies, the bureau remained a pressure group. But its advocacy of the right of African peoples to form trade unions and cooperatives, a minimum wage, an eight-hour day, and equal pay for equal work was evidence that Pan-Africanism was attempting to attract the working class.[53]

Garvey was not part of this group of men, whom it would turn out

51. Geiss, *Pan-African Movement*, 340–62; Ras Makonnen, *Pan-Africanism from Within*, 126.

52. Geiss, *Pan-African Movement*, 350–56; James R. Hooker, *Black Revolutionary: George Padmore's Path from Communism to Pan-Africanism* (London, 1967).

53. Langley, *Pan-Africanism and Nationalism*, 326–46. Only one member, I. T. A. Wallace-Johnson, was a working-class organizer.

were only temporarily ineffective. He had moved to England to live and organize in the "hub of world affairs" but was unable to make connections that would augment his single voice. His response to the Italian assault in Ethiopia was typical of his approach. The Fascist attack on one of the three independent nations of Africa had galvanized the international black world. Garvey did not join the Padmore group in the IAFA but spoke out alone in defense of Ethiopia in Hyde Park and in his magazine the *Black Man* until Haile Selassie's armies crumbled before Mussolini's bombs and poison gas and the emperor fled into exile in London in June, 1936. Garvey wanted to meet with Haile Selassie, who refused to meet with him or the IAFA radicals. Reversing himself, Garvey now attacked the emperor's reliance on the League of Nations and white advisors. He called Selassie a coward who abandoned Ethiopia, a nation where under his rule "black men are chained and flogged." Before the fall of Addis Ababa, Garvey had criticized blacks for being unprepared to aid Ethiopia. He now chastised the emperor for separating himself from blacks willing and able to aid him.[54]

Garvey's differences with the IAFA were not ideological. Initially, of course, his support of Ethiopia was spontaneous, unalloyed with the doubts that infected some of the former Communists. They hesitated momentarily before throwing their support behind an unenlightened emperor presiding over an oligarchy that did not effectively rally the population against Mussolini. In the end, they concluded that the only critical question the invasion posed was the issue of racial sovereignty, which had to be defended despite the emperor's politics. Padmore, who had attacked Ethiopia bitterly when he was a Communist, now found that "white nations regardless of their political systems, have no scruples in joining hands in assigning parts of Africa to whichever one stands most in need of colonies."[55]

None of the political stands on the Ethiopian issue was a happy one. The emperor made neither a good ally nor a good antagonist. All blacks felt helpless before the aggression against Ethiopia, which had loomed large in racial thought and mythology but had little connection with black lives and politics. The issue was a benchmark on the left-wingers' road from communism to nationalism, but it only underscored unchanging

54. Ras Makonnen, *Pan-Africanism from Within*, 105–20; MG, in *Black Man*, December 1935, July–August, 1936, January, 1937. W. E. B. Du Bois also resented Selassie's unwillingness to meet with Afro-Americans. Unlike Garvey, Du Bois did not publicly denounce the emperor. See Du Bois to Sylvia Pankhurst, March 26, 1946, and Pankhurst's response, October 11, 1946, in Du Bois Papers, University of Massachusetts.

55. Ras Makonnen, *Pan-Africanism from Within*, 115; George Padmore, "Ethiopia in World Politics," *Crisis*, XLII (May, 1935), 139.

characteristics of Garvey's political style. He did not join with the others in the IAFA, because he would not work with men whom he could not lead or dominate. Although he began with an orthodox position of racial solidarity, it was personal, not political, considerations that drove him to oppose the emperor. However, his dissent forced him to articulate truths about Haile Selassie and his rule that were suppressed by the radicals in the IAFA. But Garvey 's mercurial politics, dependent upon the vagaries of personal relations and the emotions of combat, produced distortion as often as insight, celebration of the Ku Klux Klan and Anglo-Saxon clubs as often as criticism of the Ethiopian and Liberian oligarchies.

Garvey's last years were spent alone, apart from other Pan-Africanists and then also from his own family. Reluctantly and without informing her husband, Amy Jacques Garvey and their two sons departed for Jamaica in September, 1938, while Garvey was away in Canada holding a UNIA convention. Marcus, Jr., was very ill, and doctors believed a warmer climate would speed his recovery. Although Garvey was not happy about his family's absence, he chose to remain in England. His private secretary, who remained with him, reported that he "felt that he could not lead a world movement hemed [sic] in, in this small island; so he disregarded medical advice and remained in England where he could make better world contacts and not be hampered by petty official red tape." England's climate was not good for Garvey's asthma. He had contracted pneumonia twice, which probably contributed to the stroke he suffered in January, 1940. Paralyzed on one side and temporarily speechless, he tried to resume his work despite his declining health. In May, he suffered the indignity of reading his obituary when it was widely but incorrectly reported that he had died. On June 10, 1940, the death was genuine.[56]

Although Garvey did not live to see the last and most significant Pan-African Congress, which came in 1945, or the achievements of the independence movements in Africa and the Caribbean, his wives did. Jamaica's UNIA sent four delegates to Manchester in 1945. Amy Ashwood was more active in the new Pan-Africanism than Amy Jacques. Part of the George Padmore circle, Ashwood attended the Manchester congress as a representative of the IAFA.

Their inclusion in the last burst of Pan-African militance demonstrated the varied tendencies that united briefly in 1945.[57] The Manchester con-

56. A. J. Garvey, *Garvey and Garveyism*, 232–35; Daisy Whyte, in *Voice of Freedom*, I (August, 1945), 1, 2; *Age*, May 25, 1940.

57. See letters between Amy Jacques Garvey and W. E. B. Du Bois, February 4, April 4, 5, 8, 24, 26, 1944, and Amy Ashwood Garvey and Du Bois, February 6, 19, March 1, 1958, in Du Bois Papers, University of Massachusetts; Geiss, *Pan-African Movement*, 211,

gress, unlike previous ones, demanded independence through mass organization. Padmore had written Du Bois that the "workers and peasants . . . must be the driving force behind any movement which we middle class intellectuals may establish. Today, the African masses, the common people are awake and are not blindly looking to doctors and lawyers to tell them what to do." Padmore's predictions were accurate. Representatives of trade unions, political parties, and farmers had replaced the agents of Christian missions, churches, and philanthropies. The conference did not look to the "enlightened western nations or humanity," as the first congress in 1900 had. Participants were urged to organize the masses in political parties and trade unions and use boycott and strike. W. E. B. Du Bois was present but more out of memory and continuity than out of inspiration. Harold Moody stood back as he observed the working-class elements gain the initiative. He continued to see the African question as a "humanitarian" one, not political or economic. He wished Pan-Africanism to keep a distance from the labor movement. He did not attend.[58]

Despite the renewed strength, however, the Pan-Africanists did not unify the black world in 1945. To achieve independence, they dissolved into regional and national constituencies. As an intellectual and organizational system, Pan-Africanism was weak. Just as had the first congress in 1900, the last one in 1945 confused genes and geography, culture and class. Its militant rhetoric and genuine feeling were never adequate blueprints for action. After forty-five years, Pan-Africanists had learned to speak the language of the people. Nonetheless, the class that had created the Pan-African ideology was able to dominate the process of independence and the postcolonial societies freed from empire, and it was also able to dominate the black politics created by the civil rights movement in the United States, which freed black southerners from disfranchisement and Jim Crow.[59]

272, 355, 382–83, 401, 405, 407, 415; author's interview with Amy Jacques Garvey, January 18, 19, 1971.

58. George Padmore to W. E. B. Du Bois, April 12, 1924, Henry Moon to Du Bois, April 9, 1945, in Du Bois Papers, University of Massachusetts; Geiss, *Pan-African Movement*, 385–408; Langley, *Pan-Africanism and Nationalism*, 347–68.

59. On Africa, see E. J. Berg and Jeffrey Butler, "Trade Unions," in James S. Coleman and Carl G. Rosberg (eds.), *Political Parties and National Integration in Tropical Africa* (Berkeley, 1964), 340–81. On the United States, see William Julius Wilson, *The Declining Significance of Race: Blacks and Changing American Institutions* (Chicago, 1978).

Conclusion

Born in Jamaica, Marcus Garvey aimed to organize blacks everywhere but achieved his greatest impact in the United States. This book has argued that the geography of black modernism was the best predictor of the actual map of Garveyism—its strength in the northern cities of the United States, its presence in the American South and Caribbean, and its comparative weakness in West Africa. Garvey's appeal received a hearing wherever economic development had destroyed old cultures and dangled the prospects of new prosperity.

Garvey became a mass leader, but his ideas were rooted in an elite response to economic and racial change. At the end of the nineteenth century the elites of the black world—lawyers, churchmen, merchants, educators—welcomed the forces of modernization, progress, and capitalism while most blacks, who were rural people, preferred the popular, sometimes democratic values and forms of association of preindustrial life. But despite their hopes during the Era of Emancipation, the elites were excluded from the top positions in the modern state, businesses, and professions. When confronted with racial or nonracial barriers to their careers, they tried to build the racial equivalents of elite Western institutions. Irrelevant to the lives of most blacks, the elite's creations were too slight to provide opportunities for the growing numbers of blacks who desired careers in the modern society, men like Marcus Garvey. Industrial economies and societies eroded the older cultures without providing enough urban places for the young, able, ambitious men it displaced.

Garvey initially attempted the elite solution. Failure and, then, new opportunities altered his path. The social upheavals and revolutions that took place during World War I demonstrated the power of popular mobilizations to change traditional patterns of life and power. They fostered new strategies—insurrection, trade unionism, socialism, communism—to organize the militancy that erupted throughout the black world. The Black Star Line, a modern economic enterprise blueprinted by older elites but supported by the masses in new organizations, was Garvey's way to marshal the new black insurgency to provide the opportunity and recognition that were denied him and others like him. Initial enthusiasm and initial success were deceptive. Although the launching of the BSL had depended upon the growth of a black working class entrenched in industrial society, Garvey believed that progress was created by men like himself who used the black economic surplus to create modern enterprise, which he saw as the engine of racial power. The sharp recession of 1920–1921 revealed Garvey's dependence on working-class progress. The popular exodus from the UNIA demonstrated that most black workers relied upon the larger outside world, not racial association, to provide work, the foundation of their pride.

Forced to compete with big shipping companies and pressured by the immediate needs of its shareholders, the Black Star Line did not survive. The continued viability of the UNIA required the resurrection of the BSL or the creation of another enterprise or of a politics that justified racial or Pan-African unity. The UNIA convention in 1920 had demonstrated that the new steamship line could generate a successful forum, but without common political practices to weld the local UNIA divisions into an effective worldwide organization, the UNIA's only weapon was the Black Star Line. Pan-African politics failed to produce this unity, but UNIA locals provided more modest social satisfactions for individuals—education, inspiration, opportunities for racial leaders and small businessmen, and links to the wider world. Like the churches and other fraternals, most UNIA branches in the United States joined other black groups and entered urban politics, a conceivable strategy especially after the new migration of 1923 increased the weight of black voters.

The new black or ethnic politics was not announced with a new ideology. Black nationalism did not map a sure road to the future but only rationalized new opportunities for progress. Even though the dividends of black politics were small in the 1920s, the shift from accumulating black dollars to gathering black votes was an implicit acknowledgment of the failure of the entrepreneurial route to black progress.

Black leaders other than Garvey, men like Cyril Briggs, A. Philip Randolph, and numerous little-known men, guided by various left-wing ideologies, had formulated a working-class agenda. Although their efforts were fruitless in the short run because of the weakness of all working-class organizations in the 1920s, these leaders had identified the critical new class in the black community. Over time, the ranks of black workers were swelled by new recruits from the farms and casualties from racial businesses. Garvey's UNIA survived the 1920s, but paralyzed by the discord of old and new classes and ideologies—bourgeois models, petite bourgeois leadership, and working-class members—it had been fatally wounded even before the Great Depression delivered the final blow. In the end Garveyism, dependent upon the viability of black business enterprise, was swept away by the historical tide of black class formation.

Therefore, Garveyism was more than the product of a charismatic leader or a set of ideas asserting black worth and power and mandating racial unity. Not only are the ideas of black nationalism continuous from the late nineteenth century, but they have been incorporated into the ideologies and practices of most black people and organizations. What is crucial in understanding the impact of black nationalism is the political environment in which it flourished, the political programs it was joined to, and the particular classes that embraced it.

Although black nationalism had been created by black urban elites in the late nineteenth century, Garveyism was stamped by the leadership and immediate purposes of more middling strata, people who were the source of its passionate hopes and social instability. They were ambitious and, according to Wilson Moses, "civilizationist" in their values and aspirations.[1] This characteristic was brought out very well by a Jamaican journalist who distinguished Garveyism and the Rastafarian movement in 1941: "The Rastafari movement is an excellent example of the kind of thing which develops when popular movements become entirely divorced from the educated classes. The merit of Garveyism was that it expected the educated men of African descent to come in, that it rallied all sections. It did not renounce civilization and deify an African king because it did not renounce education."[2]

As we have seen, the joining of the classes was no more stable in Jamaica than it was in the United States. Nevertheless, the intention of the UNIA was to uplift and lead the masses through enterprise and education. It is ironic that the Rastafarians, after Garvey's death, embraced him as well as Haile Selassie, the man Garvey had bitterly attacked. Obviously, they had not read or taken to heart Garvey's criticism of the emperor. But Garvey was not the first man to be taken up by a group for its own purposes. Even then, the sect's canonization of Garvey revealed the division between those who would build a heaven at home and those who aspired to build one in Ethiopia. This use of Garvey's name, which edited and revised the historical Garvey, foreshadowed the incorporation of Rastafarianism by Michael Manley's very worldly and explicitly socialist Jamaican

1. Wilson Jeremiah Moses, *The Golden Age of Black Nationalism, 1850–1925* (Hamden, Conn., 1978).
2. *Public Opinion*, July 26, 1941, cited in Ken Post, *Strike the Iron: A Colony at War, Jamaica, 1939–1945* (2 vols.; The Hague, 1981), I, 190.

nationalism during the 1970s. Today all political groups in Jamaica consider Garvey theirs.

This and other continuities in the invocation of Garvey's name have often led historians to ignore the underlying political and social dynamics and ideologies of racial movements, which are more important than the continuities of rhetoric and apostles. This study has tried to get beneath the language of Garveyism to the ideology, praxis, and social relations of the movement, which were more complex and ambiguous. The language of Garveyism was racial; its ideology was bourgeois, asserting that the road to black freedom was the creation of the core institutions of the modern nation-state. The UNIA becomes explicable only when we join the language and ideology to the particular parts of the black world that led and joined the movement.

Therefore this study speaks to the "race-class" question, which is perennial because of the false equivalency that the formulation postulates. Confusing consciousness, rhetoric, and organization with social position, the debates have often reflected preferred current political strategies more than analysis of specific historical periods and movements. Because the class structure of the black community was different from that of the Anglo-Saxon, Jewish, Italian, and Chinese communities did not mean that it was nonexistent. Conversely, the class structure of the black community in Gary, Indiana, was different from the ones in Macon County, Alabama, in Kingston, Jamaica, and in Monrovia, Liberia. The lives of black farmers, factory workers, and teachers were not identical. It would be surprising if their politics were. (This does not mean that the politics of segments of an ethnic community must conflict, only that the bridging of class experiences must be explained, not assumed.)

In other words, black experiences depended upon people's material existence. The expression of black goals is often, though not always, rooted in racial language. But when they reflect different social experiences, the same words will have different meanings. Moreover, the feeling of racial consciousness does not exclude class consciousness, which, in turn, is not equivalent to working-class consciousness. With fervent racial consciousness, the black middle class of the early twentieth century openly celebrated its status and its separation from the black masses. On the other hand, the farmer Nate Shaw often used the words *Negro* and *working people* interchangeably in his classic autobiography. Referring to some rich black farmers in his area, he remarked that they "lets their money speak for em not their color."[3]

3. Theodore Rosengarten (ed.), *All God's Dangers: The Life of Nate Shaw* (New York, 1974), 497.

Consciousness of race is an element in the lives of most black people, whether or not they participate in organizations that include whites. But whatever the subjective expression or feeling, the actual political behavior and goals are standard responses of classes buffeted by the changes of the modern world in specific political cultures. Racial politics does not originate inevitably in an immediate experience of racial discrimination or oppression. It is not dependent upon the existence of formal racial proscription, such as Jim Crow laws. And racial organizations do not attract all racially conscious blacks because these organizations usually promote the interests and employ the favored methods of portions of the black community. It is for these reasons that I find a class framework, which is not the same as that shibboleth class unity, more persuasive and generative of explanations for the origins and course of Garveyism than alternative frameworks.

Implicit in this interpretation is the idea that attitudes toward whites are less significant explanations for racial politics than is often assumed. Garveyism was infused by identical goals and forms, if not results, in the United States, where blacks were a minority; the Caribbean, where they were a majority; and West Africa, where they were virtually the entire population. Similarly, I downplay common dualisms for charting twentieth-century Afro-American history—integration versus nationalism, assimilation versus separatism. I have found that persons placed on either pole rarely perched securely or permanently, which suggests that these dualisms chart tactics more than ideology. During the same historical period, for instance, Du Bois and Garvey shared more ideas about race and progress, the underlying paradigms of their politics, than their personal disputes and differences on specific issues suggest. I have explained their disagreements on the basis of the classes the two men represented, their personalities, and their strategies at particular times.

The class framework allows us to comprehend Garveyism as an international phenomenon. The establishment of the UNIA in the United States, the Caribbean, and West Africa was possible because the middle classes in black communities chose a strategy of black business enterprise requiring minimal political organization. (Tighter political organization would have oriented groups more to their local regions.) The Pan-African consciousness and language of Garveyism reflected both the methods of the UNIA and the actual experiences of many of its leaders, who had lived and worked in various black communities. The fragmentation of the UNIA both internationally and regionally was caused by the failure of the strategy of racial enterprise and the fact that other, often nonracial relationships were more crucial in members' lives. The diverse paths Garveyites took in the 1930s and 1940s reflected the diverse social composition of the strata that had come together in the era right after World War I.

To chart the internationalism of the UNIA demanded a form of comparative history, an approach that has been used widely in the history of slavery, emancipation, and race relations. Unfortunately, comparisons of black political movements have often been made simply at the level of rhetoric and language. A close study of Garveyism required more systematic comparative analysis, which can also enrich the study of racial movements that were not formally joined in one organization. The vigor of the UNIA in the northern United States in the light of its weakness in the American South, the Caribbean, and West Africa tells us something about Garveyism but also raises questions about the genesis of all racial organizations in the United States. Garveyism was built upon a critique of the Western world but also upon the solid black gains of the period. It suggests that racial organization is often the child of social progress and that heightened and international racial consciousness can be an effective mobilization strategy in the modern world.

Social and comparative history can also provide a perspective on racial movements after Garvey. Most racial leaders of Garvey's day, reflecting the views of the middle class, looked to black business enterprise, if not to organized Garveyism, as an outlet for professional and entrepreneurial ambitions. They believed that these goals would also advance the position of the race. In the 1930s and 1940s, especially in the northern United States, some leaders, newer middling elements, and working-class organizers began to build organizations and unions around the immediate, bread-and-butter issues that dominated the concerns of most black people. The goals and targets of the new associations led them to be either non-racial or linked with similar racial groups in the larger society. More activist than those of the 1920s, the new leaders organized demonstrations and picket lines more often than petition drives and parades. The new politics emerged from changes in the black community—the devastating impact of the Great Depression on black business and employment—but also from crucial changes in the broader society.

Just as Garvey's early politics were shaped first by the models of British social imperialism and then by those of American nationalism, so black strategies of the 1930s and 1940s were altered by the new labor movement, radical politics, and a transformed Democratic party. The state now began to intervene in the affairs of civil society on the side of the working classes. The new sphere of legitimate state action was a necessary bulwark for traditional constitutional and moral arguments in favor of particular racial goals, and the social power of effective working-class organizations provided a base from which to demand civil rights legislation, active executive and judicial enforcement, and more equitable practices. Racial leaders no longer appealed to the masses, as Garvey once did, to defer immediate goals to build elite racial institutions.

Initially, this transformation took place in the northern United States. The southern struggle initiated in the 1950s was an offspring of the northern movement and a beneficiary of changing national politics, as well as a movement with indigenous roots. It began as a middle-class movement aiming to remove formal proscriptions, which were the barriers most crucial for the middle-class blacks of the region. Its new leaders quickly discovered the effectiveness of mass mobilizations and in the process began to raise the social and economic issues necessary to sustain popular movements.

Caribbean and West African politics after the Great Depression reveal many similarities to the politics of blacks in the United States. There, too, significant numbers of black workers joined trade unions during the late 1930s and 1940s. (In the Caribbean and West Africa, organization was spurred by the legalization of trade unionism; in the United States, by the admission of blacks into a new labor movement, the CIO.) With different tempos, economic development quickened during the 1940s and 1950s and propelled more persons throughout the black world into the modern economy. Offspring of this new lower-middle and working class replaced an older black elite whose demands for equal access and the extension of privilege had been gradualist, legalistic, and often class-bound. The new men mobilized the popular classes, which speeded the pace of political independence. (They were also aided by ideological pressures from the metropolitan countries, equivalent to national and northern influence on the movement in the southern United States.)[4]

The social processes in all three areas were similar. And in the United States, it was easier to secure formal equalities and racial representation, just as in the Caribbean and West Africa it was easier to win independence, than to improve the conditions of the masses. These characteristics became very clear in the worldwide economic recession and stagnation of the 1970s. By that time the equivalents of the elites of 1900 were more numerous and much more firmly entrenched in their own societies. Those in the Caribbean and West Africa possessed sovereignty and commanded considerable resources, whatever the international position of their nation

4. Post, *Strike the Iron*, I, 122; Immanuel Wallerstein, "Class, Tribe, and Party in West African Politics," in Seymour M. Lipset and Stein Rokkan (eds.), *Party Systems and Voter Alignments: Cross-National Perspectives* (New York, 1967), 499; Irving Leonard Markovitz, *Power and Class in Africa* (Englewood Cliffs, N.J., 1977), 178–79.

was. Perhaps in the postindependence world it is less useful to continue to compare black politics in the United States, where blacks are a minority, and in the Caribbean and West Africa, where they are ruling majorities. Yet I suspect that so long as the language of politics assumes racial connections, it will be worthwhile to use the comparative method.

The study of Garveyism demanded a comparative analysis of political consciousness and organization. Although rooted in the history of social structures and institutions, a comparative study of black racial ideologies and movements extends a method that has been useful in work on white supremacist thought and institutions of the United States, the Caribbean, and Africa.[5] Even for the contemporary period, it can be an important tool to break out of geographical parochialism, pose new and better questions, and, it is hoped, write better history.

5. See, for instance, George M. Fredrickson, *White Supremacy: A Comparative Study in American and South African History* (New York, 1981), John Cell, *The Highest Stage of White Supremacy: The Origins of Segregation in South Africa and the American South* (Cambridge, England, 1982), and Eric Foner, *Nothing but Freedom: Emancipation and Its Legacy* (Baton Rouge, 1983).

Note on Sources

The assumption behind this book, that Afro-American history transcends race and racism, required sources that documented the development of Garvey and the UNIA, and others that documented their context. I have used three kinds of material: sources on Garvey and the UNIA, on the general black history of the period, and on other relevant topics in American and world history.

Because only scattered remains of the papers of Marcus Garvey and the UNIA survive today, considerable detective work was necessary to ferret out new material. Garvey's most important newspaper, the *Negro World*, was crucial. Earlier scholarly studies have been based on the previously available run of the newspaper, which covered only the years from 1923 to 1933. Previous interpretations thus overweighed characteristics typical of the period after 1922, slighting crucial changes in black politics and the UNIA from 1919 to 1922 and in general ignoring the historicity of the UNIA. Although the files are still incomplete, they are now complete from February, 1921.

The historicity of the UNIA must also inform the use of other evidence, especially interviews. Talks with surviving Garveyites and with Garvey's widow were valuable. But a man who joined the UNIA in 1925 was not the best source for the UNIA in 1920. Similarly, a Garveyite from Detroit might reveal interesting information about local affairs but have little knowledge of events in New York. I interviewed one member from Philadelphia who knew little about the affairs of his own division. These caveats may sound like routine historical procedure, but they have often been disregarded in work on Garvey and Garveyism.

Evidence from government archives was diverse and rich. Government intelligence reports, used with informed caution, were indispensable, especially for the period 1918–1922. The reports of government agents in the files of the Departments of State, War, Navy, and Justice are the only records of some early UNIA meetings, and are especially useful in the absence of documentation by the *Negro World*. I have obtained files from the

Federal Bureau of Investigation on Garvey's indictment and trial and on the broader black radicalism of the period. The file prepared for the Justice Department's prosecution of Garvey surveys, sometimes daily, the activities of Garvey and Garveyites in New York and other cities. The files of the Military Intelligence Division of the War Department were valuable, especially for the period 1918–1921. The quality of its reports was generally superior to that of the Justice Department reports.

Other government material was equally useful. The wartime demand for black labor involved almost every branch of the government in some aspect of black life. The paper legacies of bureaucracies are a gold mine for historians. The files of the Departments of Labor, Commerce, and Agriculture, the Post Office Department, the War Labor Board, the Shipping Board, and the Panama Canal Company, all relatively unused, were very helpful in elucidating Garveyisms's context.

Because the UNIA was an international movement with numerous divisions in British colonies, significant information on it appeared in the files of the Colonial and Foreign Offices in London. The U.S. State Department files, especially reports from its foreign service posts, were equally valuable for the study of Garveyism outside of the United States. The best source for Garveyism in the Caribbean is the little used (Canal Zone) *Workman*, a newspaper published by the resident West Indian community.

Traditional black sources were essential to this study. I have examined the files of surviving black newspapers, which carried important information unavailable in other places. The papers of contemporary black leaders explicated their own positions and their relationships with Garvey and Garveyites, as well as the whole world of black life and politics during World War I and the 1920s. Similarly, the records of the National Urban League, NAACP, and National Negro Business League were indispensable to elucidate the UNIA's relationships with other organizations and to understand the alternatives to Garveyism.

The literature, contemporary and historical, popular and scholarly, on Garvey and Garveyism is vast, as can be seen from Lenwood Davis and Janet L. Sims, *Marcus Garvey: An Annotated Bibliography* (Westport, Conn., 1980). The studies and other published works that confront, touch, or skirt the issues and material raised in this book are far too numerous to list here. Where relevant, they are cited in the footnotes. What follows is a complete list of unpublished sources used in the present study.

Unpublished Sources

Government Records (listed by repository)

Federal Archives and Records Center, Bayonne, New Jersey
    Marcus Garvey case file of exhibits, C-33-688, FRC 539–440.
Liberian State Archives, Monrovia, Liberia
    Executive Mansion Correspondence, 1920–1925
National Archives, Washington, D.C.
    Record Group 3: Records of the United States Housing Corporation.
    Record Group 28: Records of the Post Office Department.
    Record Group 32: Records of the United States Shipping Board.
    Record Group 38: Records of the Chief of Naval Operations, Office of
        Naval Intelligence.
    Record Group 59: Records of the Department of State.
    Record Group 60: Records of the Department of Justice.
    Record Group 65: Records of the Federal Bureau of Investigation.
    Record Group 84: Records of the Foreign Service Posts of the Department
        of State: Embassy and Legation.
    Record Group 151: Records of the Department of Commerce.
    Record Group 165: Records of the Department of War.
    Record Group 174: Records of the Department of Labor.
    Record Group 204: Records of the Office of Pardon Attorney.
New Orleans Public Library, New Orleans, Louisiana
    Records of the New Orleans Police Department.
New York State Archives, Albany, New York
    Records of the Joint Legislative Committee Against Seditious Activities
        (Lusk Committee).

Private and Organizational Records (listed by repository)

Beinecke Rare Book and Manuscript Library, Yale University, New Haven,
    Connecticut
    Johnson, James Weldon. Papers.
Butler Library, Columbia University, Oral History Project, New York, New York
    Holder, Wesley McD. Reminiscences.
    Randolph, A. Philip. Reminiscences.
Fisk University Library, Nashville, Tennessee
    Du Bois, W. E. B. Papers.
    Garvey, Amy Jacques. Papers.

Haynes, George Edmond. Papers.
Johnson, Charles Spurgeon. Papers.
Hollis Burke Frissell Library, Tuskegee Institute, Tuskegee, Alabama
    Moton, Robert Russa. Papers.
    National Negro Business League. Papers.
Library of Congress, Washington, D.C.
    American Colonization Society. Papers.
    Coolidge, Calvin. Papers.
    Harding, Warren E. Papers.
    National Association for the Advancement of Colored People. Papers.
    National Urban League. Papers.
    Washington, Booker T. Papers.
    Woodson, Carter G. Papers.
Municipal Archives and Record Center, New York, New York
    Hylan, John. Papers.
New York Public Library, Manuscript Division, New York, New York
    National Civic Federation. Papers.
New York Public Library, Schomburg Center for Research in Black Culture, New York, New York
    Bruce, John Edward. Papers.
    Phelps-Stokes Fund. Papers.
    Pickens, William. Papers.
    Schomburg, Arthur A. Papers.
    Universal Negro Improvement Association. Papers.
Soper Library, Morgan State College, Baltimore, Maryland
    Scott, Emmett P. Papers.
Tamiment Library, New York, New York
    New York Socialist Party. Papers.
University of Massachusetts Library, Amherst, Massachusetts
    Du Bois, W. E. B. Papers.

Records in the Possession of Private Individuals

Braithwaite, Fred. Papers. In possession of Marion Alexander, Brooklyn, New York.
Garvey, Amy Ashwood. "Marcus Garvey: Portrait of a Liberator." Typescript in possession of Lionel Yard, Brooklyn, New York.
Yard, Lionel. "The First Amy Tells All." Typescript in possession of Lionel Yard, Brooklyn, New York.
———. "George Weston." Mimeographed study in possession of the author.

Author's Interviews

Alexander, Marion, July 18, 1976
Garvey, Amy Jacques, January 17, 18, 1971.
Harvey, Thomas, October 15, 1975.
James, Charles, August 19, 1980.
Jemmott, Rupert, June 6, 1976.
Lord, F. Levi, June 18, 1976.
Randolph, A. Philip, July 19, 1978.

Index